The
Privilege
against
Self-Incrimination

THE
PRIVILEGE
AGAINST
SELF-INCRIMINATION

Its Origins

and Development

R. H. Helmholz
Charles M. Gray
John H. Langbein
Eben Moglen
Henry E. Smith
Albert W. Alschuler

THE UNIVERSITY OF CHICAGO PRESS
CHICAGO & LONDON

R. H. HELMHOLZ is the Ruth Wyatt Rosenson Professor of Law at the University of Chicago. CHARLES M. GRAY is professor of history at the University of Chicago. JOHN H. LANGBEIN is the Chancellor Kent Professor of Law and Legal History at Yale University. EBEN MOGLEN is professor of law at Columbia University. HENRY E. SMITH is a law clerk to Judge Ralph K. Winter of the U.S. Court of Appeals for the Second Circuit. ALBERT W. ALSCHULER is the Wilson-Dickinson Professor of Law at the University of Chicago.

The University of Chicago Press, Chicago 60637
The University of Chicago Press, Ltd., London
© 1997 by The University of Chicago
All rights reserved. Published 1997
Printed in the United States of America
06 05 04 03 02 01 00 99 98 97   1 2 3 4 5

ISBN (cloth): 0-226-32660-8

Library of Congress Cataloging-in-Publication Data

The privilege against self-incrimination : its origins and development
    / R. H. Helmholz . . . [et al.].
        p. cm.
    Includes bibliographical references and index.
    ISBN 0-226-32660-8 (cloth : alk. paper)
      1. Self-incrimination—Great Britain—History. 2. Self-
    incrimination—United States—History. I. Helmholz, R. H.
    KD8386.P75   1997
    345.41'056—dc20
    [344.10556]   96-35847
                                                                  CIP

In its inception, this book was the product of coincidence. Three of us, all then teaching at the University of Chicago, discovered that we had been examining different aspects of the same subject: the history of the privilege against self-incrimination. After some thought and discussion, we agreed to pool our efforts. We shared a desire to correct one or another of what we regarded as weaknesses in the historical account of the privilege found in Leonard Levy's influential book, Origins of the Fifth Amendment (1st ed. 1968), and we thought that we would be able to improve on it. Our work on the unprinted sources, most of which we were exploring for the first time, put the whole subject in a new and different light. We recognized, of course, that a part of our efforts would be "revisionist" in nature and subject to the dangers of exaggeration that invariably attend this kind of scholarship. But even so, we all hoped that a more coherent picture of the subject would emerge from a collaborative effort. We knew that none of us could accomplish this without the help of others. Chapters 1 through 4 are the result of that decision.

These initial discussions took place several years ago. The interval between our plan's framing and its execution has been longer than any of us hoped or expected. But this delay has not been all misfortune. In the meantime several good things have happened. Most happily, we were able to find co-workers to fill in some of the blanks in the story as we understood it. We first recruited Eben Moglen of Columbia Law School to undertake research into the history of the privilege in early American law; then Henry Smith, at that time a student at Yale Law School, to examine the subject during the nineteenth century, and finally, Albert Alschuler of the University of Chicago Law School to add an evaluation of the present-day status of the privilege in light of its history. Their contributions make up chapters 5 through 7, and the three of us are very grateful for their willingness to join our effort.

Several of us have also published earlier versions of our research in the meantime. They have all been revised in preparing them for this book, both to make them fit together in presentation and to bring them up to date in light of further research. However, their principal conclusions have undoubtedly been anticipated in the earlier articles. In chronological order, they are Charles M. Gray, Prohibitions and the Privilege against Self-Incrimination, in Tudor Rule & Revolution: Essays for G. R. Elton from His American Friends 345 (DeLloyd J. Guth and John W. McKenna eds., 1982); R. H. Helmholz, Origins of the Privilege against Self-Incrimination: The Role of the European *Ius Commune,* 65 New York University Law Review 962 (1990); John H. Langbein, The Historical Origins of the Privilege against Self-Incrimination at Common Law, 92 Michigan Law Review 1047 (1994); Eben Moglen, Taking the Fifth: Reconsidering the Origins of the Constitutional Privilege against Self-Incrimination, 92 Michigan Law Review 1086 (1994); and Albert W. Alschuler, A Peculiar Privilege in Historical Perspective: The Right to Remain Silent, 94 Michigan Law Review 2625 (1996).

Beattie, Crime and the Courts	John M. Beattie, Crime and the Courts in England 1660–1800 (Princeton 1986)
Bentham, Rationale	Jeremy Bentham, Rationale of Judicial Evidence Specially Applied to English Practice, 5 vols. (London 1827)
BL	British Library, London
Blackstone, Commentaries	William Blackstone, Commentaries on the Laws of England, 4 vols. (Oxford 1765–69)
Hawkins, Pleas of the Crown	William Hawkins, A Treatise of the Pleas of the Crown, 2 vols. (London 1716–21)
Holdsworth, History	William Holdsworth, A History of English Law, 17 vols. (7th ed. London 1956–72)
Langbein, Criminal Trial	John H. Langbein, The Criminal Trial Before the Lawyers, 45 University of Chicago Law Review 263 (1978)
Langbein, Ryder Sources	John H. Langbein, Shaping the Eighteenth-Century Criminal Trial: A View from the Ryder Sources, 50 University of Chicago Law Review 1 (1983)

Levy, Origins

Leonard W. Levy, Origins of the Fifth Amendment: The Right against Self-Incrimination (2d ed. New York 1986)

OBSP

Old Bailey Sessions Papers

Peake, Compendium

Thomas Peake, A Compendium of the Law of Evidence (London 1801)

State Trials

A Complete Collection of State Trials, T. B. & T. J. Howell eds., 33 vols. (London 1809–26)

Stephen, History

James Fitzjames Stephen, A History of the Criminal Law of England, 3 vols. (London 1883)

Wigmore, Evidence

John H. Wigmore, Evidence in Trials at Common Law, 11 vols. (3d ed. Boston 1940–date) (vol. 8, rev. ed. by John T. McNaughton Boston 1961)

ONE

Introduction

R. H. Helmholz

I. THE MODERN PRIVILEGE

The privilege against self-incrimination guarantees that men and women cannot lawfully be required to answer questions that will aid in convicting them of a crime. The privilege is widely regarded as both fundamental to human liberty and venerable in the history of the development of civil rights. Some form of the privilege can undoubtedly lay claim to antiquity, boasting a link with the Latin maxim often used to state it, *Nemo tenetur prodere seipsum,* a phrase reputed to have come from the pen of Saint John Chrysostom (d. 407). The saint's words proclaimed that no person should be compelled to betray himself in public. Put into secular form, those words became a rallying cry in the history of the protection of human liberty, an established feature of Anglo-American law, and a point of departure for developing legal systems.[1]

A. Current Status of the Privilege

The privilege is very much alive today. English statute law provides that any person charged with a crime "shall not be called as a witness . . . except upon his own application." The statute goes on to state that a failure on his part to give evidence "shall not be made the subject of any comment by the prosecution,"[2] although the continued vitality of the second part of the privilege's reach may be called into question by a 1994 statutory change allowing judges and juries to draw "such inferences as appear proper" from the defendant's failure to testify.[3] Most former English colonies adopted the privilege against self-incrimination as part of their system of criminal procedure, and almost all of them continue to adhere to the established privilege, though also subject in several cases to statutory modification.[4] Canada, for example, endorsed a strong though modified form of the privilege in its Constitution Act of 1982.[5] Even residents of the Fiji Islands, a British colony from 1874 to 1970, can boast of their legal system's adherence to the basic features of this established rule of law.[6]

Of these one-time colonies, none has been more tenacious in its attachment to the privilege against self-incrimination than the United States. The Fifth Amendment to the United States Constitution provides that no person "shall be compelled in any criminal case to be a witness against himself," and judicial decisions have read this clause as extending a good deal further than its words themselves require. The privilege against being compelled to "be a witness" against oneself may be invoked not only by persons who are being tried for their allegedly criminal conduct, but also by those who might be tried at some time in the future.[7] It applies to witnesses, who are not being subjected to prosecution, just as it does to defendants. It thereby protects men and women against potential as well as present criminal jeopardy. Under current American law, the privilege extends beyond the courtroom and the interrogation room of the police station. For example, it can be invoked by witnesses appearing before committees of the houses of Congress. And the privilege reaches further than forbidding the asking of specifically incriminating questions. It permits anyone being accused of a crime to refuse to testify at all and (at least in theory) to suffer no adverse consequence from that refusal.[8] With reason has the United States Supreme Court described the "spirit of the Self-Incrimination Clause"[9] as an animating principle of American law. It is such an expansive spirit that underlies many of the judicial decisions formulating the reach of the privilege. The privilege is accordingly regarded as a fundamental, even sacred "right to remain silent."[10]

B. Criticism of the Privilege

Notwithstanding that "expansive spirit" and the lyricism that has sometimes accompanied invocation of the right to remain silent,[11] the privilege has been a subject of controversy from the time it became an effective part of our law. When subjected to analysis instead of celebration, the privilege's virtues have seemed less obvious to a long chain of critics. Jeremy Bentham, the most famous (and vocal) of its nineteenth-century critics, published a scathing examination of the whole subject in 1827.[12] Bentham came to the conclusion that the privilege was a product of irrational prejudice, one for which no convincing justification could be advanced.[13] The privilege had the inevitable effect of excluding the most reliable evidence of the truth— that which is available only from the person accused—necessarily causing greater weight to be given to hearsay and other inferior sorts of evidence.

Nor, in Bentham's view, would the reasons commonly advanced for the privilege stand any but the most superficial scrutiny. That requiring persons accused of a crime to answer questions that might help convict them would be unduly hard on those who stood in fear for life and limb, he dismissed as the product of misplaced emotion. It was nothing but an "old woman's reason," notable principally for its feeble sentimentalism. That requiring defendants to answer such questions would give an unfair advantage to the prosecutor, he ridiculed with equal vehemence as a "fox-hunter's reason." It confused sport with a search for the truth. To say that the privilege was necessary to protect defendants against judicial torture and ideological persecution, Bentham regarded as a quite fallacious argument from history. The privilege might well have performed that function in past centuries, but it was quite unnecessary under conditions of the nineteenth century. By the 1800s, English law had long since excluded the rack and the strappado. It had other, more effective and less harmful, means of protecting freedoms of thought and belief. For Bentham, it seemed clear that this privilege, which had the inevitable effect of hindering courts from discovering the truth, formed no part of a rational legal system. It was a rule both unnecessary and unwise, perpetuated simply by the "imperturbable complacency" of English lawyers and others who had been "duped and corrupted by English lawyers."[14]

Bentham's analysis and the invective he heaped on the privilege had little actual effect on the legal status of the privilege in the years when he wrote. Indeed his work coincided with the very period when the privilege was assuming its full, modern form.[15] But the long-term effects of his writing cannot be ignored. Serious criticism of the privilege has persisted. At the start of this century, its most accomplished and thorough student, John Henry Wigmore, at first called for outright abolition of the privilege[16] and later (in a more considered judgment) for its confinement within the "strictest limits" consistent with the language of the Fifth Amendment.[17] Wigmore was far from standing alone in this opinion.[18] Even its defenders have sometimes felt themselves obliged to acknowledge that the traditional justifications for the privilege read more like "empty pomposities" than reasoned judgments.[19] Criticism has been a feature of commentary about the privilege almost as frequently as praise.

Of the modern critics, probably the best known is Henry J. Friendly, the distinguished American judge, who died in 1992. In 1968, Friendly surveyed the then recent developments in the law, finding the lengths to which the privilege had been pushed by American courts unsupported by any coherent rationale.[20] Some of what he said covered the same ground Bentham had, reaching pretty much the same conclusions. Friendly was able, however, to take into account a virtue that was not so obvious during Bentham's era: the right of privacy. In the intervening years, this right had become part of the legal landscape, at least in the United States. It had become widely accepted that the "protection of personal privacy [was] a central purpose of the privilege against compelled self-incrimination."[21] Many commentators agreed that this was the true rationale for the rule, and much contemporary support for the privilege's extension undoubtedly comes from the widespread attractiveness of this concept.[22] That no one recognized it during the nineteenth century need make no significant difference. The law often finds new reasons for old rules; here is a good example.

Judge Friendly, however, found the privacy-based argument unconvincing. The privilege prevents the disclosure of evidence relating to a good deal of conduct that cannot by any stretch of the imagination be described as private. At the same time modern law does require disclosure of much that is decidedly private in nature. And in any event, under established law no one doubts that the government may violate any person's right to privacy, thus requiring that person's testimony, simply by giving him immunity from future prosecution.[23] Even if one concedes the desirability of an ample right of privacy, therefore, to Judge Friendly the privilege against self-incrimination seemed to have little to do with achieving that result.

Thus has the privilege remained controversial.[24] It continues to produce hotly contested cases in the courts,[25] a disputatious literature in the law reviews,[26] and strong reactions—indignant, laudatory, and puzzled—among informed observers.[27] Even where the rationale underlying the privilege has been agreed on in principle, the practical conclusions drawn from that rationale have not always been harmonious. Much of the case law has also seemed internally contradictory to responsible critics.[28] And disagreement about the wisdom of these decisions has often been sharp.

C. Historical Treatments of the Privilege

In much of the controversy surrounding the privilege, the starting point has been its history. Answers to present dilemmas are sought in the privilege's past. Although it has sometimes been contended that the "noble principle" animating the privilege "transcends its origins,"[29] this has never meant that the subject's history has been dismissed as irrelevant. It was with regard to the privilege against self-incrimination that Justice Felix Frankfurter once borrowed a favorite aphorism of Oliver Wendell Holmes, to the effect that "a page of history is worth a volume of logic."[30] Many judges and lawyers have followed that lead. A fuller historical understanding of the subject, surely desirable for its own sake, may also be relevant to present-day controversies, and this live possibility has led men and women who might not otherwise have done so to look into the subject's past.

Unfortunately, the understanding has proved elusive.[31] Despite repeated calls for a satisfactory historical treatment,[32] none has been written. Wigmore's great treatise on the law of evidence did not pretend to give a complete account.[33] Wigmore misunderstood some of the early evidence, he was obliged to leave many aspects of the subject unexplained, and he himself had reservations about some of his conclusions.[34] Leonard Levy's Origins of the Fifth Amendment,[35] although widely treated as a definitive account,[36] has not in fact met the need. Levy's work too often overlooks the legal context of the evidence and concentrates too exclusively on famous "show trials." The consequence is that he does not do full justice to the complexity of the privilege's actual development. A product of the era of McCarthyism in the United States, Levy's work made a strong argument for the vitality of the privilege as a basic civil liberty. That approach does not necessarily make for the most accurate history, however. Today something else is needed.

This book is intended to supply a better understanding of the history of the subject. It provides a fuller and (we hope) more realistic understanding of the privilege as it existed at various stages in the history of Anglo-American law. Our law has indeed long known a rule based on the *Nemo tenetur* maxim, but that rule has not always meant the same thing. Nor has it always been effective in practice. Although there have been continuities, overall it is surprising how differently the maxim has been interpreted and used at various times in the past.[37] The centrality of the oath and its connection with the privilege in earlier times have been particularly hard for modern writers to understand. Thus chapter 6 draws a distinction between the full privilege as we know it today and the rules about silence that had previously existed in the common law. These differences make it impossible to speak of the privilege as a coherent right that has always existed and has gradually won recognition by the courts. In fact it has served different purposes.

Admittedly, the chapters that follow do not fill all the gaps in our knowledge. Each of the contributions acknowledges that questions remain. However, a good deal of new evidence has been turned up by the authors of this book—enough to provide a more complete account than has so far existed. Above all, the authors have tried to look at the evidence within its contemporary legal context. Doing this makes one conclusion certain. The evidence shows repeatedly how halting, how slow, and how controversial have been the steps by which the modern privilege against self-incrimination became an accepted part of our law. Despite its reputation as a foundation stone of common law jurisprudence,[38] and despite the existence of some form of a rule against compelling sworn testimony in every period covered, the privilege as we know it is actually the product of relatively recent choice.

II. THE STAGES OF DEVELOPMENT

There are several chapters in the history of the creation of an effective privilege against self-incrimination, and although there are points of continuity, there are also real differences among them. Each of them is treated separately in this book. Chapters 2 through 5 take the reader from the end of the Middle Ages up to the adoption of the Fifth Amendment to the United States Constitution. Then, in chapter 6, the story moves into the nineteenth century, when the privilege in its modern, fully protective sense made its appearance. Chapter 7 assesses the current status of the privilege in light of its history.

A. The Medieval Privilege and the *Ius Commune*

Chapter 2 deals with the medieval *ius commune,* the immediate source of the maxim *Nemo tenetur prodere seipsum.* The term *ius commune,* translated literally as "common law," refers to the combination of the Roman and canon laws that was the product of the revival of juristic science in the twelfth century and was more fully developed in the centuries that followed.[39] The Latin term remains in use in order to distinguish it from the English common law. The basis for legal education in all European universities, including the English universities, before the Age of Codification, the *ius commune* was applied in Continental courts where no local statute or custom directed the contrary. It also provided the basic rules that governed practice in the English ecclesiastical courts, where the privilege's early history in England was played out. The *ius commune* itself recognized a rule against compelled self-incrimination.

The nature of that rule—of both its reach and the exceptions to it within the jurisdiction of the church—is the subject of chapter 2. Of the existence of a privilege against self-incrimination in the *ius commune* there can be no doubt. The chapter examines the nature of the rule as it was understood by the early jurists. It also reviews the evidence of the rule's assertion in practice within the courts of the English church. The chapter shows that in the *ius commune* the rule served principally as a guarantee that men and women would not be required to become the *source* of their own public prosecution. The privilege was a check on overzealous officials rather than a subjective right that could be invoked by anyone who stood in danger of criminal prosecution. In practice, the rule thus seems to have served something like the function "probable cause" does in modern American law. It served, in other words, to ensure that the canon law's fundamental purposes would be upheld. It was designed to guarantee that only when there was good reason for suspecting that a particular person had violated the law would it be permissible to require that person to answer incriminating questions. That was not a negligible safeguard for ordinary men and women, but it was admittedly a far cry from the modern privilege.[40]

B. The Early Modern Privilege and Interjurisdictional Law

Chapter 3 takes up the subject in the late sixteenth and early seventeenth centuries, a time when the maxim could be used as a weapon by English common law judges. In some of their opinions one finds the first clear statements of the principle. The statements did not, however, occur within the context of common law trials. They occurred in the context of judicial attempts to prevent the ecclesiastical courts from acting beyond the scope of their jurisdiction. The English royal courts had long claimed a right to police the boundaries that separated the spheres of jurisdiction that belonged to church and state. They accomplished this by issuing writs of prohibition and of habeas corpus, writs that kept the courts of the church from proceeding in cases in which they had overstepped the boundary line. In the late sixteenth century, opposition to the religious policies of the church coalesced with an expansive view of the supervisory powers of the common law judges to produce arguments that writs should issue to keep the ecclesiastical courts from requiring defendants to answer incriminating questions.

The common law judges sometimes accepted these arguments, but, it seems, only in egregious cases, mostly those in which interests of the common law courts themselves could plausibly be described as threatened by the actions of the ecclesiastical courts. The common law judges were being asked to serve as superintendents of a mixed system of justice. They recognized that each of the two jurisdictions had a legitimate part in that system. On that account, the judges were reluctant to go too far in interfering with the procedures of the ecclesiastical courts. To have seized on every opportunity that arose to curtail the jurisdiction of the church's courts would have upset the balance. That they did not wish to do. Indeed the judges' actions were not greatly at odds with the legal principles of the *ius commune* surveyed in chapter 2. It is too much to say, therefore, that they established an effective privilege against self-incrimination, even within the spiritual courts themselves. Only a statute of 1640 brought to an end the practice of interrogating defendants under oath in those courts,[41] and most of the common law judges of this era were very far from averring that the privilege had any particular relevance to the day-to-day operation of their own system of criminal justice.

C. Common Law Criminal Procedure to the Mid-Eighteenth Century

The privilege's status in the common law courts is the subject of chapter 4. This chapter takes the reader inside the ordinary criminal trial in early modern England. When one examines what happened in practice, it becomes evident that English criminal procedure made it virtually impossible for a privilege against self-incrimination to be asserted effectively by persons charged with a crime. The impossibility was the indirect result of the common law's refusal to allow criminal defendants to be represented by a lawyer and of the restrictions placed on other rules regarding silence on the part of the accused, rules that did not begin to be relaxed until the eighteenth century. Without professional assistance, persons accused of a crime had little choice but to speak for themselves. Help from the judges was sporadic; it was insufficient to shelter men and women charged with having committed ordinary felonies.

This chapter shows in detail some of the ways in which criminal defendants conducted their own defense. Defendants could not be sworn, but they were allowed to speak widely on their own behalf, and almost all of them did so—some with considerable ability. If they did not speak, however, no one spoke for them. In such circumstances, assertion of a right not to answer incriminating questions amounted to a right to forgo real defense. It is no wonder, therefore, that Wigmore found so little evidence that the privilege was being exercised during the seventeenth and the early eighteenth centuries. Without the active participation of defense counsel in criminal cases, *Nemo tenetur prodere seipsum* remained a maxim worthy of respect, but one with severely limited practical consequences.[42] Only with the arrival of active participation by lawyers, men able to speak in place of the accused and to make use of the potential of an emerging law of evidence,[43] could the privilege begin its effective development as a protection of criminal defendants in the common law.

D. American Developments

Chapter 5 crosses the Atlantic. There has been a particular need for adequate tracing of the events that led to the inclusion of the privilege in the Fifth Amendment to the United States Constitution. Ordinary criminal procedure in the American colonies has been less fully studied than has procedure in English courts. The common understanding and implementation of the privilege *after* its enactment has stood equally in need of research. From what can now be discovered, however, it appears that most colonial trials followed the English pattern, in which conduct of the defense was left to the accused. In fact, the general scarcity of lawyers, a distrust of all oath taking, the heterogeneity and sparseness of the population, and widespread acceptance of summary procedure made effective implementation of the privilege even more difficult in British North America than it was in England.

From this starting point, the privilege nevertheless made its way into several state constitutions and ultimately the federal Constitution. Americans apparently felt little unease about their own failure to observe the safeguards guaranteed to defendants under the privilege as we understand it today. But they were very worried about what might happen in the future.

At least to some it seemed quite conceivable that the government of the United States might adopt something like a Spanish Inquisition. There must be protection against that ever happening, and the privilege was regarded as part of a "cluster of legal rules" designed to prevent it. In light of the present situation, it is ironic that when arguments against the use of incriminating statements made by the accused were first made in American courts, they were not couched in terms of a constitutional right. They were couched in terms of preservation of traditional procedures. The connection to the Fifth Amendment, second nature to us, was not so obvious to our ancestors. Like the English, in matters of ordinary criminal procedure Americans came relatively late to effective implementation of the privilege.

E. The Nineteenth Century and the Creation of an Effective Privilege

Chapter 6 allows us to enter into the details of legal argument that, at last, allowed the nascent privilege to be asserted effectively in ordinary criminal trials. It surveys the several contributions to the development of an effective privilege made by statutory changes, treatise writers, parliamentary debate, and contemporary cases. These developments made it possible for the privilege against self-incrimination to become a truly protective right that men and women accused of a crime could actually use. Prior to these developments, English law had known several rules that had kept parties to litigation from having to testify: the disqualification for interest, the inadmissibility of unlawfully obtained confessions, and the privilege of witnesses not to answer self-incriminating questions. All of these rules had exceptions, however, and mostly they worked *against* criminal defendants in the English system. Fully considered, none provided the real protection that the modern privilege provides.

The chapter demonstrates how these rules developed and coalesced with legislative changes of the nineteenth century. Expansion of the right to counsel was, of course, a fundamental prerequisite. But it was not enough in itself. Nor was the path entirely smooth. Legislative removal of the disqualification for interest, for example, actually made things worse for defendants, since it removed their excuse for not speaking in their own behalf. It was only when the witness privilege was fully applied to defendants that it became possible to implement the privilege as a matter of day-to-day practice. The currents came together, notably in *R. v. Garbett,* an 1847 case that cemented the analogy between the privilege witnesses had long enjoyed and the rights of criminal defendants. It is only at that late date, this chapter concludes, that it makes sense to speak of the privilege in anything like its modern form.

F. The Privilege Today

Chapter 7 both reviews and steps back from the detailed historical evidence. Its object is to describe where we stand today. The chapter focuses primarily on American law. This is entirely appropriate, because the law of the United States depends so heavily on the understanding given to the Fifth Amendment to the Constitution. Indeed this focus is appropriate in a second way. The privilege against self-incrimination is the subject of a great deal of current discussion among American scholars. Their vantage points have ranged from the insights of moral theory to severely practical concerns about the effect on crime, but they have all centered attention on questioning (or defending) the privilege's justification.

Albert Alschuler concludes from his survey of the privilege's history that the law on this subject should not be constrained in a constitutional "straitjacket." At least the privilege's history does not require it. The several differences between the late eighteenth century's legal system and today's would make it literally impossible to return to the "original understanding" of the Fifth Amendment, even assuming that the evidence provided an unambiguous picture of what that understanding was (which it does not). Alschuler does not suggest that we make such an unrewarding effort. What the historical record does allow us to do, however, is to take a more realistic look at the reasons for the privilege's scope than its apparent enshrinement as a fundamental civil liberty that was established at the very dawn of our legal system has sometimes seemed to require.

III. COMMON APPROACHES

Each subsequent chapter of this book is written by a different author, someone whose interests have been concentrated on the subject and time period covered in the chapter. Despite this potential source of discontinuity, the chapters are not merely essays on the same general subject. They are part of one story. Indeed they are expressly linked by internal connections. Some of these connections are compelled by the development of the privilege itself. Others, however, follow from the authors' united approach to the privilege's history. Four common convictions have animated our efforts to describe the privilege's historical development.

A. The Ambiguous Nature of the Privilege

First, there is very little that is self-evident or organic about the privilege. Except in the most general sense, its history cannot accurately be portrayed as the progressive realization of one fundamental human right. In fact, the meaning given to the maxim *Nemo tenetur prodere seipsum* has varied from one period to another. It has not been a slow-growing plant tended by successive generations of human rights advocates until at last it bloomed fully in the Fifth Amendment. It is quite true that advocates of the privilege in every age have always made use of what had gone before them. They have taken existing legal precedents into different contexts, turning them to new uses. In that sense there has been progression, even continuity of a kind. It cannot be called organic, however. The differences between its understanding in one period and that in another have been as great as the similarities. The rule has meant different things at different times.

Moreover, actual implementation of an effective legal rule based on the *Nemo tenetur* maxim has been limited. Enforcement of the privilege was shaped by the legal circumstances and the understanding of the people who argued in its favor. The English common lawyers who used it to rein in the activities of the Court of High Commission or the Star Chamber were not seeking to establish an invariable rule of practice or "procedures indispensable to fair trial or due process of law."[44] Had this been their aim, they would have applied the rule to unsworn statements made in their own courts, or at least they would have argued that it should have been applied there. The fact is, they did not even make the connection. Legal history is filled with instances where in hindsight practice in the courts does not seem to measure up to the ideals professed by thoughtful men and women of the time. This is one such instance.[45] The contradiction seems apparent to us. It was not to them.

B. The Primacy of the Ordinary Criminal Trial

Second, the focus of a satisfactory history of the privilege against self-incrimination must be on ordinary criminal procedure. If one is to speak of the existence of a privilege, the privilege must provide protection for ordinary witnesses and criminal defendants in the common run of cases. A legal rule must be a general one, available to all who choose to assert it, if it is to be both effective and treated as an established rule of law. This means that the question of its status at any time can be answered satisfactorily only by looking at the procedure routinely employed by the criminal courts. Political trials have always been special. They involve contentious political issues; they excite great public interest; they call forth the best lawyers available; and they encourage legal innovation. Humdrum trials for larceny or assault, by contrast, attract the attention of no one but the people immediately concerned. But it is to these ordinary trials that the historian must look if he or she is to draw satisfactory conclusions about the privilege's meaning and development.[46]

Unfortunately, much of the historical inquiry into the history of the privilege has focused on the evidence found in political trials and political tracts. It may be said, and with some justification, that these were the only readily available sources at the time Wigmore wrote his pioneering account. Today, however, historians are no longer obliged to be content with these sources. Manuscript records have been explored. More thorough investigation of the early pamphlet literature has been carried out. The past twenty years have produced substantial progress in our knowledge of the way ordinary criminal trials were conducted in England.[47] From this perspective, the history of the privilege can now be written more accurately.

C. The Importance of Lawyers

Third, lawyers were crucial in the development of the privilege. Perhaps no single aspect of this subject separates us more clearly from the thoughts of our ancestors than our assumptions about the desirability of allowing trained lawyers to conduct criminal trials. Today it seems axiomatic that defendants should be represented by a lawyer. If the crime is a serious one, American law has made such representation a matter of constitutional right.[48] English law virtually guarantees representation by a lawyer through a system of legal aid.[49] Very little argument is required to show the justice of this guarantee of professional legal representation.

Medieval law made exactly the opposite assumption. It seemed right that persons who had come under legitimate suspicion of having committed a crime should speak for themselves. Both the English common law and the European *ius commune* took that view.[50] Criminal defendants should not be represented by someone else. The men who formulated the early law of criminal procedure did not come at the question from the point of view of the rights of the accused. They approached it from the perspective of what European writers call objective right. In practical terms, they asked: What procedure would both be fair and best reveal the truth? From that perspective, there was good reason to keep lawyers from speaking in place of the accused: lawyers might stand in the way of discovering the truth. Their assistance might, however, legitimately come into play when technical legal issues were raised. If the trial raised a question about the legal definition of the crime, for example, a professional might be permitted to give the defendant the benefit of his expertise. However, it was another matter entirely to allow a lawyer to "stand in" for the accused. That would hinder discovery of the facts. It would also risk leaving crimes unpunished.[51] Defendants should, therefore, speak for themselves, even if other legal principles dictated that they would not be allowed to do so under oath.

For various reasons, described in chapter 4 but still not fully understood, this "accused speaks" trial system was replaced by one that allowed defense counsel to appear in routine cases and to conduct the defense in place of the accused. In the sixteenth century, inroads in the old procedure began to be made within the *ius commune,* although it seems that this development was slow and half-hearted at the start.[52] Lawyers began to be permitted to represent defendants, first as a matter of grace and then as a matter of routine. As the final two chapters show, the English common law and then the American law arrived at the same point somewhat later.[53] Again, the step was taken for reasons that we understand imperfectly. But the step was taken. And with the arrival of the lawyers came the possibility of effective implementation of the privilege against self-incrimination. To leave lawyers out of the story, and to suppose that once the privilege had been accepted as a matter of principle it would somehow enforce itself, has proved to be a mistake.

D. The Centrality of the Oath

Fourth, apart from the question of the propriety of legal representation of criminal defendants, the aspect of understanding earlier ways of thinking about self-incrimination that divides us most decisively from our ancestors is the centrality they accorded to taking an oath. The oath's importance runs like a thread through all the book's chapters. In the *ius commune,* although there were exceptions, as a matter of rule all testimony was sworn testimony. If a statement by a witness was not made under oath, it was not testimony at all.[54] The judge could not take account of it in reaching his decision. In England, one of the reasons for the strength of feeling about the ex officio oath was precisely that it was an oath. Even in the procedure of the early common law, in which nothing prevented juries from considering whatever evidence they wished to in reaching a verdict, a line was drawn between sworn and unsworn statements.[55] Criminal defendants were allowed—even encouraged—to speak, but they were not allowed to speak under oath. *Their* privilege had to do with sworn statements. It could be seriously maintained that no violation of the principle behind the *Nemo tenetur* maxim occurred when a person had been made to answer questions, as long as he had not been required to answer them under oath.

Today, this habit of mind is all but lost to us. As Alschuler's concluding assessment puts it, "Oaths have lost their terror and even their meaning" in the modern world. What real difference does it make, we ask, whether a statement is made under oath, so long as it can be heard and acted on by the jury? We are heirs of legal realism, and perhaps we are right. The oath may well make no substantive difference in the outcome of criminal trials. But this is not how our ancestors thought about the question. To understand the history of the privilege, we must attempt to think their thoughts, not convicting them of hypocrisy too quickly. We must suspend our skepticism about the importance of the swearing and give to the oath the centrality it once held.

IV. CONCLUSION

As a matter of principle, the privilege against self-incrimination has a long and distinguished history in Anglo-American law. Taken in the first instance from the medieval *ius commune,* it was invoked against the ecclesiastical and prerogative courts during the sixteenth and seventeenth centuries. Sir Edward Coke himself knew and used it.[56] He was not alone, and the privilege was not only a means of disciplining a rival system of courts. It was long stated and admired by English lawyers. It appeared, in fact, in some of the most influential works written by English common lawyers, such as William Lambarde's manual for justices of the peace, Eirenarcha (1581),[57] and William Blackstone's Commentaries on the Laws of England (1765–69).[58] It was made part of the constitutions of several American states and then placed into the United States Constitution itself. There never was a time when the *Nemo tenetur* maxim meant nothing at all. It kept magistrates from interrogating witnesses and criminal defendants under oath.

There was never a time when it had no practical consequences whatsoever.

As an effective safeguard for persons accused of having committed a crime, however, the privilege turns out to have been less pervasive and more controversial than its long-time acceptance in principle would suggest. In the context of ordinary criminal trials, ways around the implications of the *Nemo tenetur* maxim have long been found. The privilege's limited reach and its invariable connection with oath-taking left room for incriminating questioning in other circumstances. The privilege thus had less than a dramatic impact on substantial aspects of the common law criminal trial until the late eighteenth century, at the earliest, and it became the subject of heated controversy as soon as it began to be fully implemented in the nineteenth century. The authors of this book believe that the true history of the privilege should be based on an examination of its place in the procedure in these ordinary criminal trials, and that is what the following chapters attempt to provide.

TWO

The Privilege and the Ius Commune: The Middle Ages to the Seventeenth Century

R. H. Helmholz

I. INTRODUCTION

Within the Western legal tradition, the Latin maxim commonly used to state the principle underlying the modern privilege against self-incrimination—*Nemo tenetur prodere seipsum*—had its origins in the European *ius commune*.[1] The medieval canon law, the ecclesiastical half of the *ius commune,* contained a definitive statement that "No person is to be compelled to accuse himself." Canonists made use of the words of the Latin maxim to state the rule.[2] Even the Roman law half of the *ius commune* (an unlikely source, one would have supposed) was ransacked by the medieval jurists and found to contain texts supporting a rule against compelling persons to answer incriminating questions.[3]

Not only are the maxim's origins in the *ius commune* certain; during the Middle Ages, the rule against compelled self-incrimination expressed by the maxim became a juristic commonplace. The rule was stated and explained, for instance, in the most popular procedural manual of the medieval *ius commune,* the Speculum iudiciale, compiled by William Durantis (d. 1296).[4] It was set out with particularity in a great deal of the contemporary legal literature from the Continent—for instance, in the commentaries on the law of the church written by Panormitanus, the most famous canonist of the fifteenth century;[5] in basic manuals describing the procedural rules to be followed by the judges and lawyers in the courts;[6] and in the Decisiones capellae Tholosanae, the influential collection of medieval decisions rendered by the archiepiscopal court at Toulouse.[7] Long before any appearance of a privilege against self-incrimination in the English common law, therefore, its underlying principle was to be found stated and discussed within the copious traditions of the European *ius commune*.

Although this precedence in time has been acknowledged by virtually all investigators who have written about the history of the subject, few of them have attributed the source of the modern privilege against self-incrimination to the *ius commune*. Indeed the most widely accepted account of the origins of the right to remain silent in criminal trials holds something very like the reverse. That account regards the privilege's recognition in Anglo-American law as the result of an explicit rejection of the law of the church.[8] It holds that there was a fundamental opposition over the status of the privilege between the English common law and the European *ius commune*, and for the honor of having been the effective source of the modern privilege, the palm is awarded to the English law.[9]

Such an understanding of the way law grows may seem surprising at first sight. But it is not without its reasons—respectable reasons. Some of the earliest and most dramatic statements of the rule in the English common law were made as part of attempts to keep the church from imposing on defendants an oath that would require them to incriminate themselves. The ex officio oath, or the oath *de veritate dicenda,* as it was more commonly styled in canonical parlance, was used by virtually all the courts of the English church. These courts exercised an active jurisdiction over a variety of religious offenses, including dissent from the doctrines and ceremonies of the Church of England. The oath was applied with particular effect in the branches of the Court of High Commission, the tribunal that was created under the Tudor monarchs and given a broader jurisdiction to suppress such dissent than the ordinary diocesan courts possessed.[10] Procedure in the High Commission, as in all ecclesiastical courts, did in fact sometimes require a form of self-incrimination. About its legality there was dispute, and that dispute seemed to pit the English common lawyers, as opponents of the oath, against the oath's defenders, the officials of the courts of the church.

This dispute was, at bottom, a contest for control between rival court systems. The questions it raised were treated, as chapter 3 shows in more detail, as matters of interjurisdictional law. However, the contest brought the question of the legality of the ex officio oath into play incidentally. This happened because a part of the contest involved the reach of the royal writs of prohibition and of habeas corpus. The question was whether these writs could be used to prevent the ecclesiastical courts from requiring defendants to take the oath. Orders from the royal courts prohibiting inferior courts from continuing a particular case or proceeding, writs of prohibition were granted when a court subject to supervision by the Crown had exceeded its jurisdiction, and during the sixteenth and seventeenth centuries attempts were made to prevent the ecclesiastical courts from making use of the oath through issuance of these writs. The writ of habeas corpus similarly allowed the royal courts to test the legality of imprisonment imposed by another court. Its use seemed particularly appropriate in cases where the High Commission had exercised the power to imprison it claimed under English statute.

The nature and context of these attempts to curb ecclesiastical jurisdiction are the subject of chapter 3. In connection with the subject of this chapter, however, the essential point is that in some of the ensuing cases, *Nemo tenetur* was mentioned as one of the grounds for granting relief. In specific cases, it was sometimes asserted that use of the ex officio oath was beyond the jurisdictional competence of the ecclesiastical courts. The threat of its imposition in the ecclesiastical forum thus provided one reason for prohibiting hearing of the case. Because of this circumstance, it has seemed reasonable to assume that the law of the church must have stood in stark opposition to the emergent position of English common law. The ecclesiastical courts must have embraced the use of an oath requiring self- incrimination, despite the apparent ecclesiastical origin of the *Nemo tenetur* maxim.

The reality is rather more complicated. The chapters that follow demonstrate this complexity within the history of the common law itself. In fact, however, something like the same complexity exists with regard to the *ius commune,* which was the principal source of law within the English ecclesiastical courts.[11] Understanding the full history of the privilege against self-incrimination requires taking a closer look at the privilege as it stood in the law of the church and in the European legal tradition more generally. Taking that closer look puts the history of the oath into a different perspective from that found in the most widely accepted accounts.

This chapter begins by exploring both the formal rules of the *ius commune* and the evidence concerning the application of those rules found in the court records of the English church. The *ius commune* provided the basic rules of decision for the ecclesiastical courts both before and after the Reformation. Seeking a connection between the formal law and legal practice is therefore a logical possibility. Not only is it logical; the connection is substantiated by the records themselves. Together with commentaries and case reports compiled by the ecclesiastical lawyers who served in the courts of the church, the official records demonstrate that academic treatments of the question of compelled self-incrimination were not purely theoretical. The academic law had consequences in English practice, and an appreciation of those consequences is important in arriving at a fuller history of the privilege.

II. ARGUMENTS FROM THE *IUS COMMUNE*

The pertinent question is the legality of the ex officio oath under the law that governed procedure in the ecclesiastical courts. In light of the subject's history, the primary focus must rest on the *ius commune* as it stood in the years around 1600. There was in fact no real break between the law that prevailed at that time and the law that had been in force during the Middle Ages. There had, however, been some evolution, and in particular there was more extended commentary on the subject in the sixteenth-century literature.[12] That literature shows that the question of the oath's legality was not a simple one. This turns out to be one of those questions (of which there were many in the *ius commune*) that provided abundant ammunition for both sides in the dispute.

Arguments about the privilege, pro and con, were articulated in two different ways. One approach asked whether defendants could be obliged to submit to ex officio ecclesiastical proceedings in the first place and, if they could, under what conditions and with what safeguards. The second approach asked whether defendants who were legitimately before the courts and had been subjected to the oath could then be required to answer specific incriminating questions and, if they could, with what limitations in scope. Although both forms of analysis questioned the legality of requiring self-incrimination on the part of criminal defendants, the two ways of putting the question raised slightly different issues. They called forth different arguments in contemporary legal thought. They were also raised separately in English practice before the ecclesiastical courts.

Whichever approach was selected, it is fair to say that the stated rule of the medieval *ius commune* stood opposed to the practice of compelling defendants to incriminate themselves. Texts and commentaries alike appeared to support the argument that no one could be required to take an oath that compelled this of him. The ex officio oath appeared to be illegal if one took a "plain meaning" approach to the texts. Few did so, however. As so often happened under the *ius commune,* the stated rule admitted of exceptions. It contained complications. It invited limitations and amplifications. It gave rise to restrictions and extensions. The result when put into practice came to look quite different from the impression given by the initial rule. The best way of understanding the question, together with the complexities and subtleties that attended it, is to begin by exploring the arguments made against the oath's legality and then to move in due course through the counterarguments.

A. *Nemo punitur sine accusatore*

The first argument against the ex officio oath as practiced in the English ecclesiastical courts was that the whole procedure associated with the oath was invalid because it lacked an accuser. A common maxim of the *ius commune* held that *Nemo punitur sine accusatore*.[13] The maxim encapsulated an established rule that a judge could not initiate criminal proceedings against any person on his own initiative.[14] Court officials were not permitted to undertake what we would call "fishing expeditions" to uncover evidence of wrongdoing. Nor was just anyone entitled to stir up strife by setting the machinery of justice into motion. The law required that before any criminal prosecution could take place, a formal accusation against the defendant had to be made by someone with a legitimate interest in securing the defendant's conviction.

1. Basis for the Rule

This rule was more than a matter of legal convenience. Sixteenth-century civilians gave three reasons for the requirement, the first based on precedent from Holy Writ, the second on notions of basic fairness and due process, the third on express texts in the canon law. These three reasons were also buttressed by citations from the Roman law. Like many such issues in the canon law, however, they were not limited by, or ultimately dependent on, the civil law's authority.

First, initiating criminal proceedings without an accuser was said to be contrary to divine law. Indeed it was contrary to a specific biblical precedent. The Gospels record that Jesus had said to the woman taken in adultery, " 'Woman, where are those thine accusers? hath no one condemned thee?' She said, 'No one, Lord.' And Jesus said unto her, 'Neither do I condemn thee.' "[15] This was weighty authority. Commentators understood his statement not, as most of us would, as a condemnation of self-righteousness and a counsel of compassion. They regarded it as making a specific legal point: the woman could not lawfully be condemned in the absence of a legitimate accuser. The words of Jesus himself were thought to demonstrate the illegality of prosecutions and punishments based on mere public gossip. Put into legal parlance, Jesus had forbidden bringing prosecutions in which no specific person had appeared to make the accusation.[16]

Second, it was said that permitting ex officio proceedings without an accuser perverted the right order of justice, under which the judge stood above partisanship. By definition a judge was, or at least was supposed to be, an impartial third party. He was interposed between accuser and accused.[17] If no accuser stood on the other side, however, the judge's objectivity inevitably was undermined. The practice permitted and even encouraged the judge to make the cause his own, something contrary to texts of the Roman law and to principles of natural justice alike.[18] Thus it could be said (and in fact was said in English practice) that even without considering the precise nature of the oath, the whole ex officio procedure was unlawful because it violated this established norm of justice.[19] This argument was particularly forceful where no copy of the specific charges was first given to the defendant. Respectable canonical opinion, supported by a decision of the Rota Romana, held that natural justice required a copy of preliminary process to be furnished to anyone accused of a crime before the oath could be imposed.[20] To withhold it exacerbated the problem of the judge's improper assumption of a partisan role. It put too much weight on the side of the prosecution.

Third, it was said that the ex officio procedure violated the positive law of the church in that it contradicted specific texts of the canon law. Ordinary procedure, sanctioned by a papal decretal included in the Decretales Gregorii IX, held that before a man elected to ecclesiastical office could be confirmed in it, his superiors should hold an inquest to determine his fitness for the office.[21] That inquest was expected to examine the question of whether he was guilty of any crime as one part of that determination. The decretal said specifically that in such an inquest no accuser was required. This was an argument against the procedure's legality in ordinary cases, however, because the canonists read this decretal *a contrario sensu*. Allowing the inquest in this particular situation was said by the canonists to show that it was *not* allowed in other situations.[22] Why else would a specific decretal on the subject have been required? In such cases, the spiritual office was of the most vital importance to the church, and the crimes of the cleric seeking promotion might not be discovered in any other way.[23] The decretal had therefore been necessary to authorize something that otherwise would have contradicted the church's law.

2. Exceptions to the Rule

This third method of attacking the oath pointed to a weakness inherent in the argument. It was not a rule without exceptions, and one exception might breed others.[24] Defenders of the ex officio oath in England sought to take advantage of this fact. They maintained strenuously that the rule requiring an accuser had never been regarded as absolute under the *ius commune* and that practice in the English courts came within one or another of the several exceptions to the rule. As Richard Cosin, the Elizabethan apologist for ecclesiastical jurisdiction, was later to write, the rule requiring an accuser "hath many limitations."[25] Cosin was quite right. The thirteenth-century Glossa ordinaria to the Gregorian Decretals listed fourteen exceptions to the rule,[26] and Robertus Maranta, a sixteenth-century Italian proceduralist, managed to produce an astonishing list of sixty-three separate exceptions to the requirement of an accuser that had come to be available under the fully developed *ius commune*.[27]

The most important of these exceptions was that which permitted a judge to interrogate on his own authority when public fame circulated that a specific person had committed an offense.[28] A biblical precedent for the exception was found in the story of Cain and Abel in the Book of Genesis.[29] There, "the brother's blood" had cried out for redress, and action had been lawfully taken. Following the rule authorized, or at least illustrated, by this story, *fama publica* could be said to take the place of an accuser, particularly where there was danger to the public weal and where the crime was by its nature difficult to prove in the external forum, as Cain's crime had been and as many others necessarily are.[30] In such circumstances, public fame served the function of something like probable cause in the American legal system. It permitted a magistrate to carry out an essentially neutral role in criminal proceedings: acting to discover whether an accusation spread by public fame was also likely to be the fact.

The argument based on this exception was not necessarily a crushing rejoinder in determining the legitimacy of ex officio procedure. There were counterarguments available in the *ius commune,* and some of them had direct relevance to English practice. First, not all commentators admitted the breadth, or possibly even the existence, of the exception for simple *fama publica*. Like many such points in the *ius commune,* it was disputed. There was good authority, for example, for the proposition that the existence of simple public fame was insufficient. It had to have reached a level of "open clamorousness" and have come repeatedly to the judge's notice before it would justify judicial action in the absence of an accuser.[31] Panormitanus held, or at least suggested, an even stiffer position. He stated that neither reason nor equity required that a person be compelled to answer criminal matters because of public fame alone, because "public fame is often fallacious."[32] In this view, something more substantial in the way of actual proof would always be needed.

Second, even under the most generous understanding of the exception to the requirement of an accuser, defendants could attack the sufficiency of the fame in the particular circumstances of their case.[33] Not all public suspicion or rumor counted as sufficient *fama publica* to found a public prosecution under any reading of the *ius commune*. To constitute sufficient "opening" to warrant ex officio proceeding, according to the more common opinion of the jurists, it had to meet strict requirements.[34] The public fame had to have been the true source of the prosecution, it must have existed before legal proceedings had begun, and it must have been held by trustworthy persons. The jurists' effort was to exclude all suspicion that was inherently untrustworthy; it must not have had its origins in rumor-mongering by the enemies of the accused. Moreover, before proceedings could begin, the existence of sufficient *fama publica* had to be proved in the judicial arena. It could not simply be assumed to exist.[35] Finally, it was said by some jurists that the public fame had to be so vehement that open scandal would be generated by failure to act on it.

The opponents of the oath argued that the ex officio oath as used in English ecclesiastical courts passed none of these tests.[36] The officials of these courts were themselves the source of whatever fame there was—their actions were "official" prosecutions in the fullest and worst sense of the term. The judges truly were making these causes their own.[37] Moreover, in practice, judges in the English ecclesiastical courts were acting contrary to the law by presuming the existence of the *fama publica* merely from the fact that a defendant had been presented before them. They routinely denied defendants' demands for a separate inquest on the issue.[38] Finally, if any public scandal or other evil consequence was involved, that scandal was being generated by the actions of the high commissioners and their fellows, not by those of the conscientious men and women who were the targets of the church's illegal prosecutions.[39]

3. The Argument from Customary Practice

To these arguments, which (they were constrained to admit) did raise legitimate questions, defenders of the legality of ex officio proceedings again drew an answer from the *ius commune*. Even accepting for the sake of argument that the public suspicion alleged might not have been sufficient in every case to meet the exception to the rule requiring a legitimate accuser, defenders responded that under the Roman canon law, wherever there was doubt about the proper understanding of a rule or law, custom was the surest guide. That was a common principle of construction in the *ius commune*,[40] and in this case custom was on their side. Not only did the oath's frequent use in English courts support them; they could cite direct Continental authority on point as well. Julius Clarus, for instance, the sixteenth-century proceduralist whose Practica criminalis canonica was much cited during the controversy, wrote bluntly after expressing his doubts about the legality of the oath: "But certainly whatever may be true *de iure,* practice demonstrates the reverse."[41] Proceedings ex officio without an accuser or sufficient proof of public fame against the accused occurred every day in the courts that Clarus knew, and in tribunals where the practice was regularly admitted it was not easily dislodged. Custom itself justified the use of the oath.

It goes almost without saying that those who attacked the procedures being used by the English church in 1600 did not find this particular argument from custom convincing.[42] They denied the existence of the custom, or at least the possibility of proving its prescriptive title, and they disputed its legitimacy if it did exist.[43] Custom had to meet a test of reasonability under the Roman canon law, and this one, they said, did not do so. Put another way, the argument seemed to assert that the practice was lawful simply because it was the practice. That sort of reference to custom is capable of justifying the most flagrant abuses, and opponents of the oath argued that exactly this was occurring in the High Commission. These opponents were constrained to admit that custom could be used to interpret the texts of the *ius commune,* but this did not mean that custom could itself convert a practice that was clearly unlawful into one that had to be accepted as valid law.[44]

At this point in the legal argument, the two sides in the dispute simply parted company. No intellectual solution was possible. The dispute became a test of wills and ultimately of military strength. The dominant opinion among the English civilians undoubtedly favored allowing initial imposition of the ex officio oath in the High Commission and, indeed, in all other ecclesiastical courts. Civilians who took the contrary view (or were employed to do so in litigation) either had to proceed to the second way of making the argument, which is set out below, or seek a remedy outside the system of ecclesiastical courts.[45] They did both. On the first part of the dispute over the ex officio oath, argument ended in what one might call a standoff.

B. *Nemo tenetur detegere turpitudinem suam*

The arguments so far outlined attacked the legal validity of proceeding ex officio against defendants accused of religious and political dissent. However, this was not the end of the matter under the *ius commune*. The *ius commune* also opened the possibility that defendants could object to individual incriminating questions, possibly even once they had taken the oath to tell the truth. As will be shown by the evidence described in the sections that follow, at least some defendants in the English ecclesiastical courts took advantage of this possibility. They made such objections in fact.

1. Basis for the Arguments

An established canonical principle held that "no one is compelled to bear witness against himself, because no one is bound to reveal his own shame." It was normally expressed by the Latin maxim *Nemo tenetur detegere turpitudinem suam.*[46] The maxim and the rule were already venerable by the seventeenth century. The principle had been stated and elaborated in the Speculum iudiciale of William Durantis.[47] The principle had been endorsed by the majority of the medieval commentators,[48] and it was repeated in virtually all sixteenth- and seventeenth-century European manuals of criminal procedure.[49] Requiring men and women to answer specific incriminating questions about their private acts and beliefs, whereby they risked incurring *infamia* or prosecution under a penal statute, ran counter to this principle of the *ius commune*.

The authoritative text used most often to justify the rule was an extract from a commentary on Saint Paul's Letter to the Hebrews by the great fourth-century church father Saint John Chrysostom. The text, inserted in Gratian's Decretum, stated: "I do not say to you that you should betray yourself in public nor accuse yourself before others, but that you obey the prophet when he said, 'Reveal your ways unto the Lord.' "[50] Medieval commentators read these words as making a legal point: men and women must confess their sins to God, but they should not be compelled to make their crimes known to anyone else. The normal juristic technique of the *ius commune,* reading texts *a contrario sensu,* led to this conclusion. If Christians were being directed to reveal their sins to the Lord, by negative implication they were also being directed *not* to reveal their sins to other men.[51]

Building on this text, commentators gave two additional reasons for the prohibition against requiring men and women to answer incriminating judicial questions. For one thing, none of us is untainted by crime of some sort. If the truth were fully known, all of us would stand in danger of judgment. To permit public officials to force men and women to reveal their crimes would mean that no one would be immune from public prosecution.[52] This was not a result to be desired. It would be disruptive of social order. It would encourage excesses of zeal on the part of officials. Under the canon law, many sins were therefore to be tolerated because their eradication would have led to worse consequences.[53] Commentators sometimes adduced the biblical example of Jesus' toleration of Judas to support the wisdom of this approach.[54]

Second, to the jurists it also seemed that the practice would confound the penitential with the external forum. Some parts of human life were inherently appropriate for the confessional, not for public ventilation. Chief among these were private, shameful acts. Hence the canonical rule that prevented public ecclesiastical courts from intruding into men's private lives: *De occultis non iudicat ecclesia.*[55] In what the canon law called the "internal forum," it was obvious that no person could assert a privilege against self-incrimination. Indeed, self-incrimination was the very purpose of the penitential forum. But the reverse was thought to be true in the "external forum." The privilege not to answer incriminating questions thus served a double purpose in the public forum: to keep the two kinds of spiritual jurisdiction distinct and to protect the private sphere from inappropriate scrutiny.

The biblical example of Joseph's decision to divorce the Virgin Mary "privily" after she was found to be with child (Matt. 1:19) was cited to support this result. Like many biblical texts, Joseph's refusal to make a public example of Mary made a legal point. It manifested God's judgment that public and judicial actions were rightly kept apart and that public examples should not be made in cases of private offense. As Joseph had done, so should the church. Private and shameful acts were thus rightly kept out of public tribunals.[56] Although the commentators did not phrase the objection in the terms most familiar to us—a right to personal autonomy—and although they would doubtless have been amazed at the lengths to which the idea would be carried in modern times, in a limited fashion they did endorse something akin to the modern right of privacy. There was a sphere of life into which the public authorities, whether from church or state, were not entitled to enter.[57]

One further argument on this point was made. Commentators said that obliging anyone to take the oath *de veritate dicenda* and to answer specific incriminating questions provided an occasion, even an inducement, for the commission of perjury.[58] The temptation not to tell the truth, either in taking the initial oath or in answering specific questions, would be all but overwhelming for most defendants put into this position. This was essentially the same argument that has surfaced in our own day as a "cruel trilemma,"[59] the unhappy choice among perjury, contempt, or conviction that faces all defendants who are required to give evidence against themselves. Subsequent chapters show how ubiquitous (and persuasive) this argument proved to be in later history. It was in fact even stronger at the time than it later became. Not only would the sworn lie leave the perjurer in danger of God's vengeance; even in this world, perjury was more than a technical offense or a means of punishing someone for another reason. It was an active source of ecclesiastical jurisdiction during the Middle Ages, one frequently invoked in practice.[60] Prosecution was thus more than a theoretical possibility. The argument was that courts ought not regularly to put men and women to such a test for such a doubtful gain.

2. Defenses of the Oath

To these arguments, defenders of the ex officio oath and the incriminating questions that followed the oath had answers drawn from the *ius commune*. The extract from Saint John Chrysostom given above was distinguished on the ground that Chrysostom had been referring not to process in courts of law but only to truly public utterances. His statement, they said, had not been meant to be binding in the judicial forum.[61] Furthermore, defenders asserted that the *ius commune* itself recognized several exceptions to the rule against forced self-incrimination. Indeed, some jurists took the position that these exceptions had all but swallowed the original rule, since the rule was held not to apply where there was public knowledge that a crime had been committed, where the public had an interest in punishing the crime, and where there were legitimate indicia that the defendant being questioned had committed it.[62] A privilege may be quite appropriate when the crime is truly unknown, they argued, but once it has become the subject of public repute, they reasoned, the privilege must give way. One cannot truly be "revealing" a shameful fact once that fact has already been revealed. This had become an accepted principle in the criminal law of the church. Following its mandate, under accepted principles of the *ius commune,* defendants had no personal right to refuse to plead or to ignore questions about their manifest crimes.[63] In the eyes of some commentators, to permit the rule against self-incrimination to become an absolute privilege would have been to destroy the legitimate goal of punishing criminals.

This seemed a forceful point. The existence of exceptions to the rule was admitted by all, including the participants in the English debate. The force of the exceptions shows that however much sixteenth-century arguments resembled the modern reasons given for the privilege against self-incrimination, the privilege did not then possess the quality of an absolute right. The commentators on the *ius commune* did not regard a defendant's refusal to answer incriminating questions as the exercise of a fundamental personal right, one never to be abridged. They regarded it instead as a protection against the exercise of overly intrusive powers by public officials seeking to pry into the private lives of ordinary men and women. It was one way of enforcing a principle of prudence (*De occultis non iudicat ecclesia*) rather than the recognition of the existence of a subjective right.[64]

This understanding of the privilege against self-incrimination left the opponents of the ex officio oath with what might be called a window of opportunity. Despite the existence of many exceptions, the principle still applied in the absence of public notoriety indicating that an accused had committed a crime, and it still applied to prohibit judicial "fishing expeditions" to search out the private faults of opponents of the regime.[65] Opponents argued that this sort of expedition was exactly what was happening in the English practice of their day. Especially would this have been true in the Court of High Commission, where incriminating questions were (they said) routinely put to defendants in ways that were inconsistent with the reason for the principle's existence. The oath had become a new means of ferreting out otherwise unknown religious heterodoxy.[66]

Whether this was an accurate characterization of the usages of the English ecclesiastical courts depended on the view one took of the nature of the tribunals. Its victims alleged that they were being prosecuted for their private religious beliefs. As proof, they pointed to the long series of interrogatories about their opinions with which they routinely were confronted. Defenders of the practices in England's spiritual courts countered that these actions were being undertaken simply to secure outward conformity with the laws of England. The courts did not prosecute mere private opinion. They acted only against public dissent that had public consequences. In their view, beliefs that caused men and women to absent themselves from their parish churches, to revile the English clergy, or to mock the church's ceremonies were not simply private opinions. They were public actions and they were subversive of public order.[67] This basic disagreement would seem to have signaled the end of legal controversy, since it involved basic religious beliefs.

3. Further Arguments

Contemporary legal argument, however, did not in fact end there. Even conceding the intrusive character of the ex officio oath, defenders of the legality of the oath could point to other exceptions to the rule against self-incrimination under the *ius commune*. The most famous exception was that for heresy, in which the enormity of the offense was thought sufficient justification for requiring anyone to answer.[68] This played but a small role in English practice; few of the persons brought before the English ecclesiastical courts were accused of heresy.[69] It stands to the credit of these courts that they allowed this part of the inheritance of the *ius commune* to fall into desuetude.

Another exception depended on the supposedly "medicinal" character of proceedings within the ecclesiastical courts. This exception held that, where the purpose of an incriminating question was to secure the punishment of the party, the rule applied. The defendant did not have to answer the question. Innocent IV, for example, argued that the privilege could be invoked "wherever some other penalty than a spiritual one was involved."[70] The reverse also followed, however. Where the aim was not punishment, but rather reformation of the offender, the rule did not necessarily operate to exclude questioning. It may be thought wrong to force men and women to incriminate themselves if punishment is the judge's aim, so the argument ran, but if the improvement of the accused was the judge's goal, perhaps no defendant could reasonably object. In such a case, canon law therefore allowed judges to question defendants about any crime they might have committed.[71] So it was contended in England. Defenders of the ex officio oath's use maintained that correction, not punishment, was the aim of the spiritual courts. Therefore, the oath was lawful.

There was still further argument along the lines drawn by the *ius commune*. Defenders answered the objection that forced self-incrimination encouraged perjury by noting that the canon law specifically prohibited a later charge of perjury based on false answers to formal questions.[72] It did not occur to them, apparently, to allow parties or witnesses to be examined without requiring them to take an oath; all testimony in the canonical system was sworn testimony. Defendants, however, enjoyed an immunity from subsequent prosecution for perjury, and therefore, these civilians argued, they had no reason to fear any punishment not merited by their actual crimes.[73] On that account, the danger of perjury gave defendants no substantial cause for objecting to being compelled to take the oath.

This argument was answered in turn. Critics of the oath quite sensibly said that it was wrong to encourage people to perjure themselves, even if they could not actually be prosecuted for the crime.[74] The temptation not to tell the truth would exist in any case, and eventually they would be called to answer before God for having committed the perjury it was all too natural to commit. God would make no such sophistical distinctions, whatever defendants' immunity from formal prosecution might be within the external forum of the ecclesiastical courts. Defendants, and indeed all witnesses, ought therefore to be spared the temptation that led to that more serious (and final) judgment.[75]

At the time, the argument about the purpose of the prosecution was probably the more important and controversial. It was on precisely this point that the High Commission was particularly vulnerable. English diocesan courts might perhaps, with some slight color of truth, be said to have been concerned with "improving" the behavior of those they were prosecuting. That argument was very hard to make for the High Commission, however. The diocesan courts had only the power to impose spiritual penalties, excommunication and public penance, on persons they convicted. By contrast, the high commissioners regularly exercised the power to imprison, fine, and punish corporally. It required a considerable stretch of the imagination to see how being cast into prison or having one's purse confiscated could be said to constitute an "improvement" in the life of an offender. These seemed to be—and undoubtedly were—real punishments. Among the English spiritual tribunals, these kinds of punishment were the monopoly of the High Commission.[76]

Critics of the High Commission also contended that where there was any doubt, the *ius commune* required that judges be sensitive to the dangers inherent in forcing men to reveal their secret vices and abstain from putting the incriminating question. As Andreas Gail (d. 1587) had put this point, "[j]udges should be circumspect in this matter, lest a party be harmed by any prejudicial response."[77] To their critics and victims, at least, the English commissioners seemed to be doing just the opposite. They were resolving all questions of doubt in favor of their own practices, and they were doing so in order to impose severe punishments on honest and God-fearing people.

Defenders of the use of the ex officio oath inevitably saw the matter quite differently. They regarded their actions as simply following customary practice, invoking that practice against persons who had publicly violated the legitimate laws of the realm and the established church. This difference in viewpoint led to a standoff in legal argument, as did the objection to the oath previously discussed.[78] The impasse ended the possibility of rational discourse and called instead for a test of strength. Exactly such a test ensued: the English Civil War. In that struggle the animosities directed against the courts of the church played a part.[79] They led quickly to legislation abolishing use of the ex officio oath in the ecclesiastical courts as soon as the Parliamentary Party had the upper hand.[80] That proscription lived on after the restoration of the monarchy and episcopacy in 1660.[81]

III. MEDIEVAL PRACTICE IN THE ECCLESIASTICAL COURTS

This much has been mostly legal theory. What about practice? For the most part, practice in the courts turns out to have been in accord with the theory. The manuscript records in the archives of the English church show that the arguments sketched above were known in England and that a rule against compelled self-incrimination, as understood under the *ius commune,* was largely respected in medieval practice. Use of the ex officio oath was in fact standard procedure in the spiritual forum,[82] but it was possible to resist it. Forms asserting a right not to answer self-incriminating questions in criminal causes were regularly placed, for example, into the precedent books used in the ecclesiastical courts.[83] The wording used in these documents appears to have been taken almost verbatim from Continental treatises on the subject.

The rule made itself felt in actual cases. Before the consistory court of the Diocese of Ely in 1375, disciplinary action was initiated against the archdeacon of Ely for having violated the prohibition. He was said to have habitually interrogated men and women under oath in circumstances where their "pretended excesses were wholly secret."[84] A similar charge was brought against an official in the Diocese of Carlisle early in the next century.[85] In a third instance, a woman at Lincoln, accused of an (unstated) ecclesiastical offense before the episcopal court early in the sixteenth century, refused to answer any questions put to her, apparently basing her refusal on this same reason.[86] A further example of this same objection's being raised is found in a case heard by the commissary court of the bishop of London in 1492.[87]

That the canonical form of the privilege also made itself known outside the world of ecclesiastical lawyers during the Middle Ages is suggested by a long-remembered incident involving Robert Grosseteste, bishop of Lincoln between 1235 and 1253. Grosseteste was a famous and earnest bishop, but as Sir Richard Southern has shown, the rigorous but unconventional approach characteristic of Grosseteste's thought put him slightly outside the mainstream. Exactly that approach is seen in his attempts to root out abuses and immoral conduct in his diocese.[88] He went too far. He imposed oaths on the laity, requiring them to reveal their secret faults. In this, it was widely alleged, the bishop's practice stood contrary to the law. Grosseteste was confusing the public courts of the church with the confessional, precisely in the way the *ius commune* forbade. Objections from the laity, objections that ultimately took the form of royal prohibitions, ended this experiment in pastoral control.[89] The effective result was to vindicate the privilege as it was understood in thirteenth-century law.

Despite this famous incident, a few other objections on the part of the laity,[90] and the examples cited above from the day-to-day records of the ecclesiastical courts, the issue of compelled self-incrimination never became a matter of serious dispute during the Middle Ages. The medieval act books contain relatively few refusals to take the oath *de veritate dicenda* in criminal cases, and not many disputes about its propriety have come down to us from actual litigation. The principal reason for this relative peacefulness, however, probably lies not so much in the supine responses of the persons brought before the courts of the church as it does in the observance of the canon law's requirement that *fama publica* be formally established before the oath could be required. This requirement was taken seriously by the officials of the ecclesiastical courts. In setting to one side this (admittedly inconvenient) legal requirement, Grosseteste had few successors.

Moreover, the nature of the ordinary exercise of ecclesiastical jurisdiction discouraged what objections there might otherwise have been. Persons summoned before the courts were normally "tried" by compurgation. This procedure called on them to swear to their innocence and to find a number of compurgators, or oath helpers, willing to swear that they believed that the oath of the accused was true. It amounted to less than a full determination under the canon law;[91] it all happened very quickly; and there must have been little space left for making technical legal arguments against the procedure.[92] Much easier to submit to the procedure, so long as one could find suitable compurgators. Or so it must have seemed to many. Perhaps the procedure had become so familiar and its requirements so easily met[93] that challenging its legality would have required an exceptional situation.

There were, of course, some situations in which objection was made. In them one sees the effects of the observance of the *ius commune*. Under ordinary rules of practice in the English ecclesiastical courts, it was open to persons cited to answer a criminal charge to object that no public fame existed. As noted in section II.A above, *fama publica* had to meet high standards before it was deemed sufficient to permit initiation of a prosecution. The person cited could require that *fama* in its full legal sense be established independently. The normal means for doing this was to call for a finding on the point by an inquest.[94] The inquest was to be conducted by an independent hearing, and it was in fact not wholly dissimilar from what was done by a presentment jury in the English common law.

This happened in fact. Even the routine act books show it occasionally. For example, in 1449 John Stonehill and his wife Joan were cited to appear before the consistory court of the Diocese of Rochester.[95] They were accused of having killed their infant son. Instead of answering the charge, they denied the existence of any legitimate *fama publica* against them, and the diocesan court ordered that an inquest be held on this preliminary question. As it happens, the results appear in the record. The inquest, which must have been akin to the proceedings of the same name familiar to all students of the English common law, found that the Stonehills were correct. There had been no legitimate public fame circulating against them. They were dismissed accordingly, apparently without ever having been obliged either to answer the charge or to take the oath *de veritate dicenda*.[96]

Habitual observance of this preliminary requirement diminished the number of complaints against the ex officio oath in medieval practice. It also led to an apparently surprising result, though one that was to have echoes in the practices of the common law described in chapter 6. Active assertion of the canonical prohibition against compelled self-incrimination actually appeared in the court records more often in civil cases than in criminal. This occurred because, under canonical procedure, the person suing normally produced "articles" or "positions" containing the allegations on which his case rested. Each of these had to be answered by the defendant, and they were also used to frame the questions that were put to witnesses in the case. Both the defendant and the witnesses testified under oath. They responded to "positions" that sometimes contained matters that could also be the subject of a criminal prosecution, and witnesses and parties to the litigation regularly refused to answer the positions on the ground of the canonical prohibition against compelled self-incrimination. Unlike criminal matters, where *fama publica* had to be proved and was in fact proved, in civil cases no foundation for a *positio criminosa* would ordinarily have been laid. Hence, under the *ius commune,* the parties were within their rights to refuse to answer the question. So, too, were witnesses if a *positio* touched on their own crimes. And that is what they did. A proctor in a civil case at York, for example, sought to stipulate at the beginning of the case that "if any of the positions involve a crime, they are not to be sworn to, nor is there to be an examination upon them."[97] Indeed, it became common form for parties in civil cases to state, prior to answering any of the positions, that if by inadvertence they should answer a *positio criminosa,* their answer should be counted as a nullity.[98] They hoped thereby to save themselves from formally admitting to having committed a crime; they also hoped to keep the criminal matter from being treated as legitimate proof in the civil suit. They were fully entitled to do this under the *ius commune.*

An illustrative example of this practice comes from a fourteenth-century testamentary cause at York.[99] In an attempt to secure probate of a last will and testament, the proponent alleged that the only existing copy of the will had been burned. He wished to prove the testament by oral evidence of its contents. One of his positions therefore stated that the original will had been burned. The defendant refused to respond to this position, specifically on the grounds that the position raised a criminal matter. Presumably because he might be accused of himself having burnt the testament, the defendant asserted that he could not be compelled to answer that particular position.[100] That was his right under the existing *ius commune.*

Such routine cases from the ecclesiastical court records demonstrate that long before the constitutional struggles of the Elizabethan and Stuart monarchies, the privilege against self-incrimination played a part in the legal life of England. It was not a large part. The privilege was too limited, the courts' compliance with the requirements of the *ius commune* too exact, and the lack of public dispute about the rights of the church in criminal matters too broad for the privilege to have come to the fore. But it existed. It has left tracks in the historical record.

IV. SIXTEENTH-CENTURY DEVELOPMENTS

This relative stability disappeared during the reigns of Elizabeth and her immediate successors. Objections based on the canonical principle *Nemo tenetur prodere seipsum* became more frequent in practice within the church's courts. Although in absolute terms the numbers were never large, comparatively the objections became a great deal more frequent. Refusals to take the ex officio oath are easy to find among the act books from the years after 1560. They were not restricted to the Court of High Commission, from which the larger part of the prohibition cases discussed in chapter 3 seem to have come. That court probably did face more frequent refusals of the oath than the relative number of cases it heard would otherwise have warranted, but it was not alone in facing objections.

Many of the contemporary objections, at least as they are found in the formal court records, reveal little about the specific legal grounds given for refusing the oath. When Grace Fynche was cited by the branch of the High Commission for the Diocese of Rochester in 1592, for example, the act book records only that "she expressly refused to undergo and to take the oath."[101] One cannot tell what reasons she had, although she certainly had some colorable reason, since the court appointed two clergymen to consult with her "for her better satisfying in such points as she is desirous to be resolved." There are many cases like hers. Evidence from some other cases, however, allows us to penetrate further. It shows clearly that the oath was being objected to on grounds taken from the *ius commune*.

A. The Oath in English Civilian Literature

Going further is possible, even to the point of speaking about this matter with some assurance, because in the years around 1580 the English ecclesiastical lawyers began to collect cases from their courts and also to develop a literature of English ecclesiastical law. The literature stands alongside the treatises (imported from the Continent) they used in practice, and it makes quite obvious that the assertion of a privilege against self-incrimination was not driven initially, or even primarily, by the threat of intervention from the English common law. It was driven rather by the rules of the European *ius commune* outlined in section II above. The arguments found there were more than theoretically controversial; they were regularly advanced in cases in the ecclesiastical courts. For instance, in a manuscript report of an ecclesiastical proceeding in the early seventeenth century, Dr. Wyvell, one of the civilian advocates, argued that the practice of putting men to their oaths directly on a presentment by churchwardens was one "that the law doth scarce allow."[102] By the word *law* Dr. Wyvell clearly meant Roman canon law, for in support of his position he cited treatises by Panormitanus (d. 1453), Bartolus de Saxoferrato (d. 1357), and Antonius Gabrielius (d. 1555). The author of the first of these, already mentioned above, was the greatest of the medieval commentators on the Gregorian Decretals. The second was the most famous medieval writer on texts of the Roman law; in 1600, he would have been viewed as the leading exponent of the traditional *mos italicus* school. The third, much less known, was the author of a treatise devoted to restating the "Common Conclusions" of the *ius commune*. The three were mainstream authorities on Continental law in every sense, jurists who would have known little or nothing about English common law.

A like example arose before the bishop's consistory court at Durham in 1609. Nicholas Brigges refused to answer a position "because the question posed [was] incriminating."[103] His lawyer cited Joachim Mynsinger, a sixteenth-century German writer on the *ius commune,* in support of his client's refusal.[104] Similarly, when Cuthbert Bainbridge was accused of preaching a seditious sermon in the early 1590s, he also maintained that he could not be required to take the oath in the subsequent proceedings against him. He made use of works by Julius Clarus (d. 1575), Robertus Maranta (d. 1540), and Johannes Petrus de Ferrariis (fl. 1389) to support his case.[105] The three writers Bainbridge cited were Italian jurists, authors of treatises on the Roman canon law of procedure. In still another case, one from the London courts around 1610, the *ius commune* was again relied on to determine whether a party to a probate proceeding could be compelled to say under oath whether he had suppressed a last will and testament by burning it.[106] The court's apparent decision, that the act of suppressing was sufficiently criminal to permit invocation of the privilege, was supported by citation to three texts from the Roman Law Digest and one taken from the Libri observationum of Jacobus Cujas (d. 1590).

Invocation of this civilian principle also appeared regularly outside case reports. It is found repeatedly in the contemporary manuscript treatises dealing with procedure in English ecclesiastical courts.[107] One of these, a treatise compiled to record the procedure used in the Court of High Commission and now kept in the Cambridge University Library, deals with the question of the admissibility of incriminating questions at some length.[108] Among other matters, its author asked whether a defendant could be "urged" to answer an incriminating question, even though he could not be legally compelled to do so. In another contemporary work, found among the muniments of the Diocese of Chester, the civilian writer similarly took note of the basic rule against compelled self-incrimination, citing the work of Lanfrancus de Oriano (d. 1488), and went on to enumerate several of the many exceptions to the rule found in the Italian author's work.[109]

Some of these treatises simply took note of the rule of the *ius commune* and then went on to address questions of greater legal detail, including the scope of the privilege, again using the same kinds of authorities. For exam-

ple, in a marginal gloss to a copy of Francis Clerke's work on English civilian procedure,[110] the civilian commentator grappled with the question of
whether a litigant should suffer any prejudice from having answered an
incriminating interrogatory he had not been obliged to answer in the first
place. The commentator's answer—that it depended on whether a preliminary formal protestation had been made—was drawn from works by Lanfrancus de Oriano, Octavianus Vestrius (d. 1573), and Panormitanus.[111] The
first of these was a doctor of both Roman and canon law who taught at
the University of Padua and wrote an influential treatise on civilian procedure. The second was a Roman advocate whose introductory work on
practice in the papal court went through nine printings in the sixteenth
century. The third, as noted already, was the greatest of the fifteenth-
century writers on the canon law.

Similarly, in a mid-seventeenth-century manuscript now in the Wells
Cathedral library, works by Joachim Mynsinger and Lanfrancus de Oriano
were used in considering whether a defendant could be held *pro confesso*
for refusing to answer an incriminating question for which a proper foundation had been laid. The alternative was that he might be punished merely for
contempt.[112] In the Court of Arches in the earliest years of the seventeenth
century, a fully argued case dealing with the necessity of proof of public
fame in order to found a prosecution cited a wide range of authors on the
ius commune: Hostiensis (d. 1271), Franciscus Zabarella (d. 1417), Henricus
Bohic (d. c. 1350), Joannes de Imola (d. 1436), and Hippolytus de Marsiliis
(d. 1529), among others.[113] For the lawyers who argued these cases, it was
the European *ius commune* rather than the English common law that
counted.

These treatises on English civilian practice and the case reports that
went with them demonstrate that the English civilians themselves regarded
a privilege not to incriminate oneself as a rule of the *ius commune*. It was
this rule that mattered to them. In their eyes, it was a rule subject to exceptions, and also one that raised difficult questions both of law and of fact.
Its exact reach was debatable, and its interpretation required knowledge of
the intricacies of the *ius commune,* for several aspects of the subject were
open to dispute. The facts of individual cases would often determine the
oath's legality. However, none of the treatises written about procedure by
the English civilians approached the question as pitting English common law against ecclesiastical law or practice. Legality of the ex officio oath
was not, in other words, raised in the ecclesiastical courts as if it were a
question of interjurisdictional law. Whether a prohibition lay was not the
issue.

B. The Oath in the Court Records

This conclusion is confirmed if one moves from reports and treatises and looks back more closely at the official records of the English ecclesiastical courts. As stated above, their formal nature excludes any citation of legal authority. Their wording, however, almost uniformly suggests that the oath was being objected to as contrary to the law of the church. For example, before the London branch of the Court of High Commission in 1636, a civilian advocate argued that an interrogatory "might contain some scandalous matter and unfit to be answered."[114] The High Commission consequently struck from its interrogatories the portion that asked whether the witness had been *particeps criminis*.[115] Similarly, before the bishop's commissary court at London in 1585, Richard Ramsford, defendant in an ex officio prosecution for fathering an illegitimate child, refused to answer the accusation because, he said, "he was not bound by the law to respond."[116] Edward Midleton, appearing before the High Commission at York in 1598, also refused to take the oath, on grounds that "the offense wherewithal he is charged in this article is a capitall cryme and therefore he believeth he is not bound by lawe to answere thereunto."[117] The *ius commune* remained the basis for the procedural rules in the English ecclesiastical courts after the Reformation,[118] and it appears that these post-Reformation defendants were invoking it. When defendants before the ecclesiastical courts wished to invoke a common law rule, they usually did so by introducing a royal writ of prohibition, which prevented the ecclesiastical judge from taking any action at all, or by suing out a writ of habeas corpus later on. That is not what these defendants did.

Use of a common law writ seems to have been a last resort for most defendants. There are a few such examples from the records of the ecclesiastical courts, but not many. The paucity found in the printed common law reports, to be described in chapter 3, runs parallel to the story told by the ecclesiastical court records themselves. The first step of most defendants was to raise their objections under the law of the church itself. These objections were not always, or even normally, successful. It is a tribute to the strength of a right to remain silent under the *ius commune* that refusals to take the oath or to answer specific incriminating questions appear as often as they do in late-sixteenth- and early-seventeenth-century court records.[119]

V. EXPLANATIONS FOR THE CHANGES

Where once there had been relative stability, by the late sixteenth century there was regular conflict. A form of the privilege against self-incrimination was being asserted and argued about by the English civilians. The arguments from the *ius commune* outlined in section II above moved from the classroom to the courtroom. The increase in the number of objections taken to the ex officio procedure used in the church courts requires an attempt at historical explanation. Several possible explanations present themselves, though none can be proved with certainty.

A. Social and Religious Changes

The most obvious explanation must also be a correct one: the increase in religious dissent in Tudor and Stuart England. Although medieval England had not been without opposition to aspects of the church's jurisdictional claims, that opposition was never sustained or widespread. The size and the varied nature of opposition exploded after the Reformation. Puritan and papist objected to the Elizabethan Settlement, though of course for quite different reasons, and there can be little doubt that this growing dissatisfaction with the English church as established under Elizabeth, coupled with a determination on the part of the English bishops to suppress dissent, together created the atmosphere in which the privilege against self-incrimination would come to the fore. When attempts to secure their conformity were made in the ecclesiastical courts, it was bound to happen that many of the dissenters would refuse to cooperate.[120] Some of the attempts to thwart the courts of the church took the form of refusals to swear the ex officio oath, others the form of a writ of prohibition or a petition for habeas corpus against the ecclesiastical courts, a subject taken up in chapter 3. No doubt some men and women who had been cited to appear before ecclesiastical tribunals tried both strategies.

It is also worth remembering that more than a few of the people prosecuted for religious dissent in this era were persons of substance, both intellectual and financial. This was something new. It stands in stark contrast to the normal situation that had existed throughout the Middle Ages. Then, most of the people who appeared before the consistory courts in criminal cases were drawn from the middling to lower orders of society. Few of them possessed the resources necessary to raise the legal objections to the oath that were available under the *ius commune*. Because the oath was legal in many circumstances, it would have required legal skill, a willingness to hold out against religious sanctions, some financial resources, and perhaps a disputatious temperament to have raised the objections in practice. Few did. The rise of religious dissent, however, and its spread in all levels of

English society, changed this.[121] By the end of the sixteenth century, the motives and the resources to raise the objections were coming together.

B. Legal Changes in the Ecclesiastical Courts

There were also three specific legal changes during the sixteenth century that contributed to the rise in the number and the ferocity of objections to the ex officio oath. First, the medieval usage of preliminary inquests to establish the existence of *fama publica* before subjecting defendants to the oath came to an end. Second, the creation under Elizabeth of the Court of High Commission, in which some traditional justifications for using the oath could no longer be made, raised the temperature of the dispute. And third, the use of lawyers began to be allowed in criminal cases tried before the spiritual courts. Each of these changes occurred during the last half of the sixteenth century, and each rendered it more likely that the privilege against self-incrimination would be asserted within the ecclesiastical forum.

The first of these is the hardest to explain, but the records leave no doubt that it occurred. Not only do entries relating to such preliminary inquests cease to appear in the act books of the courts during the sixteenth century, there are also cases in which a defendant denied the existence of public fame as well as the fact of the crime of which he or she stood accused and in which that defendant was nonetheless subjected to immediate trial. For example, in the early seventeenth century William Ayleworth was cited by the official of the archdeacon of Berkshire and accused of having committed adultery with a woman named Barbara Ball. In the formal words of the record, "Ayleworth denied that there was any fame of incontinence saving that Catherine Ayleworth the wife of the examinate being a clamorous woman hath often times reported . . . that this examinate and Barbara Ball have been incontinent together."[122] This denial of the existence of reliable public fame, had it been asserted two centuries earlier, would have called for the impaneling of an inquest to discover whether such public fame existed. By the sixteenth century it did not. No inquest was called. Ayleworth, who was apparently unwilling or unable to undergo public compurgation, was treated as guilty and assigned a public penance.[123] There are cases in which English judges dismissed defendants because no credible public fame existed. As civilians themselves admitted, however, in practice they had come to omit the formal inquests required by law. By the second decade of the seventeenth century, it could be alleged that "so it hath been always practised."[124]

The reasons for this change in practice are not entirely clear. The civilians themselves gave none. It may have had something to do with a shift in presumptions applied to defendants who came before the ecclesiastical tribunals, allowing officials to assume the requisite public fame as a matter of course. This change also occurred during roughly the same period on the Continent. It was acknowledged by several writers on the *ius commune* known to English civilians. Perhaps they were emboldened to omit the inquest concerning *fama publica* by the actions of their fellows across the Channel. Alternatively, it may be that the regularization of the practice of presentment of criminal defendants by parish churchwardens made a difference. The courts remained willing to accept challenges to these presentments where there was suspicion of partiality or insufficient report.[125] But the burden of proof was on the defendant to prove the insufficiency. Whatever the reason, there clearly was a change in practice, and it was one that opened the court procedure to objection. Without the preliminary establishment of *fama publica,* the ex officio oath was much harder to justify on the basis of the principles of the *ius commune.* And that is what happened. Objections followed.

The second reason for the increasing number of objections was the creation of the Court of High Commission. This court operated in separate branches in most English dioceses, and its express purpose was to suppress manifestations of religious dissent. Unlike the traditional ecclesiastical tribunals, the High Commission was given the power to inflict temporal punishments, and indeed it exercised that power with regularity.[126] This opened its use of the ex officio oath to objection based on the Roman and canon laws, because a traditional justification for allowing at least exceptional use of incriminating questions under the law was that the judge's purpose was to improve rather than to punish. That is, when the primary aim of the question was to allow the person to lead a better life, the rule against forced self-incrimination might not apply so strictly. The regular application of criminal sanctions in this court, including corporal and monetary penalties, altogether removed this justification. The High Commission was in the business of punishing, not improving. Hence its procedures were open to greater objection on the basis of the *ius commune* than were the same procedures when used by the older spiritual courts. And again, that is what happened. Objections followed. They grew louder.

The third reason was the appearance of lawyers. Like the common law courts, the medieval ecclesiastical tribunals denied criminal defendants the right to be represented by a lawyer in most circumstances. Professional lawyers, called *procuratores* or proctors, did represent most parties in civil litigation. Not so in ex officio proceedings. According to the classical canon law, the presence of a proctor would interfere with the system's legitimate aim of dealing directly with offenders against the church's laws,[127] and this was the rule put into practice in the English spiritual courts.[128] The utility of lawyers was recognized in the *ius commune,* but it was felt that they would do more harm than good in criminal cases. There was no defense counsel.

However the merits of the argument may seem today, it is apparent that in the English ecclesiastical courts, lawyers began to appear more frequently in ex officio prosecutions during the sixteenth century. It was never in the majority of the cases that their presence occurred. But neither was it a rarity. Again, it is hard to be confident in assigning a reason for the development, although the identical development was occurring at the same time on the Continent, and, given the close attention the English civilians paid to legal developments on the Continent, it is probably right to suppose that they were following the lead of practice there. Whatever the source, it seems certain that this development contributed to the number of objections raised against the use of incriminating questions in ecclesiastical court practice. In consequence of the greater presence of lawyers in criminal practice, objections that might have been quite unknown to most laymen came quickly to the surface.

VI. COMMON LAW JUDGES AND THE *IUS COMMUNE*

Chapter 3 demonstrates that the English common law judges acted with circumspection in issuing writs of prohibition to prevent compelled self-incrimination in the courts of the church. Chapter 4 shows that the common law judges did not permit defendants to assert an equivalent to the privilege against self-incrimination in their own courts. These chapters stand on their own, and they need no anticipation here. However, the evidence from the contemporary common law reports is worth noting in the context of this chapter, precisely because some part of it reads as if it were drawn from the *ius commune* and because all of it makes more sense if one understands the background against which it occurred.

One way of understanding the issues at stake in prohibition cases involving the ex officio oath is to see them as enforcing one interpretation of a rule of ecclesiastical law on the ecclesiastical courts themselves. It could be argued plausibly that the English civilians were violating their own law by imposing the oath and that the common law judges were willing to intervene to make sure that they did not commit such a violation. In chapter 3, Charles Gray notes that the common law judges were often tempted to intervene in exactly such circumstances. Under this way of seeing the whole question, they were simply making use of a strict understanding of the *ius commune* in suits involving habeas corpus and writs of prohibition to the ecclesiastical courts. It was a stricter view of the rule than most civilians held, but it was the same rule.

There are advantages to viewing the story of the period in this light. It helps, for example, to explain the appearance of the rule against self-incrimination in the Court of Star Chamber.[129] It also makes sense out of a good deal of the otherwise puzzling evidence found in contemporary common law sources. It permits, for example, reconciliation of the clear statements of the rule *Nemo tenetur prodere seipsum* found in common law reports with the halting, reluctant, and even contradictory intervention in ecclesiastical court jurisdiction that characterized so many of the decisions of the English common law judges. This understanding of the rule's place in contemporary legal thought provides a better context for many statements of the rule in cases from the royal courts. Wigmore long ago noted that many contemporary statements on the subject by the English judges, even those of Sir Edward Coke, could only be called "ambiguous and shifting."[130] Lambarde's Eirenarcha (1581) is similarly puzzling. Lambarde stated the *Nemo tenetur* maxim as a rule of law, but he seemed to be doing so principally to show that interrogation by English justices of the peace deviated from the rule.[131]

In fact, it is wholly understandable there should have been hesitation and uncertainty on the part of these lawyers and that sometimes this looks like confusion to us. The privilege of the *ius commune* was not a defendant's unqualified right to refuse to answer any and all questions about his past conduct. It was a protection against intrusive questioning into one's private conduct and opinions by officious magistrates. Whether any particular use of the ex officio oath would have violated the rule under the *ius commune* was therefore often a close question, open to doubt and argument. It would frequently have come down to a question of fact. In this light it is natural that early statements of the question by common law judges as well as by ecclesiastical lawyers should seem "shifting" to modern tastes, accustomed as we are to having the privilege put in more absolute terms as the basic right of all persons not to be compelled to answer any incriminating questions whatsoever.

Moreover, looking at the history of the privilege in light of the European *ius commune* helps to explain some of the arguments against the ex officio oath that were being made by English common lawyers at the time. The source of many of these arguments has always been something of a puzzle for legal historians,[132] and the *ius commune* provides a clue. The maxim *Nemo tenetur prodere seipsum,* oft-repeated in the common law cases, clearly was imported originally from canonical sources.[133] Other phrases and ideas, apparently drawn from commentaries on the *ius commune,* also figured from time to time in the arguments and opinions of the common law. For example, the argument that the ex officio oath necessarily involved the encouragement of perjury was made by counsel in a King's Bench case of 1607 that is discussed at more length in the next chapter.[134] The lawyer used the canonically correct term *interrogatorii captiosi* in pressing his point. Another counsel maintained that the oath was invalid as contrary to the law of nature, even making use of the biblical story of the woman taken in adultery that figured so prominently in Continental treatises as a feature of his argument.[135] In several of the common law cases one finds the point made that either *fama publica* or an accuser was necessary to justify proceedings in an ecclesiastical tribunal.[136] In others the objection to the oath was put in terms of its intrusiveness into men's private lives and secret thoughts, in much the same way the argument was framed in Continental handbooks,[137] and one common law case even made the canonical point that all men deserve punishment *in conspectum Dei.*[138] These points at least *seem* to have been drawn from the resources of the *ius commune.*

That these arguments came, either directly or indirectly, from Continental sources is certainly far from impossible. Many common lawyers knew something about the Roman and canon laws, though few of them could have been called truly expert in them. Recent research has shown that there was regular interchange between the common lawyers and the English civilians.[139] The view that the former were "wholly insular" in knowledge and outlook can no longer be maintained.[140] Sir Edward Coke's library, for example, contained a considerable quantity of civil and canon law books; the *Nemo tenetur* maxim would have been found, stated, and discussed in many of them.[141] Indeed Coke himself avowedly quoted from a civilian in discussing the lawfulness of the ex officio oath.[142] Lawyers have long chosen good ideas where they found them. It may be that these initial skirmishes over the legality of the ex officio oath owed something to the lawyerly habit of borrowing legal rules from sources that were immediately at hand.

VII. CONCLUSION

The history of the place of the maxim *Nemo tenetur prodere seipsum* in the *ius commune,* its place in the history of the English ecclesiastical courts, and even its role in the sixteenth- and seventeenth-century common law cases—in one sense merely background to the subsequent evolution in the privilege against self-incrimination—is nevertheless instructive. It illustrates the protean nature of the privilege. A rule against self-incrimination existed in the *ius commune.* There can be no doubt about that fact. The commentators acknowledged its existence, discussed its rationale, formulated its limitations, and debated its reach. In their hands, however, the right to refuse to answer incriminating questions came to be more restricted in scope than it appeared to be at first sight. It was a limited right. A Continental lawyer could not have described it as a subjective or human right had that terminology been current at the time. Perhaps it is even questionable whether one could actually speak of the privilege in the *ius commune* as an operative rule of law, at least in the way a champion of the privilege as a basic human right would see things. There were too many exceptions to the rule, and it was commonly interpreted in too narrow a fashion by most of the medieval and early modern commentators, for it to have served as an effective right for most criminal defendants.

In this sense, the negative view of the *ius commune*'s share in creating the privilege against self-incrimination, noted at the start of this chapter, has a good deal to be said in its favor. The development of a privilege within the *ius commune* shows again how a statement of legal principle, admitted by all and admired by most, may nevertheless turn out to have a more restricted effect in the day-to-day running of a legal system than appears at first sight. The limited scope of the rule may be as important as its existence. Although the details will be quite different, and although the basic reasons advanced will not be quite the same, we shall see more of that same kind of development in the chapters that follow.

THREE

Self-Incrimination in Interjurisdictional Law: The Sixteenth and Seventeenth Centuries

Charles M. Gray

I. THE CONTEXT OF COMMON LAW CONTROL

For English common law courts in the sixteenth and seventeenth centuries, whether a person was in any sense "privileged" not to be asked to incriminate himself under oath was almost entirely a question of interjurisdictional law.[1] In principle, the matter simply did not arise in a common law setting. Practice before justices of the peace or the famous *peine forte et dure,* to be dealt with in more detail later in this book, were not then regarded as even raising a problem. More specifically, the common law courts did not try issues of fact upon evidence or testimony. These issues were put to the jury, which was putatively able to answer the question addressed to it from its own knowledge. In practice, juries were usually not in a position to do this; they ordinarily decided on the basis of a trial conducted in their presence. But trials were only occasions for parties who freely chose to provide the jury with information, and the juries were neither obliged to use it nor confined to it.

Limited power to compel testimony by nonparty witnesses in civil cases was introduced by statute in 1563,[2] the first crack in the ancient supposition that all testimony was voluntary and that witnesses thus assumed the risk of being asked what they could not answer truly without making admissions harmful or even incriminating to themselves. To what extent this new power was used can probably not be investigated historically; there is in any event no indication that for upwards of a century it ever led to discussions or rulings on the propriety of asking incriminating questions of witnesses in common law trials. Except for one minor and some indirect senses in which the common law could be said to have a policy against exposing people to self-incrimination,[3] the system had no place for the privilege.

The common law courts were, however, sometimes asked to control alleged use of incriminatory questioning by ecclesiastical courts,[4] which did try facts on evidence and did compel testimony. On the criminal side, and subject to the restraints in ecclesiastical law detailed in chapter 2, the ecclesiastical courts did subject persons accused of punishable offenses to interrogation under oath. For the common law judges, whether to control such interrogation was a question of whether (and on what theories) to interfere with the workings of another jurisdiction. This generic question had numerous species. The principal burden of this chapter is to show that cases in which common law courts intervened to protect ecclesiastical parties from being forced to incriminate themselves (or were unsuccessfully urged to intervene) had a wider context of interjurisdictional law. Although those cases had peculiarities, they took a good deal of their flavor from the legal context to which they belonged. Self-incrimination is a more stirring matter than other acts of ecclesiastical courts that became candidates, successful and unsuccessful, for common law regulation. The privilege against self-incrimination may be grounded in natural right, as has often been said; it has become constitutional law in the United States and a fundamental feature of modern British law. But in the early modern period there were, for example, more and clearer cases on whether a party was "privileged" against having to produce two witnesses to prove certain facts. The history of an issue with a momentous future and perhaps deep moral roots cannot be understood without awareness of such unmomentous sibling issues.

A. The Institutional Setting

The central common law courts (King's Bench and Common Pleas) had the procedural means to control the practices of non–common law courts. At issue in hundreds of reported cases, a handful of which touch self-incrimination, was the proper use of those procedures. The main procedure available was the writ of prohibition, a judicial writ issuable upon showing cause. It did not have to be sought by the defendant in an ecclesiastical or other non–common law suit (for in theory anyone who saw an abuse of the jurisdictional division of labor could complain), but in practice it always was, save once in a while when an ecclesiastical plaintiff had reason to want to arrest the suit he himself had started.[5] The prohibition forbade the non-common law court and the parties therein to carry on with a suit before it, either definitively or pending reversal of the prohibition by a counter-writ known as a consultation. Such reversal was possible either on fuller consideration of the legal questions than they received when the prohibition was originally issued or on common law determination of a factual dispute unfavorably to the party who originally obtained the prohibition.

Prohibitions go back to the twelfth century.[6] In the Middle Ages they were issued by the Chancery in the first instance; the common law courts, however, made the final determination as to whether they had been issued appropriately. The later transmutation into a judicial writ was essentially a simplification of procedure, permitting most legally disputable cases to be resolved without elaborate pleading, either on what amounted to a motion to have a writ or a motion to reverse one already granted. One might have supposed that the more significant perturbation in the writ's history would have been the Reformation itself. Previously, the prohibition was a protective instrument for the English secular courts against the courts of the international church.[7] Extinction of papal jurisdiction might have given color to the argument that prohibitions were themselves obsolete, not properly usable by one branch of the king's judicial system against another. In fact, prohibitions went on, in great quantity.

The common law's commentary on the interrogating power of ecclesiastical courts could have been written in prohibition cases, and some of it was. The larger part, however, was laid down in habeas corpus cases. That is because many, though not all, attempts to get the common law courts to control self-incriminatory questioning were directed at the Court of High Commission.[8] The commission was an ecclesiastical court outside the regular structure of sub-diocesan, diocesan, and provincial courts and the appellate system by which those tribunals watched over each other and were finally overseen by the Court of Delegates, the statutory substitute for Rome established at the Reformation.[9] The High Commission was authorized under the Elizabethan Act of Supremacy.[10] That statute granted the monarch power to constitute such extraordinary bodies by letters patent should they be needed,[11] and they came to be a regular feature. Just what powers could be conferred on it under the authorizing statute became the subject of much litigation; eventually the common law courts arrived at fairly settled positions on the several subbranches of the problem, but only after considerable time, debate, and confusion.

Habeas corpus tended to be the preferred means of complaining about the commission because, alone among ecclesiastical courts, it claimed to possess the power to imprison. Whether it actually did was a much-controverted question, but de facto it sent people to jail. The prisoners often used habeas corpus to demand that their imprisonment be justified before one of the principal common law courts, as any person committed to jail was entitled to do. Like a prohibition, habeas corpus was a judicial writ[12] ordering the jailer to produce the prisoner and a statement, known as a return, explaining the cause of the detention. Cases were decided on the legal adequacy of the return, which was presumed to be true factually.[13] If it was not, the prisoner was returned to jail but was free to bring an action for false imprisonment.

Complaints against the High Commission touching self-incrimination were frequently combined with other complaints. Actual prisoners, usually proceeding by habeas corpus, almost always maintained that the commission lacked any power to imprison at all—in other words, that it was confined to "spiritual" sanctions, meaning excommunication in the last resort, just as the other spiritual courts were. Moreover, in many other cases there was room to complain that the commission had exceeded its substantive jurisdiction. The general ground for this argument was the widespread belief that Parliament could not have intended to undermine the jurisdiction of regular church courts altogether, but must have meant only to create this extraordinary alternative for especially refractory cases. This view prevailed in the end. There was substantial agreement that the commission could deal only with serious ecclesiastical crimes, and there was at least incipient agreement on an exact list of such crimes. But again, it took time, and in any given instance litigants could hardly be sure where the courts—two concurrent courts, for the King's Bench and Common Pleas were not always in mutual accord—stood on the High Commission's substantive jurisdiction or on the accompanying and related questions of its sanctions and procedural powers.

One has to speak somewhat tentatively about how the law came out on the range of High Commission issues, because there was not sufficient time to achieve full settlement. The commission became embroiled in political controversy and was abolished by the Long Parliament. Even so, there are reasonable grounds for saying that the pre–Civil War courts reached a fairly firm resolution on the commission's power to interrogate at the risk of exposing to self-incrimination. Although other ecclesiastical courts were much less frequently challenged for undertaking such interrogation, complaints on that score sometimes occurred. As between the High Commission and these courts, the issues were not quite the same, owing to the former's statutory basis. It was arguable that the statute gave the commission investigatory powers, as it also may have given it punitive powers, greater than those of ordinary church courts.

B. The Basic Interjurisdictional Rules

There were several settled rules of interjurisdictional law governing common law control of the ecclesiastical system. I shall discuss both the general rules and the problems to which they gave rise. The peculiar twist of those problems when the High Commission was involved will emerge later from the cases.

1. Protection of Common Law Jurisdiction against Encroachment

Non–common law courts were indisputably prohibitable from encroaching directly on common law jurisdiction—that is, from proceeding in a suit that could just as well have been brought at common law. This simple rule did not often have to be asserted in litigation, because of course people did not bring ecclesiastical suits in situations notoriously remediable at common law, where prohibition would have been a certainty and where the plaintiff would have risked incurring the criminal penalties imposed by the statutes of Praemunire. Prohibitions to prevent direct encroachment occurred in practice most often in situations where there was a legitimate question as to whether a common law remedy *was* available. For example, the common law remedied some forms of defamation, while ecclesiastical courts remedied others. It was sometimes debatable whether an utterance was actionable at common law.[14] For a contrasting example, tithes set out in the field visibly separated from the rest of the crop became the parson's property, recoverable at common law against anyone who took them, including the payer. A statute, however, permitted ecclesiastical courts to treat tithes set out and immediately retaken by the payer as mere unpaid tithes, for which the church court was the proper forum; it was often problematic just what this statute meant or how far it allowed what would previously have been simple encroachment on the common law's business.

2. Statutory Interpretation

A second safe rule was that non–common law courts were prohibitable if they misapplied a statute or purported to do something forbidden by statute. This rule, unlike the first, was questioned on virtually constitutional grounds.[15] Why, in post-Reformation circumstances, when ecclesiastical courts were recognized as agents of the king as much as secular courts, should the latter have in effect a monopoly of statutory interpretation? Were statutes not equally addressed to all courts so that misconstructions were subject to appellate review within the system, common law or ecclesiastical, for each had an independent appellate structure, and conflicting interpretations that survived remediable only by Parliament? In practice, however, the common law monopoly was massively asserted. The judicial gloss on several important statutes touching the operations of ecclesiastical courts was written in sequences of prohibition cases.[16] Although tenderness was occasionally shown to ecclesiastical courts by giving them first crack at a statute—that is, refusing to intervene until it was shown that a statutory point had actually been raised and mishandled—that was exceptional. Usually prohibitions were issued on a mere showing that something at variance with a statute had been or might be done.

3. Extensions of the Basic Rules

In several ways, control over non–common law courts extended beyond the functions of protecting the common law's own territory and enforcing the judges' understanding of statutes. Some of the extensions were relatively uncontroversial; that is, certain applications of the prohibition beyond the two least questionable ones were routine in practice. First, some rules bearing on ecclesiastical matters were regarded simply as common law rules enforceable by prohibition. For example, though tithes were recoverable in ecclesiastical courts, whether a particular product was subject to tithes was a common law question. But since all ordinary agricultural products notoriously owed tithes, the common law power was in practice exercised only around the edges—to prevent the taxation of depletable resources such as minerals and sometimes of by-products. Although nonagricultural income, except that derived from mining and some statutorily protected activities, was tithable, there was very little litigation about it.

Second, some issues arising in proper ecclesiastical suits were regarded as determinable at common law. This category never achieved complete generic acceptance. That is, it was frequently argued that if the ecclesiastical courts had jurisdiction in the first place, they should be free to decide all questions that must be decided in order to dispose of the case. The argument was worth making, however, only for relatively unusual issues. For issues that arose repeatedly, it was settled at an early date that the ecclesiastical suit would be arrested pending common law determination and returned to the ecclesiastical court by consultation only if the resolution was favorable to the plaintiff there. The strongest example, illustrating a rule that probably accounts for more prohibitions than any other, is tithe suits in which the defendant claimed a customary commutation of the tax, which was normally or de jure payable in kind. It came to be held without question that the suit would be prohibited until a jury found that the alleged custom did not exist. The rationale was that only a jury could try a custom by the standard of immemorial usage that the common law insisted on. Another routine intervention rests on essentially the same basis: when the bounds of parishes came in question—when, for example, the parson of A sued for tithes and the defendant claimed that the produce sued for was grown in B—a jury would decide where the customary parish line ran. Some other classes of ecclesiastical litigation, especially over parish rates, were also frequently stopped until disputes about customs could be tried by jury. The tithe-commutation cases, in addition to reserving factual disputes for jury trial, also gave the common law judges considerable space for legal decision making, for they assumed jurisdiction to determine what constituted a valid commutation. Other legal matters, such as the validity of a lease, might well be held exclusively suitable for common law decision, though it was not quite so predictable that these would be taken out of ecclesiastical hands as it was that questions of custom would be.

Third, ecclesiastical determination of an intrinsically appropriate ecclesiastical issue was sometimes prevented because it might prejudice common law determination of a closely related issue. The best example is mixed wills: probate of wills of personalty was an exclusively ecclesiastical function. Wills of realty pursuant to the Statutes of Wills did not require probate: they operated as conveyances of land, and if they were to be challenged on such grounds as the testator's insanity, this must be done in the ordinary course of land litigation. Problems arose from the common practice of including both goods and land in a single will. It was argued—and though the law on this subject was tangled and difficult, prohibitions so argued for were issued—that probate must be stopped lest a finding one way or the other by an ecclesiastical court (for example, that the testator was or was not insane) prejudice the jury in potential common law litigation over the land in the same will.

4. Areas of Uncertainty

Beyond the cases sketched above, the going in early modern interjurisdictional law gets much tougher. It could be responsibly argued that common law courts had *no* powers of interference save in the situations just specified. That would come to saying that whether or not the common law judges approved of the rules applied in non–common law courts or the procedures followed there—including incriminatory questioning—they must suffer them or wait for their correction by Parliament. The most interesting inter-jurisdictional cases are those in which an effort was made to controvert that. Doubting it is understandable: Could it really be true that the common law judges must stand by in silence *whatever* non–common law courts do, so long as they do not take away the common law's own business, or violate the statutes or certain entrenched nonstatutory rules such as those on tith-ability, or make determinations unsuited to their methods and expertise, or threaten inadvertent prejudice to potential common law litigation? Did the judges have no authority to keep courts outside the common law system from entertaining frivolous claims, using oppressive or inefficient proce-dures, or applying substantive rules at odds with reason, with those courts' own law, or with the basic expectations of English people (people living under a variety of laws and no doubt bound to take note of all of them, but surely entitled to rely for major purposes on the "common custom of the realm" embodied in the common law)? In particularized forms these questions arose in numerous cases, but they were never satisfactorily resolved in general terms. Sometimes the bench rose to the high-level issue of the common law's place in a mixed legal system, and sharp divisions of judicial opinion on it occasionally turn up in the reports. Sometimes the judges muddled through to a conclusion in the particular case without full awareness of implications or without readiness to face them expressly.

In their weightiest form, problems about self-incrimination went to the "high-level issue": if incriminatory questioning was morally objection-able, did it follow that common law courts had authority to control it? Whatever its moral status, was such questioning so flagrantly at variance with the underlying principles of the common law and expectations founded thereon that it was controllable even when it occurred outside the common law system? As I shall show, most self-incrimination problems were in fact resolvable, without going so high, by forms of the simpler rules on jurisdictional law outlined above. In the end, self-incrimination cases did not contribute much to solution of the major issue that was never solved, at least in the pre–Civil War period of English history: whether the common law's role in jurisdiction control was essentially a self-protective one or a supervisory one extending over every court in the realm.

C. Widest Extension of Control: Disallowance Cases

Before looking at the self-incrimination cases specifically, one needs to ask where cases of other sorts point with respect to the role of common law courts. Although in the most general terms they point to irresolution, on a closer inspection they give some significant indications. On the whole they do not support the position that incriminatory questioning in ecclesiastical courts could be controlled, except when controlling it was a matter of protecting the common law sphere against ordinary encroachment or enforcing statutes, as by confining the High Commission to the jurisdiction allowed it by statute.

Most cases touching common law power over the conduct of ecclesiastical courts in matters properly within their jurisdiction were raised by seeking a prohibition on a claim that the ecclesiastical court had disallowed a substantive plea, or evidence offered, in a suit before it. This was not true of self-incrimination cases. There was also a small range of cases in which prohibition was sought merely by claiming that the ecclesiastical suit was inappropriate—not an encroachment on the common law, not in violation of a statute or other specific rule, but a newfangled or an unwarranted attempt to impose liability for some activity that had always been free of it. Some of these cases produced jurisprudentially significant pronouncements and disagreements, but by and large they are a marginal miscellany. Most serious discussion of the common law's supervisory authority over the ecclesiastical sphere, self-incrimination aside, took place on a disallowance claim, in which a party said, "I have put in what should be regarded as a legally valid defense, but the ecclesiastical judge has disallowed it," or "I have produced what should be considered sufficient evidence, if true, to sustain my claim or defense, but it has been disallowed." Let us look first in summary at what the "substantive" disallowance cases yield. The "evidentiary" ones, which provide the closest parallel to self-incrimination cases, are virtually all the consequence of one formal rule applied in the ecclesiastical system—the rule that two witnesses must be produced to prove factual claims.

1. Substantive Disallowance Cases

The strongest general principle enunciated in substantive disallowance cases, though not always honored in fact, had two parts. One was that merely unreasonable ecclesiastical decisions (and a fortiori decisions that were incorrect under positive ecclesiastical law) should be left to ecclesiastical appeal, not remedied by writs of prohibition. The other was that if an ecclesiastical decision was based on a rule that contradicted a comparable common law rule, a prohibition was appropriate.[17]

The first branch of the principle—no prohibition to control unreasonable or internally erroneous acts—was sometimes expressly embraced and sometimes implicitly disputed. For example, several cases present disallowance of the plea of no assets in cases where an executor was properly sued for a legacy in an ecclesiastical court and pleaded that the estate was insufficient to pay legacies in addition to satisfying debts. There was no conflict of laws; common law and ecclesiastical law agreed that debts took priority. In disallowing the plea, the ecclesiastical court had either violated the agreed-on rule or, more probably, made a judgment of fact, erroneous according to the party seeking the prohibition, as to the estate's actual capacity. Some prohibitions were issued in such cases, though as the sixteenth century gave way to the seventeenth, and experience in handling interjurisdictional problems accumulated, the judges became more reluctant to interfere, sometimes even in the face of understandable temptation.[18]

The second and theoretically more interesting branch of the principle—that despite its independence as a system, ecclesiastical law must not flatly contradict the common law—received some judicial countenance, though again less than a decisive embrace.[19] Few cases treated that proposition as their *ratio decidendi,* but some gave intimations that particular ecclesiastical rules, usually ones implied in holdings rather than clearly stated, would not be tolerated. It was, for example, intimated that in ecclesiastical defamation the truth of the defamatory utterance must be accepted as a defense, as it was in common law practice,[20] or that an aspersion that a man had begotten a bastard must be accepted as true when justices of the peace, pursuing their statutory powers, had found him liable for child support as the probable father of a bastard. Because defamation was a field shared between the common law and the ecclesiastical systems, it is especially understandable that the judges wanted to see the same standards applied on both sides of the line.

Another example from the same field, however, illustrates the fundamental difficulty in applying the principle that conflict must be avoided: such conflicts were hard to find. One instance of apparent contradiction came in cases where defamation claims were released. It occurred when a married woman had sued, or was in a position to sue, for ecclesiastical defamation. Her right of action in the ecclesiastical forum without joinder by the husband was not, I believe, ever challenged. But suppose the husband released the claim to the ecclesiastical defendant or alleged defamer, and when that defendant pleaded the release it was disallowed. This presented a contradiction of the common law rules on the legal subordination of married women, and in some cases the disallowance was vetoed by a writ of prohibition. As far as they go, such cases are the strongest instance of actual insistence on conformity with the common law—as opposed to "intimations" in tangled situations where no decision was made or the grounds of decision are unclear.

Other cases went the other way. The reason is that some judges, on closer inspection of the nature of ecclesiastical defamation, saw that it was not truly parallel to common law slander. The latter aimed at damages; of course, under the prevailing conceptions of married women's property, a husband could release damages recovered or a claim to damages, just as he could alienate his wife's vested chattel property. Ecclesiastical defamation, on the other hand, was essentially criminal, aimed at the defamer's moral reformation; even in civil or "plaintiffs' rights" terms, the wife could be regarded as interested as an individual in the vindication of her honor by nonpecuniary means, whatever the husband's preference. Thus, unless a rather artificial parallelism in defamation law was desirable in itself, there was no good reason why the husband's release should be binding. Here as in other contexts, on close inspection "temporal" and "spiritual" law failed to meet, and therefore did not conflict more than superficially.

So far as I have found, no judge or lawyer thinking about self-incrimination ever pointed to implications that might be drawn from the cases on disallowed substantive pleas. That goes to demonstrate that post-Reformation jurisdictional law was a relatively new field, crowded with a great diversity of problems, which were never quite seen as a whole. No contemporary legal treatises were written on the subject.[21] If, however, we look for the possible implications, they are unfavorable to straightforward, across-the-board control of incriminatory questioning by ecclesiastical courts. On the one hand, mere objection to the morality or reasonableness of such questioning does not emerge as a very good ground for judicial interference with it, though there is an important distinction to be made: ordinarily, the ground for not correcting unreasonable holdings by prohibition was their presumptive correctability by ecclesiastical appeal. It is hard to say whether abuses of inquisition by regular ecclesiastical courts might have been brought under control by the appellate courts over them. At most, such control would have been confined to abuses, for, as chapter 2 shows, within limits incriminatory questioning was an accepted part of the *ius commune* applied in the ecclesiastical courts. The material fact is that regular church courts were involved in few cases where incriminatory questioning was complained of, and the High Commission, the scene of a majority of cases, was not subject to appeal within the system. Yet, as we shall see, despite this reality, the judges dealing with self-incrimination acted consistently with the view they tended to take generally when confronted with "bad law" on the other side of the jurisdictional divide: considering it bad—immoral, irrational, unnatural—was not enough to justify a prohibition. On the other hand, although some disallowance cases suggest that dissonance between common and ecclesiastical law was not always tolerable, they are not abundant in instances of true conflict. If incriminatory questioning were in some sense against the common law, there would be good grounds for preventing it. But was it not simply a feature of another system of law—a system dependent on evidence and testimony—perhaps a deplorable feature, for which the common law had no need? Do the two systems not just fail to meet?

2. The Requirement of Two Witnesses

The same questions pervade the many cases in which attempts were made to keep ecclesiastical courts from demanding two witnesses to prove facts in suits before them.[22] At least a vein of common law opinion deplored the two-witness rule as burdensome and unnecessary. The common law stood as an example of a system that de facto could not operate without witnesses but that, with occasional exceptions, did not impose any such formalistic requirement. It was tempting to see conflict, and not all judges avoided the temptation. But the superficiality of that view was also appreciated. The two-witness rule was a feature of a system without resources other than testimony for ascertaining facts; the common law needed nothing of the sort because it had the jury. As it was sometimes put, where there were twelve witnesses, there was no place for a rule requiring two. The systems, therefore, neither met nor conflicted. I have found no explicit reference to the two-witness problem in cases concerned with self-incrimination, but there is a parallelism, not only in the situations as such, but also in the ways the dilemmas posed by the two-witness rule were worked out in the less heavily litigated area of self-incrimination. It is impossible to know how far the analogies were noticed, but it seems likely that experience with two-witness cases had some influence on how the judges saw self-incrimination problems.

Compared to the substantive disallowance cases, those on the two-witness rule are both more clear-cut and more confused—more clear-cut because they raised the same basic issue repeatedly; more confused because no judicial consensus was ever achieved. The best way to cut through the complexities of the case law is to summarize two rival "judicial restraint" positions—that is, two positions that were at odds with the propensity of some judges to prohibit freely, either because they thought the two-witness rule foolish or because the de facto disparity between the witnessing burdens placed on people whose affairs fell in the lay or the ecclesiastical sphere seemed enough of a head-on conflict to merit interference.

The first of these positions of restraint, that of Sir Edward Coke, came very close to flat opposition to prohibitions based on the two-witness rule. It is significant, in connection with self-incrimination, to take note of his views. Coke is reputed to have been the arch-champion of an early privilege against self-incrimination. In fact, he was not. It was not, of course, logically necessary that he should have been equally indulgent toward an evidentiary formalism and toward a method of investigation that was open to serious moral objection. Still, his opposition to prohibitions against ecclesiastical court enforcement of the two-witness rule was clear. It was based partly on recognition of its benign functions—it encouraged care in business and diminished litigation—and partly on the suspicion that ecclesiastical defendants wanting prohibitions could easily get away with fictitious claims that they were victims of the two-witness rule. By contrast, most incriminatory questioning was controllable on collateral grounds, without denying the church courts a right to their methods in their own domain; similar indirect means of cutting back application of the two-witness rule were more scarce and less patently defensible. Nevertheless, Coke's stand on the two-witness rule testifies to his respect for the ecclesiastical system's integrity. This appears in numerous contexts of prohibition law besides those under discussion here. His broader reputation as a free-and-easy wielder of prohibitions, even as the judge without whom the writ would hardly have had extensive use or become a subject of political controversy, is quite false.

The second position of restraint on two-witness rule prohibitions can be associated with Chief Justice Popham almost as sharply as the more extreme one can be associated with Coke. It looked for a middle ground: sometimes nothing should be done about an insistence on two witnesses—for example, in most testamentary cases. Those were the subject of Popham's most important argument with more permissive judges (the usual modern rule that valid wills must have plural witnesses is the main vestige of the old ecclesiastical procedure). Sometimes, however, regulation was justifiable. The best argument for intervention, which even Coke might not have disputed had he faced a case in point, occurred where the two-witness rule was applied to proof of a document that might come into controversy at common law. For example, suppose A sued in an ecclesiastical court for a legacy, and the executor pleaded a release that covered both the legacy and debts owed to A by the testator. This case is analogous to that of mixed wills of land and goods noted above; a failure to establish the release for want of two witnesses *quoad* the legacy might be prejudicial to future common law litigation about the release *quoad* the debts. This is the main type of what I call "collateral" interference with ecclesiastical proceedings. It often arose in self-incrimination cases. There, too, ecclesiastical methods untouchable per se might be prohibited where they impinged prejudicially on the common law realm.

It does not, however, appear from the cases that the "middle position" was quite so confined. There are indications, for example, that if A's release in the situation just above had covered only legacies, the ecclesiastical court would still have been barred from demanding two witnesses. The rationale would then be, not "collateral impingement," but a limited duty on the part of ecclesiastical courts to follow the common law's lead: a release may be of a purely ecclesiastical interest, such as a legacy, but it is still a release, an action in extinguishment of pecuniary claims generically familiar in the temporal law. It would present excessive disconformity between two systems of law in one country for releases to be unprovable in one system and provable in the other. If, on the other hand, the matter to be proved was something for which the common law had no standard of proof because the thing itself has no existence at common law—whether tithes had been paid, whether a will of personalty was valid, and the like—ecclesiastical courts might be permitted to go their own way. However workable this distinction may be, it is consistent with the best opinion running through the substantive disallowance cases: ecclesiastical rules that contradicted the common law were controllable, but they must be made out as true contradictions, not mere differences.

Of these two positions, the second seems to have predominated. Coke's strong reluctance to interfere with the two-witness rule prevailed only in the courts over which he presided.[23] For the rest, the best generalization from the cases is that Popham's alternative way of limiting interference had considerable influence. Elizabethan courts were inclined to prohibit pretty freely. Not all seventeenth-century judges lost that propensity, but by and large later courts recognized a line between justifiable and unjustifiable prohibitions and struggled with how to draw it. It is fair to speak of Popham's approach as the "better opinion." It has affinities in general terms with the courts' handling of incriminatory interrogation.

II. THE SELF-INCRIMINATION CASES

I propose in discussing the case law bearing on self-incrimination first to summarize the conclusions to which it points and then to look in more detail at two major cases—the only cases reported extensively enough to give a real picture of judges contending with the legal problems. Both of those cases concerned the High Commission, as did most of those that are more scantily reported. Had there been no Court of High Commission, very little of the interjurisdictional law on self-incrimination would be confirmable by judicial decisions.

A. The Popham-Coke Opinion

We do, however, possess an important extrajudicial document, an opinion on the interrogating power of ordinary church courts prepared by Chief Justice Popham and Attorney General Coke in 1606.[24] There is every reason to believe that the fairly restrictive rules laid down in it were accepted so far as the ordinary courts are concerned, since there were very few subsequent attempts to prohibit those courts from asking incriminating questions. Either the regular courts observed the rules voluntarily or, if they did not and the party objected, prohibitions were so routine as to go unreported.[25] This extrajudicial opinion made four points, of which three were nearly inevitable:

(1) *No one may be constrained "to swear generally to answer to such interrogatories as shall be administered."* In other words, one must be accused of something within ecclesiastical jurisdiction before being questioned about it. Indefinite oaths to answer any question that may be asked were banned. Issues naturally arose as to the exact meaning of this requirement—the form in which and degree of specificity with which a party must be apprised of the charge; some of these come up in the High Commission cases. The rule as such, however, speaks to jurisdiction in the simplest sense. It involves no claim that ecclesiastical courts could not conduct incriminating interrogations within their jurisdiction, only that they must have jurisdiction before proceeding. If a party complained that he had been required to take

an indefinite oath, for all the common law court knew he might be asked whether he committed a common law crime, questioned about a civil matter within common law cognizance, or interrogated about something otherwise of no concern to the church. Of course a prohibition must lie. The rule effectively barred one of the worst abuses of inquisitorial procedure, the "fishing expedition," where questioning was intended to turn up an ecclesiastical offense with which the person *might* be charged. Such openended questioning could be controlled because it might also turn up a temporal offense.[26]

(2) *Persons charged with ecclesiastical crimes also punishable at common law may not be examined under oath.* A number of ecclesiastical offenses—mostly breaches of religious discipline, but also, for example, usury—were made secular offenses by sixteenth-century statutes without ceasing to be prosecutable in church courts.[27] In other words, there was a limited area of concurrent jurisdiction. The rationale of the rule, as Popham and Coke explained it, was that ecclesiastical methods unknown in the common law sphere should not be used to exact confessions that could later be employed to procure the party's accusation or conviction at common law. An obvious consideration of fairness or proportionality lay behind this restriction. It would have been odd if an arbitrary handful of minor offenders—critics of the Prayer Book, attenders of unlawful conventicles, and the like—stood in greater danger of being caught and convicted, by grace of the church's helping hand, than serious felons. The rule's strongest justification, however, was the interjurisdictional principle that ecclesiastical courts should be prevented not only from encroaching directly on the common law but also from impinging detrimentally or prejudicially on common law proceedings and on interests protected by the common law.[28]

True concurrent jurisdiction, which existed only for a few secularized ecclesiastical crimes, in a sense made for an a fortiori case of the principle. The mere possibility that proving a release or a devise of land could become more difficult in a common law setting because of related ecclesiastical dealings was reason enough for a prohibition; surely, in the absence of any protection against being prosecuted both "spiritually" and "temporally" for the same offense, a protection that did not exist, the high probability of a forced confession's being later used to a person's criminal detriment should be reason for the writ.[29] This Popham-Coke rule did not have quite the "inevitability" of the preceding one; the availability of a prohibition to prevent "collateral detriment" was not so firmly established as the rule ensuring that the church courts did not venture beyond their substantive jurisdiction. The rule was equally free, however, of any implication that incriminatory questioning was prohibitable in a properly ecclesiastical case whose resolution did not affect secular interests.[30]

(3) *"No man, ecclesiastical or temporal, shall be examined upon secret thoughts of his heart, or of his secret opinion: But something must be objected against him what he hath spoken or done."* This rule, unlike the two above, did put some constraint on ecclesiastical courts within what can at least be reasonably considered their proper sphere. They might accuse a person of making heretical utterances and then ask questions designed to discover whether he had made such statements, but under this rule, they might not (even assuming it could be done without offending against rule 1) say, "We suspect you of heresy," and ask the suspect about his religious views to see whether he would admit to believing something heretical, thereby committing an unlawful speech-act. The church's authority to enforce orthodoxy and some articles of morality by process of law stopped at overt behavior alleged to have occurred before sworn investigation started. Popham and Coke did not explain the basis of this rule. It had no clear analogue in ordinary interjurisdictional law and seems to have been drawn from the *ius commune*. Besides the obvious moral objections to entrapment, one can say that however free ecclesiastical courts should be within their jurisdiction, they were still courts. They were agencies for trying civil claims someone had advanced or crimes someone had brought a charge of, not agencies for detecting, much less provoking, misbehavior no one would otherwise have been in a position to complain about. This understanding was arguably so fundamental to the mixed English legal system that the common law courts, responsible for policing the lines of jurisdiction, must surely be obliged to enforce it. Regulating jurisdiction is meaningless save as it is directed at what *courts* do, with such substantive and procedural canons as particular courts may have.

The rule against examination of "secret thoughts" was of no great practical importance for interjurisdictional law. It restated the law normally applied in the ecclesiastical courts themselves, and English ecclesiastical courts had no inclination to root out hidden unorthodoxy (as opposed to suppressing visible nonconformity). Protestant religious assumptions militated against it. I know of only one case involving the rule, where the High Commission asked a question about an intention (not a religious opinion).[31] The rule did, however, give a certain support to the argument that demanding self-betrayal in any form was just as repulsive morally as inveiglement into committing an unlawful act, for the moral objectionableness of the latter is probably the main reason for prohibiting it.

(4) *Laymen may not be required to submit to sworn examination at all, except*

in testamentary or matrimonial causes. This was a sweeping rule. It would seem almost completely to eliminate sworn examination of lay parties as a method of criminal trial in the ecclesiastical system. Popham and Coke made clear that "testamentary and matrimonial causes" meant civil disputes on those subjects. There could be ambiguity about the term *matrimonial,* since a criminal charge of adultery, say, especially if combined with a wife's suit for separate maintenance, might be thought of as a "matrimonial cause." But Popham and Coke specifically mentioned adultery as one of the offenses laymen might not be examined about, and marital misconduct serious enough to be criminal was precisely within the rationale of the rule. The rule is hard to reconcile with general interjurisdictional principles. It was not, despite the urgings of counsel, ever applied to the High Commission. Why did Popham and Coke embrace it?

They explained the distinctions (traditionally, if lamely) by asserting that testamentary and matrimonial cases were a necessary exception because the transactions involved in them tended to be "secret" and therefore untriable except by sworn examination. Moreover, answering questions asked in these cases could not bring "shame" on the party (a dubious assertion, I should think). That people should not be forced to convict themselves of "shameful" acts was the principal reason for the rule. Clerics were outside the rule because they were presumed learned and therefore capable of taking care of themselves in examination concerning religious offenses.

These explanations had evident weaknesses, although they may be the best one could do to make sense of a rule taken as given. For example, it is hard to think of an ecclesiastical crime that it would not in some sense be "shameful" to have committed—most common sexual offenses were ecclesiastical crimes. Moreover, the rule as stated was broader, extending to numerous civil matters.[32] The real reason Coke and Popham espoused it comes out from the authorities they cited: they had a kind of statutory warrant. It was not quite an unmistakable statute flatly barring sworn examination of laymen except in testamentary and matrimonial cases, but it was a reasonable facsimile. The ancient document known as Articuli Cleri so provided.[33] The statutory status of that document was problematic, but it was at least good evidence of legal opinion around the early fourteenth century. A Henrician statute, while not mandating the rules stated in the extrajudicial opinion, also used explanatory language implying approval of the rules and reasons for them as stated by Popham and Coke.[34] For the purposes of an advisory opinion *quoad* ordinary ecclesiastical courts, Popham and Coke had a perfectly good basis for the fourth rule, as they did for the others. It was good advice to ecclesiastical courts to stay away from sworn examination outside the excepted cases and good advice to common law judges to consider that there was a strong argument for prohibition if the ecclesiastical courts exceeded the boundaries expressed in the rule. Whether Popham and Coke, both of them cautious about interfering with the mode in which church courts exercised their clear jurisdiction, would have been of the same opinion in a carefully argued prohibition case in point may be questioned, since their grounds for the rule were not beyond challenge. They got their opportunities in High Commission cases, where those grounds may not have been relevant owing to the commission's statutory foundation.

B. Cases in Ordinary Church Courts

From the period before the Popham-Coke opinion, I know of two cases in which regular ecclesiastical courts were prohibited from examining people charged with incontinence.[35] A third case involved an unusual attempt to indict an ecclesiastical official for subjecting a defendant charged with incontinence to such examination.[36] The latter seems to say that there was nothing wrong with exposing a party to potentially incriminating examination if he had been presented at an episcopal visitation, a distinction that may be implied in the Popham-Coke opinion.[37] All one can say from these skimpy reports is that there is nothing in the contemporary case law at odds with the extrajudicial opinion.

The most interesting Elizabethan case raises the question of whether sworn examination should ever be prevented when self-accusation or self-conviction of a crime or "shameful" act did not enter the picture.[38] By the letter of the Popham-Coke opinion, it should be prevented for laymen if the case was not a testamentary or matrimonial matter, and it should not be if it fell within one of those categories. This case should probably be classified as testamentary (the bounds of the categories are nowhere defined); at any rate, it was a suit to have administration of an intestate's estate revoked and a new administrator appointed. The administratrix, opposing the suit, sought a prohibition partly on the ground that the ecclesiastical court proposed, by examining her under oath, to extract information about the condition of the estate that could be detrimental in the event of common law litigation about claims against it.[39] Two judges might have been willing to prohibit, partly on the ground that ecclesiastical examining power should not be used so as to cause civil detriment in the common law sphere.

Two others were emphatically opposed, although they were willing to prohibit if the questions were irrelevant for determining whether administration should be reassigned. No decision is reported. Either the court put off resolution until ecclesiastical lawyers could be consulted on the relevance issue or they granted a qualified prohibition forbidding irrelevant questions but not the extraction of detrimental information per se. Both options were discussed. That no similar cases occurred probably goes to show that ecclesiastical courts were careful not to strain their examining power. The outcome of the case itself did not encourage widening the power beyond the lines laid down by Popham and Coke.

Two cases after 1606 expounded the Popham-Coke opinion slightly. In one, a suit against a clergyman's executor for dilapidations was prohibited because the ecclesiastical court proposed to ask the executor questions about a fraudulent lease in which he himself was allegedly complicit.[40] Clergymen were obliged to maintain the value of property attached to their livings. If they allowed it to deteriorate, their estates were liable to their successors for the loss—the so-called dilapidations. The effect of this decision was to extend Popham and Coke's second rule beyond their examples of ecclesiastical offenses turned into concurrent secular misdemeanors by statute. The court said that the executor's temporal risk was prosecution either in the Star Chamber or elsewhere under a penal statute. The decision said that those risks counted, whether or not purely civil detriment did. That seems a predictable conclusion, but even here there was a scintilla of doubt. Although Star Chamber offenses were usually common law misdemeanors, this conciliar court was outside the common law system and used the same civilian procedure as did the ecclesiastical courts. It was arguable that the common law courts lacked "interest" to protect ecclesiastical parties against trouble their confessions might bring upon them in the tribunals that were beyond the common law's reach.

This point echoes a problem that arose occasionally in interjurisdictional cases: might ecclesiastical courts ever be prevented from doing what the common law itself would not but that a court of equity, say, might? *Penal statute* here refers to the much-relied-on type of legislation that subjected an activity to a specified pecuniary penalty recoverable in part by a private prosecutor, sometimes an interested or offended party, but often a mere informer. While much of the behavior regulated by such statutes was criminal or "shameful" enough—collusion in the making of a fraudulent lease would seem to qualify, and some of the secularized ecclesiastical offenses were brought into the lay sphere using this technique—such penal statutes were also often used for purposes of economic regulation. The moral status of the penalty was therefore ambiguous. Was it a punishment or a tax? Occasional remarks in High Commission cases, however, seem to confirm the tendency of this particular decision: increasing the danger of monetary loss in the form of a penalty was not a permissible by-product of ecclesiastical examination. The decision also said that objectionable exposure to temporal detriment via compulsory examination could occur in civil cases as well as in prosecutions for ecclesiastical crimes. Whether a suit for dilapidations should be considered "testamentary" makes a question, but there was no complaint against the executor's examination save for its putting him personally in danger of this special kind of "incrimination."

The second post-1606 case extended "temporal detriment" to the civil loss involved in forfeiture of a bond.[41] It did so in circumstances that illustrate a strategy for evading agreed-on restrictions against straightforward incriminating investigation. A person accused of incontinence was required to enter a bond not to keep company with a certain woman. He was subsequently subjected to sworn examination as to whether he in fact had kept company with her. The ecclesiastical court was prohibited on the ground that the party was asked to admit to facts that would make it difficult for him to defend a common law suit for the bond's forfeiture. The legality of ecclesiastical courts' use of such good behavior bonds at all was open to question; in any event, the ecclesiastical courts were prohibited from using their examining power to ascertain the bonds' breach.

One further case is anomalous: the only instance I know of where a court of equity, rather than an ecclesiastical court, was prohibited from asking a party to betray himself.[42] The report is too skimpy to reveal possibly crucial aspects of the case, but the decision in a general way confirms the "temporal detriment" doctrine. An intestate's creditor went to the Court of Requests to seek an injunction against the administrator's opposing the creditor's common law suit with a no assets plea. The argument for the prohibition was that the plea was possible only because another suit on a fraudulent obligation had gone against the administrator and that he would be questioned about it during the application for the injunction. He seems to have been accused of fraud by colluding in that suit.[43] The report does not, however, exclude the possibility that only civil detriment was in question. At the least, one can say that the administrator would have been asked questions about the common law suits and the allegedly fraudulent obligation allegedly involved in them in determining whether the Court of Requests should enjoin him from claiming no assets.

C. High Commission Cases

I have already cited cases showing that several rules applicable to regular church courts were extended to the High Commission. The two major cases I shall now discuss are the most informative source for understanding the special problems raised by the commission and also for lawyers' and judges' thinking about self-incrimination in general. All in all, it is worth reemphasizing that the case law touching self-incrimination is niggardly with respect both to the High Commission and the regular courts.

The upshot of the High Commission cases admits of brief summary. The issue was whether the common law courts should concede to the commission the power to examine laymen about ecclesiastical crimes within the commission's jurisdiction, assuming observation of other undoubted conditions, such as due notice of the charge, no temporal detriment, and no questions about mere thoughts. The answer is that in *Maunsell & Ladd* (1607), the King's Bench under Chief Justice Popham probably did concede such power. Nothing in subsequent King's Bench practice contravenes that conclusion, although there was no express confirmation in later decisions. From the Common Pleas in the period of Coke's chief justiceship, on the other hand, several dicta state that laymen were not examinable in such cases or that they were examinable only in testamentary or matrimonial cases, neither of which, by most opinion, came within High Commission jurisdiction.[44] There are only these dicta, however. It is a reasonable guess that if Coke's Common Pleas had faced a case in point it would have gone against the King's Bench and *Maunsell & Ladd*. But of course such guesswork is perilous. *Maunsell & Ladd* was deliberately argued. The Common Pleas would have had to contend with the sister court's opinion, though it would not have been obliged to follow it, had the examinability of laymen been squarely raised. And when, as Chief Justice of the King's Bench, Coke finally got a chance to hold laymen unexaminable, he showed no inclination to do so, disposing of the case on the undisputed ground of temporal detriment. That is the second major case, *Burrowes v. Court of High Commission*. Coke's inclination to be as tender toward the High Commission as possible in an open-and-shut case against it, and as hard as possible on its Puritan victims, rather than his zeal against self-incrimination, is what stands out in it.

1. Stowe MS 424

First, a word needs to be said about a document outside the law reports that has been mistakenly used to argue that Coke in the Common Pleas issued numerous prohibitions on the ground that incriminatory questioning was unlawful.[45] This document, Stowe MS 424, is a compilation of prohibitions to the High Commission granted by Coke's Common Pleas. The collection was made by a partisan of the commission claiming that that court was being unwarrantably prohibited. Its hostile intent, however, does not detract from its value or authenticity. There is no reason to think it does not transcribe accurately what the compiler found in the Common Pleas records. It shows what it shows—all that those records can show without being supplemented by reports in which the court's reasoning appears. The Stowe MS makes clear that the Common Pleas prohibited the High Commission more frequently than is knowable from reports. It contains seventeen cases, only two of which occur in reports of which I am aware. The circumstances of a third recur in a reported habeas corpus case.[46] The Stowe cases also show that the "surmises" (written statements of the reasons why prohibition should be granted) of persons seeking to prohibit the commission usually included a complaint that they would be exposed to potentially incriminating questioning and an assertion (often in vague, general terms, invoking the Magna Carta) that such questioning was unlawful. The hitch is that nearly all the cases in the collection presented other good grounds for prohibition, mostly grounds of substantive jurisdiction so manifest that it is not very surprising that the cases went unreported.

At the time, the High Commission was campaigning for virtually unlimited power to exercise ecclesiastical jurisdiction when it saw fit. Coke's Common Pleas—outstandingly, as compared with the contemporary King's Bench—was rapidly making the law that restricted its jurisdiction and protected the local ecclesiastical courts against preemption. There is, of course, no way of proving absolutely that the prohibitions in some of the Stowe cases were not granted in response to complaints about exposure to self-incrimination, but it is not likely. It is extremely unlikely that the difficult matter of the examining power would have been taken up in cases easily disposable otherwise under currently emergent doctrine. If it had been taken up in open court, the cases would almost certainly have been reported. The cases in the Stowe MS that *were* reported confirm that self-incrimination was never reached, as do several other reported cases, in which judicial doubt about ecclesiastical examination was expressed but in which the cases were decided on other bases.

That the surmises in these cases asserted a violation of the privilege against self-incrimination means practically nothing. One could state as many reasons for prohibition as one liked; it was only prudent to allege all possible reasons in the event that something should go wrong with the most probable. The law was far from firmly settled and was under political pressure from the church hierarchy and the government. There was no untruth involved, since every defendant before the High Commission was subject to examination if his case stayed in the commission's hands. In sum, the Stowe MS leaves us where we were: Coke's court was no doubt the place to look if one needed to contend against the High Commission's examining power, but no one needed to do so seriously because the same court was vigorous in keeping the commission's jurisdiction in narrow bounds.

2. *Maunsell & Ladd*

The closest thing to a leading case on self-incrimination is *Maunsell & Ladd* (1607).[47] It did not result in a victory for the "liberal" position on the subject. Indeed, the petitioners who sought to establish the illegality of the High Commission's use of the ex officio oath failed. The arguments made in the case, however, are instructive of the possibilities then current. In hindsight, it is unfortunate that the case arose on a habeas corpus. A prohibition case would have left a fuller and clearer statement of the facts. The actual case raised a question of pure habeas corpus law—the formal adequacy of a spare return saying only that Maunsell and Ladd were imprisoned for refusing to answer a "summary question" about a conventicle. One judge, Tanfield, was at first tempted to avoid deciding the substantial issues by holding this return too cryptic. He later changed his mind, and as the swing vote delivered an opinion adverse to the prisoners. The other judges showed no interest in evasive narrow grounds. In any event, strictly speaking they had judicial knowledge only of what the return told, as in any habeas corpus case. Actually, the court knew a little more, and the historian accordingly has a bit more information, since counsel in habeas corpus cases commonly smuggled in a few facts outside the return. The key smuggled fact here is that Ladd was a layman. Maunsell was a clergyman and, at least as to religious offenses, liable to sworn examination under any comprehensive standard that might have been upheld. Counsel for the prisoners in this case would probably not have conceded such liability, and the two dissenting judges who agreed with them—Fenner and Yelverton—show no sign of recognizing a lay-clerical distinction. Of course, the majority made nothing of it, either. It had no need to invoke a harsher rule for clergymen.

A second possibly obfuscating factor in *Maunsell & Ladd,* endemic to High Commission cases, was that the commission was almost never attackable simply because of improper interrogation. Its jurisdiction and its sanctions were widely controversial. In *Maunsell & Ladd,* however, no issue was made of jurisdiction. If there had been any question as to whether participation in a conventicle was an ecclesiastical offense serious enough for the commission, it was not raised. It is an important fact that the case involved Puritans. Even judges with a narrow view of the commission's procedural powers felt little sympathy with Puritan activity, or at any rate had no disposition to soft-pedal its illegality. Despite the law's protracted uncertainty as to just which offenses were within the commission's jurisdiction, there was a persistent, and quite reasonable, inclination to think that Puritanism was what the High Commission existed to correct, and there was little inclination to distinguish among Puritan offenses. The prisoners' lawyers in *Maunsell & Ladd* were also more interested in disarming the commission procedurally than in niggling over its jurisdiction, even had there been a hope of doing so.

The commission's imprisoning power, however, was as eligible a target as its interrogating power. This issue was consequential in the case. Counsel for the prisoners and the judges on their side claimed that the commission had no such power or, failing that, that any power it did have did not extend to the facts of this case. The lines of the second, more qualified position on this point are hard to disentangle, but roughly speaking, a plausible argument could be made that even if imprisonment could be used as a punishment for persons convicted of *infra vires* ecclesiastical offenses, it could not be used to coerce taking an oath or answering particular questions once a party was sworn. That is, conceding that interrogation under oath was not unlawful per se, it could not lawfully be compelled except by purely spiritual sanctions. There was also an argument, based on statute, that if people were imprisonable at all they could not be imprisoned for more than three months, whereas—another piece of smuggled information—Maunsell and Ladd had been in jail for nine before they brought their habeas corpus. So the case was in a sense as much on the imprisoning power as on the interrogating power.

Nonetheless, it still should be considered primarily a case on self-incrimination, indeed the leading case. That is so because counsel for the prisoners, while not neglecting the imprisoning power, chose to concentrate their heaviest fire on the alleged illegality of incriminating questioning. It was a realistic choice, I think, for across time (1607 was still relatively early in the history of litigation about the High Commission) the Bench was not much inclined to deny the commission's power to fine and imprison or to split hairs about its exact extent. Having an extraordinary ecclesiastical tribunal for a limited number of otherwise intractable offenses made some-what more sense if that tribunal had extraordinary "teeth." The ably mar-shaled arguments of counsel for a broad privilege against self-incrimination had a better chance of success than their arguments against the commission's power to imprison. *Maunsell & Ladd* was thus a major case because the prisoners' lawyers wanted to make it one, to stage a full-dress argument against the High Commission and force the judges to consider the issues on all levels.

The prisoners' lawyers were Nicholas Fuller and Henry Finch.[48] Fuller had a political identity not shared by most other lawyers appearing in the many interjurisdictional cases.[49] In modern terms, he was the most promi-nent "liberal" or "left-leaning" lawyer of his day. He had both Puritan and "City" connections (he had represented London in Parliament). There can be no doubt that he believed in the causes he most famously argued. His argument in *Maunsell & Ladd* was published abroad as an explicitly Puritan attack on the High Commission.[50] Although, like most printed arguments and opinions, it was probably smoothed and amplified for publication, it does not vary seriously from the manuscript reports' record of what Fuller said in court. Since it is only his argument, it gives no sense of the court-room context and no intimation that Fuller failed to persuade three of the five judges he faced. Fuller's political position is also attested by the scandal-ous vendetta the High Commission subsequently pursued against him. He was proceeded against for schism on the strength of statements made on his clients' behalf in *Maunsell & Ladd,* convicted, and imprisoned. His at-tempts to secure common law protection were unavailing. Little as the common law judges liked these proceedings, they decided they could do nothing about them. Schism was clearly within High Commission jurisdic-tion, and no lawyer's privilege against ecclesiastical prosecution for remarks made in the line of professional duty was discoverable. There was no self-incrimination element in Fuller's case. I have no positive evidence that Finch was inspired by personal conviction, but the tone of his argument and scraps of biography—he was an intellectual lawyer who once got into trouble for an eccentric, though not orthodox Puritan, religious writing—suggest the likelihood.

Fuller and Finch went high, arguing that to demand self-incrimination violated the law of nature, Magna Carta, and several venerable English stat-utes. Whether their contentions in this vein were tactically wise makes a question. A note of judicial impatience is perhaps audible in the reports, as if to say, "Show us in the terms of ordinary interjurisdictional law why an ecclesiastical court may not always be entitled to use ecclesiastical procedures, and especially why, under the statute authorizing it, the High Commission cannot investigate crimes by interrogating the party—that rather than addressing the gallery in support of political opinions hostile to the Commission." It would not be surprising if the judges chafed a little at what they perceived as rhetoric. The relevance of Magna Carta and the other ancient statutes was dubious. Of course, if the most prestigious of statutes really did bar incriminatory questioning in all English tribunals, it would be a weighty authority.[51] Finding an intent to repeal Magna Carta in the clause of the Act of Supremacy authorizing the High Commission would be hard. No tradition held ecclesiastical courts foreclosed from incriminatory questioning because of Magna Carta. Nor, to most intents, should there have been such a tradition. At most the celebrated chapter 39 of the Charter,[52] the only section in point, could be construed to guarantee such features of "due process" as accusation by indictment and jury trial in the secular system of law.[53] Subject to the limits that made it respectable, including the strongest one—lay immunity from all or almost all liability to self-incrimination—standard ecclesiastical process almost had to count as "due" in its own sphere. Otherwise, jury trial and common law accusatory process would have been required there, against all traditional assumptions. Saying that Magna Carta entailed a duty to imitate the common law in so broad a sense as to preclude exposing any ecclesiastical defendant to self-incrimination was like saying the ecclesiastical system may not have a two-witness rule because the common law was structured not to need one. Some judges were willing to say that about the two-witness rule (and Fenner and Yelverton may have been willing to make the analogous point about self-incrimination—the breadth of their dissent is hard to assess), but it was not the prevailing opinion. For the rest, insofar as Fuller and Finch went beyond positive legal sources to invoke moral law, once again such objections were the least effective reasons for intervention.

This said, one should not necessarily dismiss Magna Carta as altogether irrelevant legally. In relation to the narrower task of construing the Act of Supremacy, it could mean something. While Magna Carta could not plausibly be taken as a limitation on the ecclesiastical system generally, it could be said to limit royal authority to confer new powers on any tribunal, ecclesiastical or secular, and to raise a presumption that Parliament did not intend to give the monarch any such authority. In other words, England might be stuck with some ecclesiastical procedures at odds with Magna Carta, but that need not mean that such procedures could be expanded without unmistakable parliamentary intent.

It is to Fuller's credit as an advocate (Finch largely stayed on high ground) that he knew *Maunsell & Ladd* could not be won by talking about moral principle and Magna Carta. Of all those who discussed self-incrimination, Fuller alone sought (and found) a sharp sense in which incriminatory questioning contradicted the common law. He produced a reason why exposing people to self-incrimination in the ecclesiastical sphere was like, say, an ecclesiastical court's refusing to accept truth as a defense in defamation.[54] Fuller was aware that head-on conflict with the common law, if it could be made out, was the best reason for blocking actions that were otherwise normal in the ecclesiastical system and subject only to internal control. What he hit on was the common law rule that when prospective jurors were challenged they would be examined under oath if the challenge reflected no discredit on their person (being related to one of the parties, for example). However, they would not be examined under oath if charged with something discreditable or illegal (having been bribed or the like). In other words, though the common law and ecclesiastical systems of accusation and trial generally failed to meet, they did not utterly fail to do so. In at least one context, the common law did try facts by examination under oath, and when it did so it avoided exposing those who took the oath to self-incrimination. That this cogent argument got nowhere with the majority judges must reflect their belief that the Act of Supremacy authorized granting inquisitorial powers to the High Commission.

The debate on the meaning of the statute was complicated by some subtleties, but ultimately, as in many other cases dealing with the High Commission's powers, the outcome depended on intuition of Parliament's likely intent and on willingness to guess at it. The statutory language was too general for a close reading to yield plausible alternatives. To the judges in the majority, Popham most explicitly, the statute's generality indicated that the monarch was meant to have at least reasonable scope to give the High Commission powers the monarch thought it needed to be effective. That scope was ample enough to include imprisoning and examining powers larger than those ordinary ecclesiastical courts enjoyed. If Parliament had intended the special tribunal to be confined to ordinary ecclesiastical powers, it could have said so. Behind this reading lay the perfectly sensible feeling that there would not have been much purpose in authorizing creation of a extraordinary court if its powers merely duplicated those of existing ecclesiastical tribunals.[55] It was Tanfield in his final opinion who most clearly articulated this point: an extra tribunal without extra teeth failed to make sense. It was also Tanfield who responded sharply to counsel's predictable objection that if, on the strength of vague statutory language the monarch could confer some such powers on the commission, why could he not go further, conferring the power to impose capital punishment, for example? To this argument, Tanfield in effect said, "Nonsense." He did not say where the line should be drawn, but Popham himself had already expressly affirmed the early cases (Leigh's Case and so on) on "temporal detriment." Under the rule endorsed by those cases, vague language did *not* imply an intent to let the commission's acts impinge on the common law or alter people's situations in the temporal sphere. The court should be taken as holding that the High Commission was subject to all the limits on ecclesiastical courts except for imprisoning power sufficient to cover this case and power to interrogate laymen in criminal suits. That was enough, practically speaking, to dispose of the hypothetical fantasy about capital punishment—the severest of detriments and by all tradition to be imposed only by common law process (the Star Chamber could not sentence to death). If it was comforting to rest this fundamental determination on Magna Carta, by the historical lights of the early seventeenth century there could hardly be an objection to doing so. The third member of the majority, Justice Williams, though a bit more nervous lest the High Commission be handed too much, was basically of the same opinion.

The two dissenting judges and the prisoners' counsel stood on the opposite intuitive response to general language. They argued that if Parliament had wanted an ecclesiastical court—and that the High Commission was an ecclesiastical court was undisputed—to have more than ordinary powers, it could easily so have provided. One should presume against an unexpressed intent to change the law. As for complicating subtleties on the statutory issue, some attention was given to the theory that the Act of Supremacy was declaratory. That is, it only declared the immemorial fact that the monarch was supreme governor of the church and restored her to the inherent powers of that office. It was entirely plausible, indeed it was supported by judicial decision, to say that the power to set up additional ecclesiastical courts was among the adjuncts of supreme governorship, not something conferred by the statute. This cut against the High Commission, because it was hard to make out that the monarch, acting alone in a spiritual capacity and unaided by statute, could create an ecclesiastical court enabled to take measures beyond the powers of other ecclesiastical courts.

This argument was not dismantled in *Maunsell & Ladd*. One must suppose that the judges favorable to the commission accepted the same commonsense point that many justices concerned to limit its substantive jurisdiction did. The statute was no doubt in a major sense restorative or declaratory (a truism of the Church of England), but that did not mean it had no legislative content. A statute may not have been necessary to create a tribunal like the High Commission, but a statute existed nonetheless, and its intention to do more than simply restate the monarch's powers could not be ruled out. If Parliament had not limited the powers of the new tribunal, the door would have been opened to usurpation of any and all functions of the ordinary courts. The contrary view, taken by the majority in *Maunsell & Ladd* and ultimately by most judges,[56] held that if Parliament's intent had been so limited, an extraordinary body would have been created without the prospect of being any more effective than the courts already in existence. This was an unlikely possibility.

The second argument for the High Commission involved the possibility that the Act of Supremacy incorporated by reference language from the statute De heretico comburendo, the one piece of legislation from the past that gave ordinary ecclesiastical courts both imprisoning power and a broad examining power.[57] The act repealed De heretico comburendo, but it was arguable that the act's wording, which permitted the prospective High Commission to exercise all powers currently being used by ecclesiastical courts, had been meant to include those given by the medieval statute. Exceptional powers were, after all, currently being used, even though the Act of Supremacy itself took them away from the ordinary courts.

Fuller raised this theory in making a different argument: if the High Commission were in fact entitled to extraordinary powers by virtue of the Act of Supremacy's reference to De heretico comburendo, then the prisoners should be released, since the statute specified that the ecclesiastical causes it covered must be disposed of within three months, as Maunsell's and Ladd's had not been. Popham tried vigorously to rebut this alleged implication by arguing that the three-months provision applied only to parties who cooperated with the ecclesiastical court, not to ones who by resisting interrogation prevented disposal within the time limit. This suggests that Popham thought the case for the commission was at least improved by finding intent in the statute's referential language, even though his main emphasis was on the sheer vagueness of the language. There is no reason to suppose that the argument from De heretico had any particular weight with the other majority judges. It seems only to reinforce what was reachable by easier means.

I have abstracted in speaking of *Maunsell & Ladd* as a 3–2 decision in favor of the High Commission's interrogating and imprisoning powers, but it comes to that. The case was argued twice, the prisoners being returned to jail while the judges deliberated. Chief Justice Popham died early in the term of the second discussion. No successor having been appointed, the decision was then a tie, amounting to a holding against the prisoners, since without a majority for their release, they stayed in prison—to what ultimate fate I do not know. Popham, however, had been vehemently against the prisoners on the first argument; a change of mind had he lived would have been extremely improbable. Tanfield, the judge who did change his mind, or at least made it up after starting in great uncertainty, had initially inclined to a dilatory solution and, on the substance, leaned the prisoners' way under the influence of the "declaratory act" theory.

The best conclusion, buttressed by the absence of decisions contra, is that *Maunsell & Ladd* settled the law on self-incrimination to the advantage of the High Commission, but that it was a close call. The two dissents are the best evidence we have that some judges were ready to create a comprehensive privilege, at least for laymen. It is worth remembering, however, that even without one, there were effective restraints on the commission's power to interrogate, principally the "temporal detriment" doctrine combined with the fact that the law on religious discipline, which the commission was centrally concerned to enforce, did often impose secular penalties. Those restraints were upheld in *Maunsell & Ladd*.

3. *Burrowes v. The High Commission*

Coke's best-reported self-incrimination case may illustrate judicial statesmanship; it may also illustrate cowardice, ambition, and anti-Puritan prejudice.[58] *Burrowes* fell toward the end of Coke's career on the Bench, just before a succession of contretemps with the king culminated in Coke's dismissal. He would have had motive to accommodate the government, in which his colleagues could well have shared. They gave no sign of disagreement with the handling of the case, which was largely managed by the chief justice. Unlike the others, however, Coke might have been motivated to add another stand on principle to those that had already got him in trouble, defying the preferences of the monarch and the churchmen. That he took no such stand need not mean that personal or political grounds discreditable to the judges explain the disposal of the case. Principle of a different kind, a statesmanlike desire to avoid disputes with the High Commission, is also a possible explanation. Whatever accounts for its actions, the court in *Burrowes* avoided deciding a very nearly open-and-shut habeas corpus case by simply liberating the prisoners.

The penumbra of uncertainty about the exact facts characteristic of cases on habeas corpus affects this one, but not seriously. Several men were imprisoned for refusing to answer potentially incriminating questions about offenses against the Prayer Book. Their offenses probably consisted entirely of speech-acts—Puritan denunciation of the established form of worship—which were generically as illegal as the overt behavior illustrated by *Maunsell & Ladd*. The prisoners were represented by Henry Finch, by then Serjeant Finch, who had been counsel in *Maunsell*. Three reasons were urged for their release: (1) "Temporal detriment"—the offenses charged were made secular by the Act of Uniformity; (2) the prisoners' lay status; and (3) an element of vagueness in the return and ultimately failure to apprise the parties of the subject of the inquiry or the questions in adequate form.[59] It is the first of these grounds that causes me to say the case was as good as open-and-shut. The prisoners could unquestionably have been prosecuted for statutory misdemeanors simply on the basis of the acts they were being asked to confess. Neither this court nor any other had the least doubt that interrogation in those circumstances was subject to prohibition. At one point in the argument, it was suggested that two of the parties might have been amenable to prosecution for schism, but no theory was seriously developed to cover that oddity. A respectable question could be raised about whether the "temporal detriment" doctrine extended to prevent inquisitorial investigation of a grave ecclesiastical crime like schism, undoubtedly within the High Commission's jurisdiction, when acts constituting or counting as evidence of that crime were also prosecutable for different reasons in the common law system.

Finch's second argument, relating to the distinction between laymen and clergy, was unpersuasive only if *Maunsell & Ladd* was interpreted as overturning the lay exemption for the High Commission and if *Maunsell* was proof against reversal. Finch did not advertise the law against him. He invited the court to hold what Coke had often suggested: that the exemption applied to the High Commission. The chief justice expressed agreement with the point quite firmly when it was first broached, after which nothing more was said about it. Letting it drop was perfectly reasonable in view of the other strong considerations; the other judges, who if anything seem less well-disposed toward the prisoners than Coke, may have disagreed with the doctrine; all one can say is that Coke apparently saw no purpose in making a fight for his convictions when there was no necessity. Finch's third ground would seem to be solid reinforcement. The court took trouble to look into the information the prisoners had been given in advance of being questioned, and it discussed the standards for appraisal, which had probably not been met. The High Commission's imprisoning power per se was unchallenged in *Burrowes*.

Coke and his brethren give no sign of thinking that the case was anything but easy on the merits. Coke was explicit, however, about preferring to put off what the merits required until, ideally, a settlement could be worked out with the High Commission. Rather than offend the commissioners by freeing their prisoners, Coke wanted to confer with them. His goal was to persuade them that in the present case and others like it (the standard Puritan case, one might say) compulsory interrogation was unnecessary. The parties were charged with open acts; by taking a bit of extra trouble to convict them on nonconfessional evidence, the commission could avoid unedifying interjurisdictional clashes and still deal effectively with "sectaries" for whom, Coke emphasized, he had little sympathy. Apparently a meeting took place. In the absence of evidence sufficient to tell the complete story, one must assume that hope of an amicable agreement foundered. Still, the King's Bench remained unwilling to decide the case until the High Commission could fulfill its expressed wish to argue its cause against the prisoners in open court. Audience was accordingly given to a prominent ecclesiastical lawyer, Dr. Martin. He delivered a high-flying royalist speech, to the effect that the High Commission was a virtually uncontrollable prerogative court. If anything could have been said to persuade common law judges that these prisoners were being lawfully held, Martin did not have the least idea of how to say it, or at any rate no inclination to proceed with caution. A careful argument, in the light of *Maunsell & Ladd* though perhaps contrary to what was assumed in it, to the effect that the intent of the Act of Supremacy overrode even the "temporal detriment" doctrine for some religious offenses, might not have been hopeless.

Even then, *Burrowes* was allowed to drag over three terms for the sake of comity, the prisoners remaining in jail all the while. In the third term, the King's Bench at last faced the inevitable. By that time there were grounds for letting the prisoners go without holding head-on that the High Commission had had no business subjecting them to incriminating interrogation. The court emphasized these independent grounds: the parties, having spent the better part of a year in prison, had been punished as much as they reasonably could be for a contempt. In other words, although the commission might imprison, even for resisting interrogation, and even when this would put the party in temporal danger, at most in such a case it might imprison for contempt. It might not hold people indefinitely until they submitted to examination. Nor could the High Commission imprison them as a punishment for the substantive offense with which they had been charged, as though they had actually been convicted. Only punishment for resisting a court order was permissible. The common law's habeas corpus jurisdiction extended to seeing that any contempt power the High Commission had was exercised reasonably.

Moreover, the final decision was not to discharge the prisoners outright but to bail them on condition that they "submit themselves" to the High Commission. That did not imply that they should answer *ultra vires* questions, only that they should go to the commission and express their willingness to abide by the lawful exercise of its jurisdiction over them. A complete picture of the facts might show that the parties had behaved contemptuously in some further sense than in not swearing or responding to questions. There may also have been reason to think the commission would be unable to catch them and deal with them by legal means if they were allowed to walk away. All appearances suggested that the prisoners were not mere victims but radical Puritans intent on openly resisting the commission, whose legitimacy they very likely denied. The conditional bail, that is to say, might have had a justification, as opposed to an essentially political motive: to offend the High Commission as little as possible while doing what had to be done under established interjurisdictional law. The final disposition was, in any event, fully consonant with the tenderness toward the commission shown throughout the case.[60]

III. AFTERMATH AND CONCLUSION

I have found no reported cases involving self-incrimination and the High Commission from the years between Coke's departure from the Bench in 1616 and the Civil War. This statistically unimpressive fact (for there are not many self-incrimination cases altogether) does not merit a melodramatic explanation. It might be tempting to imagine the High Commission as liberated from common law regulation, free to use and abuse its powers of inquisition with Coke out of the way and—-in Charles I's reign—with the success of the Laudian Party. But that is contrary to all probability. Interjurisdictional law in general went on in the 1620s and 1630s as it had before.

The passage of time and shifts in the political wind had some effects on the disposition of cases. Some Caroline judges do seem to show a more pronounced or conscious restraint about intervening in ecclesiastical matters than was characteristic of earlier decades. But at most there was delicate change in the balance and tone of judicial opinion. Old debates and differences continued, subject to the forces of cumulation always at work in case law. Some issues were settled and ceased to be worth litigating, others were not, but even then the perception of problems may have altered with experience. The law on incriminatory questioning was hardly unsettled, considering its small volume; there is not much sign of judicial division after the sharp split in *Maunsell & Ladd*. It is not unlikely that trouble about self-incrimination declined in part because the High Commission learned what Coke hoped to teach it—that even within the narrow limits in which it was probably left free to pursue sworn confessions, the technique was not valuable enough to justify the risk of overstepping those limits.

In conclusion, one can say that interjurisdictional law between the Reformation and the Civil War furnished material for later assaults on potentially incriminating interrogation. However, the material would have to be misunderstood or distorted to make out that the common law courts enforced a general "privilege" on the ecclesiastical system. There were restraints sufficient to ensure that little such interrogation could take place over the party's objection, mainly by way of the rules that admissions exacted by ecclesiastical questioning must not have common law consequences and that persons being questioned must be informed at least fairly specifically in advance what the questions would be, allowing them to seek common law protection if the questions were *ultra vires.*

These restraints were in line with interjurisdictional practice in other, more everyday contexts. Interference with interrogation in a proper ecclesiastical (or High Commission) suit, uncomplicated by common law consequences or failure of due notice, would have been out of line with that practice. There was undoubtedly a current of thought that laymen enjoyed an immunity at least broad enough to assure that they could not be convicted of ecclesiastical crimes on confessional evidence. When, however, it came to including High Commission defendants, for whom alone it would have had much practical importance, the common law courts held back from following that argument. Although the evidence is not perfectly clean, the best construction of it is that the King's Bench refused, in *Maunsell & Ladd,* to make the inclusion. That holding was never reversed. It might well have been, but there was little necessity for reversal. There were other available grounds for checking the zeal to exact self-incriminating testimony that, for a time anyway, the High Commission displayed. Even had the common law judges wished to develop a full privilege against incrimination enforceable against the ecclesiastical courts, they had no urgent reason for doing so.

FOUR

The Privilege and Common Law Criminal Procedure: The Sixteenth to the Eighteenth Centuries

John H. Langbein

The development of the privilege against self-incrimination—the guaranty that no person shall be compelled in any criminal case to be a witness against himself—was a landmark event in the history of Anglo-American criminal procedure. Prior historical scholarship has located the origins of the common law privilege in the second half of the seventeenth century, as part of the aftermath of the constitutional struggles that resulted in the abolition of the Courts of Star Chamber and High Commission. The true origins of the common law privilege, however, are to be found not in the high politics of the English revolutions but in the rise of adversary criminal procedure at the end of the eighteenth century. The privilege against self-incrimination at common law was the work of defense counsel.

From the middle of the sixteenth century, when the sources first allow us to glimpse the conduct of early modern criminal trials,[1] until late in the eighteenth, the fundamental safeguard for the defendant in common law criminal procedure was not the right to remain silent but rather the opportunity to speak. The essential purpose of the criminal trial was to afford the accused an opportunity to reply in person to the charges against him. Among the attributes of the procedure that imported this character to the criminal trial, the most fundamental was the rule that forbade defense counsel. The prohibition on defense counsel was relaxed in stages from 1696 until 1837, initially for treason, then for felony. Although persons accused of ordinary felony began to be allowed counsel in the 1730s, defense counsel did not become quantitatively significant until the 1780s.[2]

In the later eighteenth century, and more fully in the nineteenth, a radically different view of the purpose of the criminal trial came to prevail. The criminal trial came to be seen as an opportunity for the defendant's lawyer to test the prosecution case. The privilege against self-incrimination entered common law procedure (together with the beyond-reasonable-doubt standard of proof and the exclusionary apparatus of the modern law of criminal evidence) as part of this profound reordering of the trial. It was the capture of the criminal trial by lawyers for prosecution and defense, together with the important development in the rules of evidence discussed in chapter 6, that made it possible for the criminal defendant to decline to be a witness against himself.

As a convenient shorthand, and with apology for the inelegance of the terms, I shall contrast these two conceptions of the criminal trial as the older "accused speaks" theory and the newer "testing the prosecution" theory. So long as the older view of the purpose of the trial held sway, the defendant's refusal to respond to the incriminating evidence against him would have been suicidal. Without counsel, the testimonial and defensive functions were inextricably merged, and refusing to speak would have amounted to a forfeiture of all defense. The sources show that criminal defendants did not in fact claim any such self-destructive right. Until the later eighteenth century, for almost all criminal defendants, defending meant responding in person to the details of the accusation. Only with the ascendance of defense counsel did the "testing the prosecution" trial develop, and only then did a privilege against self-incrimination become possible in common law criminal procedure.

Section I of this chapter discusses the several attributes of early modern criminal procedure that combined to prevent the development of the common law privilege. Section II explains how prior scholarship went astray in locating the common law privilege against self-incrimination in the wrong events and in the wrong century.

I. THE "ACCUSED SPEAKS" TRIAL

In order for a privilege against self-incrimination to function, the criminal defendant must be in a position to defend by proxy. If the defendant is to have a right to remain silent that is of any value, he must be able to leave

the conduct of his defense to others. By restricting the use of defense witnesses and defense counsel, common law criminal procedure in the early
modern period effectively closed off most avenues of defense by proxy.
Undergirding the criminal procedure of the early modern trial at common
law was a set of rules and practices whose purpose and effect were to oblige
the accused to respond to the charges against him.

The "accused speaks" trial was already thoroughly entrenched in the
1550s and 1560s, when the historical sources first allow us to see how English criminal trials were conducted. In the treason trial of Sir Nicholas
Throckmorton (1554), the plucky defendant complains about many aspects
of the procedure to which he is subjected, but not about the incessant
questioning from the bench and from prosecuting counsel.[3] Sir Thomas
Smith, in the notable Elizabethan tract De Republica Anglorum,[4] describes
a hypothetical criminal trial held at provincial assizes about the year 1565.
Smith depicts a defendant engaged in a confrontational dialogue with the
victim and the accusing witnesses, responding immediately to each new
item of prosecution evidence. Functioning without the aid of counsel and
speaking unsworn, Smith's criminal defendant replies insistently to the
questioning and to the testimony of his accusers. After the victim of a robbery testifies to his version of the events, then "the thief will say no, and
so they stand a while in altercation. . . ."[5] This famous image of accused
and accuser "in altercation" exemplifies the "accused speaks" trial, the trial
whose purpose was to provide the accused an opportunity to explain away
the prosecution's case.

A. Denial of Defense Counsel

The bedrock principle of criminal procedure that underlay the "accused
speaks" trial was the rule that a person accused of serious crime was forbidden to have defense counsel.[6] Various justifications were put forth for the
rule.[7]

1. Court as Counsel

Dogma had it that the trial court was meant to serve as counsel for the
prisoner.[8] Alas, in many of the great political cases of the sixteenth and
seventeenth centuries, the behavior of the bench scarcely bespoke fidelity
to the interests of the defendant. For example, Bromley, the presiding judge
in Throckmorton's trial, joined the prosecuting counsel, Stanford, in urging
Throckmorton to confess to the charges, assuring Throckmorton that "it

will be best for you."[9] In John Lilburne's 1649 trial, the presiding judge, Keble, having heard the prosecution case mounted by the attorney general but not yet having heard Lilburne's defense, announced to the jury: "I hope the Jury hath seen the Evidence so plain and so fully, that it doth confirm them to do their duty, and to find the Prisoner guilty of what is charged on him."[10] Most of us hope that our defense counsel could do somewhat better by us.

The Tudor-Stuart bench had its problems in this turbulent era. Until 1701, judges held office at the pleasure of the Crown;[11] the tradition of secure judicial independence lay in the future. Thus, remarked John Hawles in a famous tract published in 1689, just after the overthrow of James II, the Stuart political trials had revealed that the judges "generally have betrayed their poor Client, to please, as they apprehended, their better Client, the King . . . ."[12]

The judges safeguarded the interests of the accused more responsibly in cases of nonpolitical crime. Because such trials go largely unnoticed in the State Trials[13] and other law reports of the period, what we know of these cases of routine crime comes mostly from the problematic pamphlet accounts of Old Bailey trials and Surrey assize proceedings.[14] The ordinary criminal case lacked prosecution counsel as well as defense counsel. Accordingly, it was the task of the trial judge to help the accuser establish the prosecution case as well as to be "counsel for the defendant" in the peculiar and restricted sense being described.[15]

The defendant's supposed entitlement to have the trial judge serve as his defense counsel was limited to matters of law, not fact. "[T]he court . . . are to see that you suffer nothing for your want of knowledge in matter of law," Chief Justice Hyde told a treason defendant in 1663, explaining the limits of the court's duty "to be of counsel with you."[16] John Beattie captures the matter with great insight, observing that the idea that the court would be counsel for the defendant meant "that the judges would protect defendants against illegal procedure, faulty indictments, and the like. It did not mean that judges would help the accused to formulate a defense or act as their advocates."[17] Indeed, the idea of the court as counsel "perfectly expresses the view that the defendant *should not have counsel* in the sense that we would mean."[18] Consequently, "accused felons had to speak in their own defense and to respond to prosecution evidence as it was given, and as they heard it for the first time. If they did not or could not defend themselves, no one would do it for them."[19]

The judges did intervene on occasion to help the defendant in the realm of fact, mainly by cross-examining a suspicious prosecution witness when the defendant appeared ineffectual. But these initiatives were episodic and unpredictable. "Judges were only occasionally moved to engage in vigorous cross-examinations. . . . For the most part they took the evidence as they found it. . . . They certainly did not prepare in detail for examination and cross-examination; they were not briefed."[20] Thus, although the judges had no reason to persecute wrongfully accused persons, neither had the judges any particular incentive to be vigilant on behalf of defendants. In fact, the judges had a considerable incentive to conduct trials in a fashion that would not interfere with the orderly processing of their large criminal caseloads.[21]

2. The Accused as a Testimonial Resource

The classic justification[22] for deliberately denying the defendant any assistance of counsel in matters of fact appears in the second volume of Serjeant William Hawkins's hugely influential treatise, Pleas of the Crown,[23] first published in 1721. The defendant needs no counsel, wrote Hawkins, because, if the defendant is innocent, he will be as effective as any lawyer. "[E]very one of Common Understanding may as properly speak to a Matter of Fact, as if he were the best Lawyer . . . ."[24] If the defendant is guilty, however, "the very Speech, Gesture and Countenance, and Manner of Defense of those who are Guilty, when they speak for themselves, may often help to disclose the Truth, which probably would not so well be discovered from the artificial Defense of others speaking for them."[25] The words *speak, speech,* and *speaking* appear a total of four times in this short passage, epitomizing in contemporary narrative the image of the "accused speaks" trial.

Hawkins's insistence that the innocent criminal defendant enjoyed a comparative advantage in defending himself at trial is preposterous. Beattie describes the ineptitude of pathetic prisoners attempting to conduct their own trials:

> [M]en not used to speaking in public who suddenly found themselves thrust into the limelight before an audience in an unfamiliar setting—and who were for the most part dirty, underfed, and surely often ill—did not usually cross-examine vigorously or challenge the evidence presented against them. Not all prisoners were unprepared or tongue-tied in court. But the evidence of the printed reports of assize trials in Surrey suggests that it was the exceptional prisoner who asked probing questions or who spoke effectively to the jury on his own behalf.[26]

As I have written elsewhere, "Hawkins's message is that it is desirable for the accused to speak, either to clear himself or to hang himself."[27] Allowing counsel to meddle with the fact-adducing process would impair the basic purpose of the trial: to hear the defendant speak, not to listen to "the artificial Defense of others."[28] Hawkins was warning that the intermediation of counsel would threaten a fundamental premise of the criminal trial of his day—that the defendant should be routinely available as a testimonial resource.[29]

The purpose of the rule denying defense counsel was, therefore, diametrically opposed to the purpose of the privilege against self-incrimination. I touch here on a deeper truth: The privilege against self-incrimination is the creature of defense counsel. The privilege could not emerge so long as the court required the defendant to conduct his own defense. In the "accused speaks" trial of the early modern period, the testimonial function was merged with the defensive function. The right to remain silent when no one else can speak for you is simply the right to slit your throat, and it is hardly a mystery that defendants did not hasten to avail themselves of such a privilege.

3. Restricting the Role of Counsel

Even after the judges relaxed the prohibition on defense counsel in the middle of the eighteenth century,[30] they limited counsel's role in order to continue to pressure the defendant to speak at his trial. The judges permitted defense counsel to examine and cross-examine witnesses, but they did not allow counsel to address the jury until legislation authorized that step in 1836.[31]

In 1777 a trial judge explained the practice of the day to a defendant at the Old Bailey: "Your counsel are not at liberty to state any matter of fact; they are permitted to examine your witnesses; and they are here to speak to any matters of law that may arise; but if your defense arises out of a matter of fact, you must yourself state it to me and the jury."[32] In an Old Bailey case two decades earlier, when the trial judge called on the defendant to make his case at the conclusion of the prosecution evidence, the defendant is recorded as saying, "My counsel will speak for me." Counsel at once corrected him: "I can't speak that for you, you must speak for yourself."[33] In 1789, sitting in a murder trial in the Old Bailey, Chief Baron Eyre of the Exchequer told the defendant that because the prosecution's case had been "proved by a chain of Evidence that is very pressing against you," he hoped that the defendant "may be able to give an answer to it. This is the time for you to make your defense; you will be heard with all manner of indulgence and say what you can for yourself." Defense counsel joined this request, observing, "I am not permitted to do it for you."[34]

Thus, even with defense counsel on the scene, the English legal system was telling the criminal defendant, "You must speak for yourself." This aspiration to capture the defendant as a testimonial resource is perfectly understandable. He is, after all, the most efficient possible witness. Guilty or innocent, he has been close enough to the events to be prosecuted for the offense. Modern Continental systems continue to emphasize the advantages of treating the accused as the central testimonial resource.[35] But this is not the conception of criminal procedure that we associate with the Anglo-American privilege against self-incrimination. It seems plainly contradictory to assert that there was a right to remain silent in the eighteenth century when eighteenth-century courts were routinely explaining, even to defendants who were represented by counsel, "You must speak for yourself."

B. Restrictions on Defense Witnesses

The goal of pressuring the accused to speak in his own defense was achieved not only by denying or restricting counsel but also by impeding defense witnesses. As with the limitations on counsel, these obstacles to the use of witnesses obliged the defendant to do his defending by himself—that is, by speaking at his trial.

Throughout the seventeenth century criminal defendants had no right to subpoena unwilling witnesses. Indeed, in the sixteenth century there were prominent occasions on which trial courts refused to hear defense witnesses who were present in court and willing to testify.[36] When defense witnesses were received, they were forbidden to testify on oath, even though accusing witnesses were routinely sworn. The defendant always spoke unsworn—he was forbidden the right to testify on oath until 1898.[37]

I suspect that the authorities came to view these limitations on the use of defense witnesses as counterproductive, in the sense that the manifest asymmetry of facilitating prosecution witnesses while denying or hampering defense witnesses offended trial jurors.[38] Perhaps that is why John Lilburne, who was straining to provoke the sympathy of the trial jurors in his 1649 trial, insisted on a right to compulsory process that he knew was not allowed him. According to the State Trials report, Lilburne asked for "subpoenas" for witnesses because some "are parliament men, and some of them officers of the army, and they will not come in without compulsion."[39]

The Treason Act of 1696 granted compulsory process and allowed defense witnesses to be sworn, but only for treason cases.[40] Legislation of 1702 allowed defense witnesses to be sworn in routine felony trials.[41] The courts construed that legislation as implicitly authorizing compulsory process as well.[42] Thus, throughout the seventeenth century, the period during which the standard historical account supposes the development of the privilege against self-incrimination at common law, the rules of trial hampered the use of the alternative means of proof—those defense witnesses who would have been needed if the accused were to have an effective right to remain silent.

C. The Standard of Proof Inchoate

Charles McCormick pointed out decades ago that the beyond-reasonable-doubt standard of proof was not precisely articulated in English law until the last decade of the eighteenth century.[43] Barbara Shapiro has collected a good deal of authority showing that there were strong intimations throughout the eighteenth century and earlier that the trier should resolve doubts in favor of the criminal defendant.[44] Still, for so long as the beyond-reasonable-doubt standard lacked crisp formulation, the imprecision pressured the defendant to speak. As Beattie observes:

> [I]f any assumption was made in court about the prisoner himself, it was not that he was innocent until the case against him was proved beyond a reasonable doubt, but that if he were innocent he ought to be able to demonstrate it for the jury by the quality and character of his reply to the prosecutor's evidence. That put emphasis on the prisoner's active role. He was very much in the position of having to prove that the prosecutor was mistaken . . . .
>
> When the evidence had been given for the prosecution, the judge turned to the prisoner and said in effect: "You have heard the evidence; what do you have to say for yourself?" The implications of the judge's question were perfectly clear. When one [defendant on trial for larceny in Surrey in 1739] responded simply "I am no thief" and the judge told him "You must prove that," he was stating plainly the situation that every prisoner found himself in.[45]

Thus, the defendant, who already lacked counsel to probe the prosecution case, also lacked the protection of the modern judicial instruction on the standard of proof that encourages jurors to probe the prosecution case. The defendant had only one practical means of defense—responding in his own words to the evidence and the charges against him.

D. Hindering Defensive Preparation

Most defendants accused of serious crime were jailed pending trial, and the conditions in the jails were appalling.[46] Pretrial confinement interacted with the rest of the procedure to disadvantage the defendant, effectively preventing the defendant from locating witnesses and developing his defense.[47]

The common law also forbade the defendant to have a copy of the indictment specifying the charges against him, not only in advance of trial but even at trial. Instead, the court clerk summarized the indictment to the defendant at his arraignment. The Treason Act of 1696 abrogated the rule against allowing the accused access to the text of the indictment, but only for cases of treason.[48] For ordinary felony cases, the rule endured throughout the eighteenth century,[49] and it impaired the defendant's ability to prepare a defense with precision.[50]

Thus, the defendant was not only locked up, denied the assistance of counsel in preparing and presenting his defense, and restricted in obtaining defense witnesses, he was also given no precise statement of the charges against him until he stood before the court at the moment of his trial. The total drift of these measures was greatly to restrict defensive opportunity of any sort other than responding personally at trial to the incriminating evidence. This aspect of the procedure did not disturb contemporaries. Responding in person is just what Serjeant Hawkins's treatise insists that the defendant ought to do and just what the trial sources depict the defendant doing. The logic of the early modern criminal trial was to pressure the accused into serving as a testimonial resource. It is difficult to imagine that a system so preoccupied with obliging the accused to reply at trial could have been simultaneously intent on constructing the counterprinciple that is embodied in the modern privilege against self-incrimination.

E. The "Accused Speaks" Theory in Pretrial Procedure

A criminal trial is an occasion for the consideration of evidence that has been previously collected. A truism of the study of criminal procedure is that the connection between pretrial and trial is intimate. We cannot understand the trial procedure of a legal system without knowing something about how the pretrial process collects evidence for trial. Likewise, to understand the pretrial we need to know how the agencies of trial will subsequently employ the materials that are gathered in the pretrial.

The Anglo-American criminal procedural tradition tends to be trial-centered, perhaps because of the drama of the criminal trial and surely because of the importance that trial has had in landmark political cases. Yet, even in the Anglo-American system, the everyday reality is that pretrial is vastly more important than trial. The evidence gathered determines many more outcomes than how the evidence is subsequently presented. The trial is mostly a pageant that confirms the results of the pretrial investigation, which is among the reasons why, when our criminal procedural system crumbled in the later twentieth century under caseload pressures, our response was to dispense with trial altogether, transforming the pretrial process into our nontrial plea bargaining system.[51]

The pretrial system that reigned in the second half of the seventeenth century—when, according to Leonard Levy, the privilege against self-incrimination "prevailed supreme"[52] in the common law criminal trial—was antithetical to any such privilege. By the mid-seventeenth century there had been in place for at least a century a system of pretrial inquiry that was devoted to pressuring the accused to incriminate himself. The Marian Committal Statute of 1555,[53] whose origins and operation I have discussed extensively elsewhere,[54] required that a magistrate, the justice of the peace (JP), should conduct a pretrial examination promptly after the defendant had been apprehended. The JP was customarily a local gentleman active in civic affairs, not a career officer of the state.[55] The Marian statute required the JP to transcribe anything that the defendant said that was "material to prove the felony."[56] The statute directed the JP to transmit this document to the trial court, where it could be used in evidence against the accused.[57] The Marian statute also required the examining JP to bind over the victim and other accusing witnesses to attend the trial and testify against the accused.[58] The emphasis on testimony against the accused was deliberate. The Marian JP was not the Continental *juge d'instruction,* not, that is, a professional judicial officer meant to gather evidence impartially. The Marian system was designed to collect only prosecution evidence.[59] In crimes of state, the Privy Council and the law officers of the Crown conducted comparably prosecutorial pretrial investigations.[60]

In a prominent article published in 1949, the evidence scholar Edmund Morgan remarked on the tension between the Marian pretrial procedure and the supposed privilege against self-incrimination in the early modern period: "There was no thought of advising the accused that he need not answer or warning him that what he said might be used against him. The justice [who had examined the defendant in the pretrial] was often the chief witness at the trial of the accused and either used his record of the examination as the basis for his answers or read the record in evidence for the prosecution."[61] Not until Sir John Jervis's Act of 1848[62]—that is, well into the age of modern lawyer-dominated criminal procedure—was provision made to advise the accused that he might decline to answer questions put to him in the pretrial inquiry and to caution him that his answers to pretrial interrogation might be used as evidence against him at trial.[63] Until then, the accused was "expected to answer" the inquiries of the examining magistrate, "and, indeed, any refusal to answer, whether of his own initiative or on advice of another, was reported and stated by the magistrate in his testimony at the trial."[64]

Thus the pretrial procedure of the sixteenth, seventeenth, and eighteenth centuries was designed to induce the accused to bear witness against himself promptly. Having impaled himself in the pretrial, the criminal defendant would find that any supposed privilege against self-incrimination available at trial was worth little. If he declined to testify at trial, or attempted to recant on his pretrial statement, the statement would be invoked against him at trial. Then as now, pretrial dominated trial.

This systematic extraction of self-incriminatory pretrial statements bears on the question of whether early modern English criminal procedure meant to recognize a privilege against self-incrimination. It seems odd to assert, as Levy does, that the privilege "prevailed supreme" at trial when the pretrial procedure was so resolutely organized to render any such trial privilege ineffectual. Remarkably, Levy was quite aware of the character of the Marian pretrial process. Levy's passage reads in full text: "By the early eighteenth century, the [privilege against self-incrimination] prevailed supreme in all proceedings with one vital exception, the preliminary examination of the suspect. In the initial pre-trial stages of a case, inquisitorial tactics were routine."[65] "For all practical purposes," Levy concludes, "the right against self-incrimination scarcely existed in the pre-trial stages of a criminal proceeding."[66] This is an important admission. Levy's account requires us to believe that the seventeenth-century common law courts and their supporting political authorities created a self-evidently schizophrenic criminal procedure—that they enshrined a privilege against self-incrimination at trial while busily gutting it in the pretrial.

F. Trial as a Sentencing Proceeding

The sentencing practices of the later seventeenth and eighteenth centuries were a powerful source of pressure on the defendant to speak at his trial. Our modern expectation is that sentencing occurs in the postverdict phase, after a separate trial has determined guilt. Further, even in jury-tried cases, we expect the judge alone to pass sentence. In former centuries, this division between trial and post-trial, between jury and judge, was less distinct. The early modern trial jury exercised an important role in what is functionally the choice of sanction, by manipulating the verdict to select a charge that imported a greater or a lesser penalty. A vestige of this power to mitigate the sentence survives in modern practice, when the jury convicts of a lesser-included offense or when it convicts on fewer than all the counts that are charged and proved.

The practice of selecting among convicted persons for the application of diminished sanctions became characteristic of the eighteenth century as alternatives to the death penalty emerged.[67] If the jury convicted a defendant of burglary, the punishment was death; but if, on the same facts, the jury convicted him of mere grand larceny, the sanction of transportation obtained.[68] Another example: the offense of picking pockets was capital if the jury valued the stolen goods at a shilling or more. If, however, the jury wished to rescue the convict from capital punishment and consign him to transportation, it could value the goods below the one-shilling threshold, for example, by finding the culprit guilty of picking the victim's pocket "to the value of ten pence."[69]

The practice of allowing juries to "downcharge" or "downvalue" in order to mitigate the death penalty, immortalized in Blackstone's phrase as "pious perjury,"[70] has been much studied in recent years. It is a main theme of John Beattie's great book, in which he uses the term *partial verdict* to describe verdicts that convict the defendant in a fashion that begets a reduced criminal sanction.[71] In a sample of London cases from the Old Bailey in the 1750s, I found that the juries returned partial verdicts in nearly a quarter of the cases.[72] For a few offenses, like picking pockets, the juries all but invariably downvalued, expressing a social consensus that the capital sanction was virtually never appropriate. At the opposite end of the spectrum were a few property crimes, highway robbery being the prototype, that were regarded as so menacing that juries virtually never mitigated the capital sanction.[73] Across the broad range of property crimes, however, jury discretion held sway. In deciding whether to return verdicts of mitigation, "juries distinguished, first, according to the seriousness of the offense, and second, according to the conduct and character of the accused."[74]

1. Informing the Jury's Discretion

The jury's power to mitigate sanctions profoundly affected the purpose of the criminal trial for the many offenses for which the jury might return a partial verdict. Speaking of the London practice in the 1750s, I have elsewhere written: "Only a small fraction of eighteenth-century criminal trials were genuinely contested inquiries into guilt or innocence. In most cases the accused had been caught in the act or otherwise possessed no credible defense. To the extent that trial had a function in such cases beyond formalizing the inevitable conclusion of guilt, it was to decide the sanction."[75] Because the main purpose of defending in such a case was to present the jury with a sympathetic view of the crime and the offender that would encourage a verdict of mitigation, the criminal defendant labored under an enormous practical compulsion to speak in his own defense. Criminal procedure of this period effectively merged the guilt-determining function and the sentencing function into a single proceeding, the trial. The procedure foreclosed the defendant from participating in what was functionally his sentencing hearing unless he spoke at trial about the circumstances of the offense and of his life and character. To be sure, character witnesses could and did carry some of this burden for the defendant in some cases; it was not impossible to remain silent and still obtain jury leniency. But it was a grave risk that few defendants had the stomach to undertake.

The partial verdict system abated slowly toward the end of the eighteenth century and during the early decades of the nineteenth century. Our modern system of postverdict judicial sentencing arose in response to many factors. The movement to revise the substantive criminal law by consolidating and rationalizing the categories of offenses invited the grading of sentences according to severity. This movement was closely connected to the transformation of criminal sanctions as imprisonment became the routine punishment for serious crime. The older sanctions, death and transportation, had lent themselves to jury manipulation because they came as either/ or choices. The new sanction of imprisonment for a term of years was all but infinitely divisible. It invited the concept of the sentencing range, which effectively transferred from the jury to the judge the power to tailor the sentence to the offender. Until the end of the eighteenth century, however, the jury-driven system of mitigation by means of the partial verdict placed an enormous premium on the defendant's willingness to talk to the jurors at trial.

2. Informing the Judge's Postverdict Review

The trial judges exercised a postverdict discretion to recommend clemency to the Crown.[76] In administering the pardon process, the judges depended on information gleaned at trial for their view of the offender. A main reason that the judges discouraged guilty pleas in seventeenth- and eighteenth-century criminal trials was the wish to learn about the offender at trial in the event that a convict sought clemency.[77] A Surrey assize judge sitting in a case in 1751 explained that he hanged a man who had pleaded guilty because the guilty plea had shut the judge "out from all evidence and circumstances favorable and disfavorable which might have appeared."[78] Thus, the clemency phase of the sentencing process reinforced the tendency of the jury mitigation system, placing the criminal defendant under further pressure to speak at his trial.

G. No Privilege Claimed in the "Accused Speaks" Trial

To summarize: A host of reasons give cause for doubting that an effective privilege against self-incrimination was in place in the later seventeenth and eighteenth centuries, the period in which it has been supposed that the privilege "prevailed supreme" at common law. Denial of counsel and restrictions on defense witnesses and on defensive preparation left the typical defendant with little alternative but to conduct his own defense. The invasive Marian pretrial process, untouched by any supposed privilege against self-incrimination, stacked the deck with self-incriminating evidence for the trial. And a system of draconian criminal sanctions frequently operated to condition escape from the death penalty on the defendant's contrite participation at trial.

When, therefore, we examine the surviving evidence of how trials actually transpired in this legal system, we cannot be surprised to find that criminal defendants actually claimed no privilege against self-incrimination. In a word, they sang. Two decades ago I pointed out that in the pamphlet reports of London trials "from the 1670s through the mid-1730s [where my study lapsed] I have not noticed a single case in which an accused refused to speak on asserted grounds of privilege, or in which he makes the least allusion to a privilege against self-incrimination."[79] I have subsequently followed this set of pamphlet reports into the 1780s without finding an accused who raised any claim to the privilege.

Beattie, concentrating on Surrey sources for the years between 1660 and 1800, makes a similar observation: "There was no thought that the prisoner had a right to remain silent on the grounds that he would otherwise be liable to incriminate himself." Indeed, "the assumption was clear that if the case against him was false the prisoner ought to say so and suggest why, and that if he did not speak that could only be because he was unable to deny the truth of the evidence."[80]

H. Defense Counsel, Adversary Procedure, and the Privilege

My theme in this chapter is that the privilege against self-incrimination is an artifact of the adversary system of criminal procedure. Only when the modern "testing the prosecution" theory of the criminal trial displaced the older "accused speaks" theory did the criminal defendant acquire an effective right to decline to speak to the charges against him. The historical bearer of the new criminal procedure was defense counsel, who crept into the ordinary criminal trial almost unnoticed and who then worked a procedural revolution with consequences that still reverberate through Anglo-American criminal justice.

1. Allowing Defense Counsel

The prohibition on defense counsel was first relaxed in the landmark Treason Act of 1696,[81] the first comprehensive charter of defensive safeguard in the history of our criminal procedure.[82] During the 1690s, contemporaries came to understand that the treason trials conducted under the regime of the later Stuarts had been grievously unfair. Especially during the dozen years from the Popish Plot trials of the later 1670s until the revolution of 1689, innocent persons of the politically significant classes had been convicted and had suffered traitors' deaths for want of the ability to defend themselves effectively against baseless prosecutions.

Defensive safeguard was a novel topic for English criminal legislation. The preamble to the Treason Act of 1696 announced the proposition that persons accused of treason should be allowed "just and equal means for defense of their innocencies in such cases."[83] The act provided a package of reforms directed at eliminating many of the procedural disadvantages that undergirded the "accused speaks" trial. The act allowed the accused a copy of the indictment five days in advance of trial; it granted the right "to advise with counsel" on the indictment; and it spelled out the right at trial to make "full defense, by counsel"[84]—meaning that defense counsel would be permitted not only to examine and to cross-examine but also to sum up and to address the jury about the merits of the defendant's case.[85] The act granted the accused the right to have defense witnesses heard, the right to have them sworn,[86] and the right to have them subpoenaed.[87]

The safeguards of the Treason Act of 1696, including the grant of defense counsel, were carefully limited to treason trials, which occurred extremely rarely.[88] There was a sense that treason defendants were especially disadvantaged on account of the hostility of the bench. Because judges were subservient to the Crown in prosecutions touching high politics, it was unrealistic to expect them to serve in the supposed judicial role of counsel for the defendant. Further, the denial of defense counsel had a special one-sidedness in treason cases, for the Crown was invariably represented by counsel. By contrast, in cases of ordinary felony, prosecution counsel rarely appeared. The rationale for allowing defense counsel in the Treason Act of 1696 was, therefore, to even the scales.[89]

Defense counsel entered the ordinary criminal trial in the 1730s, not as a result of legislative change but through the exercise of judicial discretion.[90] Something of the same "evening-up" rationale that lay behind the allowance of defense counsel in the Treason Act of 1696 seems to have led the courts to admit defense counsel in cases of ordinary felony. There appears to have been a considerable increase in the use of prosecution counsel in the 1710s and 1720s,[91] and "the resulting disparity may have influenced the judges to relax the [prohibition on defense counsel]."[92] The use of defense counsel remained a relative trickle for another half century, until the 1780s.[93]

2. The Adversary Dynamic and the Reconstruction of the Criminal Trial

During the second half of the eighteenth century and continuing into the nineteenth century, our Anglo-American criminal procedure underwent the epochal change from the "accused speaks" trial to the modern "testing the prosecution" trial. We have seen how relentlessly the earlier system of trial pressured the criminal defendant to speak. Within the space of a few decades, the expectation that the accused would defend himself disappeared. Defense counsel made possible that remarkable silencing of the accused that has ever since astonished European commentators. As early as 1820 an official French observer, Cottu, reported back to his government that in English criminal procedure prosecuting counsel was "forbidden to question the prisoner . . . . In England, the defendant acts no kind of part: his hat stuck on a pole might without inconvenience be his substitute at the trial."[94]

We do not yet have an adequate historical account of the stages by which this transformation occurred, and the historical sources are sufficiently impoverished that we may never recover the events in detail. Nevertheless, the outline seems tolerably clear. Across these decades, defense counsel broke up the "accused speaks" trial. In these developments we find not only the beginnings of a new theory of the trial but also the real origins of the privilege against self-incrimination.

The initial restrictions on the role of defense counsel at trial suggest that his primary responsibility in the eighteenth century was cross-examining prosecution witnesses. Especially in cases involving reward seekers and Crown witnesses, those shady figures whom the embattled London authorities sometimes employed to compensate for the English reluctance to institute professional policing,[95] vigorous cross-examination often proved decisive.[96] Thus, as Beattie remarks, defense counsel "began to shift the focus of the defense in a fundamental way by casting doubt on the validity of the factual case being presented against the defendant, so that the prosecution came increasingly under the necessity of proving its assertions."[97] There were several strands to this development of the trial as the occasion for defense counsel to test the prosecution case:

(1) *Production burdens.* The concept we now identify as party production burdens came to be articulated. Prosecution and defense "cases" replaced the spontaneous "altercation" described by Sir Thomas Smith. Smith's defendant replied to each piece of prosecution evidence as it was presented. When defense counsel came to prominence, the concept of prosecution and defense cases developed—that is, the idea that the prosecution had to present all its evidence, and be subject to the defense counsel's motion for directed verdict at the end of the prosecution case, before the defendant would present rebuttal evidence.[98]

(2) *Burden of proof.* Toward the end of the eighteenth century, the presumption of innocence—the beyond-reasonable-doubt standard of proof—was formulated.[99] Coupled with the prosecutor's production burden, the beyond-reasonable-doubt standard encouraged defense counsel to silence the defendant and hence to insist that the prosecution case be built from other proofs.

(3) *Evidence law.* The law of criminal evidence was formed in the later eighteenth and early nineteenth centuries. "In their objections against the admission of certain kinds of evidence, and most especially by [their conduct of] cross-examination, defense counsel sought to limit the case their clients would have to answer."[100] With the increasing use of lawyers from the 1780s onward came lawyer's literature, especially the *nisi prius* reports, on which the evidence treatises of the early nineteenth century would draw for sources.[101]

(4) *Lawyerization.* The growing use and effectiveness of defense counsel begot ever greater use of prosecuting counsel. The private associations for the prosecution of felons formed in great numbers from the 1770s and 1780s.[102] These complex organizations served a number of functions, but their central purpose was to defray the victim's costs of investigation and prosecution in certain classes of property offenses.[103] There is evidence for thinking that the surge in the formation of these groups reflected in part the need to prepare prosecution cases better, in order to deal with the new hazards of aggressive defense counsel as the "testing the prosecution" trial came to prevail.[104]

(5) *Displacing the judge.* The judge declined in importance as counsel for prosecution and defense took over the job of examining and cross-examining witnesses. The French observer Cottu, writing in 1820, thought that the use of prosecution and defense counsel was typical in the practice of provincial assize courts, although not yet in London.[105] He found that "the judge . . . remains almost a stranger to what is going on,"[106] contenting himself with taking notes and summarizing them for the jury at the end of the trial.[107]

(6) *Instructing the jury.* Changes in the practice of jury control in this period, highlighted by Fox's Libel Act of 1792,[108] reflect the decline of judicial influence over the trial jury. Counsel's increasing dominance of the conduct of the trial was inconsistent with the older informal system of jury control that presupposed the casual intimacy of judge and jury.[109]

Defense counsel silenced the criminal defendant in the second half of the eighteenth century for reasons of strategic advantage, as the logic of adversary procedure unfolded. Counsel welcomed the opportunity to pour this new wine into an old vessel, the maxim *Nemo tenetur prodere seipsum,* the centerpiece of the traditional account of the history of the privilege against self-incrimination that is the subject of section II of this chapter. By the time Bentham began complaining about the privilege against self-incrimination in the first decades of the nineteenth century,[110] adversary procedure was becoming the norm.[111] Defense counsel made the privilege against self-incrimination possible in ways that chapter 6 details. Defense counsel disentangled the defensive and the testimonial functions that previously had been merged in the hands of the defendant. By assuming the defensive function, and doing it within the structure of the adversary criminal trial, counsel largely suppressed the defendant's testimonial role. Defense counsel must have been delighted to ascribe this radical reconstruction of the criminal trial to a centuries-old maxim of soothing constitutional dignity.

II. REVISITING A TROUBLED HISTORICAL SCHOLARSHIP

The history of the privilege against self-incrimination at common law has long been a murky topic. A main source of confusion is that the modern common law privilege came to be associated with a doctrinal tag, the maxim *Nemo tenetur prodere seipsum,* that developed in earlier centuries for quite different purposes.

A. Antecedents to the Common Law Privilege

1. Medieval Roots in European Law

The Anglo-American adversary system repackaged doctrinal baggage that started its journey in the *ius commune* of the medieval church. The maxim *Nemo tenetur prodere seipsum,* liberally translated as "no one is obliged to accuse himself," helped clarify the line between two spheres of Christian obligation. The believer's duty of penitential confession did not entail instituting criminal proceedings against himself. As demonstrated at length in chapter 2, he could confess sin to a priest without being obliged to confess punishable offenses to judges and prosecutors.

The same chapter shows how prominently this maxim appeared in the sources of the *ius commune* from the later Middle Ages and the Renaissance. It demonstrates that the maxim influenced practice in the English ecclesiastical courts long before anybody in England started complaining about Star Chamber or the Court of High Commission.[112] This finding undermines Leonard Levy's effort to portray the privilege against self-incrimination as an English invention intended to protect the indigenous adversarial criminal procedure against incursions of European inquisitorial procedure. The concept that underlies the English privilege against self-incrimination origi-

nated within the European tradition as a subprinciple of inquisitorial procedure centuries before the integration of lawyers into the criminal trial made
possible the development of the distinctive Anglo-American adversary system of criminal procedure in the later eighteenth century.

2. The Ex Officio Oath

Chapter 3 describes the second phase of the history of the privilege against
self-incrimination, the saga of the Puritans' seizure of this concept of immunity from self-accusation as part of their struggle against efforts to impose
religious conformity. The Puritans were resisting the efforts of Elizabethan
and early Stuart authorities to impose established forms of worship on them.
The ecclesiastical courts and the prerogative courts of High Commission
and Star Chamber conducted disciplinary proceedings of various sorts.
These courts conducted investigation by means of the so-called ex officio
oath, the procedure sketched in chapter 2.[113] When employing this procedure, the court required the accused at the outset of the inquiry to swear
an oath to answer any questions that the court might subsequently put to
him. A defendant who refused to take that oath could be imprisoned for
contempt or subjected to other harsh sanctions. Because these defendants
were typically guilty of the nonconformist religious practices for which they
were being investigated, they resisted submitting to the ex officio oath.

Particularly toward the end of their contest with the ecclesiastical and
prerogative courts in the 1630s, the Puritans placed considerable weight
on the *Nemo tenetur* maxim, using it to stand for the claim that they ought
not to be punished for failing to cooperate in these proceedings. The Puritans sometimes succeeded in resisting ex officio oath procedure applied in
the ecclesiastical and prerogative courts by obtaining relief from the common law courts. As a matter of interjurisdictional law, the common law
courts issued writs of prohibition against some of the ecclesiastical proceedings, principally to limit subject matter encroachments on common law
turf.

When political and military reverses forced Charles I to summon Parliament in 1641, Parliament sided with the Puritans, abolished the courts
of Star Chamber and High Commission, and forbade the ecclesiastical
courts to use the ex officio oath.[114] These events, especially the fall of Star
Chamber, remain among the most celebrated landmarks of English political
and legal history. The idea that no one need accuse himself, whatever that
meant, was part of this constitutional triumph. As Henry Friendly observed,
the precocious development of this "procedural" protection against intru-

sive questioning reflected the primitive state of the substantive law concerning religious and political liberties.[115] If the protections for nonconformist
worship and for oppositional political discourse that Americans now associate with the First Amendment had been more developed, Puritans and
political mavericks would not have had to campaign as they did for procedural protections against self-incrimination in Star Chamber and High
Commission.[116]

B. Common Law Criminal Procedure

The great question is how the common law courts came to internalize a
privilege against self-incrimination. Why take a principle that had been
developed to counteract the ex officio procedures of the ecclesiastical and
prerogative courts and apply that principle to the radically different circumstances of common law criminal procedure? The historical literature,
powerfully shaped by our pioneering scholar, Wigmore,[117] affords a long-
familiar account of this development. The common law courts are said to
have recognized the privilege against self-incrimination in England in the
middle of the seventeenth century, under the influence of the fall of the
prerogative courts and the abolition of the ex officio oath in the ecclesiastical courts.

According to Wigmore, John Lilburne's "notorious agitation" against
the Star Chamber in the years between 1637 and 1641 culminated in the
1641 statute abolishing the two most controversial courts, Star Chamber
and High Commission. Then, "with a rush . . . the 'ex officio' oath to
answer criminal charges [was] swept away with them."[118] Next, Wigmore
contends—and this is the giant leap—that the demise of this procedure
and of the prerogative courts that used it affected the criminal procedure
of the common law courts by example. "With all this stir and emotion,"
Wigmore writes, "a decided effect [was] produced, and [was] immediately
communicated, naturally enough, to the common law courts."[119]

I recommend suspending judgment on how "natural" it should have
been to expect the common law courts, which had never employed the
ex officio oath, to recast their criminal procedure for the purpose of implementing a notion that the common law courts had until then asserted only
as a corrective against the quite incompatible ex officio oath procedure of
detested non–common law courts. This development may seem "natural"
in the powerful light of hindsight from the entrenched privilege against
self-incrimination of our modern law, but as emphasized in section I of this

chapter, an array of structural attributes of common law criminal procedure would have made the privilege unnatural and unworkable in the criminal trial of the later seventeenth century.

Wigmore's pithy argument continues: "Up to the last moment [in John Lilburne's 1637–1641 struggle against Star Chamber, Lilburne] had never claimed the right to refuse absolutely to answer an incriminating question; he had merely claimed a proper proceeding of presentment or accusation. But now this once vital distinction [came] to be ignored."[120] Wigmore thus argues that contemporaries confused two notions—on the one hand, the hostility to the practice of the non–common law courts, especially Star Chamber and the High Commission, that had been requiring the suspect to swear in advance to respond truthfully to questions about religious beliefs and political leanings; and, on the other hand, the expectation that someone being tried following indictment for the commission of a particular crime in a common law court would respond personally to the charges and the evidence adduced against him.[121]

Whether, as a practical matter, "this once vital distinction" was or could have been ignored seems highly unlikely. Speaking of the great moment, from 1641 and thereabouts, when the prerogative courts fell and when Parliament proscribed the use of ex officio oath procedure in the ecclesiastical courts, Wigmore writes: "It begins to be claimed, flatly, that no man is bound to incriminate himself on any charge (no matter how properly instituted) or in any court (not merely in the ecclesiastical or Star Chamber tribunals). Then this claim comes to be conceded by the judges . . . even on occasions of great partisan excitement . . . . By the end of Charles II's reign [that is, by 1685], there is no longer any doubt, in any court . . . ."[122] Wigmore's follower, Leonard Levy, echoes this claim. "By the early eighteenth century," says Levy, the privilege against self-incrimination "prevailed supreme" in the common law criminal trial.[123]

Having explained in section I why this familiar account[124] of the appearance of the privilege against self-incrimination at common law is so improbable, I turn now to examine the sources that led Wigmore astray.

C. Wigmore's Sources

What, precisely, is the historical evidence that Wigmore adduces for his proposition that the common law privilege was broadly accepted ("no longer any doubt, in any court")[125] by the 1680s? It consists of a forbiddingly long, double-column footnote in which Wigmore collects citations to seventeen reported cases.[126] These authorities turn out to supply weak support for Wigmore's proposition.

1. Civil Cases

Five of the seventeen cases are civil cases and thus inapposite. Four of these civil cases are from the Court of Chancery. The parties were disputing whether discovery or other relief should be refused on the basis of the familiar maxim of equitable jurisdiction that equity will not enforce a penalty or a forfeiture.[127] The other civil case applies a similar principle to a prohibition action pending in a duchy court.[128]

2. Criminal Cases

The dozen remaining cases come from the State Trials and involve politically significant criminal charges. One is the report of a pretrial investigation that was dropped without trial.[129] The remaining eleven involve criminal trials. In each, the defendant spoke vigorously and persistently to the merits in his own defense. What Wigmore identifies as evidence of the defendant's invoking the privilege against self-incrimination is an isolated remark or exchange that occured in a trial in which the defendant otherwise spoke constantly, utterly disregarding any supposed privilege against self-incrimination. Only the powerful searchlight of hindsight makes these cases relevant to the history of the privilege. I might put this point in a different way by saying that, if the privilege had developed no further beyond the last of the trials that Wigmore cites, which occurred in 1685, no scholar looking over these eleven cases could have concluded from such inconsequential gleanings that a doctrine resembling the privilege against self-incrimination was in force at common law.

In five of Wigmore's eleven criminal trials, what is treated as evidence of the common law court's recognition of the privilege against self-incrimination is actually hostile behavior by the trial judge intended to disadvantage the defendant. In each case, the event that Wigmore cites is the judge's refusal to allow the defendant to cross-examine an accusing witness.[130] For example, in the case of Nathanael Reading,[131] one of the Popish Plot defendants, Reading attempted to ask the sinister prosecution witness Bedloe[132] whether Bedloe was part of the supposed plot to burn Westminster. The presiding judge, Francis North, interfered, saying that "if you offer to ask him any question on his oath, to make him accuse himself, we must oppose it."[133] Thus, North employed the slogan about not requiring a man to accuse himself for the purpose of shielding a prosecution witness against legitimate cross-examination.[134] In the sixth of Wigmore's cases, it was the prosecutor rather than the judge who attempted to hinder the cross-examination of a defense witness.[135]

In four of Wigmore's criminal cases, the defendants were victims of the baseless Popish Plot prosecutions.[136] In five of Wigmore's cases, the judges whom he treats as supposedly vindicating the privilege against self-incrimination were the notorious Stuart bullies, Scroggs and Jeffreys.[137] In another of Wigmore's eleven criminal trial precedents, Jeffreys was serving as prosecuting counsel, pressing on the court the maxim against "ask[ing] him any questions that may tend to accuse himself" for the purpose of interfering with the defendant's effort to conduct a cross-examination.[138] Thus, most of Wigmore's authority for this supposed seventeenth-century breakthrough in defensive safeguard actually instances efforts by the subservient Stuart bench to disadvantage defendants in baseless political and religious persecutions. Apart from the cases previously examined, Wigmore points to three additional cases in which criminal defendants made episodic mention of an entitlement not to accuse oneself.[139] In each of these cases, the incidental invocation of the notion that the accused was not obliged to reply to a particular question was an isolated event during the course of a trial in which the defendant otherwise responded constantly to questioning.

3. Overview of Wigmore's Evidence

The privilege against self-incrimination at common law did not exist during the period in which Wigmore thought he was seeing its origins. The successful campaign to topple the courts of Star Chamber and High Commission and to prevent the ecclesiastical courts from using the ex officio oath made a tremendous impression on contemporaries, just as Wigmore thought. But, although these events did indeed put the *Nemo tenetur* maxim into currency as an abstract principle or maxim worthy of respect, this maxim had no determinate meaning when applied to criminal procedure within the common law courts. That is why the bullying Stuart bench could turn the maxim upside down and use it as a club against the pathetic defendants in the Popish Plot cases, and that is why the defendants in a handful of other cases chanced to mention it in the course of proceedings that otherwise exhibit no fidelity to any privilege against self-incrimination.

D. Wigmore's Reservations

Having located what he thought to be the origins of the common law privilege in the seventeenth-century authorities, Wigmore had the marvelous good sense to record serious doubts about his own conclusion. His follower, Levy, displays no such circumspection. Levy depicts the modern Anglo-American privilege against self-incrimination as such an obvious historical inevitability that the only puzzle is to wonder why it took the dummies so long to see the light.[140]

1. The Stuart Connection

Wigmore was perplexed that "the privilege, thus established, comes into full recognition under the judges of the restored Stuarts, and not under the parliamentary reformers."[141] Wigmore sensed the irony inherent in his view of the development of the privilege against self-incrimination at common law. An event that has come to be understood in historical perspective as among the most distinctive attributes of defensive safeguard in the whole of our criminal procedural tradition was, on Wigmore's view of it, the handiwork of the notoriously craven late-Stuart bench. The judges who supposedly created the privilege at common law were Scroggs, Jeffreys, and their brethren—men whose names are synonymous with subservience to the Crown and murderous unfairness to criminal defendants.[142] I find it difficult to imagine that a group of judges who displayed such hostility toward criminal defendants would simultaneously have been so alert to recognize and enforce a novel and dissonant measure of defensive safeguard.

Levy, unlike Wigmore, was untroubled to find himself celebrating the spectacle of the late-Stuart judiciary supposedly crafting the privilege. Indeed, it is the Popish Plot trials, which were as manifest a persecution of innocent people as ever occurred at common law, that move Levy to exult in "how scrupulously the courts adhered to the right against self-incrimination."[143]

2. Judicial Indifference

Wigmore noticed how tentative the supposed privilege against self-incrimination was in the hands of the very judges who supposedly recognized it. Referring to the behavior of the bench in the seventeenth-century State Trials, his primary resource, Wigmore remarked that the supposed privilege against self-incrimination "remained not much more than a bare rule of law, which the judges would recognize on demand. The spirit of it was wanting in them. The old habit of questioning and urging the accused died hard—did not disappear, indeed, until the 1700s had begun."[144] This is Wigmore's way of noticing that, even in the handful of cases that contain supposed authority for his view that there was a seventeenth-century privilege against self-incrimination, the evidence is at most an isolated reference to the privilege in the course of a trial at which the defendant otherwise replied routinely to the accusations against him.

3. The Failure of Constitutionalization

When the age of safeguard in common law criminal procedure actually dawned, the English displayed a peculiar lack of interest in securing the privilege against self-incrimination among their landmark safeguards. As Wigmore observed, "In all the parliamentary remonstrances and petitions and declarations that preceded the expulsion of the Stuarts, [the privilege against self-incrimination] does not anywhere appear."[145] The privilege "was not worth mentioning to the English constitution-menders of 1689," that is, it was not in the Bill of Rights of 1689.[146] It is even more revealing that the determined Whig reformers of the 1690s, who drafted the great catalog of protections in criminal procedure in the Treason Act of 1696,[147] found no room to include the supposed privilege against self-incrimination among the protections they valued.

E. Overview on a Historical Error

How could a historical writer so sensitive to the sources and to the subject as Wigmore have erred by a century in identifying the origins of the privilege against self-incrimination? He did not fabricate. The *Nemo tenetur* maxim did indeed gain currency during the Tudor-Stuart constitutional struggles. Wigmore in effect traced some of the history of the maxim's use.

The key insight, however, is that the maxim did not make the privilege. It was rather the privilege—which developed much later—that absorbed and perpetuated the maxim. The ancestry of the privilege has been mistakenly projected backwards on the maxim, whereas the privilege against self-incrimination in common law criminal procedure was, in truth, the achievement of defense counsel in the late eighteenth and early nineteenth centuries.

Without defense counsel, a criminal defendant's right to remain silent was the right to forfeit any defense; indeed, in a system that emphasized capital punishment, the right to remain silent was tantamount to the right to commit suicide. Only when defense counsel succeeded in restructuring the criminal trial to make it possible to silence the accused did it finally become possible to fashion an effective privilege against self-incrimination at common law. How this was done is the subject of chapter 6.

III. CONCLUSION

I have been tempted to speak in a shorthand of sorts in order to make the pithy claim that there was no privilege against self-incrimination in common law criminal procedure during the early modern epoch. Formulating the claim in this way almost captures what has been shown, yet it would neglect an important strand. The core value of the privilege against self-incrimination was indeed on the lips of those whose words have found their way into the conventional but misguided historical account of the supposed Tudor-Stuart origins of the privilege.

The better way to encapsulate the theme of this chapter is not to say that there was no privilege but rather to recognize that the structure of criminal procedure in the early modern epoch made it impossible to implement the privilege. The "accused speaks" criminal trial stood in perpetual tension with the notion of a right to remain silent. The privilege against self-incrimination became functional only as a consequence of the revolutionary reconstruction of the criminal trial worked by the advent of defense counsel and adversary criminal procedure. The privilege as we understand it is an artifact of the adversary system of criminal procedure. The error has been to expect to find the privilege in operation before the adversary system was in place.

Across the centuries the privilege against self-incrimination has changed character profoundly, from the original privilege not to accuse oneself to the modern privilege not to respond or to testify. Many policies have come to be associated with the privilege against self-incrimination. Indeed, Wigmore enumerated a full dozen for his treatise.[148] They range from the prohibition on torturing the accused[149] (a reform effected before the first traces of the privilege at common law)[150] to the modern American rule forbidding adverse comment on the accused's silence (a rule so recent, historically speaking, that the ink is still wet).[151] But the core value of the privilege, the accused's right not to speak, presupposes an effective right to have another speak in the accused's stead. In our legal history, the use of defense counsel became common only toward the end of the eighteenth century. The elaboration of a modern privilege during the nineteenth century flowed directly from the establishment of adversary criminal procedure.

FIVE

The Privilege in British North America: The Colonial Period to the Fifth Amendment

Eben Moglen

I. INTRODUCTION

The legal records of early America confirm the crucial importance of defense counsel in shaping the changing nature of the privilege against self-incrimination. Had the right been recognized in the era of John Lilburne, and enshrined in the sequel to the Glorious Revolution, its invocation would be visible in the colonial records of those British North Americans whose descendants, in the 1770s and 1780s, did indeed express the privilege as a right in the new constitutions. If, on the other hand, the English privilege developed in the eighteenth century onward through intervention by defense counsel, replacing a system structurally biased in the opposite direction, we should see little of the "right" in colonial records. Indeed, the more closely conforming to English practice were the colonial legal orders, the less of the defendant's privilege against self-incrimination should we expect to see, and it is this state of affairs that the records reveal. But the conclusion gives rise to another doubt. If the privilege against self-incrimination was born as a consequence of the sweeping changes brought about by the activities of defense counsel over time, how did the Americans—whose legal profession was necessarily less developed than that of the metropolis in the colonial period—come to treat the privilege as a constitutional right as early as the mid-1770s?

Reconsideration of American developments is thus crucial to understanding the history of the privilege. Much essential research has not been done; only for one colony do we possess a detailed qualitative reconstruction of the criminal justice system. In brief, the records of the colonial legal orders in the seventeenth century, like those of England, show the predominance of the "accused speaks" elements of the old criminal procedure, in which no effective defendant's privilege against self-incrimination existed. Pretrial process—which effectively determined the possibility of defendants' silence at trial—followed the English models, inhibiting rather than furthering the privilege. Counsel infrequently appeared in felony cases until the end of the colonial period even in New York, where the profession reached the highest degree of prerevolutionary development and influence. In misdemeanor proceedings, where counsel were theoretically available, administrative and economic considerations precluded defense counsel from having a major effect on investigative and trial procedure.

Yet the Americans did adopt constitutional provisions protecting against coercive self-incrimination, and at a comparatively early date. The paradox is only apparent. The constitutional provisions were meant to be conservative, protecting against practices or institutions that Americans saw as possible innovations by tyrannical government. The ambiguities surrounding the *Nemo tenetur* maxim, the wary attitudes toward oaths among American sectarians, and the "rights antiquarianism" of the American Revolution all contributed to the drafting of such provisions. But the provisions were not treated, at least initially, as requiring variation from existing local practice. In those states that did enact such constitutional provisions, any effect on the existing criminal procedure is difficult to discern. In New York, which did not, no conflict was seen in recommending such a protection in the federal Bill of Rights. In this regard, the legal positions of New Yorkers epitomize the history of the privilege against self-incrimination. Rather than the story of a timeless natural right, growing in recognition as society became more "free," the history of the privilege reveals how procedure made substance and how legal evolution adaptively turned old structures to new functions.

II. EARLY MODERN CRIMINAL PROCEDURE IN AMERICA

The legal systems of British North America came into existence over a period of more than a century, from the foundation of the Jamestown colony in 1607 through the organization of Georgia in the 1730s. The diversity of conditions of settlement—including religious belief, ethnic composition, and socioeconomic structure—makes it impossible to treat "colonial American law" as an entity. The difficulties of comprehensive description are increased by the obscurities of the sources. Records of criminal justice at the lowest levels are scant in almost all jurisdictions, and even the upper reaches of the colonial legal systems are documented in incomplete and substantively frustrating fashion. Although the secondary literature offers many studies, including careful editorial introductions to printed records,[1] which quantitatively assess the performance of the criminal justice system and categorize its effect on different elements of the society,[2] we possess only one study attempting to restate the entirety of one colonial system of criminal procedure doctrine on the basis of a comprehensive survey of surviving records.[3] Outside New York, for which the research begun by Goebel and Naughton is sufficiently advanced to support confident conclusions, reconstructions of the details of criminal procedure are necessarily tentative. Despite the difficulties, however, the evidence so far unearthed shows important regularities in the conduct of criminal justice in colonial America, from which the history of the privilege can be discerned.

A. After English Ways: The Roots of Colonial Criminal Procedure

To begin with, all of the colonial societies in British North America, despite varying degrees of modification to soothe religious, ideological, or ethnic conflicts, proclaimed an intention in principle to provide criminal justice in conformity with the laws of England. We are liable to mislead ourselves if we conceive this in terms of "reception" of English law.[4] Charter provisions limiting legislative authority to acts "not repugnant to the laws of . . . England" had some effect in this regard,[5] as did early experience with attempts to administer colonial societies under qualitatively different rules, such as the martial law regime in Virginia from 1610 to 1618.[6] But the most potent force was probably that which is least simple to specify in technical terms— the desire of settlers in distant, often hostile, territory for the social and institutional structures that helped them see the wilderness as "home."[7] Still, three primary considerations make it impossible to talk about "reception" of the English criminal law in British North America in the first century of settlement. First, some Englishmen in North America wanted a home that varied in significant respects from the society they left behind. Second, not all of the communities whose political assent determined the effectiveness of the justice system were English. Third, the material conditions of life and the available social resources differed profoundly throughout North America and just as profoundly differed from those in the English countryside. These diversities preclude us from basing our interpretation on the reception of English law and make the reconstruction of colonial law a process specific to locality and time. Given the forces militating against uniformity, the basic elements in which the colonial systems agreed may be taken as the least common denominator of common law criminal procedure—the essence of Englishness under colonial circumstances. As we shall see, the "accused speaks" trial and its concomitant practices represented the common core of English criminal procedure in America during the first century of settlement.

Colonial defendants by and large experienced the "accused speaks" trial familiar in early modern English criminal procedure. Throughout the process, the defendant was deprived of the assistance of counsel, limited in his ability to call witnesses of his own, and denied access to adverse evidence before trial, including the charging instrument itself. At pretrial committal he was examined unsworn by a justice of the peace who was required to take down all evidence against the defendant, including if possible his own confession for admission at trial; at trial he confronted a prosecution unhampered by an explicit burden of proof beyond a reasonable doubt. The effect of these practices in combination was to pit the accused at trial against the prosecution's evidence, including his own unsworn confession—to explain it away if he could or to dig himself in more deeply by untutored and self-revelatory behavior before judge and jury.

Deprivation of counsel was the sine qua non of the old criminal procedure in felony cases, as we have seen. It should come as no surprise that American criminal procedure of the seventeenth century by and large conformed to the English pattern, since in addition to the English justifications for deprivation of counsel, the virtual absence of trained professionals from the provincial courts in the first decades of settlement made any other policy impracticable. Indeed, the diversity of American innovation sometimes led away from, rather than toward, availability of counsel in criminal cases. Religious perfectionism—and a distrust of the legal profession (composed half of sad experience with legal persecution and half of a general hostility to lawyers)—led the more sectarian of colonial communities to stringent regulation. Massachusetts Bay banned the activities of counsel in its courts altogether in the initial decades of settlement, thus denying representation to all criminal defendants, not merely those charged with felony.[8] Elsewhere in British North America, the common law principle that felony defendants might have counsel only to argue matters of law to the court seems to have formed the basis of practice. Virginia permitted counsel in felony cases by

statute after 1735, but what little evidence we have shows that their participation was infrequent.[9] New York never provided statutory sanction for
the appearance of counsel in felony, and the expense of employing a lawyer,
whose activities were limited to matters of law, was almost always prohibi-
tive.[10] New York apparently also followed the common law in permitting
counsel in misdemeanor cases as early as 1686,[11] but for administrative and
economic reasons more fully described below, counsel rarely appeared in
misdemeanor cases until late in the eighteenth century. So far as the seventeenth century is concerned, and indeed long after, there seems no reason
to doubt Julius Goebel's conclusion that in New York "[t]he felonies were
still a preserve as restricted to defense counsel as were the hunting grounds
of the Indians to the colonists, and in the misdemeanor field the lawyers'
pickings for a long time were as lean as the quitrents paid to the King."[12]
Even the rather libertarian polity of Rhode Island, when it passed the earliest colonial statute regarding access to counsel after indictment, in 1669,
limited itself to declaring the common law privilege of counsel "to plead
any point of law."[13]

Systematic exclusion of counsel did more to prevent the accused from
testing the prosecution's case or effectively presenting his own than all other
rules combined, but such indications as we have of the details of trial procedure in seventeenth-century America show that in other respects too English restrictions on the presentation of defense witnesses were followed.
Until 1702, English practice required defense witnesses in felony cases to
testify unsworn, assertedly for the repulsively fictional reason that no one
could be admitted to swear against the king.[14] The English rule was changed
by a statute whose benefit was not extended to the colonies,[15] but evidence
from New York suggests both that the common law rule was fully observed
in the seventeenth century[16] and that practice altered in conformity with
English practice after passage of the statute.[17]

Spotty documentation makes it difficult to say at what point courts of
most jurisdictions began issuing subpoenas to compel attendance of defense
witnesses; in New York, however, such orders survive from a few trials
scattered through the eighteenth century.[18] If the justices' manuals and other
normative sources correctly depict Virginia procedure, defendants there had
limited access to subpoena by the second quarter of the century.[19] But sworn
or unsworn, defense witnesses at trial were scarce commodities by and large.
The practice papers of John Tabor Kempe, attorney general of New York
from 1759 through the end of the colonial period, contain several dozen
notes on trials for which Kempe presented the Crown's case. In a few cases

an energetic defense was mounted when the nature of the charge permitted counsel and the defendant could afford representation. When defense witnesses testified, Kempe made note of it.[20] But the great preponderance of his trial notes shows that no defense evidence at all was offered.

B. Pretrial Examination: The "Accused Speaks"

Taken together, these elements of colonial criminal procedure demonstrate that the American legal systems at the turn of the eighteenth century conformed to the model of the "accused speaks" trial, with which the notion of an accused's right to silence in the face of the evidence was simply incompatible. Trial itself was only the latest stage in the process. It was in pretrial proceedings that the full weight of the criminal process was enlisted behind the attempt to induce self-incrimination. In order to understand the nature of that process, it is necessary to begin with a clear grasp of the personnel who administered it and the sources of the law they applied.

1. The Justices of the Peace

Without exception, administrators of criminal justice in British North America made use of the process established by the Marian committal statute.[21] In its essence, the statute required a defendant, once apprehended, to be brought before a justice of the peace, who was to transcribe all available evidence "material to prove the Felony." The JP, in normal English usage, was a lay member of the squirearchy rather than a professional investigator. In matters of felony or other serious crime, his function was to secure the Crown's evidence for transmission to the Quarter Sessions or the Assizes. The nonprofessional character of the JP was assumed in North America, where the pool of legally trained potential magistrates was minuscule. In New York, English practice was followed to the extent of designating some of the JPs as "of the quorum," though conditions throughout the colonial period were such that even justices of the quorum were unlikely to possess legal training.[22] Sitting together in the General Sessions of the Peace, these JPs took cognizance of misdemeanors, criminal trespasses, and felonies up to and including petit larceny.

2. The Justices' Manuals

"One of the fundamental constraints upon a legal system which assigns important roles to laymen is the need to devise modes of instruction to remedy their inexperience."[23] In British North America, as in England, the most important mode of instruction was the didactic literature known generically as justice of the peace manuals. Beginning with William Lambarde's Eirenarcha, or of the Office of the Justices of Peace, first published in 1582, these manuals provided JPs with an alphabetical digest of information relating to their common law and statutory responsibilities, including forms for the dispatch of the most frequent civil and criminal business. Lambarde's Eirenarcha, after several editions, gave way in English practice to Michael Dalton's The Countrey Justice (1618).[24] Dalton's work remained the basic vade mecum of the English JP through the seventeenth century, giving way at the opening of the eighteenth to William Nelson's The Office and Authority of a Justice of Peace and Giles Jacob's The Modern Justice.[25] These in turn gave way by mid-century to a series of manuals, the most expansive and widely circulated of which was Richard Burn's Justice of the Peace and Parish Officer.[26] Justices' manuals were not simply primers of criminal procedure, either in Great Britain or in British North America. The JPs were the primary administrators of the countryside, and the manuals reflected this fact by increasing in bulk during the eighteenth century as Parliament added vastly to the volume and scope of legislation for whose implementation these men were ultimately responsible. But this growth in volume and complexity changed very little of the basic articles in the manuals on the subject of criminal investigation and adjudication. Dalton's words on the conduct of examination of criminal suspects remain present in Nelson, Burn, and other manuals down through the end of the eighteenth century.[27] The most significant change in the phrasing of the English manuals on the core subjects of criminal procedure was the appearance of Serjeant Hawkins's overwhelmingly influential Pleas of the Crown, which became the single most authoritative source for characterization of the common law procedures developed in the wake of the Marian legislation.[28]

The English manuals had a significant circulation in British North America. The disposition of the library of John Montgomerie, governor of New York from 1727 to 1730, gives us a useful illustration. Montgomerie's books were sold in 1732, two years after his death. The sale list shows us the young chief justice of the province, James DeLancey, buying Montgomerie's copy of Nelson's manual; a cash purchaser, whose name was therefore unrecorded, paid more than twice as much for Montgomerie's copy of Dalton, while yet a third buyer acquired the governor's copy of Matthew Hale's Pleas of the Crown.[29] In 1720 the most recent manual in the possession of James Alexander, ultimately the owner of one of the largest law libraries in North America, was Fleetwood's Office of a Justice of Peace (1658).[30] By 1732 he evidently owned both Nelson and Dalton, however, and as the first purchaser of Montgomerie's books at sale declined to buy the governor's copies. By mid-century, in addition to the manuals, each of the surviving library lists of New York lawyers shows that Hawkins's Pleas of the Crown was a required reference—Joseph Murray, John Chambers, and William Smith Jr. all owned copies.[31] At the other end of the English settlement on the Atlantic littoral, the North Carolina legislature in 1749 statutorily required JPs to buy, along with other law books, the latest available edition of Nelson's Justice.[32]

Along with the transplanted copies of English sources, administrators of the criminal justice system in America were informed by a series of domestic manuals, issued throughout the course of the eighteenth century. Though often cited by writers on substantive law in colonial America, these works have not received the attention that, as a genre, they deserve, perhaps because of their stereotyped and largely repetitive nature; only one has received the benefit of modern reprinting, and that without much editorial explication.[33] The present occasion is not one on which to consider the full range of information that can be extracted from the corpus of the American manuals, but a few points of importance to the colonial history of criminal procedure should be made.

The American JP manuals can be divided into two primary categories: those that simply reprinted large portions of English works and those that in addition contained local material drawn from the acts of colonial legislatures. The first of the American manuals, Conductor Generalis (1722), was of the former variety. Drawn, by its compiler's own admission, entirely from Nelson's Justice, the Conductor attained, like the English work it recapitulated, a cross-colonial circulation, being reprinted several times in the various cities of British North America. Like Nelson, Dalton, Burn, and the other English manuals in colonial circulation, the Conductor Generalis militated in the direction of uniformity of American criminal procedure by putting in the hands of the system's lay administrators instructional material that presumed the processes of criminal investigation and preparation for trial to be substantially the same regardless of the geographical location of the JP.[34]

Even the second class of American manual, which made substantial reference to local sources or at least—like George Webb's Office and Authority of a Justice of Peace (1736)—made local applicability part of its appeal to readers, nonetheless circulated outside the boundaries to which it nominally applied, increasing the sense of uniformity of colonial practice.[35] And whether the manuals simply reprinted English writers or inter-mingled portions of the English manuals with descriptions of local statutory requirements, the treatment of the JP's responsibility in examining sus-pected felons was altogether invariable. All sources agreed on three critical points: at the preliminary examination, the defendant was to be questioned unsworn; his statements were to be made a matter of formal written record; and his confession, if any, was to be admissible against him at trial.

The requirement that the defendant testify unsworn was significant, and more will be said of it below. In providing for the admissibility of confessions, the American sources, particularly after the publication of Hawkins's enormously authoritative Pleas of the Crown, routinely stated that such confessions were admissible only against the maker, and not against any other party. In New York, at any rate, the defendant's testimony at examination was assumed to be an important, if not invariably essential, element in the Crown's presentation, upon which the attorney general or his deputy relied in framing an indictment, and which the examining justice was expected to provide on pain of official displeasure.[36] The incentives faced by the examining justice in his relation to the Crown's officials in the colony confirmed the essential fact: the prosecutorial system depended upon routine self-incrimination in preliminary proceedings.

The aim of securing self-incrimination in pretrial proceedings affected even those portions of the process apparently directed at fairness to the accused. Most of the manuals directed the JP to note evidence favorable to the prisoner as well as that favorable to the Crown. Sometime early in the eighteenth century it became the practice in New York, when the defendant was available at the time of examination of the prosecution's witnesses, to confront him with those witnesses at that time.[37] Although this might have afforded some few defendants an opportunity to poke holes in the Crown's case, the primary purpose seems to have been to inspire a confession from the accused.[38] Leonard Levy's conclusion that in England "the right against self-incrimination scarcely existed in the pre-trial stages of a criminal proceeding" is equally true for British North America.[39]

C. The Limits of Coercion

The importance of the preliminary examination in the system of colonial criminal procedure is underestimated if it is seen solely as prelude to the unequal combat of the jury trial. As in England, where JPs sitting alone had substantial summary jurisdiction, colonial criminal justice included among its essential features a broad reliance on summary justice. In New York, the criminal or quasi-criminal jurisdiction of a single JP included enforcement by fine of the statutes governing fraudulent repacking of meat, sale of unmerchantable flour, violation of weights and measures, and the usual run of public morality enforcement, including offenses such as profaning the Sabbath, swearing, public intoxication, dealing in lottery tickets, and providing liquor to slaves and apprentices. Forms of criminal or quasi-criminal trespass, such as breaking windows and milestones, firing of guns or fireworks in the city, and passage of counterfeit copper coinage were similarly punished by summary jurisdiction.[40] In these areas of summary jurisdiction, examination was equivalent to trial. As we shall see, socioeconomic forces militated in favor of expansion of summary jurisdiction, or its equivalent, in British North America during the eighteenth century. In this absolutely crucial sense, self-incrimination became more, rather than less, important in the administration of colonial criminal justice in the decades preceding independence.

Yet despite all the energy expended in the creation of opportunities for the accused to commit himself, there remained important limitations on the degree of coercion employed in the search for the guilty. By all measures, the most important was the distinction separating witnesses from those accused. In the aftermath of Bacon's Rebellion, in 1677, the Virginia House of Burgesses, perhaps under the pressure of those apprehensive that they would be swept up in Governor Berkeley's measures of pacification and retaliation, stated that

> UPON a motion from Accomack county, sent by their burgesses, It is answered and declared, that the law has provided that a person summoned as a witness against another, ought to answer upon oath, but no law can compel a man to swear against himself in any matter wherein he is liable to corporal punishment.[41]

Plainly, the legislature was declaring what it understood to be settled law, in which the traditional understanding of the *Nemo tenetur* maxim can be clearly discerned. Witnesses were persons who could be compelled under spiritual and monetary penalties to appear and tell the truth, but they could not be compelled to swear against themselves. Nor could defendants, to be sure, but since their testimony, particularly self-incriminatory testimony, was of the greatest value—even if it consisted of exculpatory falsehoods that showed consciousness of guilt—the solution was simply not to examine them under oath.

To the modern mind, the oath in the legal process is merely a formal ritual, reminding the witness of the possibility of secular punishment for perjury. But this is merely the last step in the withering away of the Christian world's favored instrument of spiritual coercion. British North American communities in the seventeenth and early eighteenth centuries were even more sensitive to the controversial nature of the oath than the bulk of English society in the time of John Lilburne. For New England Congregationalists of the 1630s and 1640s, oaths were not intrinsically to be distrusted, as they were for many others in North America. New Englanders enthusiastically employed oaths for any number of civil purposes,[42] but the ex officio oath, and its role as an investigative device in the persecution of dissenters under Archbishop Laud, was more uniformly reprehended than in England. Hence the great codes of Congregationalist New England limited the use and wording of oaths to prevent the use of spiritual coercion.[43] This did not inhibit Congregationalist judges from attempting to entrap defendants into self-incrimination by questioning them, so long as, in conformity with the common law as they understood it, no oath was first administered.[44] Similarly, the Friends in Pennsylvania, who altogether denied the propriety of oaths—regarding them as blasphemous invocations of divine interference in worldly affairs—by no means concluded from their long confrontation with English justice that traditional examination practices in the country violated the spiritual privileges of the accused.[45] Tender religious sensibilities in British North America intensified the impression that there was something dreadfully wrong with forcing men to choose between damnation and secular punishment for crime—a sentiment without which the subsequent constitutional developments would be less explicable. But nowhere in the American colonies did this imply that the traditional criminal procedure of the English countryside, with its extensive reliance upon self-incrimination, ought to be changed.

Similarly, the Americans recognized severe limitations on the use of physical coercion to secure testimony, yet they did so upon principles that left the rationale of the "accused speaks" trial, and all it implied, intact. For those seeking, on the basis of the received wisdom, to find among the Massachusetts contemporaries of Prynne, Bastwick, and Lilburne a recognition of the eternal right against self-incrimination, article 45 of the 1641 Body of Liberties is at best a problem:

No man shall be forced by Torture to confess any Crime against himself nor any other unless it be in some Capital case where he is first fully convicted by clear and sufficient evidence to be guilty, After which if the cause be of that nature, That it is very apparent there be other conspiritors, or confederates with him, Then he may be tortured, yet not with such Tortures as be Barbarous and inhumane.[46]

To say, as Leonard Levy does, that this provision "provided in somewhat equivocal terms for the right against self-incrimination" is rather an exaggeration.[47] When not conscripted for the task of supporting the "right," to which it is unsuited, article 45 does however reveal something of value. Even among moderate dissenters of the 1630s, the English use of torture seemed in one sense inferior to the Continental pattern, as John Selden pithily remarked:

> The Rack is used nowhere as in England. In other Countries, 'tis used in Judicature, when there is semi-plena probatio, a half proof against a man, then to see if they can make it full, they rack him to try if he will Confess. But here in England, they take a man & rack him I do not know why, nor when, not in time of Judicature, but when somebody bids.[48]

The primary problem with torture, in short, was that it was used as a matter of royal discretion, and therefore was inherently lawless in the sense of being ungoverned by law. Article 45 was intended to resolve that grievance, closely connected with the grievance against the use of ex officio oaths in the prerogative courts, by subjecting all such means to the authority of the traditional criminal law.

These ideas of the Massachusetts Bay orthodoxy on the relation between compulsion and confession in the administration of the criminal law can be seen in their clearest form—as so often in the early history of Congregationalist New England—in the dialogue between civil and religious leaders. A perceived outbreak of offenses against public sexual morality in the early 1640s, including one famous case of sexual relations with children and a cluster of cases of bestiality, brought the magistrates to a consideration of the problems inherent in punishing capital crimes that by their nature eluded the holy watching of potential witnesses.[49] In the winter of 1641–42, Governor Bellingham sought counsel from the ministers and magistrates of the towns on a series of questions concerning these issues. "How far," Bellingham asked, "may a magistrate extract a confession of a capital crime from a suspected and an accused person?" Only two of the original responses to this circular have survived, and only one is directly responsive to the question of compulsion. Ralph Partrich answered in words perfectly

descriptive of the intersection of common law tradition and Congregationalist orthodoxy:

> I conceive that, a magistrate is bound, by careful examination of circum-
> stances and weighing of probabilities, to sift the accused, and by force of
> argument to draw him to an acknowledgment of the truth; but he may not
> extract a confession of a capital crime from a suspected person by any violent
> means, whether it be by an oath imposed, or by any punishment inflicted
> or threatened to be inflicted, for so he may draw forth an acknowledgment
> of a crime from a fearful innocent; if guilty he shall be compelled to be his
> own accuser, when no other can, which is against the rule of justice.[50]

Partrich's conclusion seems to have been that of the ministers at large in
1642; John Winthrop reported the consensus this way:

> [W]here such a fact is committed, and one witness or strong presumptions
> do point out the offender, there the judge may examine him strictly, and
> he is bound to answer directly, though to the peril of his life. But if there
> be only light suspicion, &c. then the judge is not to press him to answer,
> nor is he to be denied the benefit of the law, but he may be silent, and call
> for his accusers. But for examination by oath or torture in criminal cases, it
> was generally denied to be lawful.[51]

The important features here are the placement of questioning under oath
and torture in the common category of "violence" and the distinction
drawn between such violent means and magisterial "force of argument"
directed at securing a confession. The silence of the accused was a tolerable
response only where suspicion was light; otherwise the magistrate should
inquire "strictly" and the accused was bound to answer, even at his ultimate
peril.

In summary, we are justified in reaching several conclusions concerning
the formation of systems of criminal procedure in the American colonies
in the decades following settlement. First, despite diversities of belief, purpose, and conditions of settlement, by the end of the seventeenth century
a broad convergence on traditional English forms had occurred throughout
the criminal procedure systems of the British colonies. The common features included not only the grand and petit juries and other palladia of
English liberties, but also the system of preliminary examination, the rules
excluding counsel, and the other elements of early modern criminal procedure that developed from the merger of English traditions of local government and the sweeping effect of the Marian committal statutes. Colonial

American criminal justice depended upon self-incrimination in practice, because the basic design of the system assumed it would.

At the same time, the American records also disclose a strong array of beliefs that physical and spiritual coercion was an inappropriate way to secure evidence of crime. *Nemo tenetur prodere seipsum* was no meaningless tag. It expressed ideas about treatment of witnesses that were older than the system of criminal procedure of which they now formed part. It played a role in the debate over the uses of physical coercion, casting weight onto the scale against the practice of judicial torture. But however broad the theoretical principle that might be framed upon the maxim, its real effect on the system of criminal procedure was peripheral. For at the center of that system stood the defendant, friendless and alone, confronting the evidence and his fate. So long as he remained in that condition, and it was the fixed purpose of the system to keep him there, any notion of the defendant's privilege against self-incrimination was but a phantom of the law.

The English system Serjeant Hawkins described was a system the Americans, mutatis mutandis, were committed to emulate. In it, despite its existing features, there was material upon which defendants' counsel, actively engaged in reshaping the criminal trial, could seize in order to save their clients from the snares and pitfalls of examination. English developments do seem to have followed that path. But the systems of criminal justice in colonial America existed in an environment distinctively different in important respects from that of England. The social and economic conditions of criminal justice in eighteenth-century America made adherence to the traditional system more necessary, and emulation of the English developments less likely, as the colonial period came to a close.

III. SOCIAL DETERMINANTS OF THE LATE COLONIAL TRIAL

We have seen that, in the first instance, British North Americans adopted English modes of criminal procedure imitatively. But practices and institutions could only survive by performing the necessary functions under prevailing conditions. The "accused speaks" trial and the associated modes of pretrial procedure met the requirements of public order in the social conditions of colonial America reasonably well. It demanded little in the way of resources for criminal investigation. Because it presumed a defendant largely without resources to challenge the prosecution's case, it also economized on prosecutorial energies, allowing a minimal cadre of lawyers to manage comparatively large numbers of prosecutions. And, not least, because it assumed that defendants either could not or would not be represented, it dispensed with the need for any social investment in a criminal defense bar. All of these elements, like the basic dependence on a stratum of local lay judges accorded broad discretion, suited colonial conditions at least as well as English ones.

Conditions in the eighteenth-century colonies did not, however, parallel contemporary English ones in all relevant respects. Demographic, economic, geographic, and political forces were at work shaping American criminal procedure, and those forces did not militate in the direction of the "testing the prosecution" trial. Indeed, much social energy was directed—even in the comparatively professionalized system of New York— at rendering the disadvantages of the defendant yet more disadvantageous. On a practical level, an observer of colonial criminal process in 1770 would not have detected an inclination to increase the privileges of criminal defendants. Julius Goebel's conclusion that the privilege against self-incrimination was an exotic fruit of Westminster Hall, with whose flavor the provincial lawyers were unacquainted,[52] would have seemed not only descriptively correct but likely to remain so. Before we can understand how, and to what extent, revolutionary rhetoric coincided with an alteration of the system, we must comprehend the material conditions of prerevolutionary criminal justice and their relation to doctrine.

The essence of the common law criminal procedure transported to the American colonies was its use of a hierarchy of courts graded to a hierarchy of offenses, allowing local lay judges—acting first alone and then in groups meeting in central locations with quasi-professional advice—to dispose of all but the most serious offenses. Serious crimes were disposed of by itinerant or centrally located judges of high professionalization, accompanied by a cadre of professional lawyers responsible for the preparation of the Crown's case. The assumption was that all justice other than local summary justice was expensive, and the time of professional judges and counsel was most expensive of all.

Everywhere in British North America the demographic density was so low, compared to England's, that the differences in expense between summary and professional justice were intensified. Outside New England in particular, and always in a gradient from east to west within each colony, distance increased the costs of professional justice. So too did the extremely small number of men capable of serving as judges and counsel. Geographical dispersion and a small professional cadre together constituted a strong force for the expansion of summary jurisdiction in order to effect the necessary economy in expensive justice. Increasing population did not itself relieve the pressure for expansion of summary jurisdiction, because increasing population did not always bring a proportionate increase in the resources available for criminal justice.

Other forces too made cheaper localized summary criminal justice attractive in colonial America. American populations were geographically mobile, young, and male. In rural areas as well as in the port cities, those apprehended for crime were more often than not strangers—indigent and transient. To hold them for trial meant maintaining them at public expense. Every case in which the defendant could not make recognizance to appear—in New York ordinarily £20 with two sureties—was a matter of expensive justice. Maintenance of the jails was one of the permanent fiscal burdens on the colonial communities—one that both taxpayers and public officers were loath to discharge. The records are replete with demonstrations of the gross inadequacy of colonial jails. In New York's Ulster County, for example, the sheriff appears to have made complaint of the insufficiency of the jail at virtually every Sessions.[53] Even the minutes of the Supreme Court reflect the constant complaint of those officers responsible for the safekeeping of defendants.[54] Sheriffs were of course anxious lest the inadequacy of the jails lead to escapes for which, as at common law, they would be liable in damages.[55] Nor were sheriffs the only source of agitation over jail conditions; one scholar located almost 240 complaints from the court records and common council minutes throughout the period.[56] The legislature took occasional action,[57] and there were even attempts to use the machinery of the criminal law against public officers who negligently permitted the decay of the jails,[58] but then as now jail construction was politically popular only so long as no one had to be taxed to pay for it, and the public parsimony so characteristic of colonial America ensured that the complaints never died down. Summary criminal jurisdiction, which affected lower-class defendants rather than taxpayers, was an altogether more acceptable solution.

In light of these pressures, it is not surprising to see eighteenth-century legislative interventions designed to expand the scope of summary jurisdiction. Beginning in 1732, for example, New York repeatedly expanded its reach. Two statutes were passed in that year providing that anyone in custody charged with offenses below the degree of grand larceny (in New York limited by the traditional "goods to the value of 12s.") who was unable to make recognizance or bail within forty-eight hours might be tried by three JPs, sitting without a jury, and sentenced to corporal punishment "not extending to Life or Limb." The 1732 acts also specifically defined the evidentiary standard for such convictions, allowing conviction "by Confession or by the oath of one or more credible witnesses."[59] The wording of these statutes made clear the element of class justice involved:

> WHEREAS not only Several disorderly Persons inhabiting in the City of New York but many vagrant and Idle persons passing through the same from the Neighboring Counties and Colonies have often Committed divers misdemeanors breaches of the Peace and other Criminal offences . . . who not being able to procure bail to appear at the ye General Quarter Sessions . . . and having no Substance of their own have been at great Expence to the Inhabitants in the mean while in Gaol . . .

It was surely prudent to whip such persons soundly on their own confession or on the oath of a single prosecution witness and let them go, taking care if they were strangers to have them transported "by warrant from the said Justices to the place of his or their last Settlement or place of abode or out of the Colony of New York." The socioeconomic advantages of limiting trial to those with "Substance" and standing in the community were easy to grasp; the 1732 act was revived and extended in 1736 and in 1744.[60] In 1762 summary procedure was made available for use against those obtaining goods by false pretenses in New York City.[61] In 1768, for reasons examined below, the assembly determined that those charged with larceny of goods to the value of £5 might, unless clergy was unavailable, be treated as though they had committed petit larceny. For those of the wrong social status, common law felony charges might be tried summarily in New York at the end of the colonial period, using a procedure that made confession sufficient for conviction in itself and that provided no procedural protections against abuse.

Precisely because of the nature of the proceedings, records of the employment of summary criminal justice in colonial America are extremely sparse. In New York, we have only the records in New York City between 1733 and 1743, involving about seventy-five cases.[62] With one insignificant exception, no records whatever of the course of summary justice in the New York countryside survive. Suspicion that the sequence of "examination followed by confession followed by whipping" sometimes merged with the sequence of "examination followed by whipping followed by confession" is inevitable, but we simply have no way to know.

The socially discriminatory use of summary justice guaranteed its political acceptability. The political classes were indifferent, or positive, about its use because it was not aimed at them or theirs. No New Yorker during the colonial period, so far as records reveal, complained that the widespread use of such procedure violated any common law rights until in 1769 the provincial attorney general himself raised the issue, in revealing circumstances. Complaint was made by a substantial Suffolk County landowner that three JPs had whipped one of his servants after summary proceedings. John Tabor Kempe wrote in strong terms to the justices, reminding them that the statute was intended only for vagrants and persons unable to make bail. Extension to other defendants, Kempe pointed out, would "be destructive of that Grand Bulwark of our Freedom and safety, the Trial by Jury." He plainly threatened that if the justices did not observe the distinction between vagrants and the servants of the rich, he would take action against them.[63]

In addition to transient or indigent defendants requiring pretrial confinement, most colonial societies contained substantial populations of slaves, for whom all justice and injustice was summary. For their offenses against others than their masters, summary corporal punishment was the only fitting process, duplicating in the public law the principle of summary corporal punishment that prevailed between the individual master and slave. But the presence of slaves in the population had more far-reaching effects than the addition of another impetus to summary criminal justice. The routine imposition of violent physical coercion that defined the pattern of slave discipline could hardly be expected to stop at the moment a slave stood accused of crime. As the most thorough account of slave criminal justice in Virginia sums up the matter: "The nearly absolute power of white officials over slaves could lead to the use of torture in order to 'fix' a case, speed up the questioning process, find further evidence, or force suspects to reveal the identity of accomplices."[64] When the white communities' fears of servile insurrection were aroused—whether or not in response to outbreaks of violent resistance—criminal procedure ordinarily too harsh for use with anyone but a slave might easily spread to the ordinarily more favored classes. "In insurrection episodes . . . torture could yield the 'confession' that anxious or angry whites wanted,"[65] and not necessarily from slaves alone. In the midst of the 1741 slave conspiracy panic in New York, Chief Justice Daniel Horsmanden used the threat of immediate execution to force testimony incriminating a white man from the white daughter of a convicted conspirator.[66]

The widespread employment of summary criminal procedure in the colonies had effects reaching far beyond the defendants chargeable under the summary statutes. Misdemeanor defendants at Quarter Sessions in New York, who could not under all but the most exceptional circumstances afford to retain counsel, found themselves at preliminary examination facing what could easily be converted into a summary trial. At the end of such a process they would be awarded the same whipping likely to result from the formal proceedings to which they were nominally entitled, less the time spent languishing in jail or the expense of recognizance. We should not be surprised, therefore, to find, as Julius Goebel does, that in the City Quarter Sessions from 1691 to 1776, 248 defendants confessed, 94 pled not guilty and went to trial, and 17 were convicted for want of a plea, for a gross rate of 69 percent confession at preliminary examination.[67]

Material pressures on the traditional criminal procedure system intensified in the 1760s as colonial America suffered from recurrent large-scale disturbances of public order. Prosecutorial and adjudicative resources were intensively diverted to the trial of riot and related offenses. The beginnings of the Regulation movements in the southern hinterland, like the squatter disruptions on the Vermont frontier and the agrarian violence in the Hudson River Valley, challenged the capacities of the public order systems in several colonies. Douglas Greenberg, in his quantitative study of criminal justice in colonial New York, concludes that between 1750 and 1776 "riots and the like were the most frequent source of prosecution in the countryside."[68] Under these and associated pressures, the criminal justice systems began a process of radical adjustment. In New York, less prosecutorial attention was devoted to such traditional concerns as theft offenses in the countryside. Imposition of punishment other than fines for misdemeanor offenses largely vanished; in a doubtless connected process, Supreme Court trial rates dropped and plea rates soared.[69] In such an environment, expansion of summary jurisdiction was one of the few tools available to the legislature. The New York act of 1768 making punishable in summary proceedings what had been felonious larceny throughout the history of the common law is but the clearest example of the effects of the pressure.[70] Moreover, imperial disruptions of American public finance, including the Currency Act of 1764,[71] and interferences with administration of justice, including the closure of the courts of most colonies during the Stamp Act crisis, made the traditional parsimony of colonial taxpayers with respect to the criminal justice system all the more intense.[72] Far from seeking more expensive criminal procedure that was increasingly protective of the defendants' interests, the societies of British North America were heading in the late colonial period in quite the opposite direction.

Thus we reach the great apparent paradox in the history of the privilege against self-incrimination. How could Americans, who on the evidence of their colonial records employed the early modern "accused speaks" form of criminal procedure throughout the period of imperial affiliation, and who intensified this pattern for socioeconomic reasons in the closing decades of the colonial era, nonetheless have adopted constitutions that proclaimed the accused's right to avoid self-incrimination in the criminal process?

The answer is that the explosion of constitutional polemic in British North America after 1760 put into play intellectual forces that led American criminal procedure doctrine in a direction very different from the direction that had been taken in the late colonial period. The Americans wound up adopting broad legal and constitutional positions with which their own historic practices were seemingly in conflict. However, as with so many social groups in a similar situation, the Americans did not feel themselves immediately compelled to put their principles into practice.

IV. RIGHTS, CRIMINAL PROCEDURE, AND THE AMERICAN REVOLUTION

The great constitutional conflict that ended in the dissolution of the first British Empire involved several different clusters of constitutional ideas—about rights, legislative authority, and representation. So far as these clusters of ideas concerned rights, they involved not lists of independent "human rights," following the model of twentieth-century constitutional jurisprudence, but rather closely interwoven meshes of privileges that the Americans believed intrinsic to the common law tradition, unmodifiable by an increasingly sovereign British Parliament.

American constitutional polemic thus focused on historical practices and institutions in the English common law tradition that protected subjects—individually and collectively—against legal innovation destructive of their interests. First among these was the jury, which, particularly in American circumstances, was perceived to have a vital constitutional function in tempering the effect of innovative or foreign legislative decisions. This the jury did by limiting enforcement to the extent palatable to the community itself. So the Americans exalted the jury and all the common law rules and maxims ancillary to its function. In the process, the Americans discovered a tenderness concerning process that extracted confessions. If directed against witnesses, such process short-circuited the accusatory role of the community; if directed against defendants, it deprived them of mean-ingful jury trial altogether. To follow the American thought process in de-tail we must recreate the theoretical context of eighteenth-century consti-tutional law, a step that requires us to view in a new light much that we have regarded as familiar.[73]

A. Constitutional Theory and the Jury

We must begin by recognizing the full importance of the Americans' claim to their rights as Englishmen.[74] British North Americans in the eighteenth century claimed to be entitled to all the rights of English subjects on numer-ous grounds—including charter, statute, and purchase by the hardship of transatlantic migration. The constitution of the British Empire, they argued, guaranteed them an equality of treatment with the king's English subjects, who enjoyed a constitution more protective of rights than any (as they saw it) in the world.

Protection of the Englishman's rights began with protection for the most important rights of all, the rights to security and property. These rights were the ends of government, as eighteenth-century Whigs viewed the question, and their protection separated the free government of Britain from the despotisms of the rest of the known world.[75] The British Constitu-tion protected security and property because it provided liberty, that is, government under law.[76] The law, by which British North Americans meant English common law, confined all authority, including and most especially the sovereign. If Parliament claimed the power to make absolute law, then parliamentary sovereignty was destructive of liberty. In this re-spect, which is hard to grasp beneath the conflicting uses we have made of the same constitutional vocabulary in the past two hundred years, British North Americans claimed a constitutional right to the common law.[77]

As British North Americans carried this constitutional theory into the climactic confrontations with Parliament and the Crown, American liberty seemed increasingly threatened by the same forces that earlier generations of Englishmen had resisted. Because liberty was government under law, attention was again directed at those basic institutions of law that protected liberty. These institutions were many, and one stood out from all the rest: the jury trial. But when Americans spoke of the fundamental-law role of the jury, an entire cluster of rights was connoted, including claims to traditional common law privileges of indictment, venue, representation, confronta-tion, and a general verdict. As the legal historian John Phillip Reid says:

The right to trial by jury, unlike the rights of property, security, and eighteenth-century government, is a right we think we know. We do, but only in an attenuated form. We no longer know the right as it existed in the age of the American Revolution. Certainly we cannot capture the extreme euphoria of British and colonist alike when they thought of jury trial.[78]

The problem is that the analytic overlay of subsequent constitutional development has broken down the cluster of rights into individual components, of which the jury right is merely one.

To see the contents of the rights cluster centered around the institution of the jury, we can do no better than heed the words of the Continental Congress. After the passage of the Quebec Act, which provided for the continuation of civil law in one portion of the king's North American dominions, the Congress addressed the Quebecois, hoping to impress upon them the degree of discrimination implied in the denial of jury trial. The right of trial by jury, the Congress said,

> provides, that neither life, liberty nor property can be taken from the possessor, until twelve of his unexceptionable countrymen and peers, of his vicinage, who from that neighbourhood may reasonably be supposed to be acquainted with his character, and the characters of the witnesses, upon a fair trial, and full inquiry face to face, in open Court, before as many of the people as chuse to attend, shall pass their sentence under oath against him; a sentence that cannot injure him, without injuring their own reputation, and probably their interest also.[79]

Congress, expressing the official colonial position, was telling the Quebecois something we must grasp ourselves—that polemics about the right of jury trial intrinsically included within their scope questions that we have tended to place in multiple constitutional pigeonholes. Just as the institution of the jury protected other, even more fundamental rights, it was in turn protected by a series of legal rules—about when, where, and how juries were convened, what evidence they heard, and what they did about it—which the Americans considered it beyond the constitutional authority of Parliament to alter. As an English pamphleteer wrote in "On the Perversion of Law from its Constitutional Course" in 1771, the right to a jury uncontrolled by the judge "is so essential a part of our constitution, that the liberty of the subject is violated, whenever the least attempt is made to break through this sacred rule, which will admit of no exception."[80] This was an exaggerated picture of the freedom of the English jury, but the distortion emphasizes for us the importance attached to the principle.

As the constitutional crisis of the 1760s and 1770s deepened, the cluster of rights surrounding the jury became more important for two reasons. First, imperial measures to counteract increasingly violent colonial political dissent—ranging from the use of vice-admiralty to try revenue offenses, to the shotgun form of general writs of assistance, to parliamentary threats to apply the Treason Act of Henry VIII, to the closure of the Massachusetts courts—employed legal processes the Americans considered tyrannical and unconstitutional innovations. Second, and more important, Americans accorded a unique constitutional function to jury trial; it provided a check against overweening power, and particularly a local check on the authority of Parliament, which was without political accountability to the objects of its colonial legislation. The local jury, hearing the evidence for itself, provided an alternate source of authority to the judges, who might be appointed by the Crown from among a group of officials unsympathetic to or hostile to American liberties. Interference with jury trial, the voters of Boston said during the Stamp Act crisis, when imperial legislation enforcing internal revenue measures in vice-admiralty was first imposed, "deprives us of the most essential Rights of Britons, and greatly weakens the best Security of our Lives, Liberties and Estates; which may hereafter be at the Disposal of Judges who may be Strangers to us, and perhaps malicious, mercenary, corrupt and oppressive."[81] Thus, a group of grievances and anxieties concerning "unconstitutional" and oppressive use of the criminal procedure system became a part of the constitutional history of the American Revolution, and the colonial remedies for the grievances and preventives for the anxieties embedded themselves in the state and federal constitutions. Among them were various restatements of the traditional *Nemo tenetur* maxim, which was related, by history and logic, to the colonial concerns.

B. Constitutional Theory and the Privilege

Among the colonial grievances to which the idea cluster denominated by the right to jury trial—let us call this the "trial rights cluster"—responded was the perceived expansion of prerogative courts, initially expressed in the colonial hostility to the institution of vice-admiralty. After taxation without representation, Boston instructed its representatives in 1769, "the Jurisdiction of the Admiralty, are [*sic*] our greatest Grievance."[82] The problem was that vice-admiralty, acting without juries, no longer protected natural or positive rights, as Englishmen had a right to expect. As the voters of Providence put it during the Stamp Act resistance, "we look upon our natural Rights to be diminished in the same Proportion, as the Powers of that Court are extended."[83] In this fashion the Americans, objecting to an employment of prerogative courts in North America with parliamentary sanction, began to adopt rhetoric concerning the unconstitutionality of prerogative justice first employed against the king in the period of personal rule by Charles I. Whereas the Court of High Commission had been the primary concern in the earlier era, admiralty became the focus of hostility in America, and among the reasons given for the American objection was its alleged employment of the ex officio oath for coercive purposes.

Admiralty had not always inspired such detestation in British North America. Admiralty provided one of the few fora for the effective adjudication of certain kinds of intercolonial trade disputes, and during the long period of imperial confrontation in Atlantic waters, the prize jurisdiction of the admiralty courts had helped to make many a privateer, and more than a few lawyers and judges, rich. But in the aftermath of unqualified British victory over France in North America, admiralty justice lost many of its attractive uses, and the American hostility to prerogative justice grew apace.[84] So the ex officio oath and the abuses of Star Chamber procedure again became staples of the pamphlet literature. A Boston pamphleteer drew an explicit connection between vice-admiralty jurisdiction and the use of coercive self-incriminatory oaths in imagining satirically what would befall Samuel Adams should the customs commissioners sue him in admiralty. Once he was sworn, he should expect: "Pray Sir, when did you kiss your maid Mary?—Where? and in what manner? Did you lay with her in a barn? or in your own house?"[85] An English electoral polemic of 1769 made the same point more in anger than in satire, arguing that the use of admiralty to try revenue offenses committed on land "is a great and dangerous breach of the constitution. Attempts have been made in times past to introduce the civil law; the rack which now lies in the tower was brought in for a beginning of it, but these attempts were repelled by our ancestors."[86] As the admiralty grievance grew in intensity after 1765, the idea of a fundamental-law privilege against coercive testimonial pressure further embedded itself in the language of constitutional debate.

Concern about the "unconstitutional" imposition of prerogative justice in America reached the boiling point after the parliamentary output of 1774. The Quebec Act's provision for nonjury trial in a portion of British North America,[87] along with the Massachusetts Administration of Justice

Act,[88] implied to the Americans that Parliament claimed the sovereign power to institute any system of criminal justice it pleased in the American dominions, regardless of the traditional usages of the common law. Thus was heard again in North America the Englishman's most comprehensive denunciation of oppressive government: "They will make Frenchmen of us all."[89]

Less often noted in the secondary literature, but of incalculable effect on Americans, particularly lawyers, during the revolutionary era, was a step Parliament merely threatened: adoption of an address to the Crown recommending the application of the Treason Act of Henry VIII in North America.[90] Not surprisingly, the threat to revive Tudor approaches to justice left an indelible mark on the men whom it threatened with transportation to England for a trial in the venue of the Crown's choice, where proof of "constructive treason" under the statute of Edward III would end in speedy execution.[91]

But there was another, less obvious, implication of the threat to apply Henry VIII's Treason Act. Its application would have deprived its American objects of the protections of the Treason Act of 1696,[92] a monument of Whig constitutionalism raised in the aftermath of the political abuse of criminal justice by Charles II and James II. The 1696 act was the source of much reformist criminal procedure in the eighteenth century, most particularly the right of defendants to counsel and a copy of the charges. Judges extended the protections it originally accorded only to the political classes to other defendants charged with felony offenses under the common law. By threatening to deprive Americans of its benefits, Parliament, in American eyes, proposed to do to the American political classes what they themselves did to the vagrants, strangers, and slaves in their own communities.

C. The Privilege and the State Constitutions

From these and other related causes grew the American inclination to treat elements of common law criminal procedure as fundamental law protecting against legislative innovation or tyrannical suppression. To all American Whigs, the trial rights cluster was a prominent object of concern. Every state constitution, whether or not it contained a bill of rights, protected the entitlement to jury trial. It is of cardinal importance that throughout the constitutional debate, the trial rights cluster denoted principles that the Americans believed Parliament had trampled, or would trample in the future if left unchecked. Americans sought to protect their practices against tyrannical innovations, claiming that what they did themselves fully conformed to what the ancient constitution required. It is in this context that we must read section 8 of the Virginia Declaration of Rights, in which George Mason provided the model for constitutional expression of the trial rights cluster, adopted with few alterations in all the state bills of rights of the 1770s and 1780s:

> That in all capital or criminal prosecutions, a man hath a right to demand the cause and nature of his accusation, to be confronted with the accusers and witnesses, to call for evidence in his favor, and to a speedy trial by an impartial jury of twelve men of his vicinage, without whose unanimous consent he cannot be found guilty; nor be compelled to give evidence against himself; that no man be deprived of his liberty, except by the law of the land or the judgment of his peers.[93]

Mason's compressed drafting reflects the fact that these various procedural guarantees, including the privilege against self-incrimination, were part of a cluster of legal rules conceived not primarily as independent, freestanding rights but rather as part of the constitutional system for protecting all rights by ensuring that government activity met the fundamental check of jury trial. Mason's language encapsulated the constitutional history of the jury right cluster, from Magna Carta to the Treason Act of 1696. Significantly, it did not include a right to be represented by counsel before the law of the land and judgment of one's peers. This development was too recent to be an element of timeless right.

The Virginia Declaration passed on June 12, 1776, and was published in Philadelphia newspapers even before the Continental Congress voted for independence at the beginning of July. It traveled with the delegates into the rest of the states and became a model for constitutions all along the Atlantic coast. By late September, the Pennsylvania convention had drafted a constitution prefaced by a Declaration of Rights, itself published by the end of August and closely modeled on Mason's. Section 9 repeated Mason's section 8, but with one critical addition: "that in all prosecutions for criminal offenses, a man hath a right to be heard by himself and his counsel."[94] Benjamin Franklin had tightened Mason's prose, but the addition of a right to counsel was neither inadvertent nor far-sighted; Pennsylvania had recognized the right to counsel since 1701, as a consequence of William Penn's contemptuous familiarity with the failings of English criminal procedure.[95] For Pennsylvanians, counsel was as much a part of the jury right cluster as the other procedural protections familiar to George Mason.

But Pennsylvanians did not think they had one more right than Virginians—both groups thought they enjoyed all the rights of Englishmen and no more.

The swift process of constitution drafting produced a few inflections of the style in which the *Nemo tenetur* principle was made fundamental law. Less than a month after Pennsylvania's declaration was adopted, and even before the Pennsylvania Constitution was finished, Delaware had adopted a Bill of Rights using the Pennsylvania text as its model.[96] The Delaware convention's committee broke the independent clauses of Pennsylvania's section 9 into separate articles, so that section 15 read, in its entirety, "That no man in the Courts of Common Law ought to be compelled to give evidence against himself."[97] To Leonard Levy, this "subtle but crucial change" corrected the "bad draftsmanship" of George Mason by "extending the right against self-incrimination to witnesses, as well as parties, in civil as well as criminal cases."[98] Perhaps this is correct, though one might equally argue that it reduced the scope of the privilege from all criminal prosecutions to those at common law, specifically denying the right to defendants in summary proceedings. We can only speculate on the motives of the draftsmen, for the Delaware convention adopted the committee draft without recorded debate.[99] Some confirmation for the latter view may be provided by the action of the Maryland convention, which modified the Delaware provision in turn, declaring that "no man ought to be compelled to give evidence against himself, in a common court of law, or in any other court, but in such cases as have been usually practised in this State, or may hereafter be directed by the Legislature."[100] Here the concern to except summary jurisdictions was made explicit.

Not all the states adopted a constitutional formulation inspired by Mason's Virginia Declaration. South Carolina, Georgia, New Jersey, and New York all included clauses proclaiming the fundamental right to jury trial; none specifically adopted language invoking the *Nemo tenetur* concept.[101] It may at first be "baffling" or "inexplicable" how particular phrases entered into, or were left out of, the American constitutions, ultimately to be explained by "bad draftsmanship" in George Mason or "careless" and "thoughtless" behavior by Thomas Jefferson, who would have replaced Mason's words on compelled self-incrimination by a ban on the use of judicial torture.[102] But once the anachronistic vision of a catalog of independent rights is put aside and is replaced by the American Whig vision of a syncretic cluster of fundamental-law principles embedded in common law practice, such weak explanations are rendered unnecessary. Section 8 of the Virginia Declaration was a concise epitome of the history of criminal procedure in the British Constitution, from Magna Carta through the Treason Act of 1696, and of its eighteenth-century corollaries, such as the right to counsel in felony as well as treason trials. Among the elements of that fundamental-law history was a belief that *Nemo tenetur prodere seipsum,* for if a future legislature or tyrannical executive could impose ex officio oaths or judicial torture, then the constitutional function of jury trial—to provide the local community with a check on governmental power—could not be preserved.

It cannot be sufficiently stressed that the constitutional provisions were primarily devices to protect existing constitutional arrangements as Americans saw them rather than a program of law reform. This we can see in the Maryland legislature's decision to qualify the provision that no man should be compelled to give evidence against himself by providing for exceptions "in such cases as have been usually practised in this State, or may hereafter be directed by the Legislature."[103] New Yorkers, who had not adopted a state bill of rights, had no difficulty perceiving that they needed protection against a federal government that might adopt innovative and fundamental departures from the common law trial practice; hence the suggestion of the New York ratifying convention in 1788 that a federal bill of rights include the provision that "in all criminal prosecutions, the accused . . . should not be compelled to give evidence against himself."[104] Compulsory self-incrimination was what happened in Star Chamber, or in France, not what occurred every time the JPs entered a summary conviction under the Larceny of Goods by False Pretenses Act of 1762, for instance, an act the revolutionary legislature saw no difficulty in extending through 1780.[105]

D. The Fifth Amendment

The delegates to the Federal Convention of 1787 concluded their efforts without adopting a declaration of rights to accompany their plan for federal government of the United States; apparently this resulted more from distaste for the late-summer weather of Philadelphia than from any ideological cause. But as the ratification process took shape in the state conventions, popular pressure for a bill of rights in the now-conventional form began to be heard. The half-hearted Federalist claim that no bill was necessary because the proposed constitution delegated no power to infringe individual liberty collapsed of its own weight and its inconsistency with the document itself. Ultimately more than one-half of the ratifying states recommended amendments, and four recommended entire bills of rights. These four, Virginia, New York, North Carolina, and Rhode Island, included versions of section 8 of the Virginia Declaration of Rights, thus constitutionalizing the privilege.[106]

Debate over the meaning or propriety of section 8 is almost entirely absent from the records of the state conventions. Twice, however—once in Massachusetts and once in New York—antifederalist delegates supported inclusion of a bill of rights by pointing to the potentially oppressive use of the criminal justice system by the new federal government. In Massachusetts, Abraham Holmes warned his colleagues that the guarantee of jury trial in article III might be rendered empty, since the mode of trial was not determined. Counsel might be denied, or confrontation of witnesses; indeed, Congress might institute "the Inquisition." In a similar vein, Thomas Tredwell of New York urged that Congress might establish criminal proceedings not under the common law but under the "civil, the Jewish, or Turkish law." Star Chamber and the Inquisition too figured in his dark imaginings.[107] Although both speeches are primarily examples of Richard Hofstadter's "Paranoid Style" (Protestant variant), whose rhetorical effect on auditors was doubtless minimal, they remind us once again of the intrinsically conservative context in which the privilege was discussed in the era of constitution-making. Common law procedure, however dependent in practice on self-incrimination, was not the object of reforming zeal. The goal of even the most enthusiastic advocate was to prevent sovereign authority from overturning the traditional forms of jury trial, instituting "foreign" or "innovative" means of coercion that would bypass the jury. The rack in the Tower, not the JP flogging a vagabond, was the emblem of the need for a guarantee against coerced confession.

James Madison's proposed bill of rights, presented to the first Congress in June 1789, diverged substantially from any of the proposals submitted by the state conventions. Madison proposed an article containing a series of guarantees surrounding jury trial and a more general article concerning judicial process but not limited to jury proceedings in criminal cases. This provision read:

> No person shall be subject, except in cases of impeachment, to more than one punishment or trial for the same offence; nor shall be compelled to be a witness against himself; nor be deprived of life, liberty, or property, without due process of law; nor be obliged to relinquish his property, where it may be necessary for public use, without just compensation.[108]

The placement of this provision—separate from other criminal trial rights and combined with matters of more general import—was novel.

Unfortunately, the nature of Madison's reasoning process is inaccessible to history—he left no document and made no recorded comment on the principles behind his drafting.

The House Select Committee that first passed on the bill made no change in Madison's provision concerning the privilege, and there was no debate in the Committee of the Whole. John Laurence of New York, saying that it was "a general declaration in some degree contrary to laws passed," moved that Madison's language be limited to criminal cases. There seems to have been no opposition to the amendment, and the clause as amended was unanimously adopted.[109] The Senate, while collecting the trial rights provisions into what became the Sixth Amendment, made no further change in the article containing the privilege against self-incrimination. Unless one cares to spin complex theories from a skein of negative evidence, the legislative history of the Fifth Amendment adds little to our understanding of the history of the privilege.

E. After the Fifth: The Privilege in Practice

The constitutionalization of the self-incrimination privilege, completed by the first Congress, was part of the larger process by which a diverse collection of criminal procedure doctrines became fundamental law in the United States. Those rules were components of the common law's structure for protecting subjects' rights under the eighteenth-century British Constitution. Once conceived as fundamental law, the rules—originally subsidiary or ancillary doctrines of uncertain scope—themselves became rights that individuals could invoke. Jury trial was a right, but it also was a process for protecting other, more basic rights, such as those of security and property. The jury trial right was protected by other rules preventing the sovereign from instituting inquisitions that would trump the community's right to find the facts and nullify the law. One of those rules, or rather of many somewhat inconsistent rules, could be summarized by the maxim *Nemo tenetur prodere seipsum*. Now that rule, too, had become independent of its context. It could be called a right.

Fashioning fundamental law meant constraining the new governments to behave in traditional ways, within the context of common law expectations. The Maryland convention said explicitly what context and language also indicated elsewhere: the new constitutional provisions were meant to inhibit tyrannical innovations, not to alter existing institutions or procedures. As Leonard Levy has said:

As for the self-incrimination clause in Section 8 [of the Virginia Declaration,] there is no evidence that it was taken literally or regarded as anything but a sonorous declamation of the common-law right of long standing. . . . Thus the great Declaration of Rights did not alter Virginia's system of criminal procedure. . . . The practice of the courts was simply unaffected by the restrictions inadvertently or unknowingly inserted in Section 8.[110]

Levy here implies that a right to be free from self-incrimination continued to be more fully observed than the language of the declaration required. The conclusion is wrong, but the observation on which it is based—that the courts of Virginia and other parts of the new nation changed their practice not at all in response to the new constitutional provisions—seems to be right. The records of immediately postrevolutionary criminal justice have been, if anything, less well studied than those of the late colonial period. If any generalization is licensed by current knowledge, however, it is that little change occurred in direct response to the new constitutions.

Perhaps the best general evidence of the absence of change in local criminal procedure after the adoption of the new constitutions is provided by the justices' manuals. The issuance of JP manuals was by no means infrequent in the 1780s and 1790s, and in keeping with the general postrevolutionary mood of independence from English manners, the manuals tended to proclaim themselves renewed and shorn of English disadvantages. The title Conductor Generalis, for example, was revived by James Parker in a new manual published in Patterson, New Jersey, in 1788. Parker's preface urged readers to prefer American to English manuals for studying the JP's duties, because the English manuals had grown too full of unnecessary matter, inapplicable to American (not merely Jerseyite) situations. Despite the gallant proclamation of American divergence from English practice (significantly treating American practice as one, rather than a multiplicity, in line with the prerevolutionary tendency), Parker's Conductor was actually nothing more than a pared-down edition of the then-current edition of Richard Burn's Justice of the Peace and Parish Officer. Shorn of its "unnecessary matter," Burn could be reduced from four volumes to one, but the section on examination, along with the other basic articles of criminal procedure, remained as in Burn. No citation of any constitutional provision, local or federal, appeared in Parker's work.

Nor was this tendency to describe American criminal procedure in traditional English terms disrupted by the debate over the federal Constitution or the subsequent adoption of the Bill of Rights. The next edition of the Conductor, printed by Robert Campbell at Philadelphia in 1792, adopted the 1788 text but added a new preface describing the changes brought by the federal Constitution:

> On the adoption of the New Constitution, a considerable part of that power & authority which had hitherto belonged to each of the States respectively, was, for the common good, wisely transferred to the general government. In consequence of which several acts have been passed, which do not affect any one State in particular, but pervade the whole union. Of these the most generally interesting are, the laws for the regulation of the militia, and the excise—and these the Editor has here inserted.[111]

In its hypothesis that the most remarkable changes for local JPs brought about by the adoption of the new federal Constitution were items of congressional legislation concerning taxation and military service, the Conductor conformed to the pattern of early republican manuals of instruction, as it did in omitting citations to any state constitutional provisions in its text. The rudiments of criminal procedure, in particular, continued through the turn of the century to be provided to the new nation's local judges by Dalton, Hale, Hawkins, Nelson, or Burn, in their own right or as copied by American editors. Practice may have changed more rapidly than the JP manuals, to be sure, but it should be observed that the JPs themselves were even more durable than the manuals, and, given the broad discretion of local justices, continuity of personnel was an important determinant of continuity of practice.

The practice papers of lawyers conducting criminal representation in the first decade of the new regimes likewise show no sweeping alteration in procedure. In New York, the constitution of 1777, though it did not include a provision concerning the privilege, did guarantee that all criminal defendants could be heard through counsel "as in civil actions."[112] Notwithstanding this provision, expansion of the criminal defense practice was but slow. The leading figures of the postrevolutionary New York bar, such as Alexander Hamilton and Aaron Burr, were only infrequently engaged in the criminal process; they concentrated on their active and profitable civil practices.[113] Where counsel were involved, it was often without fee, at the trial stage, presumably as a mixture of public service and advertising; in this context, defense counsel neither sought nor acquired much leverage over the conduct of pretrial examination.[114] But it was the lawyers in postrevolutionary America, like those in England, who began the slow process of refashioning the criminal trial.

In ironic confirmation of the proposition that the new constitutional provisions had little effect on American criminal procedure, lawyers' arguments for limitation of the scope of incriminatory pretrial examination were predominantly nonconstitutional. Beginning in the 1790s, one can detect in the sources one such argument against the admission of pretrial statements, an argument that based the privilege on a revealing form of republican antiquarianism. Perhaps the first expression of this idea in the formal sources (after how much previous development, only an exhaustive review of manuscript records could reveal) appeared in the 1795 edition of Hening's Virginia Justice, which noted, after giving the traditional rules concerning the examination of suspected felons:

> It should be observed, that this examination of the offender, being taken in pursuance of the statute of England, 1 & 2 P. & M. c.13 which is not in force in this country, the trial of a criminal in this state must be governed by the rules of the common law, and our own acts of Assembly; neither of which will justify his own examination in order to convict him.[115]

According to this source, the Revolution returned the law of criminal procedure to its pre-Marian state, since republican lawyers could now find that the central statute of English early modern procedure had never been in force in America.

The argument that pretrial examinations could not be evidence at trial because the ancient common law, rather than the law as modified by the Marian statutes, determined American criminal procedure seems to have been disseminated widely, at least south and west of Virginia, as a consequence of its presentation in Hening's manual. Hening's passage appears verbatim, for example, in Henry Hitchcock's Alabama Justice of the Peace.[116] The absence of even a supporting citation, as late as the third decade of the nineteenth century, to relevant state and federal constitutional provisions gives indirect confirmation that those provisions were thought to do no more than express the common law position.

But what was the common law position? This, rather than the effect of the constitutional provisions, seems to have been the subject of lawyers' ruminations. A revealing example is found in the trial notebooks of Thomas Rodney, territorial judge in the Mississippi Territory, from the Jefferson County Circuit in March 1808. In the trial of one Fulgum, charged with stealing a young slave, the local magistrate who had examined and committed the defendant according to form testified to the incriminating statements then made by the accused. Fulgum's lawyer, identified in Rodney's notes only as F. Turner, objected to the admission of this testimony:

> [W]hile Col. Burnet (Who Examined and Committed the Prisoner) was giving in Evidence Of the Voluntary Confessions the Prisoner had Made before Him—Mr. F.T. Objected, that any Confessions of The Prisoner Should be given in Evidence—That it was not legal and that Such a thing was never heard of before—The Court Informed him That he Must be Mistaken in This position—He replied he was not & defied any one To find a Case in all the books to authorise it—The Court asked him if an Examination Taken [in] writing by the Justice who Committed [the] Prisoner Could Not be admitted in Evidence. He replied Certainly not—The Court replied that he was Certainly Mistaken. He called On the Court if there Was any Such Law To Shew it—Judge Rodney replied To him—That if he Asserted the Law was different from what the Court apprehended To be It was his business To produce the authorities that Supported the position he had Taken—He Then Turned To his books and Every book he Cited Contradicted the position he had avowed and Justified the Opinion of the Court but he said it was Statute not Comm. Law—whereupon he acquiesced—and Col. Burnet proceeded. . . . The Statutes however on this head are made in affirmance of the Common Law—and the Practice in [A]merica has always been conformable thereto and Especially in this Territory.[117]

Turner may have been what Rodney obviously supposed him to be—an ignorant backwoods lawyer. Rodney, brother of a signer of the Declaration of Independence and a Delaware Federalist lawyer, gave the correct traditional argument, as the justification passage in his notes shows. But Turner's argument, even as noted down by the judge he had outraged, bears a more sophisticated interpretation. His comment that the adverse authority derived from statute, not common law, tracks the argument elsewhere advanced in the formal sources: that the admissibility of defendants' statements in pretrial examination derived only from the Marian statutes and was not law in the United States unless enacted by the legislature.

How widespread this position was, or how many defense counsel in the early Republic argued this position before the courts in an attempt to exclude their clients' incriminating statements, we cannot know. The records of trial process in the period are extremely scant. Ultimately, of course, the more traditionalist argument represented by Rodney prevailed. When the constitutional provisions, state and federal, did begin to appear in the instructional sources in the course of the second decade of the nineteenth century, they did so in confirmation of the traditional doctrine. Augustin Clayton's Office and Duty of a Justice of the Peace (1819) provided for Georgia JPs appendices containing the state and federal constitutions, and in his section on evidence he offered, without citation to other authority, a neat combination of the new language and the old ideas: "No man shall be compelled to give evidence against himself. Hence it is held that if a criminal be sworn to his examination taken before a justice, it shall not be read against him."[118] The concern with the coercive power of the oath, which traditionally gave rise to the rule that sworn examinations were inadmissible, was here directly embodied in the constitutional language, without the intervening filter of citation to Dalton, Nelson, or Hawkins. But even as we can see defense counsel in the new republic acting to temper the effect of old procedural doctrine on their clients by seeking to exclude their incriminating statements, no one argued that the constitutional provisions themselves altered the balance. The presence of counsel, not the new constitutional language, was putting pressure on the traditional strategy of prosecution.

V. CONCLUSION

Previous constitutional history has inaccurately depicted the origins of the American constitutional privilege against self-incrimination. American criminal procedure in the colonial period—like the English model it closely followed—assumed the testimonial availability of the defendant at the crucial pretrial stage of the prosecution and at trial freely made use of the defendant's admissions. Americans, like Englishmen, understood the common law to prohibit torture in the search for evidence, and at least some Americans exceeded the English concern with the coercive power of oaths. On both sides of the Atlantic, witnesses and criminal defendants were sharply distinguished in the legal process—what was not only acceptable but necessary to convict the felon was regarded as inappropriate in the treatment of witnesses.

But the social and economic context of criminal justice in colonial America militated even more strongly than English conditions in favor of widespread employment of summary criminal justice, aimed primarily at the economically dependent or socially marginal elements of the society. Summary procedure, largely left out of the traditional account of the privilege, was the purest version of "accused speaks" criminal justice. There the privilege (except in the narrowest possible acceptation—avoidance of torture to extract confessions) was irrelevant.

The constitutional polemic of the later eighteenth century brought Americans to a pitch of rhetorical enthusiasm for jury trial and its legal ancillaries, which for them represented a strong check on the centralizing tendency of imperial authority. In the process of separating themselves from imperial rule, the Americans wrote constitutions that restated—as "fundamental law" immune from legislative alteration—elements of the common law tradition upon which they had depended in their constitutional controversy with Great Britain. Among those elements were protections against tyrannical "innovations" in the system of criminal procedure. Rather than a program for the reform of the criminal law, these constitutional provisions, including the expressions of the privilege against self-incrimination, were aimed conservatively, against deviations from existing practice. As the instructional sources that informed local justices of the peace—the real administrators of criminal justice—show, new constitutional language was largely irrelevant to the development of criminal procedure in the early republic.

However, the expanding activities of criminal defense counsel ultimately brought about changes in the system, paralleling the development in Great Britain. Lawyers, seeking to exclude from the trial the incriminating statements made by their clients in the process of investigation or committal, began to put pressure on the traditional strategy of the criminal prosecution. Initially these efforts depended not on constitutional language but rather on the republican uncertainty about the relation between new American and old English law. The constitutional provisions, to the extent they were involved at all, were seen as embodiments of the common law tradition, and it was the nature of this tradition about which common lawyers argued. The important fact was that they were present to argue at all. Counsel, not constitutions, were remaking criminal procedure.

In this refashioning process, the language of the constitutions, like the *Nemo tenetur* maxim and the history of John Lilburne, were available pegs on which to hang new arguments. Old parts of the system came to serve new functions—the new procedural environment adapted prior doctrine in the Darwinian fashion typical of the common law. This process requires lawyers as the agents of creative reinterpretation. The history of the privilege against self-incrimination in American law, like so much else in our criminal procedure, cannot be told without a recognition of the epochal alteration that began with the large-scale entrance of defense counsel into the process.

SIX

The Modern Privilege:
Its Nineteenth-Century Origins

Henry E. Smith

I. INTRODUCTION

Previous chapters have shown how ineffective the maxim *Nemo tenetur prodere seipsum* was in ensuring a right to silence to defendants in criminal trials before at least the late eighteenth century. The true origins of the modern privilege against self-incrimination thus remain an open question. This chapter will show that the privilege in its modern form had its effective origins in a mid-nineteenth-century analogy between one rule, the witness privilege, and another, the confession rule.

The phrase *privilege against self-incrimination* is sometimes used to mean any rule or aspiration facilitating silence. At other times it refers to the modern right to remain silent. This chapter explores the appearance of the privilege in the latter sense. It guarantees that no person can be required to answer a question tending to expose him to a criminal prosecution and also that a criminal defendant may refuse to testify altogether. The right is a strong one; any statement acquired in violation of the privilege is inadmissible at trial, and, in the United States, any evidence discovered because of such a statement is inadmissible generally. A witness can invoke the privilege even after answering earlier questions; merely answering some does not waive the privilege. And witnesses and defendants are entitled to a warning about the consequences of a waiver.

Such a full privilege did not exist at the beginning of the nineteenth century. In England until 1837 the criminal defendant had no right to have *145* counsel address the jury. If he wished a speech to be made to the jury, he had to make it himself. The more draconian the consequences of invoking a right to silence, the less often it can be invoked by sensible defendants, and therefore the less effective it can be. So it had proved with the privilege, and instead of the full privilege, the early nineteenth century knew an array of rules and maxims related to the subject of silence, none of which, alone or together, afforded defendants or witnesses an effective right. The maxim *Nemo tenetur* was certainly known. But it was not an effective rule in contemporary legal practice. The actual rules in force were three:

(1) *The disqualification for interest.* The disqualification for interest required silence by disallowing the testimony on oath of defendants, other parties in both criminal and civil trials, and all those with an interest in the outcome of the case. Far from being a right to silence, the disqualification was a burden on parties.

(2) *The confession rule.* Statements made under the hope of favor or fear of consequences were inadmissible at trial. The rule only applied to statements made on oath before a magistrate at pretrial. This exclusionary remedy extended to all pretrial statements, since the rule treated any statement on oath as compelled. It did not protect mere witnesses, however.

(3) *The witness privilege.* Third-party witnesses were protected by a privilege that can be regarded as the precursor to the full privilege. They were not required to answer questions that might later incriminate them or even hurt their reputation. The rule was, however, far weaker than the modern privilege. It applied to witnesses only, since parties were forbidden to testify because of their disqualification for interest. Waiver of this privilege was easy to find if the witness answered any question. Most important, the privilege carried no exclusionary remedy; its violation did not result in exclusion of the affected evidence.

None of these rules afforded a full or effective right to silence, much less the exclusionary rule that is familiar today. The full privilege against self-incrimination developed through an analogical extension of the witness privilege. That privilege was expanded to include the requirement of explicit waiver, invocation even after partial testimony, and, above all, the exclusionary remedy of the confession rule. A pivotal vehicle for the analogy was the case of *R. v. Garbett* (1847).[1] That decision, however, did not occur suddenly. Rather, it arose in the context of several developments in the law:

(1) *Lawyerization of the criminal trial.* During the eighteenth century, defense counsel played an increasingly central role in the criminal trial, allowing defendants to refrain from serving as an informational resource. In England, this trend culminated in 1836 with the grant of a full right to counsel, including the right to have counsel address the jury.

(2) *Jervis's Act of 1848.* The first of three famous statutes proposed by Attorney General Sir John Jervis, "An Act to facilitate the Performance of the Duties of Justices of the Peace out of Sessions within England and Wales with respect to Persons charged with Indictable Offenses,"[2] required for the first time that the accused be cautioned about his right to silence in the pretrial investigation. The justice of the peace (JP) was directed to warn the accused that the accused need not say anything, but that anything the accused might say would be taken down and might be used against him at trial. This statute can be regarded as officially ending the Marian pretrial procedure of examination of the prisoner by a magistrate.[3]

(3) *Elimination of the disqualification for interest.* The disqualification for interest was abolished piecemeal and after much debate in the nineteenth century. The trend was to treat the interest of the potential witness as affecting his credibility rather than his competence. First, interested nonparties were allowed to testify, then parties to civil suits, and lastly criminal defendants.

(4) *The "gap" between the witness privilege and the confession rule.* A long line of cases in the 1820s and 1830s inconclusively addressed the question of how to treat the statement of a witness who later became a criminal defendant. Did he fall under the witness privilege (no exclusion) or under the confession rule (exclusion)? I call this a "gap" not only because it was a gap in what would be covered by a full right to silence, but also because contemporaries themselves felt that defendants who did not fall under the stronger confession rule needed more protection than the witness privilege afforded.

Applying the exclusionary remedy to a violation of a witness's right not to answer, as *Garbett* did, was most obviously a solution to (4), the problem of the witness-turned-prisoner. But the decision was not wholly new; it fit into a pattern of increasing opportunity (and need) for an effective right to silence. On the opportunity side, the increasing role of lawyers and, to a lesser extent, the official removal of Marian pretrial procedures made a right to silence practicable. On the other hand, the need for an effective right to silence was becoming more acute: the disqualification for interest, which prevented the accused from speaking on oath at all, was being progressively dismantled. When, as happened fully in England by 1898, the disqualification was removed by statute,[4] the defendant had to speak on oath unless he could rely on an effective right to silence. *Garbett* headed off this problem as well by granting an exclusionary remedy to parties. The rationale of the decision was that compelled self-incrimination generally should lead to exclusion in all proceedings; in this an effective right to silence was born.

This right to silence remained partially obscured in England until 1898, however, because the disqualification still forbade the accused to speak on oath, even if he wished to. As far as sworn statements are concerned, early evidence for the privilege must therefore be indirect. Beginning in the 1840s, treatises began adventurously to present a general right to silence.[5] While the disqualification was being removed from criminal defendants, the privilege also appeared frequently in the debates, and, finally, the removal of the disqualification for interest from defendants in criminal trials caused the privilege against self-incrimination to emerge from the partial shadow of the disqualification. The privilege applied freely as a right to silence in all its potential contexts.

II. RULES PROMOTING SILENCE IN THE EARLY NINETEENTH CENTURY

At the beginning of the nineteenth century, several rules governed the subject of silence on the part of various persons in court proceedings, but neither individually nor collectively did they afford an effective right to silence to criminal defendants. The three most important such rules were the disqualification of parties for interest, the witness privilege, and the confession rule. The disqualification of parties for interest mandated silence as far as testimony on oath was concerned. That rule was unrelated to the privilege against self-incrimination: it was not limited to criminal defendants, nor was it designed to protect them. Of the remaining two rules—which permitted silence and which were associated loosely in the treatises with the maxim *Nemo tenetur*—only one, the witness privilege, can be regarded as the direct forerunner of the privilege against self-incrimination. It was, however, far narrower and weaker than the modern privilege.

A. Disqualification of Parties for Interest

The disqualification of parties for interest is centrally important to the history of the privilege against self-incrimination. This section therefore describes the wide scope of the party-witness disqualification and shows that its effect on one particular class, defendants in criminal trials, was not only to mandate silence (as elsewhere) but to foreclose thereby the very choice of testifying or not testifying on oath that the privilege against self-incrimination provides modern-day defendants.

1. Scope and Rationale of the Disqualification for Interest

The disqualification of parties for interest that continued to hold at the beginning of the nineteenth century was a rule different in scope and rationale from the privilege against self-incrimination, applying not only to criminal defendants but to all directly interested parties in order to prevent them from testifying falsely.[6] That this disqualification was one purely of interest should come as no surprise since it obtained in both civil and criminal proceedings. In civil trials it applied to both plaintiffs and defendants, preventing them from giving self-serving false testimony by keeping them from testifying at all. The treatise writer Thomas Peake complained that the rule, even narrowed down to "direct interest," was prone to uncertain application.[7] Indeed it seems that its uncertainty resulted from its breadth: it was extremely difficult to do without the testimony of the parties and others with a direct interest. Excluding such evidence could easily work substantial injustice where the most important evidence could come only from one who had such a direct interest.

Such a wide rule—and it was always treated as a unitary rule—was not primarily motivated by concern for the accused in a criminal trial. Rather, it reflected the concern to forestall perjury. As late as 1839, the treatise writer Samuel March Phillips gave a justification for the noncompellability of a party in terms quite at odds with *Nemo tenetur:* "As a party to the suit is not suffered to be a witness in support of his own interest, so he is never compelled in courts of law to give evidence for the opposite party against himself."[8] Note that the later part of this statement receives a verbal formulation similar in some respects to the privilege against self-incrimination. But it is not the privilege. Rather, as this passage makes clear, it is a corollary drawn from a disadvantage that had nothing to do with the defendant's protection and everything to do with an attempt to limit his chance to commit perjury. One must be careful in interpreting statements that sound like formulations of the privilege against self-incrimination.

Later treatise writers were not so careful. They sought a connection between the interest rationale for the disqualification and the maxim *Nemo tenetur.* Simon Greenleaf, for example, discussed the traditional reasoning that the disqualification minimized the temptation to perjury,[9] but in the next section he also cited *Nemo tenetur*.[10] Interestingly, the English cases he cited in support, *R. v. Woburn* (1808)[11] and *Worrall v. Jones* (1831),[12] had nothing to do with *Nemo tenetur,* having been decided solely on grounds of interest.[13] The one American case he cited, *Commonwealth v. Marsh* (1830),[14] was likewise unrelated to *Nemo tenetur.* It had been decided mainly on the basis of interest and the "public policy" of preventing perjury. The concern in the cases was not with protecting defendants but with keeping them from "evad[ing] the ends of justice."[15]

Greenleaf thus overstated his case, trying to unify the rules and maxims further than the sources should have justified. In all cases, but most obviously in civil cases, the rationale for the disqualification was the existence of interest. The prevention-of-perjury rationale may well be related to interest: interested parties are more likely to perjure themselves. But Greenleaf's association of the maxim *Nemo tenetur* with the disqualification was novel. Describing the disqualification as a privilege rather than the burden it was shows in this innovative context how malleable the *Nemo tenetur* maxim was. Since it had no determinate meaning, it was available as an ad hoc incantation wherever silence was at issue.

More generally, Greenleaf should be counted as an innovator in the law of silence. In addition to trying to connect the disqualification with *Nemo tenetur,* he tried to bring closer the two rules permitting silence, the witness privilege and the confession rule. He was, however, quite uncomfortable with the fit between treating an oath as (per se) compulsion and the reliability rationale for the confession rule:

> It may, at first view, appear unreasonable to refuse evidence of a confession, merely because it was made under oath, thus having, in favor of its truth, one of the highest sanctions known in the law. But it is to be observed, that none but voluntary confessions are admissible; and that if to the perplexities and embarrassments of the prisoner's situation are added the danger of perjury, and the dread of additional penalties, the confession can scarcely be regarded as voluntary; but, on the contrary, it seems to be made under the very influences, which the law is particularly solicitous to avoid.[16]

Greenleaf immediately went on to note that the witness privilege, although similar, worked differently:

> But where a prisoner, being examined as a witness, in a prosecution against another person, answers questions, to which he might have demurred as tending to criminate himself, and which, therefore, he was not bound to

answer, his answers are deemed voluntary, and as such, may be subsequently used against himself, for all purposes; though where his answers are compulsory, and under the peril of punishment for contempt, they are not received.[17]

This passage shows that Greenleaf was aware of the mismatch between the confession rule and the witness privilege. He strove mightily to reconcile the two on the basis of "compulsory" answering. He was concerned with exactly the gap—third-party witnesses who later were defendants—that troubled the courts in the cases to which I will turn shortly.[18] The law on this question was indeed unsettled in the 1820s and 1830s.[19] Greenleaf nonetheless sought to interpret the treatment of witnesses in a manner consistent with that of criminal defendants under the confession rule. While admitting that what counted as compulsion for purposes of the confession rule did not necessarily count as compulsion for the witness privilege (e.g., a statement on oath might be deemed voluntary under the witness privilege but could not be under the confession rule), he analogized the case of an objecting witness as closely as possible to that of an accused. But the analogy could not erase the difference in how the two rules were invoked: the accused—unlike the witness—would *not* have to object in order for the answers to be deemed involuntary. Nor, on an intuitive level, does it make much sense to say that a witness was testifying "voluntarily" just because he failed to raise the witness privilege objection. Ignorance is not willingness.

The disqualification for interest had not been associated with the maxim *Nemo tenetur* in the early nineteenth century. It was instead a burden on those with any interest in litigation that might induce them to testify in a self-serving way. However, as Greenleaf had sought to bring the disqualification and the *Nemo tenetur* maxim closer together, so later treatise writers similarly found novel uses for the maxim. It was cited in an uneasy connection with the disqualification, to such an extent that less innovative treatise writers could take the more adventurous writers to task for making this stretch.[20]

2. Noncompellability under the Disqualification

A misreading of such verbal formulas referring to the disqualification lies at the heart of previous views on the origins of the privilege against self-incrimination. In particular, the word *compulsion* in nineteenth-century legal parlance had two distinct senses. One, closer to the everyday sense of the term, meant "force operating to negate the role of an individual's free will." This is the sense on which the confession rule was built,[21] but, as will be discussed shortly, the confession rule excluded only some forms of what might be regarded as compulsion in the everyday sense of the word. The second sense of *compulsion,* and the one Phillips was using in the above-quoted passage, is the reverse side of competence. The permission to give evidence in one's own behalf is competence, that is, the ability to call oneself as a witness. Compellability is being subject to being called as a witness by the opposing party. The difference between competence and compellability lies in who is doing the calling of the witness. The term *compellable* featured as part of a formula that sounds as if it were referring to confession-rule-like compulsion, but the reasoning behind the disqualification belies any such connection.[22] *Compellable* and *compulsion* in the context of the disqualification simply meant that one was subject to being "called by the other side."

Leonard Levy, like many others, falls into exactly this trap of confusing the two senses of *compulsion.* As a result, he wrongly identifies the disqualification with the privilege. For example, Levy finds evidence for the privilege in misreading the manuscript records of William Smith, a member of the New York governor's council, who investigated and prepared a 1760 report on illicit trading:

> Smith accepted [one of the ship's master's] evidence against others but did not require him to inform against himself. The master himself, "being Particeps Crimin[is] [a party to the crime] can not be compelled to answer." Offenders, said Smith, should be prosecuted only if sufficient proof of guilt could be obtained. In a case of 1702, Chief Justice Atwood had prevented David Jamison from testifying on behalf of Bayard because Jamison "is *particeps criminis* for which reason he cannot be allowed as evidence." But the case of the master in 1760 involved one who could not be *compelled.* Jamison, as an alleged party to the crime, could not be *allowed* to testify because his interest in the case had disqualified him. The master, by contrast, was not disqualified for interest; he was protected against self-incrimination.[23]

Levy attempts to distinguish the two cases on the basis of a distinction between *compelled* and *allowed* and concludes that the 1760 case did not involve disqualification because the former rather than the latter word was used. Here, as elsewhere, he sees the privilege where he encounters the word *compelled.* However, both the 1760 and the 1702 cases explicitly rest on the fact that the person in question was a participant in the crime, hence interested. The use of the term *compelled* is fully consistent with reading both passages naturally as referring to the disqualification for interest. For the disqualification, *compelled* simply means "not callable." It is just one side of allowability. The only difference between Levy's two cases is the specificity of the term used to refer to the disqualification. The fact that the word *compellable* is used brings us no closer to the privilege, and Levy's example provides no evidence for the privilege. Confusion about the meaning of *compulsion* is a major source of error in the search for the origins of the privilege against self-incrimination.

B. The Confession Rule

A second rule that has been confused with the privilege against self-incrimination is the confession rule. There are several reasons why commentators have tended to identify the confession rule with the privilege against self-incrimination, none of which is ultimately persuasive. First, there was a rhetorical association of the confession rule with the maxim *Nemo tenetur prodere seipsum*. However, the maxim was generally invoked when a rule treated silence favorably; the confession rule's favorable treatment of silence fell far short of that afforded by the modern privilege. Second, the confession rule was associated with an exclusionary remedy; confessions extorted by compulsion were not admissible at trial. This exclusionary remedy, however, was limited only to coerced confessions. It did not create a generalized right to silence.[24] Third, although the confession rule was formulated in terms of compulsion, it was a very different kind of compulsion from that involved in the disqualification rule.[25] The "compulsion" element, along with the exclusionary remedy, would be important later to the confession rule's role in the analogy that created the privilege against self-incrimination, but the compulsion here was quite specific to the problem of an accused being examined in the pretrial process. Because the confession rule was narrowly focused on that context, it was distinct from both the party-witness disqualification and the witness privilege, not an instance of the (later) full privilege against self-incrimination.

1. Scope of the Confession Rule
The confession rule was well established by the beginning of the nineteenth century. For our purposes, the earliest origins of the rule are not as important as its scope and associations at that time. The classical formulation, on which treatise accounts were based, is found in *Warickshall's Case* (1783).[26] In it, the defendant claimed that evidence should be excluded because it had been found as a result of a confession she had been induced to make

by "promises of favor."[27] Her contention was that "as the fact of finding the stolen property in her custody had been obtained through the means of an inadmissible confession, the proof of that fact ought also to be rejected; for otherwise the faith with which the prosecutor had pledged would be violated, and the prisoner made the deluded instrument of her own conviction."[28] The court rejected this claim, essentially the "fruits of the poisonous tree" doctrine,[29] stating that "no such rule ever prevailed."[30] It held instead that the evidence was properly allowed, applying what came to be known as the "confession rule":

> A free and voluntary confession is deserving of the highest credit, because it is presumed to flow from the strongest sense of guilt, and therefore it is admitted as proof of the crime to which it refers; but a confession forced from the mind by the flattery of hope, or by the torture of fear, comes in so questionable a shape when it is to be considered as the evidence of guilt, that no credit ought to be given to it; and therefore it is rejected.[31]

The "flattery of hope" was a constant danger of the Crown witness system, in which one accomplice in a crime went free in return for testimony against the other; each had an obvious motive to perjure himself.[32] The confession rule can be seen as one response to this source of unreliability.[33] The "torture of fear" could similarly induce a false confession. The rationale for the rule was reliability; since both the fruits of any confession and a "voluntary" confession were regarded as highly reliable, they were admitted. Involuntary confessions were excluded, since they could not be trusted.[34]

    A foundation of this rule was lack of compulsion. The notion of compulsion for purposes of the rule was so narrow, however, that it did not reach the examination of the prisoner by a magistrate that the Marian Committal Statute of 1555 expressly directed.[35] Interestingly, immediately after stating that the prisoner may not be put on oath, Phillips says that the magistrate "is directed to take *the examination of such person*"[36] and notes that "[t]he words in the act [the statute of Philip and Mary], respecting the taking of *the examination,* imply an authority given to examine the prisoner, and, therefore, to put questions (for without questions no examination can be carried on) as to the facts proven against him."[37] Furthermore, in a footnote Phillips cites evidence that the "power, given by the statute, was exercised with great harshness" and worked against a prisoner's silence.[38]

2. Confession-Rule "Compulsion"

The exact contours of "compulsion" for purposes of the confession rule are difficult to discern. The rule reflected a concern about excessive inducement, so that if a judge found no excess in the inducement to confess, there would be no "compulsion." A notable example is the case of *R. v. Gilham* (1828), in which the prisoner was exhorted by a visiting cleric on more than one occasion that "before God it would be better for him to confess his sins."[39] The jail keeper, seeing the prisoner's distress during their conversations, had given the prisoner Bible passages to read and had encouraged him to seek the chaplain's counsel. The chaplain spoke with the prisoner several times and at trial "stated the prisoner's agitation and perturbed state of mind during the interview was so great, that he could not help being aware that the prisoner had something pressing on his mind."[40] In between interviews the cleric consulted with the magistrate, and at the interview the cleric told the prisoner he could not help him unless he confessed. The court allowed the confession the prisoner eventually made, resting its decision on two reasons:

> The whole argument, therefore, on the other side [in favor of excluding the confession], as to the religious impressions [i.e., alleged compulsion], is founded on fallacy; because the motives are not of a class that can justify a fair and reasonable suspicion, that the confessions given under such motives are untrue. And with regard to any temporal hopes, none such existed; or, if they did exist, the effect of them is entirely got rid of by the cautions given the prisoner [that he need not confess] before the confessions were made.[41]

The court did not say that the "cautions" given the prisoner were sufficient to counteract the religious impulse he felt to confess. The court also did not say that the prisoner was not influenced. It is true that the influence was "religious," but it is curious why that should matter. After all, the confession rule treated statements on oath as per se compelled because a prisoner would feel compelled by the religious character of the oath.[42] Only later, in a less religious age, did the prospect of a perjury prosecution become the source of compulsion.[43] The prisoner in *Gilham* may well have been as flustered as someone facing a perjury prosecution, but what influenced him failed to fall within the rule's definition of *compulsion*.[44]

Examining the accused on oath counted as per se compulsion, whether the oath was likely to produce false testimony or not. The general rule was that the prisoner might not be examined on oath, and if he were, the examination could not be used in evidence against him.[45] So much was clear. What was not clear, even to early-nineteenth-century commentators, was the exact justification for this per se rule. Thomas Starkie exhibited discomfort with the rationale even as he trotted it out: "The prisoner is not to be examined on oath, for this would be a species of duress, and a violation of the maxim, that no one is bound to criminate himself."[46] But in a footnote, he acknowledged the problem that this did not explain why an oath did not count as compulsion in the case of witnesses, and he noted that he was not alone in his worry: "It generally happens that a party who is examined upon oath before the magistrate, is examined as a *witness* against others, and under the expectation that he will not be prosecuted. It has been said that a prisoner ought not to be questioned by a magistrate. . . ."[47] This is the same concern with the Crown witness inducement that John Langbein has identified as motivating the confession rule.[48] Starkie then cited *R. v. Wilson* (1817) as his sole example of a case in which a prisoner's examination not on oath was excluded because a magistrate should not have examined the prisoner at all.[49] But he acknowledged that this flew in the face of the Marian Committal Statute, which directed the magistrate to examine the prisoner.[50] Starkie even noted that, in a then-recent case, Holroyd, J., had admitted the prisoner's examination over this very objection.[51] And in *R. v. Ellis* (1826),[52] which overruled *R. v. Wilson,* Littledale, J., noting that *R. v. Wilson* and the contrary case were both cited by Starkie, pronounced Holroyd's decision correct: a prisoner's unsworn answers to questions put by a magistrate were, if made without threat or promise, admissible as evidence.[53]

Two lessons can be drawn from *R. v. Wilson* and Starkie's ambivalence. First, around the edges of the confession rule there was some temptation to expand the notion of compulsion. In particular, commentators were quite aware that the maxim *Nemo tenetur* proved too much to be actually applied as formulated, but they were uncomfortable with the lack of fit between the maxim and current practice. The narrowness of the confession rule and—as we will see—the witness privilege, in contrast with the broad-sounding maxim, presented a problem with which courts grappled throughout the 1820s and 1830s. Second, early-nineteenth-century judges and lawyers were fully aware of the anomalies inherent in the legal notion of compulsion on which the confession rule rested. We will return to examine this awareness more closely.[54]

C. The Witness Privilege

The full privilege against self-incrimination has its origins in another rule, the witness privilege, that permitted rather than mandated silence. The witness privilege allowed a nonparty witness to refuse to testify to any question that would have the tendency to expose him or her to future prosecution. This rule—unlike the disqualification for interest—was associated with the maxim *Nemo tenetur*. It would, however, be a mistake to identify the witness privilege of the early nineteenth century with the later full privilege against self-incrimination. First, the remedy for violation of the witness privilege was not exclusion. Second, and more fundamentally, the witness privilege was a right of third parties, not of the parties to the instant case, who had no choice but not to testify because of their disqualification for interest. The early-nineteenth-century witness privilege was simply irrelevant to the plight of a criminal defendant at trial.

1. The Scope of the Witness Privilege
The core of this rule was that no witness was compellable to answer a question that would incriminate him or even tend to incriminate him.[55] Although authorities seem to have agreed on this core, none mentioned the consequences of wrongfully compelling a witness. The witness could raise the objection and might not be subject to contempt of court, but there is no evidence until several decades later that exclusion of the testimony from use in a subsequent proceeding against the witness was a consequence of a violation of the witness privilege.[56] If a third-party witness was wrongfully compelled to testify, the witness privilege did not bar the use of that testimony in his subsequent criminal prosecution. And, as we will see, the idea that exclusion would be a remedy was treated as a novelty in the 1847 *Garbett* case, suggesting strongly that the early-nineteenth-century witness privilege was not backed up by an exclusionary remedy.[57] This is all the more striking since the confession rule, by contrast, was a "remedially" exclusionary rule that led to later exclusion of the confession obtained.[58]

At the beginning of the nineteenth century, the witness privilege seems to have extended beyond the core of statements that might lead to future criminal prosecution, but further applicability of the rule was more controversial. According to the treatises, the privilege was quite broad, including statements that could potentially subject one to any penalty, civil action, debt, or even degrading revelation.[59] Peake devoted a considerable footnote to the privilege based on potential civil liability, after observing that "[i]t has also been held, that this rule of law [witness privilege] protects a man's pecuniary interests, as well as his person, from punishment; and that therefore he is not compellable to give any answer which may subject him to a civil action, or charge himself with a debt."[60] As late as 1877, J. F. Archbold devoted a section to the protection the witness privilege afforded against having to provide answers that would degrade the witness's character.[61]

If one traces the witness privilege back earlier than the nineteenth century, one finds evidence that in the eyes of the treatise writers this breadth of the witness privilege suggested associations that had very little to do with the confession rule or with policies that we would associate with the right to silence. Interestingly, Hawkins even placed the witness privilege with the disqualification of a previously convicted witness to testify, which he explained first:

> As to the fourth Particular, *viz.* Where a Person shall be disabled to be a Witness in Respect of his having been attainted or convicted of a Crime: It seems agreed, That a Conviction, and therefore *a fortiori* an Attainder . . . being in a Court which had Jurisdiction, are good Causes of Exception against a Witness, while they continue in force.
>
> But it is agreed, That no such Conviction or Judgment can be made use of to this Purpose, unless the Record be actually produced in Court. *Also it is a general Rule that a Witness shall not be asked any Question the answering to which might oblige him to accuse himself of a Crime;* and that his Credit is to be impeached only by general Accounts of his Character and Reputation, and not by Proofs of particular Crimes, whereof he never was convicted.[62]

Textually, William Hawkins's treatment of the witness privilege is closely intertwined with the disqualification for former conviction but quite separate from the confession rule.[63] This suggests that the concern of both the prior-conviction rule and the witness privilege was not to avoid a possible future conviction—in the case of the prior-conviction rule, the conviction was safely in the past—but rather to prevent discouraging witnesses from testifying truthfully. Neither the witness privilege nor the prior-conviction rule was necessarily about convictions at all. Both rules were about reputational harms, whether they stemmed from convictions or other embarrassing material that would inhibit truthful testimony on the part of the witness.[64] Although it is true that both the prior-conviction rule and the witness privilege *could* involve a prosecution of the witness, their rationale was to insulate the witness from certain influences harmful to the testimony. The witness privilege's breadth was required, on this policy, since it had to cover all material that was felt to have this inhibiting effect on the witness. It was not a response to the narrow "compulsion" of the confession rule.

In the following decades, the scope of the witness privilege contracted sharply. The parts eliminated first were the more tenuous reputational harms. By the time Peake wrote in 1801, the witness privilege had already become too narrow to be identified closely with the prior-conviction rule:

> [Proving a former conviction by means of a copy of the judgment] was formerly the only mode by which the objection could be raised, for it was then considered as a rule, that no man could be examined to prove his own infamy; but by the modern decisions on this subject, though a man cannot be asked any question tending to convict him of a crime, and thereby be put in danger from his own examination, yet he may be asked whether he is already convicted, and has suffered the judgment of the law; for his answer to these questions can put him in no further peril.[65]

While acknowledging the earlier connection, Peake distinguished the two rules. The witness privilege covered the threat of future prosecution only. Thus, at the beginning of the nineteenth century, the witness privilege was actually narrower than it had been a few decades earlier, and, as we will see, it may not have extended even as far as Peake would have it.[66]

2. The Witnesses Act of 1806

The history of the Witnesses' Declaratory Bill (now known as the Witnesses Act of 1806) demonstrates the unclarity of the contemporary witness privilege.[67] In 1806 the House of Lords was preparing to impeach Lord Melville for "gross malversion and breach of duty" as treasurer of the navy, and certain key witnesses' testimony was required.[68] To remove the witness-privilege objection, it was proposed to grant the witnesses immunity through a witnesses' indemnity bill, and in order to remove their disqualifying interest they were to be indemnified for certain debts that might turn on the outcome of the impeachment. However, the scope of the immunity that would be required to remove the first (witness-privilege) objection immediately became a contentious issue. It was clear that, without immunity from criminal prosecution, the witnesses could raise the witness privilege. Thus, the witnesses' indemnity bill had to include immunity from future criminal prosecution.[69] It was also proposed to give them immunity from civil suit, including suit for debt. However, there were immediate objections that this was unnecessary. The objectors claimed that the existing witness privilege did not provide protection for a witness fearing exposure to civil suit and therefore the witnesses did not merit civil immunity to remove the witness-privilege objection. The solution to this impasse was to ask a panel of judges whether (1) a witness might object to a question on the grounds of possible future civil liability, (2) might object because of a possible suit for the recovery of profits from public money, or (3) might object on the grounds of interest even though the witness was indemnified. The answer that came back was less than clear:

> The Judges were, however, upon those two questions, which they considered to be resolved into one [witness privilege], divided in opinion. Those who were of opinion that a witness in such a case could not demur, might be prepared to give a decisive answer to that effect, but with respect to those who were of a contrary opinion, that opinion was qualified by a great number of exceptions. . . . With respect to the 3d question [disqualification for interest], they were unanimously of opinion, that a witness in the situation described, could not be repelled on the ground of being interested. . . .[70]

In the face of this answer, Lord Eldon, who had expressed the opinion that there could be no doubt that the witness privilege extended to fear of civil liability,[71] acknowledged that he was obliged to retract his earlier pronouncement.[72] A lengthy debate ensued on what the law was—or should be—on the extent of the witness privilege.[73] During that debate, Lord Chancellor Erskine called Peake's version of the witness privilege into question for overstating its scope.[74] The debate showed that practice left much room for doubt. Since some of the judges were of the opinion that the privilege did extend as far as Peake said, it was possible that practice could extend that far as a matter of judicial discretion, but that instances of such application did not amount to the firm rule stated by Peake.[75] Furthermore, it may have been that, since the witness privilege was contracting in this period, Peake was simply behind the times. This debate provides another view of some of the same points raised in cases and treatises. What emerged from the debate was that practice in applying the witness privilege varied. Moreover, the debates underscore the need to approach the treatises with caution. They typically state propositions in positive form, with little hint of the division of opinion that may have obtained.

After much debate, the solution reached was to settle the law of the witness privilege generally in a bill renamed the Witnesses' Declaratory Bill. The final version stated this proposition negatively: a witness could not refuse to answer a question solely because the reply might expose him to civil liability.[76] The legislative history of the bill provides some evidence against the existence of a general privilege against self-incrimination and in particular against identifying the witness privilege with the full privilege against self-incrimination. Application of the witness privilege in cases of fear of civil liability was treated as a question of the law of evidence; the lord chancellor, an opponent of the bill, expressly contrasted it with "viola-tion[s] of a principle of the constitution" that he regarded as more appro-priate subjects for declaratory acts.[77] Significantly, *Nemo tenetur* was never mentioned. The closest the debates got to principled reasons for a wide scope of the witness privilege were rhetorical invocations of the "genius and principles of the old law of England" and the "common sense of man-kind" in support of applying the witness privilege to fear of exposure to debt actions.[78] The debates are most consistent with the conclusion that no effective right to silence then existed in fact.

3. The Witness Privilege and the Confession Rule Contrasted

Neither the witness privilege nor the confession rule served the function at the beginning of the nineteenth century that the privilege against self-incrimination does today. Both rules were distinct from each other and also from the later, full privilege against self-incrimination. Unlike the modern privilege, the confession rule was backed by an exclusionary remedy: viola-tions of the confession rule's requirement of voluntariness led to exclusion of the resulting material from the criminal trial. The witness privilege was not exclusionary except in the weaker sense that its invocation led to less evidence being introduced. Treatise writers were not wrong to discuss the two rules under separate headings.[79]

A related and crucial difference between the witness privilege and the confession rule was the prohibition on partial testimony, associated only with the former. A prisoner could claim the protection of the confession rule at any time during an interrogation. The witness privilege afforded far less protection. A witness who answered some questions had waived his privilege and could not refuse to answer further questions.[80] This prohibi-tion on partial testimony survived in England until *R. v. Garbett* (1847)[81] and in the United States until the 1880s.[82] In one of the leading English cases, *East v. Chapman* (1827), Abbott, C.J., made the revealing remark that "[w]hether the evidence received in mitigation of damages [the witness's previous statement] was admissible or not, may perhaps be matter of doubt; but where there is doubt, I think it best to receive it."[83] Such an attitude is not what one would expect in the face of an effective right to silence. It is understandable as a rough-and-ready approach to a law of evidence that prevailed.

Since the witness privilege and the confession rule were different and distinct rules at the beginning of the nineteenth century, one can now ask what positive evidence there is that they were connected at all. The answer is that whatever connection there was consisted of an association of each rule with a pro-silence policy; discussion of both rules often led to a citation of *Nemo tenetur*. An early example is Peake's transition to his discussion of the witness privilege: "I observed before, that no one could be compelled to give evidence which tended to charge himself with a crime."[84] The 1824 American edition also cited the *Nemo tenetur* maxim in discussing the witness privilege.[85] When Starkie attempted a fuller explanation of the desirability of the *Nemo tenetur* policy, he touched on many of the themes that would later be applied to the general privilege:

> Upon a principle of humanity, as well as of policy, every witness is protected from answering questions by doing which he would criminate himself. Of policy, because it would place the witness under the strongest temptation to commit the crime of perjury; and of humanity, because it would be to extort a confession of the truth by a kind of duress, every species and degree of which the law abhors. It is pleasing to contrast the humanity and delicacy of the law of England, in this respect, with the cruel provisions of the Roman law, which allowed criminals, and even witnesses, in some instances, to be put to the torture, for the purpose of extorting a confession. That a people, so polite and so learned, should tolerate an usage so barbarous, and a policy so mistaken, creates both surprize [*sic*] and regret.[86]

Starkie identified the witness privilege and the confession rule on the level of policy, but he distinguished them as two separate rules, treating the confession rule under the heading "Admissions."[87] He recognized that the witness privilege was related, but noted only the contrast between the two: the confession rule was exclusionary to a greater extent than the witness privilege since "[w]here a witness answers questions upon examination upon trial, tending to criminate himself, and to which he might have demurred, his answers may be used for all purposes."[88] Furthermore, *Nemo tenetur*—not cited here but referred to—was called a "policy." It may well be doubted how strong this was, even on the level of policy, since so much else of English criminal procedure was designed to force the accused to speak and to minimize expense and trouble.[89]

III. COVERING THE SELF-INCRIMINATION TERRITORY

At the beginning of the nineteenth century the accused lacked rights that would ensure that keeping silent at trial might actually be advantageous to him. Two of these missing rights were the right to a full defense by counsel, including the right to have counsel address the jury, and the right to a warning that the accused could legitimately remain silent during pretrial and trial. Since the defendant's counsel could not address the jury, the accused had to choose between silence and addressing the jury himself. Thus, silence on the part of the accused still came at a high price. Imposing such a price is inconsistent with an effective right to remain silent at trial. In this respect, what Langbein has termed the "accused speaks" trial—a trial centered on the accused as an informational resource—remained in force.[90]

This situation was to change, and the debates surrounding the adoption of the full right to counsel in 1836 provide indirect evidence about the right to silence. The arguments make the most sense if one assumes that there was no such effective right. Significantly, in light of the wide-ranging discussion that occurred about the opportunities, advantages, and disadvantages for an accused who remained silent, the maxim *Nemo tenetur* and the concept of silence as a right were not mentioned once during the debates. The second right acquired by criminal defendants during this period, the right to a warning, also afforded the accused a greater opportunity to benefit from keeping silent; it ensured that he would be aware of the ability to remain silent in the first place. Although not constituting a full, effective right to silence, securing these new rights made its later formation a possibility.

A. The Right to Full Defense by Counsel

At the beginning of the nineteenth century, a criminal defendant had a right to a lawyer who could advise him on points of law and examine and cross-examine witnesses but could not address the jury. The right to counsel had developed over time, the last step before this period being the new right of counsel to examine witnesses. We will see that there was a contemporary awareness that the subjects of right to counsel and an effective opportunity to keep silent were intimately related. For one thing, the greater the right to have counsel speak for one, the easier it was to keep silent oneself. In addition, a legal rule that held through much of the nineteenth century provided that one had no right both to have counsel speak for one and to make an unsworn statement oneself.[91] The extent of the right to counsel and the ease of keeping silent were both legally and practically related.

Allowance of a full right to defense counsel in felony cases was an important step toward creating an effective right to silence. Indeed, the debates on the subject were one of the last stages in the development of the unimpeded right. The terms of that debate reflect a clear understanding that what was at stake was the possibility of actual silence on the part of the accused. But they were not framed in terms of the *rights* of the accused. If *Nemo tenetur* already provided a core right to silence at trial during the decades of these debates, then one would expect discussion of a privilege against self-incrimination to feature prominently in the debate. That it did not provides evidence, albeit indirect, that the effective right to keep silent was new.

Introduction of the right to defense by counsel in cases of felony was a topic hotly debated on at least three occasions. A bill to allow full defense by counsel for prisoners in cases of felony was introduced in 1824, but it failed.[92] Likewise in 1826.[93] A new bill was introduced in 1833,[94] and it became law in 1836.[95] In the debates, both proponents and opponents of the bills adduced many arguments, some quite fanciful and anachronistic.[96] But *Nemo tenetur* did not figure among them.

1. Concern for the Plight of the Accused

Proponents of the bills frequently invoked the plight of criminal defendants. They spoke at length and in minute detail about the dangers to an innocent accused who was fearful, flustered, or inarticulate. The Second Report of the Commissioners on Criminal Law, published in 1824, opened with a typical statement to this effect. After conceding that some defendants might be able to defend themselves well, the report contended that

> [s]uch, however, is not the ordinary case; it much more frequently happens, that an innocent person is surprised and confused by false evidence, and rendered incapable of making an efficient defence by a forcible exposition of the improbabilities and discrepancies arising on a nice comparison of facts, which may be the only means of discovering the truth and rescuing an innocent man.[97]

Such arguments would be a natural opening for citation of a right to silence, but none occurs. These arguments assumed that the main problem was that defendants would not speak well, not that they were being asked to do something they had a right to refuse to do. The argument was that defendants would have little chance "of attending to the merits of the case,"[98] not that they were being illegally required to speak to the merits.

Although this concern with the unreliability of flustered defendants may have been overstated, it is still striking that *Nemo tenetur* or a right to silence was nowhere mentioned. George Lamb, for instance, evidently saw no fundamental problem with making defendants talk even while he deplored the treatment of an accused, "who, when put upon his trial for murder, was told repeatedly by the judge: 'Come, now, Mr. Cooper—no more flourishes; speak to the point.' Could such language have been used to any counsel, employed for Mr. Cooper, on such an occasion?"[99] The judge's behavior was typical of the "accused speaks" trial,[100] but Lamb's objection was to the lack of respect for the accused—not to what would be an obvious violation of a right to silence. Such a right would have permitted the accused not to speak at all if he did not wish to. Lamb, however, did not make that argument, for no such effective right was practicable.

A variant on this theme was the argument that the then-current system was unfair to defendants who were physically unable to speak, for example, mute, insane, or alien defendants.[101] The argument presupposed that the main problem with forcing such defendants to speak was that they were not equipped to speak at all, or at least very well. Despite a clear understanding about the disadvantages to the accused of having to speak, a *right* not to speak never came up. If contemporaries had thought there already was an effective right to silence, an argument that such a defendant was being asked to do something he had a right to refuse would have been called for. But it is conspicuously absent.

2. Advantages and Disadvantages to the Accused of Silence
Even though a right to silence was not mentioned in the debates, the possibility of silence on the part of the accused was considered in great detail. However, it was either considered a disadvantage or taken to be an incidental opportunity, not a matter of right. The dilemma of a physically mute defendant, just mentioned, is one example. More generally, when the topic of silence arose, it was usually treated as a disadvantage. Proponents envisioned a real problem "if these forlorn and disabled creatures [certain criminal defendants] were to have no counsel to plead for them—no voice to interpose in their behalf—when perhaps only a voice had been wanted to make their innocence manifest to all."[102] Their discussion, however, never left the tactical level. They did not mention the privilege—not even the *Nemo tenetur* maxim.

Opponents of these bills argued that the right to have counsel address the jury would actually work to the disadvantage of the accused. A speaker in the House of Lords objected that "[i]n any cases, it was to be remembered, in which counsel having the power of addressing the Court for a prisoner, declined to avail himself of that privilege, the possession of it could only act in condemnation of his client."[103] An opponent in the House of Commons objected that the measure would be "depriving accused persons of the most judicious defence that could generally be made, except by cross-examination—a total silence."[104] Not only did this opponent not mention impairment of a privilege against self-incrimination, he also discussed "adverse inference" in a fashion wholly inappropriate to the privilege:

> If the hon. Member should succeed in giving to a prisoner full defence by Counsel, he would drive him from the high vantage ground he now occupied; and bring him down into an arena of contention upon facts, forcing him to have a complete representative to whom, if he had any answer, that answer must be known, and from whom, therefore, it would be expected.[105]

This speaker's vantage point was not the privilege against self-incrimination, as one today might expect. Instead, this opponent was speaking of the law of proof, making an exaggerated claim about its effectiveness.[106]

3. The Accused as an Informational Resource

In the debates, there was an awareness that the accused who spoke was an informational resource. I use this term because the word *testimony* was associated with statements made on oath. Whether or not what the prisoner said was, strictly speaking, evidence—a matter of confusion and controversy during this period[107]—the proponents of these bills were well aware that any time the accused opened his mouth, he functioned as an informational resource. In a present-day trial, whenever an accused conducts his own defense, more inferences may be drawn from what the accused says and how the accused says it. The proponents of defense by counsel similarly noted the inference from the innocent defendant's poor conduct of his own defense:

> It frequently happens that hardened villains possess more coolness and composure than the innocent; and that the latter, instead of having even their ordinary reason and speech at command, are deprived of their usual presence of mind, and exhibit a degree of confusion which might seem to indicate a consciousness of guilt.[108]

Proponents also pointed out that the defendant was in a no-win situation since

[i]f he, by some accident, were enabled so to [present the merits of his case effectively], then there arose another class of objections and prejudices not less violent and dangerous: the feeling was, that he must be an experienced rogue. If under the circumstances described, he was able to make out a good case, he must be an old hand, an ancient practitioner, and thus he must either bring out no case at all, or bring it out to his disadvantage.[109]

The proponents brought up this point to prove the general unfairness to the accused, but they did not mention any impact such adverse inferences would have on the right to silence. This omission of an otherwise obvious argument calls into serious question the existence of an effective privilege against self-incrimination.

This line of argument by the proponents was countered by the opponents of the measure with a justification also at odds with an effective right to silence. The defenders of the status quo took a page from the history of the "accused speaks" trial: "As to information respecting the merits of the case, who could have shown more information than that individual [the defendant]?"[110] This argument is certainly inconsistent in spirit with a generalized right to silence. Made today, it would call forth a rejoinder based on the privilege against self-incrimination. Pointing to a right to silence, if one existed in practice, would have been the obvious answer. But, again, no one gave it.

4. The Judge as Counsel for the Prisoner

Although the maxim *Nemo tenetur* did not appear in these debates, the maxim that the court should serve as counsel for the prisoner did. The latter maxim was traditionally used to justify lack of counsel and a pressure on the accused to speak, and it is therefore significant despite being anachronistic or unrealistic. First, it shows how wrong it is to assume that because something is called a maxim—as *Nemo tenetur* equally was—it must have had an effect on practice.[111] Second, that *Nemo tenetur* was not mentioned at all is more striking when one considers that the court-as-counsel maxim was mentioned so often. Conceding that the court-as-counsel maxim was more germane in this debate, the discrepancy is nonetheless vast; court-as-counsel was invoked at least thirteen times during the debates,[112] and also at three points in the commission's report, *Nemo tenetur* not at all.[113] Finally, the use of the court-as-counsel maxim is significant because, anachronistic or not, it expressed the common assumption that if the defendant wanted an advocate, he had better be one himself.[114] The defendant would not be let off the hook as an informational resource. The judge lacked the information to be counsel for the defendant.[115] That an argument revolving around this subject did not touch on a privilege of silence suggests that the privilege was not a resource of the accused.

5. Presumption of Innocence and Standard of Proof

Other maxims that bore on the debate more indirectly than court-as-counsel were invoked quite often. Very prominent among these was the high burden of proof placed on the prosecution, which by this time was more than simply a maxim.[116] Opponents especially deplored one (bizarre) alleged disadvantage of granting a full right to defense by counsel: if the defendant's counsel could address the jury, they said, the defendant would lose some of the protection of the presumption of innocence.[117] Supposedly, an explanation from defendant's counsel would be expected by the trier of fact, whereas without counsel the defendant's silence was more excusable. He could depend on the presumption of innocence. Despite the tenuous quality of this argument, it abounds in the debate. By contrast, *Nemo tenetur* is never mentioned, and if it had been an effective rule in practice, it would have been at least as relevant to the debate as the burden of proof.[118]

6. Indulging the Accused

The debates also make a theme of supposed indulgence of the accused in traditional English criminal procedure.[119] Both supporters and opponents framed arguments from this "tenderness." Supporters pointed out that the denial of full defense by counsel was inconsistent with indulgent treatment of the accused.[120] Opponents stressed that the indulgence of the accused had in their opinion gone far enough already.[121]

A second, somewhat contradictory, current of the debate was to discredit the status quo by identifying it with the roughness of criminal trials in previous times. One proponent located "[t]he origin of our present practice . . . in the same system which adjudicated men to death on paper depositions, without confronting the prisoner with the witnesses against him, and inflicted torture on the prisoner, in order to extract from his own mouth evidence against him."[122] Rhetorically, this is reminiscent of the traditional *Nemo tenetur* maxim, but his point was a general one about previous harshness. He made no specific argument that denying a full right to defense counsel was inconsistent with the privilege against self-incrimination.

In a similar vein, some of the debate touched on unfavorable comparisons between English and Continental (especially French) procedure. Special scorn was heaped on the system of interrogating the prisoner in inquisitorial fashion.[123] None of these statements went beyond the supposed general difference in style between the adversarial and the inquisitorial systems.[124] At most, the English were celebrating the practice of not directly questioning the accused at trial. This comparison of the systems may have touched on the confession rule, which was mentioned once by an opponent of the full right to counsel, complaining that the confession rule already went too far, since "[c]riminals and witnesses were continually cautioned against saying anything that could possibly implicate themselves; and time even given them, to reflect upon what they should say, lest they should unwittingly let an unwelcome truth escape."[125] A right to silence going beyond the confession rule would have been even more unwelcome to that opponent.[126] But again, despite coming so close to the issue of silence, no one argued directly that denying counsel prevented the accused from taking advantage of silence if he or she wished. The confession rule and the inquisitorial practice of French courts were mentioned, but, despite these openings,[127] no one invoked either a general right to silence at trial or the *Nemo tenetur* maxim.

7. Summary

Statements about criminal procedure uttered during parliamentary debate should not be taken at face value. However, the most striking fact about the debates in the 1820s and 1830s remains that in hundreds of pages, the maxim *Nemo tenetur prodere seipsum* was not mentioned even once, although the advantages and disadvantages of silence on the part of the accused were constant themes. The debate about the right of counsel thus suggests an entire absence of effectiveness in the English criminal defendant's right to remain silent at trial.

B. Jervis's Act of 1848

In addition to the 1836 full right to counsel law, one development that did secure greater ease of silence for criminal defendants was the passage of Jervis's Act of 1848.[128] It provided, inter alia, that an accused should be warned that he need not say anything, but that anything he did say could be used as evidence.[129] Writing later in the nineteenth century, Sir James Fitzjames Stephen assigned much importance to this statute. He subscribed to the now-familiar view that the privilege against self-incrimination had its roots in the maxim *Nemo tenetur prodere seipsum* and the controversies of the later Stuarts, especially those surrounding the Star Chamber.[130] He claimed that soon after the Revolution of 1688, the practice of questioning prisoners "died out"[131] but that "[t]his was . . . subject to two important qualifications."[132] The first was that in cases of felony there was no right to counsel; the second was the Marian pretrial procedure's provision for examination of prisoners.[133] Stephen put the end of this regime in

> the year 1848, when by the 11 & 12 Vic. c. 42, the present system was established, under which the prisoner is asked whether he wishes to say anything, and is warned that if he chooses to do so what he says will be taken down and may be given in evidence on his trial. The result of the whole is that as matters stand the prisoner is absolutely protected against all judicial questioning before or at the trial, and that, on the other hand, he and his wife are prevented from giving evidence in their own behalf. He is often permitted, however, to make any statement he pleases at the very end of the trial, when it is difficult for anyone to test the correctness of what is said. This is one of the most characteristic features of English criminal procedure, and it presents a marked contrast to that which is common to, I believe, all continental countries. It contributes greatly to the dignity and apparent humanity of a criminal trial.[134]

The statute may simply have recognized changes that had previously taken place in practice, however, since JPs were ceasing to act as public prosecutors before the act's passage.[135]

Stephen may have exaggerated the practical importance of the statute, but he was not wrong on the trend. Like the granting of a full right to counsel in 1836, the 1848 statute did have a privilege-like effect: it made it easier for the prisoner to remain silent. More important, however, it marked the end of a legal regime, the Marian system, which sanctioned questioning in a form contrary to a true right to silence. Significantly, the vestiges of that system seem to have coexisted with the maxim *Nemo tenetur,* the confession rule, and the witness privilege. In the early nineteenth century, no one seems to have suggested that the Marian system was in conflict with a "right to silence" or even *Nemo tenetur.*[136]

Stephen himself did see the contradiction between the residue of the Marian system and *Nemo tenetur.* But he was approaching the subject with hindsight. In 1848, when Jervis's Act was passed, the modern privilege against self-incrimination existed—in its infancy, as I will argue. When Stephen noted the contradiction in 1883, over three decades had passed since the period that saw the development of the modern privilege against self-incrimination.

IV. DEVELOPMENT OF THE MODERN PRIVILEGE AGAINST SELF-INCRIMINATION

The development of the modern privilege against self-incrimination resulted from developments made clear by *R. v. Garbett,* decided in 1847.[137] That decision was long foreshadowed by treatise writers' attempts to unify and thereby extend their treatment of the confession rule and the witness privilege. It also capped a long line of cases that struggled with the plight of the witness-turned-criminal defendant, who as a defendant seemed to fall under the spirit of the confession rule but who, technically speaking, should have received the lesser witness-privilege protection—with no exclusion, a lesser waiver requirement, and no per se exclusion of sworn testimony. *Garbett* solved this problem, since its reasoning extended the exclusionary remedy to all proceedings and all instances of compelling testimony.

At the beginning of the nineteenth century the confession rule and the witness privilege had had little in common except for a vague connection to the maxim *Nemo tenetur.* The confession rule, but not the witness privilege, carried with it an exclusionary remedy, treated the oath as per se compulsion, and required a more explicit waiver. During the century these differences were leveled.[138] The emphasis on the role of the oath diminished in mid-century, and the other differences were addressed in a line of cases culminating in *Garbett.* They carried the exclusionary remedy of the confession rule over to witnesses and raised the standard of waiver to the higher level of the confession rule.

A. The "Gap" between the Confession Rule and the Witness Privilege

Because the confession rule was distinct from the witness privilege, the question arose of how the law should deal with situations that might be thought to come under both rules. The confession rule was specifically designed for criminal defendants, and the witness privilege was designed for nondefendant witnesses, but situations arose in which today's defendant was yesterday's witness. If such a person made a statement on oath as a witness and was subsequently charged, the person was a witness at the time of the statement but a prisoner at the time the statement was to be used against him.

The conventional practice in such situations was to classify the case according to the facts obtaining at the time of the statement rather than at the time of its use as evidence. The distinction was crucial, because if a defendant's statement was on oath it was inadmissible, but a witness's previous statement on oath could be used for all purposes, including a later prosecution of the witness.[139] Thus, precisely because the confession and the witness rules were so different, it was possible for the witness's statement to have been on oath and yet be admissible against him, although a similarly situated defendant whose statement had been taken on oath while he was a prisoner could have the statement excluded.

There were limited situations in which a witness had no right to refuse to answer: evidence taken on oath before a commission of bankruptcy, for example.[140] There was uncertainty about the situation. Such evidence was not admitted in *R. v. Britton* (1833),[141] a misdemeanor trial for concealing property from a bankruptcy commission. Shortly thereafter, however, a similar case was decided in opposite fashion. In *R. v. Wheater* (1838),[142] a sworn declaration made before a commission of bankruptcy was admitted into evidence at the later trial. The judges in the majority stressed that the witness (and later defendant) had been cautioned and had been allowed to elect which questions to answer.[143] In other words, the situation was treated as falling under the witness privilege. The court in *Wheater* refused to treat the oath as per se compulsion, as the confession rule would have required.

Starkie, appearing for the prosecution in *Wheater,* argued that the confession rule should be understood as allowing an out-of-court statement as evidence, subject to the requirement that the statement "be a voluntary one, not procured by threats or duress."[144] He argued against the per se approach:

> I admit that the policy of the law is wise in not permitting an oath to be taken; but it is a different question whether, if a party gives an answer on oath without objection, it is inadmissible. As a mode of carrying the law of taking examinations into effect, it may be politic to reject such evidence, although not inadmissible in point of principle.[145]

One judge noted that the oath did not necessarily imply any lack of voluntariness: "I understand, if a prisoner's examination be on oath it shall not be received in evidence without reference to a duress or threat; I see no reason for it; in principle, the answer may be quite voluntary."[146] In any event, the court found the confession properly received.

The result narrowed the gap between the confession rule and the witness privilege. Either rule might apply, with opposite results, and the choice depended on whether it was more important that the now-defendant had been a mere witness at the time of the statement or that he was a criminal defendant when the statement was used. By de-emphasizing the oath that was critical to the traditional confession rule, the judges gave the defendant the lesser protection of the witness privilege. The oath of a mere witness was not treated as per se compulsion. The judges thus brought the confession rule closer to the witness privilege.

This boundary between the confession rule and the witness privilege was the subject of a line of cases in the ten years after 1829. In them, the confession rule came to apply if the person had been under suspicion when he made the statement. The boundary between persons accused and others was drawn in *R. v. Haworth* (1829).[147] The defendant, Haworth, had given sworn evidence before a magistrate about a felony for which someone else had been charged. Subsequently, Haworth was charged with a different felony, and the prosecution proposed to introduce his prior statement into evidence. Parke, J., allowed the evidence, reasoning that since Haworth was not an accused at the time and could have raised the witness privilege objection like any other witness, the deposition was admissible.[148] Similarly, in *R. v. Tubby* (1833),[149] a prior statement on oath was admitted on the grounds that the defendant was not a defendant at the time of the statement. In *Tubby* the judge emphasized that the controlling factor was whether the current defendant had been a defendant at the time of the statement, but it is worth noting that according to the report of the decision, the prosecution and the judge also emphasized that the defendant had not even been under suspicion at the time he made his statement on oath. Both *Haworth* and *Tubby* treated statements made by persons subsequently prosecuted as falling under the witness privilege. Therefore, the fact that the statements were on oath did not bar their admissibility.

The most revealing of these cases involved defendants under suspicion at the time they made the sworn statement. In *R. v. Lewis* (1833),[150] several persons had been summoned before a magistrate investigating an attempted poisoning. At the time no one had been charged, but immediately after the depositions, Lewis was in fact charged with the crime. The prosecution relied on *R. v. Tubby,* but the judge distinguished it on two grounds: the deposition had been made at the same time as the other depositions on which Lewis was committed by the magistrate, and she was committed on the same day those depositions were made.[151] The judge considered the defendant as the functional equivalent of a prisoner and treated the confessions as per se involuntary and thus inadmissible under the confession rule.[152] Similarly, in *R. v. Owen* (1839),[153] the court rejected earlier evidence by the prisoner taken on oath before a coroner. The court expressed some doubt that *Wheater* could be distinguished but (citing *R. v. Britton*) nevertheless excluded the evidence.[154]

If there is a unifying thread to these cases, it is that there was recognition that people who were not technically defendants may have been similarly situated. Where this was true, the protections of the witness privilege appeared insufficient. The confession rule afforded better protection in these cases since, under it, statements on oath were per se involuntary. Furthermore, the confession rule was typically surrounded with warnings and was exclusionary in the strongest, remedial, sense. By contrast, the witness privilege was easy to waive, did not make the taking of an oath compulsion per se, and seems not to have been treated as exclusionary until the mid-nineteenth century.[155]

The advantages to bringing the two rules closer were palpable. Treating the confession rule and the witness privilege together eliminated the need to agonize over whether witnesses who later became prisoners fell under the one or the other. There would be one privilege supplying a generalized right to silence in the judicial setting. On the other hand, by stretching the confession rule to cover some cases where witnesses could expect little protection under the witness privilege, this line of cases foreshadowed the full privilege against self-incrimination. However, the full privilege had to await the leveling of the differences between the confession rule and the witness privilege—oath, waiver, and exclusion.

B. *Garbett* and Its Aftermath

Implementing the full privilege against self-incrimination required a rule that protected all witnesses but with several features of the (pretrial) confession rule: an exclusionary remedy for testimony improperly coerced, a broader notion of compulsion, and a requirement of explicit waiver that could be refused even in the midst of testimony. The witness privilege acquired these traits largely as a result of the decision in the case of *R. v. Garbett* (1847).[156] A full privilege against self-incrimination resulted, but for a time it was partly masked by the disqualification for interest, which prevented any testimony on oath by defendants.

1. The *Garbett* Decision

Garbett extended the witness privilege into a full privilege against self-incrimination by importing into it the exclusionary remedy for "wrongful compulsion."[157] The question in the case was again whether the defendant's testimony in a previous case was admissible as evidence. In the earlier proceeding, the defendant had answered some questions but had objected to answering others on the ground of the witness privilege. As previously applied, it did not allow selective testimony; if the witness answered any question, then he was obliged on pain of contempt to answer all further questions.[158] The defense tried, as in the line of cases discussed previously, to bring the defendant's situation under the confession rule, arguing that the statement was involuntary because it had been made on oath. The prosecution sought to read the confession rule narrowly, as excluding only confessions of doubtful veracity and those induced by promises or threats (of better treatment for confessing or worse treatment for not confessing). The prosecution argued that by answering the defendant had waived the witness privilege. The court held that a witness could object after answering some questions and that if the witness were nonetheless compelled to answer (by the threat of being found in contempt of court), the testimony was not admissible in evidence against him. In so holding, the judges explicitly overruled *Dixon v. Vale* (1824)[159] and *East v. Chapman* (1827).[160]

In reaching this result, the judges did not claim to have brought the particular fact situation there under the confession rule. The report of the case indicated that

> [i]n reference to an observation, that the statement of the prisoner resembled a confession made under undue influence, Alderson B. said—"Is not this the true ground of exclusion—that his liberty of refusing to say anything on the subject has been infringed—rather than that his evidence is not receivable, because it is possibly not true?"[161]

This dictum was unprecedented; it was ahead of its time in the sense that the rule of *R. v. Garbett* was open to, and did actually later receive, this interpretation. The court held that the witness privilege had the same exclusionary attributes as the confession rule.[162] In other words, the witness privilege was expanded into a full privilege against self-incrimination by importing into it those aspects of the confession rule that had distinguished it from the less protective witness privilege. By its logic, compelling testimony should lead to exclusion in any proceeding, and this is the interpretation the decision received.[163]

Garbett is intriguing in another respect: the oath played no part in the decision. This could suggest that evidence would run afoul of the new exclusionary rule even if unsworn. Again, the decision seems to apply the exclusionary remedy in a witness-privilege case because it violated a right to silence.[164] The court, in bringing the exclusionary remedy to bear on a witness-privilege case, created a new rule on the foundation of the old witness privilege. This new rule was the modern privilege against self-incrimination. At the time, it was partially in conflict with the disqualification for interest, because the party-witness disqualification still prevented the accused from testifying on oath in a criminal trial. But once the disqualification was removed, the privilege against self-incrimination would have all the more bite.

2. The Importation of the *Garbett* Rule into the United States
Garbett seems also to have played some role in the establishment of the modern privilege against self-incrimination in the United States. The leading American case on the exclusionary aspect of the witness privilege—or more precisely, the exclusionary aspect of the privilege against self-incrimination—in a situation that would have come under the older witness privilege is the Pennsylvania case of *Horstman v. Kaufman* (1881).[165] The Pennsylvania Supreme Court was confronted with an 1879 Pennsylvania statute that allowed a plaintiff in an action for civil execution to examine the defendant on oath about the defendant's property.[166] The court found the statute unconstitutional, holding that testimony given under judicial order was inadmissible if it was the product of compulsion.[167] Rather than explaining its reasoning, the court cited *Garbett*.[168] After summarizing the English case, the court made the interesting observation that, among other things, the English case stood for the proposition that "such statements must be regarded as given under compulsion and duress, upon the same principle that confessions not free and voluntary cannot be received to affect the defendant."[169] This was a broad reading of *Garbett*, since that case's terse opinion had left it entirely implicit that the violation of the witness privilege was to be treated in the same manner as a confession-rule problem. The *Horstman* court drew out the implication, however, and accepted that there was one "principle" at work in the exclusion both of confessions and of improperly compelled statements by witnesses.

3. The Privilege in the Treatises
For the first time, the treatises in the mid-to-late nineteenth century exhibited the privilege against self-incrimination in its modern form. In 1876

Stephen discussed the privilege under the heading "Confessions Made upon Oath, &c." and drew out the parallels between a witness statement and a confession:

> Evidence amounting to a confession may be used as such against the person who gives it, although it was given upon oath, and although the proceeding in which it was given had reference to the same subject-matter as the proceeding in which it is to be proved, and although the witness might have refused to answer the questions put to him; but if, after refusing to answer any such question, the witness is improperly compelled to answer it, his answer is not a voluntary confession.[170]

The citation for this passage was to *Garbett*. Stephen was describing the privilege but, following that case, made clear that it is an exclusionary version of the witness privilege designed to deal with statements "amounting to confessions." Here we have a practical identification of the witness privilege with the confession rule; this section is Stephen's treatment of the witness privilege. The American edition of 1885, reflecting the American experience with allowing criminal defendants to testify,[171] contained a virtually identical passage supported by references to American cases.[172] At the end of the sentence is the citation to *Garbett* and an internal reference to the treatise's section on witnesses (Article 120).[173] Likewise, in the section on witnesses the edition cited the earlier discussion on confessions, as well as *Garbett,* for the proposition that "[t]estimony given under compulsion of the court, contrary to the privilege, cannot be used against the witness."[174] This was the modern, exclusionary privilege.

If the privilege in England was partially obscured by the party-witness disqualification in this period, one might also expect to find the party-witness disqualification undergoing some reinterpretation. Since a silence-mandating rule (disqualification) blocked the application of a silence-promoting rule (privilege against self-incrimination), there were two ways to remove the blockage: the disqualification rule could be either dropped or reinterpreted as part of the privilege. Both tacks were taken. The notion of interest as a justification for excluding testimony became less popular, leading to piecemeal removal of the disqualification, most notably in civil suits in the Evidence Act of 1851.[175] The treatises took the second method of eliminating the uncomfortable relationship of the disqualification and the privilege. Anticipating somewhat the direction the law would take, they began recasting the disqualification by de-emphasizing the traditional interest rationale for it and reinterpreting its application to criminal defendants as an instance of *Nemo tenetur.* The very fact that this was so unrealistic—it does not explain the application of the disqualification to civil parties—suggests a forced fit between the maxim and the disqualification. The recent creation of the modern privilege against self-incrimination can explain this effort: if the disqualification could be recast as the privilege by way of *Nemo tenetur,* then the disqualification and the privilege would no longer be in conflict.

The treatises in the later nineteenth century indeed made this effort. In sharp contrast to the treatise writers of the early nineteenth century, in 1883 Stephen assumed that the disqualification implemented the policy of *Nemo tenetur.*[176] In one of the later editions of Phillips, one likewise finds a justification for the disqualification that flatly contradicts the one given twenty years earlier. In 1839, the American edition had derived the noncompellability of a party from the incompetence of the party to give evidence on his own behalf.[177] The 1849 American version cited the traditional interest justification. However, instead of deriving the noncompellability from incompetence, it merely stated that a party to a suit was neither competent nor compellable. It went on to speculate that "[t]his rule [party-witness disqualification] seems to have originated from some apprehension of vexation or inconvenience which might ensue, if a person were bound to prejudice or accuse himself."[178]

The original motivation for the rule was the vexation to the judicial process of the lies a party might tell, but this 1849 conjecture is interesting as an attempt to allow the privilege to emerge from the partial cover of the disqualification by reinterpreting the disqualification as an instance of the privilege. It was a stretch, nonetheless, and a new editor for the 1868 edition, Isaac Edwards, went to some pains to restore the old approach (incompetence therefore noncompellability) and to disavow the previous edition's speculation: "*Ground of incompetency.* The incompetency of the parties to the record to give evidence in their own behalf, appears to have been founded upon the *sole ground of their being interested* in the event."[179] This was of course more accurate than the 1849 speculation, but the speculation is more interesting in its attempt to reconcile the disqualification and the privilege by recasting the former as an application of the latter.

V. THE TIMING OF THE RISE OF THE PRIVILEGE AGAINST SELF-INCRIMINATION

The final chapter in the rise of the modern privilege against self-incrimination in England was the removal of the disqualification for interest. The privilege was invoked repeatedly in the debates over whether and how to remove the disqualification. This occurred in stages, first for interested nonparties, then for civil parties, and finally for the criminal accused.[180] Once it had been removed, the privilege would stand on its own. The silence of the accused then depended on the strength of the privilege itself.

A. The Debates over Removing the Disqualification for Criminal Defendants

In the late nineteenth century, references to the privilege abounded in discussions over removing the disqualification against criminal defendants. As Joel Bodansky has demonstrated, those who opposed removing the disqualification made the argument that the removal of the disqualification would impair the accused's exercise of the privilege against self-incrimination.[181] Commentators recognized the threat that removal of the disqualification would pose to it.[182] Bodansky has also shown, however, that the interest rationale and the fear for the efficiency of the judicial process were the important concerns for the opponents,[183] suggesting that, despite attempts by the treatise writers, the disqualification was not regarded as entirely reconciled with the privilege. The character of the debate was, however, quite consistent with full implementation of the privilege. The disqualification was not the privilege itself; it simply sometimes blocked the application of the privilege, which was, however, always recognized for purposes of debate.

Removal of the disqualification in 1898 in England led to codification of the privilege. If the removal of the disqualification had not been accompanied by statutory recognition of the privilege, the statute's silence could have been taken as a rejection of the privilege as well as of the disqualification. The Criminal Evidence Act of 1898 therefore provided in addition that "[a] person [charged with an offence] shall not be called as a witness in pursuance of this Act except upon his own application."[184] The final 1898 act thus codified the privilege, explicitly providing for the noncompellability as well as the competence of the criminal defendant.

B. *Garbett* at the Intersection of Trends in the Law of Silence

Stepping back somewhat, one can see two trends emerge from the nineteenth-century developments in the opportunities for silence on the part of the accused, trends that may explain the timing of the emergence of the privilege against self-incrimination. First, the accused gained legal protection for silence at pretrial in Jervis's Act of 1848. With Stephen, we can regard this as the official close of the "accused speaks" criminal procedure era. Second, the removal of the disqualification for parties was under way from the early 1840s. Interested nonparties were made competent in 1843, and civil parties gained competency in the county courts in 1846. Thus the first provision for parties to testify occurred in 1846, and the trend toward elimination of the disqualification was already apparent.

These two trends intersected in the 1840s, one ending as the other began. The first, the increasing legal protection of silence, was the culmination of the withering away of the "accused speaks" trial in the face of the increasing role of counsel in criminal trials. The second was the beginning of the elimination of the mandated silence of the disqualification for interest. Viewed in isolation, the second trend could threaten to undo the first. If the disqualification, however, based on interest as it was, were to be removed, the accused could then be questioned at trial more freely than Jervis's Act of 1848 allowed at pretrial. Something was needed to ensure that the accused, once he was no longer required to keep silent, did not become required to speak.

The pivotal case, *R. v. Garbett,* fell in the period when these two trends, the silence-promoting and the silence-threatening, overlapped. It is impossible to say whether the intent of *Garbett* was to address the effect of the possible later removal of the disqualification from criminal defendants. But its effect was to establish a core right to silence at trial to match the legal right to silence at pretrial that was the object of Jervis's Act of 1848. That core right was created in the period of flux between the legal recognition of the demise of the "accused speaks" trial and the weakening of the disqualification for interest. *Garbett* was at least a response to a felt necessity, one that had run through the cases of the 1820s and 1830s, of addressing the gap between the confession rule and the witness privilege. This *R. v. Garbett* did, and only after that case do we find routine references to the privilege. A full and effective right to silence on the part of defendants in criminal trials is at the heart of the modern privilege against self-incrimination, and it dates from the 1840s.

SEVEN

A Peculiar Privilege
in Historical Perspective

Albert W. Alschuler

I. THE PUZZLING ETHICS OF THE RIGHT TO SILENCE

United States Supreme Court decisions have vacillated between two incompatible readings of the guarantee that no person "shall be compelled in any criminal case to be a witness against himself."[1] One—a reading that countless repetitions of the *Miranda* warnings have impressed on the public—sees this language as affording defendants and suspects a right to remain silent. This interpretation asserts that government officials have no legitimate claim to testimonial evidence tending to incriminate the person who possesses it. Although officials need not encourage a suspect to remain silent, they must remain at least neutral toward his decision not to speak. In the Supreme Court's words, "[T]he privilege is fulfilled only when the person is guaranteed the right 'to remain silent unless he chooses to speak in the unfettered exercise of his own will.' "[2] He must have "a free choice to admit, to deny, or to refuse to answer."[3] On this view of the privilege, the concept of waiving the privilege seems unproblematic; one might waive a right to remain silent for many plausible reasons.

On the Court's second interpretation, the self-incrimination clause does not protect an accused's ability to remain silent but instead protects him only from improper methods of interrogation.[4] This second interpretation emphasizes the word *compelled,* a word that appears on first reading to express the self-incrimination clause's core concept. In ordinary usage, compulsion does not encompass all forms of persuasion. A person can influence another's choice without compelling it; to do so, he need only keep his persuasion within customary bounds of civility, fairness, and honesty. Compulsion is an open-ended concept encompassing only improper persuasive techniques. On this view of the self-incrimination privilege, the concept of waiver of the privilege becomes paradoxical. Although a defendant or a suspect might sensibly waive a right to remain silent, few sane adults would waive a right to be free of compulsion.

The clash between the two interpretations has centered mostly on whether a fact finder may appropriately treat the refusal of a suspect or defendant to speak as one indication of his guilt. Although the Supreme Court remains somewhat ambivalent about the issue, the "right to silence" interpretation now seems dominant, at least in popular understanding of the privilege.[5]

Distinguished scholars and judges have contended, however, that the right to silence afforded by the privilege is incompatible with ordinary morality. In a probing treatment of the issue, R. Kent Greenawalt drew a contrast between questioning on slender suspicion and questioning on solidly grounded suspicion.[6] He offered a number of illustrations of the moral difference between these two practices. When Ann has little basis for suspecting that Betty has stolen her property, Greenawalt suggested, it would be insulting and unfair for Ann to ask Betty to account for her activities at the time of the theft. Betty might properly respond, "That's none of your business." If, however, a friend had told Ann that he had seen Betty wearing a distinctive bracelet like the one that Ann had reported stolen, then Ann might appropriately describe the reason for her suspicion and ask Betty to explain. Ann's query would be less insulting and intrusive than most other means of confirming or dispelling her suspicion—surreptitiously watching Betty, searching her possessions, or interrogating her associates. In such circumstances, Betty would have powerful reasons for responding, and if she declined, Ann's suspicion could appropriately increase.

Although Greenawalt analyzed close personal relationships and less personal relationships separately, he concluded that the line between slight suspicion and well-grounded suspicion marked the boundary between proper and improper questioning in both. In Greenawalt's view of ordinary morality, a person interrogated on slender suspicion may appropriately remain silent; a person questioned on well-grounded suspicion may not.

If the United States Constitution had adhered to Greenawalt's view of morality, the Fifth Amendment might have provided a qualified right to silence comparable to the qualified freedom from governmental searches and seizures afforded by the Fourth Amendment.[7] The Fourth Amendment provides only partial immunity from governmental intrusion; its protection can be overcome by a showing of probable cause. The privilege afforded by the Fifth Amendment, however, is unqualified. The framers of the Constitution apparently concluded that no amount of evidence could justify compelling a person to supply testimonial evidence against himself in a criminal case. The Fourth Amendment, which forbids only unreasonable searches and seizures, invites balancing. The Fifth Amendment does not. The Constitution says flatly that no person shall be compelled in any criminal case to be a witness against himself.[8]

Like a police search, governmental interrogation invades a suspect's privacy and should not be permitted without antecedent justification. A qualified right to silence—one that could be overcome by a showing of probable cause—could easily be justified. The rationales that the Supreme Court has offered for a more sweeping right to silence are unconvincing, however,[9] and the more elaborate rationales offered by academic writers seem unpersuasive too.[10] Accepting the common assumption that the privilege affords a right to silence, Stephen Schulhofer recently wrote, "It is hard to find anyone these days who is willing to justify and defend the privilege against self-incrimination."[11] Akhil Amar and Renée Lettow added, "Small wonder . . . that the Self-Incrimination Clause—virtually alone among the provisions of the Bill of Rights—has been the target of repeated analytic assault over the course of the twentieth century from thoughtful commentators urging constitutional amendment to narrow it or repeal it altogether."[12]

Although the Supreme Court has said that the privilege is the "essential mainstay" of an accusatorial system[13] and that it "requir[es] the government in its contest with the individual to shoulder the entire load,"[14] our legal system is substantially less accusatorial than this rhetoric suggests. The Supreme Court has required defendants to shoulder much of the load by producing incriminating documents,[15] giving pretrial notice of defenses and of the evidence to be used to support them,[16] providing copies of defense investigative reports,[17] and supplying all forms of nontestimonial evidence—blood samples,[18] voice samples,[19] and even, in one case, the body of a child whom a suspect was thought to have killed.[20]

The virtues of an "accusatorial" system in which defendants are privileged to remain passive are far from obvious. The person who knows the most about the guilt or innocence of a criminal defendant is ordinarily the defendant himself. Unless expecting him to respond to inquiry is immoral or inhuman (contrary to Greenawalt's view of ordinary morality), renouncing all claim to his evidence is costly and foolish.[21]

Our legal system is in fact wise enough to reject in practice much of the rhetoric it proclaims in theory. It actively seeks incriminating, testimonial evidence from the people it accuses of crime. Unfortunately, it often does so in troublesome ways. Every year, courts find that suspects in the back rooms of police stations have made multitudes of knowing and intelligent waivers of their Fifth Amendment rights. If these suspects had understood their situations in the slightest degree, most of them would have remained silent.[22] In addition, 92 percent of all felony convictions in the United States are by guilty plea.[23] Behind this figure lies the practice of plea bargaining. Prosecutors and other officials exert extraordinary pressure on defendants, not merely to obtain an answer, but to secure an unqualified admission of guilt. The Federal Sentencing Guidelines currently promise a substantially discounted sentence to a defendant who supplies "complete information to the government concerning his own involvement in the offense."[24] Few other nations are as dependent as ours on proving guilt from a defendant's own mouth.

No parent or schoolteacher feels guilty about asking questions of a child strongly suspected of misconduct. Similarly, no employer considers it improper to ask an employee accused of wrongdoing to give his side of the story. Criminal cases aside, there are apparently no investigative or fact-finding proceedings in which asking questions and expecting answers is regarded as dirty business. Noting that "parents try hard to inculcate in their children the simple virtues of truth and responsibility," Justice Walter V. Schaefer once wrote that "the Fifth Amendment privilege against self-incrimination . . . runs counter to our ordinary standards of morality."[25]

People who regard criminal defendants as an appropriate source of evidence for resolving criminal disputes may wonder how the contrary position became, at least much of the time, a revered principle of American constitutional law.[26] The common assumption that the privilege mandates an accusatorial system and forbids all efforts to induce a defendant to reveal what he knows explains much of the persistent criticism of the privilege described in chapter 1. The chapters that followed have not fully answered this question, but they have told a substantial part of the story. They demonstrate with unmistakable clarity, moreover, that much criticism and other discussion of the privilege has rested on a historical misconception. The privilege in its inception was not intended to afford criminal defendants a right to refuse to respond to incriminating questions. Its purposes were far more limited. When the privilege was embodied in the United States Constitution, its goal was simply to prohibit improper methods of interrogation.

II. A HISTORY OF THE PRIVILEGE IN THREE ACTS

The history of the modern privilege against self-incrimination can be divided roughly into three stages, each of them captured by its own distinctive formulation of the doctrine. At the earliest stage, the privilege against self-incrimination was expressed in maxims like *Nemo tenetur seipsum accusare* and *Nemo tenetur prodere seipsum*. At the second stage, the formulation was that of the United States Constitution: "No person shall be compelled in any criminal case to be a witness against himself." At the third stage (the modern stage), the warnings mandated by *Miranda v. Arizona*[27] express the general, although not universal, understanding of the privilege: "You have a right to remain silent." These formulations often are treated as equivalent, but they are very different in fact. The evidence presented in this volume shows that the people who created and invoked them meant different things as well.

A. *Nemo tenetur prodere seipsum*

As chapter 2 suggests, the roots of the privilege in the early seventeenth century (and earlier) are to be found not in the common law of England but in the *ius commune*—the law applied throughout the European continent and in the English prerogative and ecclesiastical courts. When seventeenth-century common law courts restricted the power of the High Commission to ask incriminating questions of suspected religious dissenters, these courts were, for the most part, requiring the commission to adhere to the law it purported to observe.

Several maxims of the *ius commune* expressed its most important limitation on interrogation. In addition to the familiar *Nemo tenetur* maxim, given above, the *ius commune* made use of two more: *Nemo punitur sine accusatore* ("No one is punished in the absence of an accuser") and *Nemo tenetur detegere turpitudinem suam* ("No one is bound to reveal his own shame"). The principle reflected in these maxims was unknown in classical Roman law,[28] and when it entered the *ius commune* is uncertain. A plausible hypothesis is that the privilege began as a limitation on the religious duty to confess.[29] By the third century, penance for wrongdoing was an obligation of Christian faith,[30] and the penance occurred in public. Whether this penance generally included a public confession or whether, instead, private confession preceded it is a matter of dispute,[31] but the church ultimately demanded only private (auricular) confession. The fourth-century church leader Saint John Chrysostom wrote, "I do not say that you should betray yourself in public nor accuse yourself before others, but that you obey the prophet when he said, Reveal your ways unto the Lord."[32] Chrysostom's statement was cited centuries later as justification for the *Nemo tenetur* principle.[33] The fifth-century historian Sozomen explained:

> [I]n seeking pardon it is necessary to confess the sin; and since from the beginning the bishops decided, as is only right, that it was too much of a burden to announce one's sins as in a theater with the congregation of the Church as witness, they appointed for this purpose a presbyter, a man of the best refinement, a man silent and prudent. To him sinners came and confessed their deeds.[34]

Far from reflecting the notion that wrongdoers have a right to remain silent, the privilege against self-incrimination originally may have reflected only a pragmatic judgment that a sinner's duty did not include public disclosure that could lead to criminal proceedings against himself. To demand either public disclosure or submission to criminal punishment would have diminished the willingness of wrongdoers to confess, and confession, not silence, was good for the soul.

By the seventeenth century, the privilege had grown into a right not to be interrogated under oath in the absence of well-grounded suspicion. All of the formulations of the *Nemo tenetur* maxim in the *ius commune* were consistent with the concepts of ordinary morality voiced by Kent Greenawalt. They concerned the initiation of criminal proceedings, declaring that a person could not be required to "accuse" or "produce" or "betray" himself.[35] No person could be required to "reveal" his own wrongdoing. There must instead be an "accuser," someone other than the defendant who had revealed or asserted his crime. Officials must not commence prosecutions by interrogating at large, by conducting fishing expeditions, or by questioning on what Greenawalt would call slender suspicion. Officials in the seventeenth century and earlier were expected to have probable cause before asking suspects to respond under oath to incriminating questions.

Unlike the common law courts of the seventeenth century, which did not permit criminal defendants and other litigants to testify under oath, the High Commission required parties to swear to answer truthfully all questions that the court might put to them. The High Commission often did so, moreover, without specification of the charges against a suspect or notification of the questions to be asked. When litigants challenged the High Commission's power to administer the ex officio oath, they did so primarily on the ground that the *ius commune* did not permit judges to commence ex officio procedures. Unless someone with an interest in securing the defendant's conviction had accused him, or other strong evidence of his guilt appeared, interrogation of the defendant under oath was improper.

The difference between the procedures of the High Commission and other ecclesiastical courts, in all of which defendants were sworn to tell the truth, and those of common law courts, in which defendants often spoke but were disqualified from testifying under oath, is important in understanding the history of the privilege against self-incrimination. The history of the privilege, from the struggles over the authority of the High Commission through at least the framing of the American Bill of Rights, is almost entirely a story of when and for what purposes people would be required to speak under oath.[36]

In preliterate societies and, to a lesser extent, in societies in which a substantial portion of the population remains illiterate, religious oaths are the primary means of solemnizing and memorializing important statements and transactions. In these societies, oaths are sometimes accompanied by the sacrifice and dismemberment of animals to make the oaths vivid and also to symbolize the fate awaiting people who default on sworn obligations.[37] God's third commandment to the Israelites was "Thou shalt not take the name of the Lord thy God in vain."[38]

The Book of Matthew includes Christ's condemnation of oaths,[39] but the leaders of the early Christian church, prompted in part by social need, concluded that Christ's statement was not meant literally. These leaders pointed to oaths taken by Abraham (Gen. 21:23–24), Saint Paul (2 Cor. 1:23), and even God (Is. 62:8) in support of their position. Some later Christians, however, including some of the seventeenth-century religious dissenters who resisted the ex officio oath, took Christ at his word. They conscientiously opposed all oaths.

Oaths were "the institutional glue par excellence" of the procedural law of the medieval church, and a sixteenth-century treatise listed 174 ways in which they had special significance in the *ius commune*.[40] Their power was great enough that in church courts, and even at an early stage in the king's courts, they sometimes were treated as conclusive proof. A defendant could swear his innocence and produce the number of *compurgatores,* or "oath-helpers," that the court required. Once the *compurgatores* swore that they believed the defendant's oath, he was, without more, acquitted. By the seventeenth century, however, far from treating a criminal defendant's oath as conclusive, common law courts neither required nor permitted criminal defendants to swear to the truth of their statements. In assessing the coercive power of an oath in that century, one must recall the spirit of the age. It was still a time when questions about whether bread and wine became Christ's body and blood or instead merely symbolized them were matters over which men willingly fought and died.[41]

To the charge that use of the ex officio oath was unlawful without an accuser, defenders of the High Commission responded that *fama publica* could take the place of an accuser. Some authorities disputed this proposition, and the sources that recognized a *fama publica* exception to the requirement of an accuser emphasized that rumor alone was not enough. The public fame must "have reached a level of 'open clamorousness' "; it "must have been the true source of the prosecution"; it "must have existed before legal proceedings had begun"; it "must have been held by trustworthy persons"; and it must have been "so vehement that open scandal would be generated by failure to take action upon it."[42] Under the *ius commune,* the propriety of inquisition before the High Commission thus turned upon the proper application of the principles of morality that Kent Greenawalt articulated more than three hundred years later.[43] Disputants considered what sort of antecedent justification the law required before the High Commission could administer the ex officio oath and ask questions. Once an appropriate preliminary showing had been made, suspects were required to submit to the oath and to answer.[44]

Critics of the High Commission sometimes objected to its procedures for reasons other than the lack of a sufficient evidentiary basis for questioning. For one thing, they argued that forcing people to answer incriminating questions on oath tempted them to commit perjury. This objection would have been as forceful in cases of questioning on strong suspicion as in cases of questioning on light suspicion. When defendants testify under oath, an objection to forcing them to choose among perjury, contempt, or conviction—a choice that the Supreme Court has called a "cruel trilemma"[45]—has the potential of creating a broader privilege than the privilege of insisting on an adequate evidentiary foundation for questioning. This objection appears to condemn forcing people to answer incriminating questions on oath altogether.

Something like this objection may have been among the circumstances that led common law courts to disqualify criminal defendants and other interested parties from providing sworn testimony—testimony that, if false, might have jeopardized their souls.[46] In the *ius commune,* however, the objection did not lead either to testimonial disqualification or to the establishment of a privilege of sworn witnesses always to decline to answer incriminating questions. Interrogation on oath remained permissible so long as public fame or an identified accuser provided an adequate evidentiary foundation.

During this early era, the discomfort generated by forcing suspects to answer on oath was great enough that the *ius commune* exempted false answers to incriminating questions from the penalties for perjury. False answers still were punishable as contempt, however, and in the seventeenth century, the temporal penalties for perjury were not the most important ones. Although critics of the High Commission objected that the moral trilemma confronting sworn suspects remained, this objection did not lead common law courts to prohibit involuntary administration of the ex officio oath by the commission.

Another, more technical objection to questioning by the High Commission found greater favor in the common law courts. As chapter 3 emphasizes, common law courts forbade questioning by the High Commission that could effectively resolve either a civil or a criminal case that the common law courts had jurisdiction to decide. Other privileges, too, were available to suspects brought before the commission, including a privilege not to be questioned concerning "secret thoughts."[47] No suspect, however, successfully asserted an unqualified privilege to refuse to respond to incriminating questions.

In chapter 3, Charles Gray notes a habeas corpus action brought by Maunsell and Ladd in 1607.[48] In this case, two Puritan suspects who had been brought before the High Commission challenged the court's authority to ask incriminating questions, and they lost. Their case established the propriety of the High Commission's interrogation under oath when (1) the case was within the commission's jurisdiction, (2) the commission's questioning did not expose the person interrogated to a risk of detriment in a common law proceeding, and (3) the commission gave sufficient notice of the subject of its interrogation.

In summary, the common law courts enforced more than one privilege against the High Commission, but all of these privileges were compatible with the principles of ordinary morality articulated by Kent Greenawalt. The most important of these privileges—the privilege not to be subjected to incriminating interrogation under oath until a specific accuser or public fame provided a clear basis for suspicion—was in fact grounded on precisely the moral principles that Greenawalt later voiced.

B. No Person Shall Be Compelled in Any Criminal Case to Be a Witness against Himself

The privilege against self-incrimination that the framers included in the Bill of Rights of 1791 differed from the privilege that the English common law courts enforced against the High Commission. The Fifth Amendment, declaring that no person shall be compelled in any criminal case to be a witness against himself, plainly refers, not just to the initiation of criminal proceedings or to a first accusation, but to the conduct of the criminal trial.

By the time a felony defendant reaches trial, a strong basis for suspecting his guilt ought to be apparent,[49] and a privilege afforded to defendants who have been placed on trial after a showing of probable cause goes beyond Greenawalt's principles of morality. Unlike the limited privilege of the *ius commune,* the Fifth Amendment's privilege was not designed merely to guarantee an adequate evidentiary basis for interrogation. The Constitution affords an absolute privilege, one that no evidentiary showing can overcome.[50]

In assessing what this constitutional privilege meant to the people who enacted it, manuals used to instruct justices of the peace on the conduct of their offices offer a helpful starting point. For nearly three hundred years, from 1584 through the mid-nineteenth century, these manuals declared that the *Nemo tenetur* principle precluded the interrogation of suspects under oath.[51] One of the most frequently used manuals in colonial America, Dalton's Countrey Justice, first published in England in 1618, declared, "The offender himself shall not be examined upon oath; for by the common law, *Nullus tenetur seipsum prodere.*"[52]

A manual published in 1745 explained:

> The Law of England is a Law of Mercy, and does not use the Rack or Torture to compel Criminals to accuse themselves. . . . I take it to be for the same Reason, that it does not call upon the Criminal to answer upon Oath. For, this might serve instead of the Rack, to the Consciences of some Men, although they have been guilty of Offenses. . . . The Law has therefore wisely and mercifully laid down this Maxim, *Nemo tenetur seipsum prodere.*[53]

Nineteenth-century American manuals substituted the language of the Bill of Rights for the familiar Latin maxim:

No man shall be compelled to give evidence against himself. Hence it is held that if a criminal be sworn to his examination taken before a justice, it shall not be read against him.[54]

The prisoner is not to be examined on oath, for this would be a species of duress, and a violation of the maxim, that no one is bound to criminate himself.[55]

All of these manuals noted the coercive force of an oath (a force derived from both the secular penalties for perjury and the supernatural sanctions for falsely invoking God's name), and they linked the disqualification of suspects and defendants from testifying on oath to the privilege against self-incrimination.

The claim that incriminating interrogation under oath is forbidden for the same reason that torture is forbidden was asserted by religious dissenters in England and embraced by religious dissenters in America. In about 1591, Thomas Cartwright and eight Puritan colleagues objected that the ex officio oath "put the conscience upon the racke."[56] In 1637, John Lilburne declared before the Star Chamber that "no man's conscience ought to be racked by oaths imposed."[57] Five years later, in the winter of 1641–42, the governor of the Plymouth Colony asked the colony's ministers and magistrates "how far a magistrate may extract a confession from a delinquent to accuse himself of a capital crime seeing *nemo tenetur prodere seipsum*." One of the few surviving responses exhibited little shyness about asking incriminating questions of unsworn suspects or about pressing these suspects through force of argument. It declared, however, that physical force, threats of increased punishment, and interrogation under oath were all impermissible:

I conceive that a magistrate is bound, by careful examination of circomstances & weighing of probabilities, to sift the accused; and by force of argument to draw him to an acknowledgment of the truth. But he may not extract a confession of a capital crime from a suspected person by any violent means, whether it be by an oath imposed, or by any punishment inflicted or threatened to be inflicted, for he may draw forth an acknowledgmente of a crime from a fearful innocent. If guilty, he shall be compelled to be his own accuser, when no other can, which is against the rule of justice.[58]

Summarizing the responses that the governor received, John Winthrop saw two principles at work: first, a principle that one might call "the Greenawalt principle," affording suspects a right to silence in cases of light suspicion but not when a strong evidentiary basis for interrogation existed, and second, an unqualified prohibition of torture and of requiring suspects to answer under oath:

> [When a crime has been committed] and one witness or strong presumptions do point out the offender, there the judge may examine him strictly, and he is bound to answer directly, though to the peril of his life. But if there be only light suspicion, &c. then the judge is not to press him to answer . . . but he may be silent, and call for his accusers. But for examination by oath or torture in criminal cases, it was generally denied to be lawful.[59]

In 1677, the Virginia House of Burgesses declared that forcing suspects to answer incriminating questions under oath was incompatible with their natural rights. In the aftermath of Bacon's Rebellion and its suppression, the House resolved "that a person summoned as a witness against another, ought to answer upon oath, but no law can compel a man to swear against himself in any matter wherein he is liable to corporal punishment."[60]

These sources and others discussed below support this judgment: the Fifth Amendment privilege prohibited (1) incriminating interrogation under oath, (2) torture,[61] and (3) probably other forms of coercive interrogation such as threats of future punishment and promises of leniency.[62] The amendment prohibited nothing more, or at least the sources mention nothing more.[63] The self-incrimination clause neither mandated an accusatorial system nor afforded defendants a right to remain silent. It focused on improper methods of gaining information from criminal suspects.

If this understanding of the original understanding is correct, critics of the Fifth Amendment privilege have missed the mark. Although the intensity of the framers' disapproval of sworn statements by suspects may seem foreign to us today, the policies that informed the privilege were coherent and compelling, and they were not in tension with ordinary morality. When Ann has a strong basis for suspecting that Betty has stolen her property, ordinary morality may permit Ann to interrogate Betty and to draw an adverse inference if she refuses to respond. Ordinary morality, however, does not permit Ann to place Betty on the rack or to insist that Betty swear on threat of imprisonment for falsehood or silence that her explanation is true. When critics have spoken harshly of the privilege against self-incrimination, they have assumed that it afforded more than a right to be free of inhuman methods of interrogation. They have assumed that it afforded a right to silence—a right not to respond to incriminating questions at all. The evidence is overwhelming that the privilege did not afford this right at the time that it appeared in the Bill of Rights.

What the Fifth Amendment privilege did not prohibit is in fact clearer than what it did. The privilege did not prohibit the forceful incriminating interrogation of suspects by judges and magistrates so long as the suspects remained unsworn. Unsworn suspects who refused to respond to the questions of English and American courts doubtless would have suffered no more severe sanction than the drawing of an adverse inference.[64] The procedures of the pre-nineteenth-century trial, however, would have made that disadvantage substantial in every case and devastating in most. The privilege did not afford suspects a right to suffer no consequences for their refusal to speak.[65]

Unlike an unsworn defendant, a witness who had been sworn and who then was asked incriminating questions could refuse to respond. This witness had a limited right to remain silent. If the witness chose to reveal incriminating information, moreover, he could fairly be said to have waived his privilege. The objection to interrogating this witness rested on the compulsion effected by an improper technique of interrogation, however, and did not extend to all methods of encouraging suspects and defendants to speak.

Language that appropriately described the situation of sworn witnesses ultimately was extended to unsworn suspects, whose silence came to be seen as a moral right. Where the framers of the Constitution saw an obligation to the community to speak, later judges and scholars saw a right to refuse to cooperate in what they regarded as an inspiring, poetic contest between the individual and the state.[66]

Chapters 4, 5, and 6 tell the story of this transformation. In Chapter 4, John Langbein distinguishes between two historic models of the criminal trial: the "accused speaks" trial and the "testing the prosecution" trial. Langbein argues that the shift from the former model to the latter began in the late eighteenth century, when lawyers came to represent defendants in significant numbers. So long as defendants were unrepresented, no one could speak for them unless they spoke for themselves. In this situation, a right to remain silent would have been a right to commit suicide. Langbein notes that several other aspects of common law procedure also induced defendants to speak, and the evidence is clear that in the sixteenth, seventeenth, and eighteenth centuries virtually all English defendants did speak.[67] One source described the criminal trial as an "altercation" between the defendant and his accusers.[68]

Trial, moreover, was not the only stage of the criminal process at which the accused was expected to speak. The Marian Committal Statute of 1555

required justices of the peace to interrogate suspects following their apprehension and to record anything "material to prove the felony." Until the
mid-eighteenth century, the record of the defendant's pretrial examination
was read routinely at his trial.[69] Courts then began to express a preference
for hearing the defendant's account from the defendant himself, but the
record of his pretrial examination remained available for impeachment purposes. If the defendant said something different at trial from what he had
told the magistrate, the jury heard about it.

Chapter 5 reveals that American criminal procedure throughout the
colonial period and into the early republic corresponded to the "accused
speaks" model. It offers little direct evidence concerning the defendant's
role at trial (little evidence seems to survive), but the chapter demonstrates
that the Marian procedure was firmly in place. Justices of the peace
throughout America interrogated unsworn defendants, and these defendants' statements were used at trial.[70]

In England, lawyers were first permitted to represent criminal defendants in ordinary felony trials in the 1730s, and, according to Langbein,
"The use of defense counsel remained a relative trickle for another half
century, until the 1780s."[71] Within another half century, however, counsel
had begun to work a substantial change in English criminal procedure. As
early as 1820, the French visitor Charles Cottu wrote of the English trial,
"[T]he defendant acts no kind of part: his hat stuck on a pole might without
inconvenience be his substitute. . . ."[72] Cottu may have exaggerated, however, for chapter 6 suggests that "accused speaks" procedures persisted into
the 1820s and even the 1830s. Criminal suspects and defendants had no
right to remain silent until well into the nineteenth century.

As chapter 4 emphasizes, the criminal defendant's right to remain silent
was "the creature of defense counsel." The framers of the American Constitution, however, apparently saw no contradiction between their "accused
speaks" procedures and the privilege against self-incrimination that they
included in the Bill of Rights. The Fifth Amendment privilege did not
afford a right to remain silent, and it was not the product of lawyer-
dominated trials or of the disappearance of "accused speaks" procedures.[73]

Congress submitted the Bill of Rights to the states in 1789, at the end
of the decade in which, Langbein reports, defense attorneys first appeared in
English criminal trials in significant numbers. In John M. Beattie's estimate,
lawyers represented 20 percent of the defendants tried in the Old Bailey a
few years before Congress's submission of the Fifth Amendment to the

states,[74] and representation by counsel was rarer in America than in England.[75] Moreover, the Fifth Amendment's formulation of the privilege was not new; similar declarations had appeared in a number of state constitutions.[76] Indeed, in 1776, just prior to American independence, the Virginia Declaration of Rights had listed among the defendant's privileges, "[N]or can he be compelled to give evidence against himself."[77] At this time, even in London, only about 2 percent of all felony defendants were represented by counsel,[78] and only about 180 residents of the American colonies were lawyers in the sense that they had been trained at the Inns of Court.[79] The privilege against self-incrimination articulated by the Bill of Rights and by American state constitutions could not have been driven by lawyer-dominated trials.

If someone had argued to judges of the founding generation that their "accused speaks" procedures violated the privilege against self-incrimination, they might have offered any or all of three responses. These responses would have denied each and every element of a violation of the privilege:

First, far from compelling any defendant to be a *witness* against himself, we do not permit any defendant to be a witness against (or for) himself. The defendant is disqualified from giving evidence partly because we are concerned that placing him on oath would be incompatible with his privilege.[80]

Second, if our procedures compel defendants to do anything, it is not to *incriminate* themselves. We do not press defendants to admit their guilt. To the contrary, we want to hear anything that they may be able to say in their defense. When an occasional defendant attempts to plead guilty, we in fact discourage him.[81] If there is any tilt to our procedures, we press defendants to *exculpate* rather than to incriminate themselves.

Third, our procedures do not in fact *compel* anyone to do anything. If a defendant were to refuse to respond to judicial questions or to the charges against him, we would impose no punishment for his refusal. We would merely permit the jury to draw whatever inference seemed appropriate in determining whether he was guilty of the offense with which he was charged. Permitting a jury to draw a fair inference is a far cry from torture, placing a defendant upon oath, or any other form of compulsion.

None of these judicial responses would have been plausible if defendants had been examined under oath. Then the defendant would have been a witness; he would have been subject to compulsion (the punishment for perjury) if he failed to speak the truth; and if the truth were incriminating, his oath would have pressed him to incriminate himself.

Some early sources emphasized that placing a suspect on oath tempted him to commit perjury. The principal concern of these sources was to prevent what modern lawyers would call entrapment—that officials might prompt a suspect to commit a crime that he would have avoided in the absence of the officials' enticing conduct. The new crime, moreover, would be perjury, an offense that would not only subject the suspect to temporal punishment but also jeopardize his soul.

Other sources referred to the oath as compulsion—as a form of "violence" akin to torture. Their concern appeared to be not that the suspect would be induced to commit perjury but rather that he would be compelled by improper methods to confess his crime. Concerns about tempting suspects to commit perjury may in fact have blended with concerns about compelling them to incriminate themselves; the choice among perjury, contempt, and self-incrimination was indeed a "cruel trilemma."[82]

Whatever their reasons, manuals for justices of the peace in England and America consistently emphasized that the suspect was not to be sworn when examined.[83] In two eighteenth-century English cases, justices of the peace overlooked the manuals' admonitions and administered oaths to suspects before examining them. In both cases, judges excluded the suspects' statements from evidence at trial. In one case, the judge remarked, "If [the examination] is upon Oath it cannot be read, for Persons are not to swear against themselves; all Examinations ought to be taken freely and voluntarily, and not upon Oath, and then we can read [th]em." A pamphlet report of the second case explained: "[T]he confession was produced; but it being taken on oath, it could not be read. If it had been taken voluntarily it would have been admitted as good evidence; but the law supposes that an oath is compulsion; and consequently that no man is obliged to swear against himself in cases where it affects his life."[84]

The courts' unwillingness to receive sworn, self-incriminating testimony explains what otherwise would seem a paradox: that witnesses for the prosecution and witnesses in civil cases were much more likely to invoke the privilege, and to do so successfully, than criminal defendants. Unlike defendants, prosecution witnesses and witnesses in civil cases were sworn, and when they invoked the privilege, the courts forbade other trial participants from asking them incriminating questions. At least by 1700, both sworn defendants in religious courts and sworn witnesses in common law courts were permitted to decline to answer any questions that could lead to criminal punishment or forfeiture.[85] Once a witness was sworn, he was subject to compulsion, and his only protection lay in the ability to decline to answer specific questions. The protection of common law defendants, by contrast, lay in not being sworn at all.

Chapter 5 offers persuasive evidence that American courts did not view the answers of unsworn defendants in the same light as those of sworn witnesses. Following ratification of the Fifth Amendment, some American lawyers objected on nonconstitutional grounds to the pretrial interrogation of defendants by justices of the peace. These lawyers noted that although American law generally incorporated the common law of England, it did not, in the absence of legislative provision to the contrary, incorporate English statutory law. Because the pretrial examination of defendants was authorized by a statute, the Marian Committal Statute of 1555, the lawyers contended that American law did not allow this procedure.

Neither the lawyers nor the commentators who advanced this argument supplemented it with a claim that the pretrial examination of suspects violated either the Fifth Amendment privilege against self-incrimination or the similar provisions of state constitutions. If anyone had thought that the Constitution guaranteed a right to remain silent or that "accused speaks" procedures were inconsistent with the privilege, this was the occasion to say so, but for three decades of debate over whether the Marian Committal Statute was a parliamentary innovation or merely declarative of the common law, no one did. Even the opponents of "accused speaks" procedures did not consider them inconsistent with the constitutional privilege against self-incrimination.

C. You Have a Right to Remain Silent

Chapter 6 reveals that the transformation of the privilege into a right of criminal defendants to remain silent occurred only during the nineteenth century. Lawyerization of the trial contributed to a changed ideology of criminal procedure—one in which the dignity of defendants lay not in their ability to tell their stories fully but rather in their ability to remain passive, to proclaim to the prosecutor, "Thou sayest," and to force the state to shoulder the entire load. As defendants participated less in the proceedings that determined their fate, they were seen more as objects or as targets of the coercive forces of the state.

In parliamentary debates of the 1820s and 1830s, reformers complained that "accused speaks" procedures often worked unfairly. Many defendants were not sufficiently educated and articulate to tell their stories coherently. The remedy that the reformers sought, however, was not the declaration of a right to remain silent; instead, they proposed giving defense attorneys the power to argue on the defendants' behalf before juries. The expansion of the role of counsel that they secured in 1836 permitted defendants to take a still more passive role at trial and contributed to the rapidly changing ideology of English procedure.

An 1838 opinion declared that "[a] prisoner is not to be entrapped into making any statement" and that a magistrate should advise him before taking his statement "that what he thinks fit to say will be taken down, and may be used against him on his trial."[86] A clearer doctrinal recognition of the right to remain silent came ten years later in Sir John Jervis's Act. This act provided that, before the pretrial examination, the accused should be cautioned that he need not answer and that if he did answer, his answers could be used against him at trial.[87] In New York City, magistrates began routinely to caution defendants in 1835. The number of defendants who declined to submit to pretrial interrogation increased thereafter.[88]

A more significant doctrinal development than the magistrates' cautioning of suspects was the abolition of the testimonial disqualification of defendants. In 1864, Maine became the first American jurisdiction to allow defendants to offer sworn testimony in criminal cases,[89] and other states quickly followed. The British Parliament, a latecomer to the movement, enacted its competency statute in 1898.[90] By the end of the nineteenth century, Georgia was the only American state to retain the common law disqualification. It permitted defendants to offer sworn testimony only in 1962.[91]

The statutes that ended the testimonial disqualification of defendants were controversial, and the controversy centered on constitutional issues.[92] Proponents maintained that defendants should have the same right as other witnesses to testify under oath and that the common law disqualification substituted a presumption of perjury for the presumption of innocence.[93] Opponents contended, however, that the statutes threatened the privilege against self-incrimination.[94] They argued that jurors would view the failure of a lawyer to call his client to testify as a confession of the client's guilt and that the jurors would draw this inference whatever cautionary instructions they received. In practice, defendants would be pressed to take the oath and thus be subject to precisely the compulsion that state and federal constitutions condemned.[95] Many defendants, moreover, would respond by committing perjury. Sir James Stephen wrote, "It is not in human nature to speak the truth under such pressure as would be brought to bear on the prisoner, and it is not a light thing to institute a system which would almost enforce perjury on every occasion."[96]

In deference to constitutional concerns, most competency statutes, including the federal statute of 1878,[97] provided that the prosecutor could not comment on the failure of a defendant to testify and that no presumption against the defendant would arise from his failure to take the stand.[98] Some courts later suggested that the statutes would have been invalid without these provisions.[99] Placing defendants on oath apparently was constitutional only because defendants were thought to have an unfettered option to decline to testify without suffering any consequence.

Some competency statutes expressly preserved the defendant's power to make an unsworn statement to the jury. Following the English Criminal Evidence Act of 1898, for example, defendants were allowed either to testify from the witness stand or to make an unsworn statement from the prisoner's dock. The sense that unsworn statements were worthless, however, led Parliament to abolish the option of speaking from the dock in 1982.[100] Most American jurisdictions had reached the same conclusion long before. Today, Massachusetts may still allow defendants to decide whether to offer sworn or unsworn statements,[101] but no other state gives defendants this option.

Following the enactment of competency statutes, the law in some jurisdictions might technically have been that although jurors could draw no lawful inference from a defendant's failure to testify under oath, they could lawfully consider the defendant's failure to make an unsworn statement.[102] This distinction, however, was too thin to be maintained. When defendants, in practice, spoke only from the witness stand and when jurors were forbidden to draw an inference from their failure to take the stand, defendants had a right to remain silent at trial.

In 1965, *Griffin v. California* held that prosecutorial or judicial comment on a defendant's failure to testify violated the Fifth Amendment privilege.[103] The framers of the Fifth Amendment, who might not have approved of sworn testimony by defendants at all, probably would have agreed that a defendant's refusal to submit to the compulsion of an oath could not be the subject of adverse comment. *Griffin,* however, forbade comment, not simply on the refusal of a defendant to submit to an oath but "on the accused's silence."[104] The Court offered no indication that refusal to submit to an oath might differ from any other form of silence, and one year after *Griffin,* the Court extended the right to remain silent to unsworn suspects in custody in *Miranda v. Arizona.*[105] That the presence or absence of an oath might have made a difference seemed inconceivable in 1966. Because an unsworn statement made in response to police interrogation would be used against a suspect at trial, it was the functional equivalent of testimony. The distinction between sworn and unsworn statements, central to the framers' understanding of what it meant to be compelled to testify, had disappeared.

In 1987, *Rock v. Arkansas* held that the Constitution guaranteed defendants a right to testify under oath[106]—a right the framers might have characterized as the right to be compelled. Turning the original understanding of the constitutional privilege on its head, the Supreme Court declared, "The opportunity to testify is . . . a necessary corollary to the Fifth Amendment's guarantee against compelled testimony."[107]

In the years since *Miranda,* Americans have seemed increasingly enamored of its accusatorial rhetoric, especially as they have learned that *Miranda*'s system for protecting the Fifth Amendment privilege has little practical effect.[108] During the Reagan administration, the Justice Department proposed abandoning *Miranda,*[109] but its proposal generated considerable criticism even among police administrators.[110]

England, by contrast, has reassessed the value of "testing the prosecution" trials. The Criminal Justice and Public Order Act of 1994 provides that once an accused has been warned of the consequences of a failure to testify, "the court or jury . . . may draw such inferences as appear proper from the failure of the accused to give evidence."[111] In addition, the act invites jurors and judges to draw inferences from the pretrial silence of defendants in many situations.[112] The act encourages suspects to cooperate with police investigations, to disclose defenses at the earliest opportunity, and to submit to cross-examination at trial, but its supporters contend that it is consistent with the privilege against self-incrimination because it does not treat a suspect's failure to speak as a crime or as contempt of court.[113]

The European Court of Human Rights will decide whether the 1994 Criminal Justice and Public Order Act violates England's obligation under the European Convention on Human Rights to give every defendant a fair trial. Past decisions make it doubtful that the act will survive this scrutiny.[114] After centuries of self-congratulation by English judges and lawyers who have denigrated the "inquisitorial" practices of the European continent, Continental judges may take ironic pleasure in denouncing England's new "inquisitorial" procedure.

More than the adaptation of old doctrines to new functions, the history of the privilege against self-incrimination seems to reveal the tyranny of slogans. Shorthand phrases have taken on lives of their own.[115] These

phrases have eclipsed the goals of the doctrines that they purported to describe and even the texts that embodied these doctrines. The phrases and
the images they evoked—what the phrases "sounded like"—shaped the
law. Latin maxims declaring that "no one shall be compelled to betray
himself" have sounded like the declaration that "no one shall be compelled
in any criminal case to be a witness against himself." The latter declaration
has been summarized as "the privilege against self-incrimination" (a description not in general use before the twentieth century[116] and one that
omits all reference to the constitutional concept of compulsion). The "privilege against self-incrimination," in turn, has sounded like the "right to
remain silent." Much of the history of the privilege has been a story of
slippage from one doctrine to another without awareness of the change.
Officials have drifted from limiting the burdens of the religious obligation
to confess in the interest of obtaining more confessions to condemning
incriminating interrogation under oath without adequate evidentiary justification. They have drifted from condemning interrogation under oath
without evidentiary justification to condemning torture and all interrogation of suspects under oath. The officials then have drifted to a judgment
that the framers of all of the earlier doctrines unquestionably would have
disapproved: that it is unfair to expect defendants on trial and people arrested on probable cause to participate actively in the criminal process by
telling what they know.[117]

Linguistic confusion may also have affected historians of the privilege.
It might even be said that the historians have described two different privileges that arose centuries apart, each of them treated as "the" privilege
against self-incrimination.[118] Sworn witnesses were privileged not to answer
incriminating questions by the end of the seventeenth century. Criminal
defendants, however, gained recognition of their right to remain silent only
some 150 years later. When the authors of this volume maintain that the
privilege did not come into existence until the latter date, they emphasize
that the appearance of the *Nemo tenetur* maxim does not indicate any recognition of the right to silence of defendants. Until the 1830s or later, unsworn criminal defendants were expected to speak both before trial and at
trial.

III. WHERE DO WE GO FROM HERE?

The history of the privilege against self-incrimination seems to pose its own
"cruel trilemma" for American courts. One possible option for modern
courts is to return to the original understanding of the Fifth Amendment

with its strong distinction between sworn and unsworn statements. In our era, however, the fires of hell have smoldered. Oaths have lost their terror and even their meaning. Bruce Ackerman, moreover, has pointed to a number of "constitutional moments" that have effectively altered the Constitution without formal amendment.[119] The enactment of statutes ending the testimonial disqualification of defendants, if not a constitutional moment, was at least a constitutional nanosecond. In a very different world from that of the early American republic, restoring the original understanding of the Fifth Amendment privilege is impossible.

If the distinction between sworn and unsworn statements cannot be maintained today, two options remain. One is to treat sworn statements in the same way that eighteenth-century English and American courts treated unsworn statements—by strongly encouraging them and by drawing adverse inferences when defendants fail to provide them. England, in effect, chose this option in the Criminal Justice and Public Order Act of 1994, which authorized judges and jurors to draw such adverse inferences in many situations. The second option is to treat unsworn statements in the same way that eighteenth-century courts treated sworn statements—with wariness if not complete disapproval. At least on paper, the United States Supreme Court chose this option for defendants in custody in *Miranda v. Arizona*.[120]

If the United States were now to follow England's lead—which seems extremely unlikely—it would treat sworn statements in the same manner in which the framers of the Fifth Amendment treated unsworn statements. Just as the framers expected defendants to speak at trial, courts would now expect them to testify. *Griffin v. California* would be overruled along with *Miranda*. The privilege would remain a safeguard against torture and other forms of coercive interrogation (although not against the coercion once thought inherent in the oath). As a concession to the past, courts might permit defendants to testify under oath but exempt their testimony from the penalties for perjury (confirming the informal exemption that prosecutors usually provide in practice).[121] With the threat of secular penalties removed, the sworn statements of our era might be no more the product of compulsion than the unsworn statements of the founders' era, and treating today's sworn statements like the unsworn statements of the past might be the most accurate "translation" of the framers' understanding.[122] This position might also be supported by reading the Fifth Amendment at the highest level of generality, by declaring that the word *compelled* invites each generation to determine for itself what interrogation methods are offensive and by proclaiming that in the final years of the twentieth century, requiring someone to swear to tell the truth does not seem very much like torture.[123] Still, one might be troubled by an interpretation of the Fifth Amendment that, in one very clear sense, would afford less protection to defendants than the framers intended them to have.

The last alternative—treating unsworn statements by defendants in the same way that the framers treated sworn statements—might bar sworn and unsworn statements from evidence. At least it would require suspects to make unfettered waivers of the right to silence whenever they responded to official inquiry. It also would forbid fact finders to draw adverse inferences from the failure of defendants to answer. This solution, the one that *Miranda* adopted for suspects in police custody, is the worst alternative of all. More likely to be honored on paper than in practice, it would, if taken seriously, all but abandon defendants as an evidentiary resource. No sensible criminal justice system would pay this high price; no coherent ethical principle could explain why it should; and the architects of the Constitution never imagined that the Fifth Amendment would be read to demand it.

The history of the privilege against self-incrimination provides only limited guidance in resolving the Fifth Amendment issues that confront modern courts. Recognition that the amendment does not afford a right to remain silent or require an unfettered waiver of this right whenever officials ask incriminating questions could lead to a reconsideration of *Miranda,* but history cannot tell judges what sorts of interrogation amount to compulsion under the amendment. As Carol Steiker has observed, "Our twentieth-century police and even our contemporary sense of 'policing' [were] utterly foreign to our colonial forebears."[124] Nothing closely resembling station-house interrogation occurred at the time of the Fifth Amendment's framing.

The nearest analogue to police interrogation known to the framers was interrogation before a magistrate under the Marian Committal Statute of 1555,[125] and for decades, people whose names "read like an honor roll of the legal profession"—Wigmore, Pound, Kauper, Friendly, Schaefer, Frankel, and many others—have proposed a return to something like the Marian procedure.[126] Pretrial interrogation before a magistrate of the sort they envision might require the magistrate to find probable cause for a suspect's arrest before interrogation could begin. It might permit the suspect to be represented by counsel as his statement is taken. It might bow to the original understanding of the Fifth Amendment privilege by allowing the suspect to remain unsworn. It might permit a magistrate or, perhaps, a prosecutor to question the suspect, taking his statement in much the same manner that a lawyer engaged in civil practice takes a deposition. The procedure might also afford the suspect a reciprocal opportunity to obtain the statements of prosecution witnesses. In 1980, Scotland reinstated its pretrial examination of defendants, and Scotland's experience might guide American reform.[127]

A suspect's answers to orderly questions in a safeguarded courtroom environment should not be regarded as the product of compulsion. These answers might tend to prove the suspect's guilt because they were incriminating, seemed internally contradictory, rang untrue in certain details, or were inconsistent with the suspect's defense at trial. Equally, the answers might tend to prove the suspect's innocence by showing that he had denied his guilt promptly, in a manner consistent with his trial defense and in straightforward answers to specific questions. Interrogation before a judicial officer would be likely to promote accurate fact-finding both when accurate fact-finding would help the suspect and when it would hurt him. If the suspect refused to answer, his refusal should be admissible at trial both because it would have a rational bearing on his guilt and because its admission would express the judgment that, following a showing of probable cause, suspects can reasonably be expected to respond to orderly inquiry. For the same reason, a defendant should be expected to speak at trial (perhaps under oath but exempted from the penalties for perjury).[128] If he declined, the jury or judge should be permitted to draw appropriate inferences.

The history of the privilege against self-incrimination may raise as many questions for modern courts as it answers, but if a state legislature were to approve a procedure like this one, a court could take much of its guidance from the past. Because this procedure would require a showing of solidly grounded suspicion before interrogation could begin, it would be consistent with the maxim *Nemo tenetur prodere seipsum* as that maxim was understood in the *ius commune* and as it was enforced by the common law courts against the High Commission. The procedure also would be consistent with the original understanding of the Fifth Amendment privilege, for the framers saw no tension between the privilege and their own interrogation practices—practices that differed from the proposal only in that they lacked some of its safeguards. Finally, the procedure would be consistent with the principles of ordinary morality articulated by Kent Greenawalt. When neither text, history, nor sensible policy condemns a practice, a court should find it constitutional; and if the practice seems inconsistent with the right to remain silent, courts should read the Constitution again. With the help of history and of ordinary morality, they should look at what the Fifth Amendment really says.

ONE

1. A version of the privilege has recently been proposed, for example, in the new Code of Criminal Procedure of Taiwan; see Jaw-Perng Wang, Taiwan's Proposed Adoption of the Right to Silence: A Theoretical Analysis and Empirical Study of the Privilege against Self-Incrimination (1995) (unpublished Ph.D. dissertation, University of Chicago Law School). The author comments, however, that it "is the most controversial topic in the criminal justice area."

2. 61 & 62 Vict. c. 36 (1898).

3. Criminal Justice and Public Order Act of 1994, §§32–35. For recent English developments in light of the underlying reasons for the rule, see Ian Dennis, Instrumental Protection, Human Right or Functional Necessity? Reassessing the Privilege against Self-Incrimination, 54 Cambridge Law Journal 342 (1995) (taking note also of the possibility of expansion of the privilege through intervention by the European Court and the European Commission of Human Rights). See also James Michael and Ben Emmerson, Current Topic: The Right to Silence, 1 European Human Rights Law Review 4 (1995).

4. See, e.g., Petty v. The Queen, 65 Australian Law Journal Reports 625 (1991).

5. Constitution Act of 1982, §§11(c), 13. See generally David Paciocco, Charter Principles and Proof in Criminal Cases 479–508 (1987); Yves de Montigny, La Protection contre l'Auto-Incrimination au Canada: Mythe ou Réalité?, 35 McGill Law Journal 746 (1990).

6. Constitution of the Sovereign Democratic Republic of Fiji, §11(7) (1990), in 6 Constitutions of the Countries of the World 40 (Albert Blaustein and Timothy J. Kennedy eds., 1990 update); Criminal Procedure Code, ch. 9, §146(a), in 1 Laws of Fiji (W. G. Bryce ed., 1955).

7. See, e.g., Akhil Reed Amar and Renée B. Lettow, Fifth Amendment

First Principles: The Self-Incrimination Clause, 93 Michigan Law Review 865–74 (1995).

8. Griffin v. California, 380 U.S. 609 (1968). For critical comments on the practical results of the decision, see, e.g., Donald B. Ayer, The Fifth Amendment and the Inference of Guilt from Silence: *Griffin v. California* after Fifteen Years, 78 Michigan Law Review 841 (1980).

9. 380 U.S. at 613–14.

10. See, e.g., R. Kent Greenawalt, Silence as a Moral and Constitutional Right, 23 William & Mary Law Review 15, 34–52 (1981); Charles Fried, Privacy, 77 Yale Law Journal 475, 488–89 (1968); and the English authorities collected in J. D. Heydon, Statutory Restrictions on the Privilege against Self-Incrimination, 87 Law Quarterly Review 214, 216–21 (1971).

11. E.g., Erwin Griswold, The Fifth Amendment Today 73 (1955).

12. 5 Bentham, Rationale, bk. 9, ch. 3, at 207–83.

13. William Twining, Theories of Evidence: Bentham and Wigmore 86 (1985); Michael A. Menlowe, Bentham, Self-Incrimination and the Law of Evidence, 104 Law Quarterly Review 286–307 (1988).

14. 5 Bentham, Rationale 218; 2 id. at 183.

15. This is the argument developed in chapter 6.

16. Nemo Tenetur Seipsum Prodere, 5 Harvard Law Review 71, 87 (1891). See also Henry Terry, Constitutional Provisions against Forcing Self-Incrimination, 15 Yale Law Journal 127 (1906).

17. 8 Wigmore, Evidence §2251, at 296.

18. Id.

19. Robert B. McKay, Self-Incrimination and the New Privacy, 1967 Supreme Court Review 193, 214.

20. Henry J. Friendly, The Fifth Amendment Tomorrow: The Case for Constitutional Change, 37 University of Cincinnati Law Review 671 (1968).

21. Fisher v. United States, 425 U.S. 391, 416 (1975) (Brennan, J., concurring). See also Couch v. United States, 409 U.S. 322, 327 (1973) ("private inner sanctum of individual feeling and thought" guaranteed by the privilege); Griswold v. Connecticut, 381 U.S. 479, 484 (1965) ("Self-Incrimination Clause enables the citizen to create a zone of privacy which government may not force him to surrender"); Murphy v. Waterfront Commission, 378 U.S. 52, 55 (1964) ("inviolability of the human personality" protected by the privilege). See also Robert Gerstein, Privacy and Self-Incrimination, 80 Ethics 87 (1970).

22. E.g., McKay, supra note 19, at 214 (urging abandonment of traditional "empty pomposities" in favor of this rationale).

23. Friendly, supra note 20, at 687–90.

24. Compare, e.g., A. R. N. Cross, The Right to Silence and the Presumption of Innocence—Sacred Cows or Safeguards of Liberty?, 11 Journal of the Society of Public Teachers of Law 66 (1970), with Richard Field, The Right

to Silence: A Rejoinder to Professor Cross, id. at 76. See also Steven Greer, The Right to Silence: A Review of the Current Debate, 53 Modern Law Review 709 (1990); Robert S. Gerstein, The Self-Incrimination Debate in Great Britain, 27 American Journal of Comparative Law 81 (1979).

25. See, e.g., Baltimore City Department of Social Services v. Bouknight, 493 U.S. 549 (1990) (mother suspected of having killed her son asserted privilege not to comply with order by juvenile court to produce the son). See also the review of recent cases by Eric R. Delinsky in Criminal Procedure Project, 83 Georgetown Law Journal 1182–90 (1995).

26. See, e.g., the reaction to Bouknight in Note, 25 Wake Forest Law Review 885, 886 (1990) (warning that if the "right is compromised whenever the courts are particularly outraged at the suspected crime, the right will be ultimately emasculated"). For measured evaluations, see Stephen J. Schulhofer, Some Kind Words for the Privilege against Self-Incrimination, 26 Valparaiso Law Review 311 (1991); David Dolinko, Is There a Rationale for the Privilege against Self-Incrimination?, 33 UCLA Law Review 1063 (1986).

27. Walter Schaefer, The Suspect and Society 61 (1967) (describing the privilege as "a doctrine in search of a reason"); Griswold, supra note 11, at 7 (describing it as "one of the great landmarks in man's struggle to make himself civilized); Ed Ratushny, Self-Incrimination in the Canadian Criminal Process (1979).

28. Amar and Lettow, supra note 7, at 860–98.

29. Miranda v. Arizona, 384 U.S. 436, 460 (1966) (quoting United States v. Grunewald, 233 F.2d 556, 581 (2d Cir. 1956) (Frank, J., dissenting)).

30. Ullmann v. United States, 350 U.S. 422, 438 (1956) (quoting Justice Holmes in New York Trust Co. v. Eisner, 256 U.S. 345, 349 (1921)).

31. E.g., A. A. S. Zuckerman, The Principles of Criminal Evidence 315 (1989): "[T]he origins of the privilege remain obscure."

32. E.g., McCormick on Evidence §114, at 279 (3d ed., Edward W. Cleary ed., 1984); David M. O'Brien, The Fifth Amendment: Fox Hunters, Old Women, Hermits, and the Burger Court, 54 Notre Dame Lawyer 26, 27, 30 (1978); Stefan Riesenfeld, Law-Making and Legislative Precedent in American Legal History, 33 Minnesota Law Review 103, 118 (1949). See, however, William J. Stuntz, The Substantive Origins of Criminal Procedure, 105 Yale Law Journal 393, 411 (1995) (arguing that there is no more than an apparent contradiction between what he calls the "Wigmore-Levy" account and that given herein).

33. 8 Wigmore, Evidence §2250 contains the basic story.

34. See chapter 4, section II.D.

35. Levy, Origins (1st ed. 1968; 2d ed. 1986).

36. E.g., Gaspare J. Saladino, The Bill of Rights: A Bibliographic Essay, in The Bill of Rights and the States: The Colonial and Revolutionary Origins of

American Liberties 502 (Patrick T. Conley and John P. Kaminski eds., 1992) ("It remained, however, for Leonard W. Levy . . . to write the definitive study on the privilege against self-incrimination").

37. An instructive parallel is the history of the common law jury; see Stephen C. Yeazell, The New Jury and the Ancient Jury Conflict, 1990 University of Chicago Legal Forum 87.

38. The term *privilege against self-incrimination* itself seems also to be of comparatively recent vintage. See Levy, Origins xvi. Earlier writers found different names for it, so there is some anachronism involved in our usage.

39. James A. Brundage, Medieval Canon Law 60–61 (1995).

40. See M. R. T. Macnair, The Early Development of the Privilege against Self-Incrimination, 10 Oxford Journal of Legal Studies 66 (1990).

41. 16 Car. 1, c. 11. The prohibition against use of the oath coincided with the abolition of the ecclesiastical courts themselves. When the courts were reestablished after the Restoration, however, the rule abolishing use of the ex officio oath was retained. 13 Car. 2, c. 12, §4 (1660).

42. It might, for example, more easily be applied to or asserted in favor of the testimony of a witness than of a person charged with a crime. See, e.g., Trial of Titus Oates (1685), 10 State Trials 1099–1100, 1104, where the attempt to put such "ensnaring" questions to a witness was reproved by the chief justice.

43. See John V. Orth, Combination and Conspiracy: A Legal History of Trade Unionism, 1721–1906, at 33–35 (1991).

44. Levy, Origins 321.

45. It should not be pretended, of course, that such examples are limited to the past. See, e.g., T. Jeremy Gunn, Adjudicating Rights of Conscience under the European Convention on Human Rights, in Religious Human Rights in Global Perspective: Legal Perspectives 305 (Johan D. van der Vyver and John Witte Jr. eds., 1996).

46. For a similar problem, with similar conclusions, in the law relating to criminal insanity, see Joel Peter Eigen, Witnessing Insanity: Madness and Mad-Doctors in the English Court 3 (1995).

47. See, e.g., John H. Langbein, Prosecuting Crime in the Renaissance (1974); Crime in England 1550–1800 (J. S. Cockburn ed., 1977); Beattie, Crime and the Courts; Twelve Good Men and True: The Criminal Trial Jury in England, 1200–1800 (J. S. Cockburn and Thomas A. Green eds., 1988).

48. U.S. Const., amend. VI. For a full discussion, see 2 Wayne LaFave and Jerold Israel, Criminal Procedure §11.1 (1984).

49. Legal Aid Act of 1988, §21(3).

50. The basic rule applied in the *ius commune* was found in X 5.1.15 (for the canonical system of citation, see infra chapter 2, note 1); for the English common law, see 2 Hawkins, Pleas of the Crown, ch. 39, §2 (asserting, however, that this favored the prisoner, whose "simplicity and innocence, artless

and ingenuous behaviour . . . [possessed] something in it more moving and convincing than the highest eloquence of persons speaking in a cause not their own").

51. Richard M. Fraher, The Theoretical Justification for the New Criminal Law of the High Middle Ages: "Rei publicae interest, ne crimina remaneant impunita," 1984 University of Illinois Law Review 577.

52. I have collected what evidence I could on the subject in R. H. Helmholz, Roman Canon Law in Reformation England 117–19 (1990).

53. See Beattie, Crime and the Courts 356–62.

54. Hostiensis, Summa aurea II, tit. De testibus, no. 5 (Venice 1574): for example, the parties could remit the necessity for an oath if they chose.

55. E.g., [Richard Crompton], L'Office et Aucthoritie de Justice de Peace 1584, at 152 (P. R. Glazebrook ed., 1972).

56. Cullier v. Cullier (K.B. 1589), Cro. Eliz. 201, 78 Eng. Rep. 457. This case, its several reports, and its meaning are discussed in more detail in chapter 3.

57. William Lambarde, Eirenarcha, or of the Office of the Justices of Peace bk. 2, ch. 7 (London 1581). See Levy, Origins 371–74 for a fuller list.

58. 4 Blackstone, Commentaries 296.

TWO

1. The term *ius commune* refers to the combination of Roman and canon laws that dominated European legal education before the modern era. In large measure, it determined the rules of practice in the courts of the English church, both before and after the Reformation of the sixteenth century. See generally O. F. Robinson, T. D. Fergus, and W. M. Gordon, European Legal History: Sources and Institutions 106–23 (2d ed. 1994); James A. Brundage, Medieval Canon Law (1995); Manlio Bellomo, L'Europa del diritto comune (1988), translated as The Common Legal Past of Europe, 1000–1800 (Lydia G. Cochrane trans., 1995). The following abbreviations to the texts of the Corpus iuris canonici, which contained the basic texts for the canon law, are used throughout:

Dist. 1 c. 1	Decretum Gratiani, Distinctio 1, canon 1
C. 1 q. 1 c. 1	———, Causa 1, quaestio 1, canon 1
De pen.	———, De poenitencia
De cons.	———, De consecratione
X 1.1.1	Decretales Gregorii IX, Book 1, tit. 1, cap. 1
Sext. 1.1.1	Liber sextus, Book 1, tit. 1, cap. 1
Clem. 1.1.1	Constitutiones Clementis V, Book 1, tit. 1, cap. 1

Extravag. 1.1.1	Extravagantes communes, Book 1, tit. 1, cap. 1
Dig. 1.1.1	Digestum Justiniani
ad	Latin term used to indicate the text being commented on
d.a.	dictum ante (in Decretum)
d.p.	dictum post (in Decretum)
gl. ord.	glossa ordinaria
s.d.	sub datum (reference to the date given for a document)
s.v.	sub verbum (reference to text in glossa ordinaria or other commentary on a legal text)

All references to treatises from the *ius commune* are given in full in the first instance and thereafter by the most common abbreviation used in earlier practice. Also used herein is the method of citing by text rather than by page; this follows common usage in early legal practice, and it is also more useful because of the large number of printed editions of many of the works. The following abbreviations to libraries and record repositories have also been used throughout:

BIHR	Borthwick Institute of Historical Research, York
BL	British Library, London
Bodl.	Bodleian Library, Oxford
CUL	Cambridge University Library
LPL	Lambeth Palace Library, London

2. Gl. ord. ad X 2.20.37 s.v. de causis: "Sed contra videtur quod non teneatur respondere quia nemo tenetur prodere se." See also gl. ord. ad De pen. Dist. 1, c. 87 s.v. accuses, and ad Sext. 2.9.2 s.v. absque rationabili causa.

3. See, e.g., Julius Clarus (d. 1575), Sententiarum receptarum liber quintus . . . (seu) Practica criminalis, quaest. 45, no. 6 (Venice 1595), with citation to Roman law texts and medieval commentaries.

4. William Durantis, Speculum iudiciale III:1, tit. De inquisitione §1, no. 1, §2, nos. 2–5 (Basel 1574, repr. 1975). For a later example from the papal court, see Octavianus Vestrius, In Romanae aulae actionem et iudiciorum mores introductio, bk. 5, at 95 (Venice 1547).

5. Panormitanus, Commentaria super decretalium libros ad X 2.18.2, no. 16 (Venice 1615): "Videtur enim quod non tenebatur respondere interrogationi seu positioni criminosae quia non debet seipsum prodere."

6. E.g., Lanfrancus de Oriano (d. 1488), Practica aurea, tit. De responsioni-

bus, no. 16 (Venice 1541): "Decima regula sit ista, positioni criminose non est respondendum."

7. Johannes Corserius, Decisiones capellae Tholosanae, quaest. 69 (Frankfurt 1575). See also Jean-Louis Gazzaniga, Droit et pratique: Notes sur les décisions de la Chapelle toulousaine, in L'Église et le droit dans le Midi (XIIIe–XIVe siècles) 321–37 (Fanjeaux 1994).

8. The first chapter of Levy, Origins, is titled "Rival Systems of Criminal Procedure."

9. See, e.g., the routine statement of this understanding in Conrad Russell, Whose Supremacy? King, Parliament and the Church 1530–1640, Lambeth Palace Library Annual Review 57 (1995).

10. The Act of Supremacy, 1 Eliz. c. 1 (1559) gave parliamentary sanction to the exercise by commission of jurisdictional power delegated by the Crown. For a representative commission issued in due course under this statute, see G. R. Elton, The Tudor Constitution, no. 103 (1962). The standard work on the subject remains Roland G. Usher, The Rise and Fall of the High Commission (1913, republished with a new introduction by Philip Tyler 1968).

11. See M. R. T. Macnair, The Early Development of the Privilege against Self-Incrimination, 10 Oxford Journal of Legal Studies 66 (1990); see also the interesting account of controversy on the subject among French scholars in A. Esmein, Le Serment des inculpés en droit canonique, in Bibliothèque de l'École des hautes études: Sciences religieuses 231–48 (1896).

12. See Harold J. Berman and Charles J. Reid Jr., Roman Law in Europe and the *jus commune:* A Historical Overview with Emphasis on the New Legal Science of the Sixteenth Century, 20 Syracuse Journal of International Law and Commerce 1–31 (1994).

13. C. 2 q. 1, c. 4.

14. See X 3.11.1 and DD. ad id. Or see Bartolus de Saxoferrato, Commentaria ad Dig. 1.18.13, no. 3 (Venice 1570–71): "Et ista regulariter est prohibita, quia nemo sine accusatore punitur."

15. John 8:10–11.

16. See Robertus Maranta, Speculum aureum seu lumen advocatorum . . . praxis civilis, pt. 6, tit. De inquisitione, no. 6 (Venice 1605); see also the comment by an English civilian, BL, Lansd. MS 131, fol. 150: "Nulla enim aequitas suggerit, ut quis debeat prodere crimen suum, etiamsi de eo sit infamatus cum infamia saepe sit fallax . . ."

17. E.g., Franciscus Arrentinus, Practica criminalis canonica, ch. 14 (Perugia 1609): "Qui quidem iudex medius est inter accusatorem et reum eis iusticiam administrans, medium autem in neutram partem inclinare debet."

18. Petrus Follerius, Praxis canonica criminalis (Venice 1570), pt. 2, quaest. 6, no. 1 (Venice 1570), where it is said that the practice would be contrary to "commutative justice" because the judge is properly *interpres iustitiae*. See also

Maranta, supra note 16, at pt. 6, tit. De inquisitione, no. 24; Sigismundus Scaccia (d. 1620), Tractatus de iudiciis causarum civilium criminalium et haereticalium, bk. 1, ch. 68, no. 10 (Venice 1663).

19. See discussion with citation to works of Continental authors by English civilians, BL, Add. MS 11,406, fol. 257 (Miscellanea of Sir Julius Clarus); BL, Lansd. MS 131, fols. 148v–50; LPL, MS 2,004, fols. 66–71v, 76–76v; Trinity Hall Library, Cambridge, MS 43/2.

20. See Sebastianus Vantius (d. 1570), Tractatus de nullitatibus processuum, tit. De defectu processus, nos. 29–30 (Venice 1567): "Naturali namque rationi convenit ut quis prius cognoscat id super quo iudicare [sic; recte iudicari] debet et propterea dici consuevit quod causae cognitio a iure divino descendit." But cf. Clarus, supra note 3, at quaest. 45, no. 8, noting with disapproval the prevalence of customary practice to the contrary.

21. X 1.6.3.

22. See Innocent IV, Apparatus in quinque libros Decretalium, ad X 5.1.21, no. 4 (Frankfurt 1570, repr. 1968).

23. Gl. ord. ad id. s.v. conversatus: "Alias non posset de ipsius vita constare."

24. See, e.g., Durantis, supra note 4, III:1, tit. De inquisitione §2, nos. 1–3.

25. Richard Cosin, Apologie for sundrie proceedings by Jurisdiction Ecclesiasticall pt. 2, ch. 7, at 54 (1593).

26. Gl. ord. ad X 3.12.1 (dealing also with cases where the accuser failed to prove the crime he alleged).

27. Maranta, supra note 16, tit. De inquisitione, nos. 22–202.

28. See gl. ord. ad X 5.1.17 s.v. exceptis occultis: "Super his inquisitio fieri non debet, sed super illis tantum de quibus infamia praecessit." The argument is found in the comments of English civilians. See, e.g., BL, Lansd. MS 131, fol. 150: "Si [crimen] est notorium vel famosum respondere tenetur."

29. Gen. 4:10, in which Cain's murder of Abel comes to God's attention because, God said, "vox sanguinis fratris tui clamat ad me de terra." See Follerius, supra note 18, pt. 2, quaest. 6, no. 2.

30. See, e.g., Julius Clarus, supra note 3, quaest. 6, no. 1, where public fame is said to "open the way for the judge to proceed" because "[talis] diffamatio succedit loco accusationis."

31. See X 5.1.24 and DD. ad id.

32. Panormitanus, Commentaria ad X 2.18.2, no. 19: "saepe est fallax." See also Lanfrancus de Oriano, supra note 6, tit. De responsionibus, marg. add. ad n. 17.

33. "Wee have fownde and shewed that this manner of proceedinge to extorte first our owne othe etc. is repugnante both to the worde of God and Lawe." LPL, MS 2,004 (Fairhurst papers), fol. 71v (concluding discussion about absence of proper grounding for oath).

34. For fuller and more representative discussions of the law's requirements, see Julius Clarus, supra note 3, quaest. 6, nos. 1–23; J. B. Diaz de Luco (d. 1556), Practica criminalis canonica, ch. 118 (Lyons 1554), s.v. Iuramento praemissis

interrogari); Maranta, supra note 16, pt. 6, tit. De inquisitione, no. 19; see also Cosin, supra note 25, pt. 2, chs. 6–7.

35. The fullest discussion of this requirement I have seen is found in Marquard Freher (fl. 17th c.), Tractatus de fama publica, bk. 1, ch. 11, nos. 1–15, 21 (Basel 1591).

36. Asserted by a defendant before the commissary court of London, in Ex officio v. Curtis, London Guildhall, Act book MS 9,064/18, fol. 21 (1620); the defendant refused to undergo purgation, "quia huiusmodi detectio fuit et est fabricata ex nudis accusatione et assertione dicte Suzanne nulla publica fama inde laborante." For commentary, see Julius Clarus, supra note 3, quaest. 6, nos. 12–21.

37. See BL, Harl. MS 358, fol. 198 (1588–89) (arguing that the practice had become *nutricula peccati* to every judge of the High Commission, "imboldeninge him oftentymes at his owne pleasure iniuste vexare innocentem." See also J. Morice, Brief Treatise of oaths exacted by Ordinaries and Ecclesiastical Judges 9 (1590), criticizing the ex officio oath as allowing a judge to "play the part of a subtil circumventor and accusor."

38. LPL, MS 2,004, fol. 71, arguing that initial proof of *fama publica* by suitable witnesses was required before the oath could be administered, this being admitted "even by the judgment of Julius Clarus himselfe." Defenders of ecclesiastical jurisdiction admitted that such inquests were not always held. See Thomas Ridley (d. 1629), A View of the Civile and Ecclesiasticall Law pt. 1, ch. 5, at 113 (Oxford 1662).

39. BL, Harl. MS 358, fol. 198 (1588–89), contrasting the innocent victims with the anonymous defamers who shielded their own culpability by making use of the ex officio procedures.

40. See Guido Papa (d. 1487), In augustissimo senatu Grationapolitano regis consiliarii decisiones, quaest. 1 (Geneva 1667).

41. "Sed certe quicquid sit de iure totum contrarium docet practica," in Julius Clarus, supra note 3, quaest. 6, no. 1. He was arguing that the phrase *fama publica praecedente,* commonly appearing in official court documents, was not borne out by the facts of ordinary practice. See Lanfrancus de Oriano, supra note 6, tit. De responsionibus, no. 17 (contrasting the practices followed in different locations); Ludovicus Gilhausen (d. 1642), Arbor judiciaria criminalis, ch. 3, tit. De inquisitione, no. 23 (1662): "Porro quicquid sit de iure, de consuetudine tamen sequitur condemnatio, etiam non probata qualitate in inquisitione deducta."

42. See, e.g., Bainbridge's Case, BL, Harl. MS 358, fols. 197–98 (1588), arguing that if indeed there were any such custom, "yett by lawe yt were nott tollerable bycause yt ys inimica canonibus; 2, bycause yt doth inferre gravamen ecclesiae; 3, yt ys nutricula peccati in the judge, in the partye himselfe and in those which doe secrettlye informe."

43. One opponent, taking note of the nationality of its proponent, sneered

that "yf we consyder the partye him selfe being counsellor to the King of Spaine . . . yt wyll not seame straunge." See BL, Harl. MS 358, fol. 199v.

44. Id., arguing that, since custom must be based on the consensus of those using it (*consensus utentium*), English practice must similarly reject it.

45. Not all civilians were partisans of the king in the English Civil War. Most were royalist in sentiment, but a few became active parliamentarians supporting the new regime. See Brian Levack, The Civil Lawyers in England: A Political Study 1603–1641, 196 (1973).

46. "Nemo tenetur prodere seipsum, quia nemo tenetur detegere turpitudinem suam." See Julius Clarus, supra note 3, quaest. 45, no. 9.

47. Speculum iudiciale, bk. 2, tit. De positionibus, §7, no. 40 (1574); see also gl. ord. ad Dig. 12.2.26, additio s.v. acquisiti ("Ista glossa est valde notabilis ad hoc, quod dicitur in practica, ista positio est criminosa; et ideo ei non respondendum"). Similarly for the canon law: gl. ord. ad Sext. 2.9.2 s.v. absque rationabili causa: "Item super crimine eius contra quem fiunt, non admittuntur positiones."

48. See, e.g., Antonius de Butrio, Commentaria super libros Decretalium ad X 1.6.54, no. 55 (Venice 1578): "Dic, quicquid dicant quidam, quod si crimen est omnino occultum respondere non tenetur, quia de illo non iudicat ecclesia." See also Panormitanus, Commentaria ad X 2.20.37, no. 13.

49. See, e.g., Jodocus Damhouder (d. 1581), Praxis rerum civilium, ch. 154, no. 22 (Antwerp 1646): "Nemo cogitur respondere se criminosum esse, quod sane intelligendum est, scilicet de criminibus occultis et ad reipublicae perniciem non pertinentibus"; Josephus Mascardus (d. 1588), De probationibus, vol. 3, concl. 1177, nos. 59–60 (Venice 1593): "Positio criminosa non est admittenda nec ei respondendum est, cum nemo cogatur detegere turpitudinem suam"; Lanfrancus de Oriano, supra note 6, tit. De responsionibus, no. 16: "Decima regula sit ista, positioni criminose non est respondendum."

50. C. 33 q. 3; De pen. Dist. 1 d.p. c. 87, §6.

51. For some of the "tensions" inherent in this approach, together with the practical consequences, see Mary C. Mansfield, The Humiliation of Sinners: Public Penance in Thirteenth-Century France 116–24 (1995).

52. Hostiensis (d. 1271), Lectura in libros decretalium ad X 1.6.54, no. 30 (Venice 1571, repr. 1963): "Unde et dicitur nemo sine crimine vivit . . . sed nec tenetur quis se prodere." Innocent IV, Apparatus ad id., no. 11: "[S]ed super criminibus non debet iurare de veritate dicenda cum si a quolibet inquireretur de suis criminibus occultis vix quisquam sine crimine reperiretur." See generally Hans Peter Glöchner, Cogitationis poenam nemo patitur: Zu den Anfängen einer Versuchslehre in der Jurisprudenz der Glossatoren (1989).

53. See Innocent IV, Apparatus ad X 2.18.2, no. 2, for a fuller discussion.

54. C. 2 q. 1 c. 6.

55. See Stephan Kuttner, Ecclesia de occultis non iudicat: Problemata ex

doctrina poenali decretistarum et decretalistarum a Gratiano usque ad Gregorium PP. IX, in Acta Congressus iuridici internationalis, Romae 1934, at 225–46 (1936).

56. C. 2 q. 1 c. 19, an extract from St. Augustine. The scriptural text specifically described Joseph as "being a just man."

57. The characteristic formulation is given by the early canonist Huguccio: "Secretorum enim Deus et non homo est iudex," quoted in Stephan Kuttner, Kanonistische Schuldlehre von Gratian bis auf die Dekretalen Gregors IX, at 20 (1935).

58. See, e.g., Julius Clarus, supra note 3, quaest. 45, no. 9 ("mihi certe haec practica nunquam placuit, est enim manifesta occasio perjurii . . . ut quotidie experientia docet"); Andreas Gail, Practicarum observationum, obs. 85, no. 5 ("Lex occasionem periurii non dare, immo ubi subest periculum periurii iuramentum prohibere debet"). For an older statement, see Petrus de Ferrariis (fl. c. 1400), Practica nova judicialis, tit. Forma excipiendi contra positiones, sec. detegentes, no. 2 (Lyons 1556).

59. The phrase seems to owe its popularity to its inclusion in an opinion by Justice Goldberg. See Murphy v. Waterfront Commission, 378 U.S. 52, 55 (1964). It is in fact older. See John T. McNaughton, The Privilege against Self-Incrimination: Its Constitutional Affectation, Raison d'Etre and Miscellaneous Implications, 51 Journal of Criminal Law, Criminology & Police Science 138, 147 (1960).

60. See Brian Woodcock, Medieval Ecclesiastical Courts in the Diocese of Canterbury 89–92 (1952).

61. See, e.g., Antonius Gomezius (d. 1562/72), Variorum resolutionum, bk. 3 (De delictis), ch. 12, no. 5 (Antwerp 1693) : "quia intelligitur extra judicium vel etiam in iudicio nulla praecedente diffamatione vel iusta causa."

62. This answer was summed up by the commonly used phrase "Licet nemo tenetur seipsum prodere, tamen proditus per famam tenetur . . . innocentiam suam ostendere et seipsum purgare." See, e.g., its statement in the opinion of nine English civilians, temp. Jac. I, Trinity Hall, Cambridge, MS 43/2.

63. Damhouder, supra note 49, ch. 154, no. 22. The parallel case of the canonical presumption of innocence is also instructive. See Richard Fraher, "Ut nullus describatur reus prius quam convincatur": Presumption of Innocence in Medieval Canon Law? Proceedings of the Sixth International Congress of Medieval Canon Law 943 (1985).

64. Kuttner, supra note 55.

65. See Julius Clarus, supra note 3, quaest. 6, no. 2, arguing that before undertaking any proceedings the judge must take care to compile "informationes super infamia rei."

66. See the attitude of Lord Burleigh, cited in Levy, Origins 137. The argument was sometimes stretched slightly, as in the case of a prosecution based on

an allegedly seditious public sermon. Opponents of the Court of High Commission contended that questioning was unlawful without first establishing the existence of *fama publica* that an offense had been committed. See BL, Harl. MS 358, fols. 196–200.

67. These two perceptions are well articulated, on the basis of contemporary controversial literature, in Levack, supra note 45, at 156–57; Usher, supra note 10, at 121–48.

68. See, e.g., Clarus, supra note 3, quaest. 6, no. 7: "Item scias, quod predicta conclusio non habet locum in crimine haeresis, . . . propter enormitatem delicti."

69. The stress laid on heresy as the crime at issue is thus too great in an otherwise useful article, William J. Stuntz, The Substantive Origins of Criminal Procedure, 105 Yale Law Journal 393, 412–15 (1995).

70. Apparatus ad X 1.6.54: "[I]dem credo etiam quod principales personae non coguntur respondere si ad aliam poenam quam spiritualem agatur." In the English context, see Trinity Hall, Cambridge, MS 43/2, fols. 10v–12: "Because penances enioyned by the ordinary are not to be taken in law to be poenae, but medicine tending to the reformation of the delinquent, the example of others and satisfaction of the church, therfore they are not to make such scruple to discover themselves after fame." See also BL, Harl. MS 358, fol. 224, where the oath was justified, "the proceedings beinge onelie for matters towchinge the sowles health of the parties summoned."

71. Trinity Hall, Cambridge, MS 43/2, fols. 10v–12. See generally P. Bellini, Denunciatio evangelica e denunciatio judicialis privata (1986).

72. See Julius Clarus, supra note 3, quaest. 45, no. 10, stating that there could be no punishment in public courts for perjury.

73. That this immunity existed in practice is shown in Ronald A. Marchant, The Church under the Law: Justice, Administration and Discipline in the Diocese of York, 1560–1640, at 4–6 (1969).

74. Id.

75. See, e.g., Antonius Gomezius, supra note 61 (holding that men should always prefer punishment—even death—to perjury, but acknowledging that in practice most men made the opposite choice). See also BL, Harl. MS 358, fol. 200: God "will not hold him guylltlesse that taketh his name in vayne."

76. See supra note 21.

77. Andreas Gail, Observationes practicae, bk. 1, obs. 82, no. 12 (1595): "Debet tamen iudex ea in re circumspectus esse, ne pars praeiudiciali aliqua responsione gravetur, quo casu etiam ad ius commune recurrendum et pars ad respondendum non compellenda [est]."

78. See 1 Stephen, History 342–45; Stuntz, supra note 69, at 412–16.

79. For the part played by hostility to episcopacy and the ecclesiastical courts in leading to the outbreak of the English Civil War, see C. Hill, The State-Ecclesiastical, in 2 The Collected Essays of Christopher Hill 51 (1986); Rose-

mary O'Day, The Debate on the English Reformation 38, 195–200 (1986); Laurence Stone, The Causes of the English Revolution, 1529–1642, at 118–22 (1972).

80. 16 Car. 1 c. 10 (1641) (Act for the Abolition of the Court of High Commission) (after the Restoration).

81. 13 Car. 2 c. 12, §4 (1661) (Act for Repeal of a Statute of Elizabeth concerning Commissioners for Causes Ecclesiasticall). The privilege was not wholly irrelevant in the ecclesiastical courts even then. See, e.g., Gifford v. Perkins (1671), a case in which a witness refused to "fully answer" a question put to him because (he said) it would require him to admit that he had been present at a clandestine marriage, thus subjecting him to ecclesiastical jurisdiction. The case is recorded in a post-Restoration collection of ecclesiastical cases: Columbia Law School, MS M 315, fol. 12v.

82. See Woodcock, supra note 60, at 84; Ralph Houlbrooke, Church Courts and the People during the English Reformation 1520–1570, at 44–47 (1979).

83. Canterbury Cathedral Library, Lit. MS D.8 (14th c.), fol. 26v: "Exceptio contra articulum ex officio eo quod fama non precessit." Other examples: Norfolk Record Office, Norwich, ANW/21/6 (16th c.), fols. 3–5; Canterbury Cathedral Library, MS Z.3.5.31, at 662–63; Lincolnshire Archives Office, Lincoln, For.23, fol. 159 (15th c.).

84. CUL, EDR Act book D/2/1, fol. 25: "[u]bi excessus non est manifestus nulla monitione vel citatione legitima precedente et aliquotiens ubi excessus pretensus est totaliter occultus."

85. This was an appealed cause to the Provincial Court of York as part of a dispute over jurisdiction. One charge was that the judge at Carlisle had sought to exercise ex officio jurisdiction over Ralph Spuriere, rector of Cliburne, for incontinence with Agnes Grene, despite lack of public fame against him. It is found in BIHR, CP.F.26/2 (1407).

86. Ex officio v. Harvy (1526), Lincolnshire Archives Office, Lincoln, Act book Cj/3, fol. 14; she was nevertheless excommunicated, it apparently being the point in contention whether proper foundation for this had been laid. No outcome survives. Another example is Ex officio v. Hostler (Bath and Wells 1533), Somerset Record Office, Act book D/D/Ca 8, fol. 29v, in which the defendant was pronounced convicted for his refusal. A third, although complicated by a jurisdictional objection, is found in BIHR, CP.E.31f (1336–37), an attempt to proceed against monks of the abbey of Furness "super lapsu carnis."

87. Ex officio v. Lucas, Guildhall Library, London, MS 9,064/5, fol. 13.

88. Richard Southern, Robert Grosseteste: The Growth of an English Mind in Medieval Europe (1986); this subject in particular is covered at 260–64. See also J. H. Srawley, Grosseteste's Administration of the Diocese of Lincoln, in Robert Grosseteste: Scholar and Bishop 165 (D. A. Callus ed., 1955).

89. The story is told, although without apparent recognition that the law

of the church rather than the law of the king was most directly involved, by Mary Hume Maguire, Attack of the Common Lawyers on the Oath *ex officio* as Administered in the Ecclesiastical Courts in England, in Essays in History and Political Theory in Honor of Charles Howard McIlwain 205–8 (Carl Wittke ed., 1936).

90. Id. at 208.

91. See gl. ord ad X 5.1.21 s.v. quaesivisti for illustrative discussion.

92. See the characterization in William Hale, A Series of Precedents and Proceedings in Criminal Causes lxii (1847) (describing the procedure as "deciding the matter in a most summary way, and apparently so justly, that there occurs hardly a notice of an appeal").

93. Opinions among historians have differed about its effectiveness as a means of finding facts. Probably most commentators have adopted a milder version of Maitland's famous characterization of the procedure as "little better than a farce." See 1 F. Pollock and F. W. Maitland, History of English Law 443 (2d ed. 1968).

94. E.g., Ex officio v. Homewood (Rochester 1514), Kent Archives Office, Maidstone, Act book DRb Pa 6, fol. 30: "Alicia Homewod notatur adulterii cum Johanne Turke quod die comparuit vir et negat famam unde decernitur ad inquirendum." Similarly, Ex officio v. Brekman (Canterbury 1454), Canterbury Cathedral Library, Act book X.1.1, fol. 100: "Et decretum est ad inquirendum de fama in ecclesia de Harbledon die iovis proximo post festum sancti Hugonis."

95. Kent Archives Office, Maidstone, Act book DRb Pa 2, fol. 109.

96. Similar is Ex officio v. Thomlynson (Durham 1494), Department of Paleography and Diplomatic, University of Durham, Act book DCD.CB. Pr.Off., fol. 73, in which the judge did not require the oath of a defendant after finding that there was no public fame "penes bonos et graves . . . sed pocius ex malicia."

97. Bolton v. Bolton (York 1511), BIHR, D/C.AB.2, fol. 113v, in which the defendant's proctor protested "quod quatenus [positiones] sunt criminales non iuretur nec examinetur super eisdem." The question was litigated in a mid-sixteenth-century case: Nedham v. Lee (York 1559), BIHR, Cons.AB.21, fol. 490; the party had answered such an incriminating *positio* after making the initial protestation. When sentence was given against him, he appealed on the ground of the sentence's nullity. Unfortunately, no result survives.

98. E.g., Bray v. Betyk (Exeter 1533), Devon Record Office, Exeter, Act book Chanter MS 778, s.d. 17 December: the party protested that if "aliquid responsum ad quod de iure non tenetur respondere quod tunc pro nullo habeatur."

99. Pykering v. Hurworth (York 1399), BIHR, D/C.CP.1399/1.

100. The legal principle was so stated in a civilian manuscript notebook of around 1600 in Guildhall Library, London, MS 11,448, fol. 146: "A partie

principall cannot be examined on his oath to answeare a position touchinge the suppression of a will or the burning thereof, . . . because it is criminall."

101. Kent Archives Office, Maidstone, PRC 44/3, at 103: "recusavit expresse subire et prestare iuramentum." Other cases in which defendants refused to take the oath or to give self-incriminating answers: Ex officio v. Quarterman (London High Commission 1640), Public Record Office, London, SP 16/434A, fol. 6v; Ex officio v. Brandling (Durham High Commission 1633), in Acts of the High Commission Court, 34 Surtees Soc. 53 (1857); Ex officio v. Postande & Bridgeton (Exeter 1630), Devon Record Office, Exeter, Chanter MS 764, fol. 25v; Ex officio v. Birthbye (Archdeaconry of Hertford 1597), Hertfordshire Record Office, Hertford, AHH 5/3, fol. 49v; Ex officio v. Becke (Lincoln 1630), Lincolnshire Archives Office, Lincoln, Act book Cj/30, fol. 83; Ex officio v. Bretten & Chisnall (Chester 1601), Cheshire Record Office, Chester, Act book EDC 1/32, fol. 9; Ex officio v. Elliott (Archdeaconry of Nottingham 1597), University Library, Nottingham, A 11 (pt. 2), at 67–69; Ex officio v. Cobden (Chichester 1596), West Sussex Record Office, Chichester, Ep I/17/9, fol. 11v; Ex officio v. Twyninge (Bath and Wells 1594), Somerset Record Office, Taunton, D/D/Ca 100, fol. 18v; Ex officio v. Fynche (Canterbury High Commission 1592), Kent Archives Office, Maidstone, PRC 44/3, v. 109; Ex officio v. Morley (York High Commission 1586), BIHR, HC.AB.11, fols. 52v–53; Ex officio v. Jones (St. Asaph 1580), National Library of Wales, Aberystwith, SA/CB/1, fol. 11; Ex officio v. Walton (Worcester 1576), CUL, MS Mm.4.29, fol. 3.

102. BIHR, MS Prec.Bk.11, fol. 31v: "But Wivell & Blomfeild said that the lawe doth scarcely allowe of this practice, vide Gab. Rom. lib. 1, conclus. 1, de testibus, nu. 32; Bart. l. divus, ff. de cust. et exhibit. reorum (Dig. 48.3.6); Abb. c. in omni, 4, de testibus (Panormitanus, Commentaria, ad X 2.20.4)."

103. Harrison v. Brigges (Durham 1616), Department of Paleography and Diplomatic, University of Durham, DDR XVIII/3, fol. 258v: "Notwithstanding he refuseth to answer the article, quia positio criminalis."

104. Id. "He alleageth Minsingers Counsailes dec. 1 resp. nu. 22."

105. LPL, MS 2,004, fols. 66–77v. The same case is also reported in BL, Harl. MS 358, fols. 196–200.

106. Guildhall Library, London, MS 11,448, fols. 146, 149 (c. 1610).

107. The rule that "no one may be compelled to answer an incriminating position" is found, for example, in "Processus seu modus procedendi in causis correctionum," Cumbria Record Office, Carlisle, DRC 3/62, fol. 82 (1629); in marginalia to a manuscript copy of Francis Clerke's Praxis in curiis ecclesiasticis, Archdeaconry of Nottingham Records, University of Nottingham Library, MS P 284, at 10; in a manuscript called "Summarium processus iudicii in curiis ecclesiasticis huius regni," BL, Add. MS 6,254, fol. 10 (c. 1600); and in a Canterbury formulary, Canterbury Cathedral Library, MS Z.3.24, fol. 49, in which

the proctor was advised to object whenever a position was "criminosa aut captiosa."

108. CUL, EDR F/5/45, at 94–99.

109. Marginalia, Cheshire Record Office, Chester, EDR 6/3, fol. 11v: "Quando respondendum libellis criminosis vide Lanf. de respons. nu. 13."

110. This work, Praxis in curiis ecclesiasticis, published in Dublin in 1666, was written in the 1590s and widely circulated in manuscript. See J. D. M. Derrett, The Works of Francis Clerke, Proctor, 40 Studia et documenta historiae et iuris 52 (1974).

111. See Bodl., Tanner MS 112, no. 57.

112. Marginalia written c. 1640 by Mark Tabor, Registrar of the Wells Archdeaconry Court, Wells Cathedral Library, in the uncatalogued manuscript copy of Francis Clerke's Praxis in curiis ecclesiasticis, fol. 226v.

113. Bodl., Tanner MS 427, fols. 167–68v.

114. Ex officio v. Bale & White (1636), Public Record Office, London, SP 16/324, fol. 5v.

115. Id.

116. Guildhall Library, London, MS 9,064/12, fol. 66v: "dictus Ricardus presens in judicio noluit respondere sed tantum dixit se non teneri de iure respondere."

117. Ex officio v. Middleton (1597), BIHR, HC.CP.1597/8. See also Ex officio v. Udall (High Commission 1590), 1 State Trials 1271, 1275.

118. See the manuscript copy of Francis Clerke, Praxis in curiis ecclesiasticis, Catholic University of America, Washington, D.C., Spec. Coll. MS 180 (containing contemporary annotations to many sources from the tradition of the *ius commune*). A slightly later but equally illustrative example is Henry Conset, The Practice of the Spiritual or Ecclesiastical Courts (1685).

119. Examples discovered: Ex officio v. Beeke, Lincolnshire Archives, Cj/30, fol. 83 (Lincoln 1639), in which the defendant argued that "non tenetur de iure ad prestandum iuramentum de fideliter respondendo etc."; Penrise v. Briscoe (Carlisle 1629), Cumbria Record Office, Carlisle, DRC/3/62 s.d. 16 January, where a defendant, commanded to take the oath in a defamation case, argued that "de iure non tenetur respondere"; Curtice v. Cox (Salisbury 1629), Wiltshire Record Office, Trowbridge, D 1/39/1/51, fol. 28, where a defendant in a defamation suit "dicente se non teneri de iure ad respondendum eidem"; Ex officio v. Langdon (Norwich 1577), Norfolk Record Office, Norwich, ACT/25, s.d. 4 April, where a defendant objected that requiring him to answer was "not warranted by law."; Ex officio v. Okeden (Canterbury 1560), Canterbury Cathedral Library, Act book Y.2.24, fol. 20v, in which the defendant at first refused to undergo the oath because it would be "rashe to take an othe upon a book to the casting away of my soole as some now a daies doo."

120. See, e.g., the discussion in Leo F. Solt, Church and State in Early Modern England 1509–1640, at 120–21 (1990) (taking note also of the use of incriminating questioning in the courts created in contemporary Geneva).

121. See, e.g., Anne Richardson, William Tyndale and the Bill of Rights, in William Tyndale and the Law 11 (John A. R. Dick and Anne Richardson eds., 1994).

122. Ex officio v. Ayleworth (Archdeaconry of Berkshire 1633), Berkshire Record Office, Aylesbury, D/A 2/c.74, fol. 62.

123. It was possible to allege the invalidity of the presentment, but this seems to have cast on the defendant the burden of showing, by witnesses, that the presentment against him was malicious or otherwise unlawful. See, e.g., Ex officio v. Tennaunte (London 1612), Guildhall Library, London, MS 9,064/17, fol. 49, where Tennaunte alleged that the presentment was "ad omnem iuris effectum invalidam . . . and did arise out of the report of the said Damaris being an infamous woman of noe creditt."

124. BIHR, Prec.Bk.11, fol. 31v: "The judge doth putt him to his purgacion although he deny the crime & the fame, so it hath beene always practised. Clarke tit. 336. But Wivell & Blomfeild said that the lawe doth scarcely allowe of this practice."

125. See, e.g., Ex officio v. Browninge (Archdeaconry of Canterbury 1585), Canterbury Cathedral Library, Act book X.2.1, fol. 154, in which the judge "decrevit oeconomos citandos [fore] in proximo ad iustificanda detecta etc."

126. The standard work on the subject remains that by Usher, supra note 10.

127. See gl. ord. ad X 5.1.15 s.v. criminali: "Habes ergo hic expresse quod in causa criminali non intervenit procurator, nec ad agendum, nec ad defendendum [followed by citations to the Decretum Gratiani and Roman law]." There were, however, exceptions.

128. The conclusion is based largely on negative evidence. However, in the one attempt to have a proctor intervene in an ex officio case, the judge rejected it. Ex officio v. Mustell (Ely 1377), CUL, EDR D/2/1, fols. 82v–83.

129. See William Hudson's Treatise of the Court of Star Chamber, pt. 3, §20 (temp. Car. I), in 2 Francis Hargrave, Collectanea Juridica 208–9 (1791).

130. 8 Wigmore, Evidence §2250, at 287. See also Lawrence Herman, The Unexplored Relationship between the Privilege against Compulsory Self-Incrimination and the Involuntary Confession Rule (pt. 1), 53 Ohio State Law Journal 101, at 195–204 (1992).

131. William Lambarde, Eirenarcha, or of the Office of the Justices of Peace, bk. 2, ch. 7, at 403 (London 1581). On Lambarde's view of fundamental problems of jurisprudence, see Wilfrid Prest, William Lambarde, Elizabethan Law

Reform, and Early Stuart Politics, 34 Journal of British Studies 464–80 (1995).

132. See, e.g., 9 Holdsworth, History 197–203.

133. E.g., Rochester v. Mascall (C.P. 1608), BL, Stowe MS 424, fol. 160v: "Quod per legem terrae nemo tenetur in causis criminalibus prodere seipsum." See also 2 Charles M. Gray, The Writ of Prohibition: Jurisdiction in Early Modern English Law 322–23 (1994).

134. Maunsell & Ladd's Case (1607), BL, Add. MS 25,206, fol. 55 per Fuller. The principle that a man should not be required to accuse himself was attributed to "le ley de nature" at fol. 56 of the same report.

135. Id., fol. 56v per Finch, J.

136. Dighton v. Holt (K.B. 1615), Cro. Jac. 388, 79 Eng. Rep. 332, which stressed the need for witnesses before imposing oath on defendant; Dr. Hunt's Case (C.P. 1591), Cro. Eliz. 262, 78 Eng. Rep. 518, speaking of the necessity for presentment by two men before imposing oath on a defendant; Boyer v. High Commission Court (K.B. 1614), 2 Bulstr. 182, 80 Eng. Rep. 1052, taking note of the exception carved out in canon law for examination of parsons seeking entry into benefices.

137. Edward's Case (K.B. 1608), 13 Co. Rep. 9, 77 Eng. Rep. 1421; Jennor's Case (1610), BL, Stowe MS 424, fol. 159v: "Quod nullus liber homo per leges terrae compelli debent [*sic*] ad respondendum de cogitatione sive secretis cordis etc."

138. Glover v. Pipe (K.B. 1586), CUL, MS Ff.5.4. fol. 303v per Tanfield.

139. See Reinhard Zimmermann, The Law of Obligations xi (1990); Kenneth Pennington, Learned Law, Droit Savant, Gelehrtes Recht: The Tyranny of a Concept, 5 Rivista internazionale di diritto comune 199 (1994); Christopher Brooks and Kevin Sharpe, History, English Law and the Renaissance, Past and Present 133 (1976); Hans Pawlisch, Sir John Davies,the Ancient Constitution and Civil Law, 23 Historical Journal 689 (1980); Paul Christianson, Young John Selden and the Ancient Constitution, ca. 1610–18, 128 Proceedings of the American Philosophical Society 271 (1984); Charles Donahue Jr., Book Review, 84 Yale Law Journal 167 (1974). And see generally the conclusions and authorities collected in Glenn Burgess, The Politics of the Ancient Constitution: An Introduction to English Political Thought, 1603–1642, at 80–82 (1992).

140. Compare J. G. A. Pocock, The Ancient Constitution and the Feudal Law 56 (1957), with his reissue of the book containing his comments on the subject thirty years afterwards: id., "Reissue with a Retrospect" 262–63 (1987). See also William Lambarde's use of a civilian source, Harvard Law School, MS 5,116, fol. 21, cited in Prest, supra note 131, at 476 n. 38.

141. For Coke's collection of treatises on the canon and civil law see Catalogue of the Library of Sir Edward Coke 38–41 (W. Hassell ed., 1950).

142. See his "Of Oaths before an Ecclesiastical Judge ex officio" 12 Co. Rep. 26, 77 Eng. Rep. 1308 (1606): "for as a civilian said . . ."

THREE

1. This chapter is based on reported cases, those in print supplemented by MS reports from the British Library collections. It reworks parts of Charles M. Gray, The Writ of Prohibition: Jurisdiction in Early Modern English Law, 2 vols. (1994) (hereafter Gray, Writ of Prohibition), centrally vol. 2, ch. 5. That work is a detailed, case-by-case study of interjurisdictional law divided into a large number of subtopics, each treated chronologically, accompanied by introductions analyzing the general contours of the various problems. The work covers the late sixteenth century (when reported cases become frequent) and the seventeenth down to about 1640. There are post-Restoration sequels for most of the topics, but not for the subject of self-incrimination in any significant degree. Printed cases are cited here by the reporter's name (all available in the Standard Reprint of the English Reports), unprinted ones by the name of the British Library MS collection and folio number.

2. 5 Eliz. c. 9.

3. Questioning of suspects by justices of the peace under the Marian bail statute, the best example of an apparent violation of the privilege in its modern understanding, was done without requiring the suspect to take an oath. See generally John H. Langbein, Prosecuting Crime in the Renaissance: England, Germany, France 25–26 (1974).

4. The possibility of incriminating questioning existed wherever the procedure of the *ius commune* was used, which is to say in equity and admiralty courts and the Star Chamber as well as the ecclesiastical courts. I know of only one case, however, in which the common law intervened to stop such questioning outside the ecclesiastical system (that case, involving the Court of Requests, an ancillary equity court, is discussed below). Equity courts and the Star Chamber were sometimes held up as good examples as against the ecclesiastical courts: tribunals that did not, to be sure, avoid exposing to self-incrimination altogether, but observed restraints similar to those that, according to most common law opinion, the ecclesiastical courts should have. (This is done in the important Popham-Coke extrajudicial opinion discusssed below, and there is some evidence confirming what is suggested there about the relative scrupulosity of chancery and Star Chamber practice.) Equity and admiralty courts were generically subject to common law control, but it was almost entirely exercised to keep them within the bounds of their substantive jurisdiction (very occasionally to control a procedural step other than incriminatory investigation). Since these courts were entirely civil (the admiralty's jurisdiction over crimes on the high seas was exercised by statutorily authorized commission using common law pro-

cedure), there was no more than a slight chance that they might incidentally ask an incriminating question. The chancery was never prohibited, but lesser equity courts were, as shown in Charles M. Gray, The Boundaries of the Equitable Function, 20 American Journal of Legal History 192 (1976). Prohibitions to the admiralty are abundant, owing to serious problems about the meaning and enforceability of the principle that they were confined to matters arising on the high seas. The Star Chamber was untouchable: it was never suggested that the King's Council in its judicial capacity was amenable to common law interference.

5. Usually this was to cause a factual issue that had arisen in the course of litigation before the ecclesiastical court to be tried at common law.

6. G. B. Flahiff, The Writ of Prohibition to Court Christian in the Thirteenth Century (pt. 1), 6 Mediaeval Studies 261 (1944); (pt. 2), 7 id. 229 (1945).

7. The equity and admiralty courts that were also regulated by prohibition in the early modern period—though much less frequently so than the ecclesiastical courts—were as yet minor components of the legal system.

8. See Roland G. Usher, The Rise and Fall of the High Commission (1913, reissued with a new introduction by Philip Tyler, in 1968).

9. See G. I. O. Duncan, The High Court of Delegates (1971).

10. 1 Eliz. c. 1. (1558).

11. See, e.g., the royal commission of 1559 printed in G. R. Elton, The Tudor Constitution: Documents and Commentary 221–25 (1962).

12. However, whereas prohibitions were often turned down on the initial application for want of sufficient cause shown, just being in jail was usually enough to secure a writ of habeas corpus.

13. Besides remanding the applicant to jail when the return was legally sufficient, the options were outright release, in the event of a simply inadequate return, or, in appropriate circumstances, admission to bail.

14. Another recurrent type of case arose from the difficulty of discriminating between an annuity recoverable by common law action and an annuity-like interest known as a "spiritual pension," which ecclesiastical courts were free to enforce.

15. See, e.g., Thomas Ridley, A View of the Civile and Ecclesiasticall Law, pt. 2, ch. 2, §6 (1607).

16. Perhaps the most important example from bread-and-butter law, relatively unaffected by politics, is intestacy: ecclesiastical courts had jurisdiction to arrange for the administration of intestates' estates, but a statute—21 Hen. 8 c. 5, §2 (1529)—was made to direct how that should be done. Decades later there were still wide-open questions about the statute's meaning—essentially how much discretion in choosing administrators, repealing letters of administration, and ordering distributions was allowed to the ecclesiastical judge. The seventeenth-century common law courts painfully settled these matters through

a long series of prohibition cases brought to stop ecclesiastical courts from taking measures allegedly contrary to the statute.

17. For fuller discussion see 2 Gray, Writ of Prohibition, ch. 2 ("Substantive Surmises of Disallowance") and ch. 3 ("Problems of the Disallowance Surmise"). The latter does not bear directly on the conclusions summarized here, but it does elaborate the jurisprudential and procedural issues raised by the prominent place of disallowed pleas in the prohibition practice.

18. If ecclesiastical law had adopted the absurd rule that legacies must be paid on demand however encumbered by debt the estate was, there would obviously have been an intolerable conflict; application of any such rule would have had to be prevented. Executors forced to deplete the estate by paying legacies would have been liable at common law to pay the debts out of their own pockets. When ecclesiastical courts disallowed no assets pleas because they found legacies payable despite the protests of cautious or dilatory executors, it made a certain sense—depending on apparent circumstances, such as the sums involved and the probable validity of creditors' claims—for the common law judges not to abide the process of ecclesiastical appeal. In the long run, however, the argument that ecclesiastical appeal was an adequate remedy—plus the countervailing point of utility: that recovery of modest legacies should not be delayed indefinitely pending settlement of possibly dubious common law claims— tended to prevail.

19. This rule has a basis in statute, but I think it likely that it would have been asserted even without that support. 25 Hen. 8. c. 19 (1533) provided that ecclesiastical law must not contradict either the statutes or the common law. I have not, however, found any explicit dependence on the statute by the lawyers and judges urging the rule.

20. Similarly, it was said that ecclesiastical courts must in defamation cases give the word *bastard* its common law sense rather than its well-known ecclesiastical sense (by the common law a person was a bastard if his parents were not married at the time of his birth, whereas by ecclesiastical law one born between contract to marry and actual marriage was legitimate).

21. That is, there were no treatises designed to be useful to professional lawyers. By contrast, the controversial literature was very large, though much of it remains in manuscript.

22. Full discussion is in 2 Gray, Writ of Prohibition, ch. 4 ("Evidentiary Disallowance Surmises: The Two-Witness Rule").

23. The Common Pleas when he was chief justice there deliberately reversed its own contrary precedent. That court held the line while Coke served on it, and I have found no reported two-witness rule prohibitions from the King's Bench during his subsequent chief justiceship of the other principal court.

24. 12 Co. Rep. 26, 77 Eng. Rep. 1308. Reference of the matter to these

dignitaries indicates concern about it, but I have no direct evidence of the disputes or complaints that led to the document's preparation.

25. The High Commission, where most challengeable interrogation occurred, was outside the terms of the Popham-Coke opinion. Most of the restraints endorsed in it were applied to the commission, and it was sometimes argued, without much success, that the residue should be.

26. This restriction was applicable to suits before the High Commission for, whatever privileges that statute-warranted tribunal might have, it never pretended to substantive jurisdiction beyond the bounds of ecclesiastical law. The most thorough discussion of the rationale for adequate apprisal of the subject of the interrogation and the standard of adequacy occurs in the High Commission case of *Burrowes,* discussed below. See also Birry's Case (K.B. 1605), Godb. 147, 78 Eng. Rep. 90; Add. MS 25,205, fol. 22: dictum that a bond obliging a High Commission defendant to answer unspecified questions is void for the unlawfulness of the condition. Parson Wransfield's Case (C.P. 1609), Harg. MS 52, fol. 15: affirming a duty to apprise defendant, but doing so in "summary" terms is sufficient; swearing to answer with such general notice of the subject does not oblige the party to answer particular questions that are *ultra vires* or otherwise open to objection.

27. See generally Norman L. Jones, God and the Moneylenders: Usury and Law in Early Modern England (1989).

28. The principle sometimes applied in mixed-will cases and to some extent in the disallowance cases discussed above.

29. Short of a positive ban on prosecution of concurrent offenses in both tribunals, the obvious way to prevent "temporal detriment" by fallout from ecclesiastical proceedings is to exclude confessions and other information gained by compelled testimony, as well as non–common law judicial findings, as evidence at common law. It is, however, obvious only with a modern conception of the jury as judge of evidence and modern assumptions about trial ritual and judicial control over it. I know of one rather tantalizing Caroline discussion of the "exclusionary rule" approach—suggested by Justice Hutton, treated with skepticism by his colleagues. Anon. (C.P. 1628), Lit. 167.

30. This rule was applied against the High Commission several times. Three early Elizabethan cases—Leigh's Case (dated 1567 in Darrington's Case (7 Jac. I), Harg. MS 52, fol. 20v); Hynde's Case (dated 1576, in id.); and Mitton's Case, 4 Co. Rep. 32, 76 Eng. Rep. 965 (1584)—were cited on several occasions for the doctrine that the High Commission may not examine concerning ecclesiastical offenses secularized by statute, beginning with Maunsell & Ladd (see infra text accompanying note 47). None of them is independently reported, and descriptions of them in later discussions are not completely consistent in detail, but their basic effect seems clear. They provide an unusual instance in interjurisdictional litigation of operative judicial precedents—that is, cases from

earlier than the plethora of prohibition and habeas corpus cases at the end of the sixteenth century and beyond that were actually regarded as settling a point of law. Note especially their decisive role in *Burrowes* (below).

In the High Commission case of Parson Latters v. Sussex (C.P. temp. Coke, C.J.), Noy 151, 74 Eng. Rep. 1112, the concept of "temporal detriment" was taken beyond statutorily secularized offenses, as was done with respect to the ordinary courts. Thus the examination of a clergyman as to whether he had obtained his living by simony was prohibited because the statute of 31 Eliz. c. 6 (1588–89) deprived simoniacs of the living (a freehold interest) ipso facto. This holding is obliquely confirmed by Sir William Boyer v. High Commission Court (K.B. 1614), 2 Buls. 182, 80 Eng. Rep. 1052, where the commission was *not* prohibited from examining about simony because there was no showing that the examinee was in danger of temporal loss (he was someone allegedly involved in simoniacal dealings, but the clergyman who had primarily profited from them was dead). The court stated expressly that such a party—probably the patron of the living—*might* be in a position to claim temporal loss of some other sort than the ipso facto deprivation of a simoniacal incumbent, but this must be shown to have a prohibition. Note how this case supports my basic argument that incriminating interrogation by the High Commission was never banned as such, where the matter was *infra vires* and the first three rules laid down by Popham and Coke were observed.

31. Edwards's Case (C.P. 1608), 13 Co. Rep. 9, 77 Eng. Rep. 1421.

32. Similarly, it may be objected that the lay privilege went beyond religious offenses, and it is not evident why clerics should be less protected against shaming themselves than laymen.

33. It was found printed as a statute: 9 Edw. 2 st. 1 (1315–16).

34. 25 Hen. 8 c. 14. (1533). What this statute actually did was repeal the sole statute that authorized sworn examination of some ecclesiastical defendants, the famous De heretico comburendo (2 Hen. 4 c. 15 (1401)). Authorization of such examination by a secular statute was of course not necessary to make it lawful, but it is a ground, over and above the language of the repealing act, for arguing that it was not lawful without the authorization.

35. Anon. (Q.B. 1589), Add. MS. 25,196, fol. 213v, and Harl. MS 1,633, fol. 63v; Cullier v. Cullier (K.B. 1589), Harl. MS 1,633, fol. 160; Cro. Eliz. 201, 78 Eng. Rep. 457; Moore 906; 4 Leo. 194.

36. Dr. Hunt's Case (Q.B. 1591), Cro. Eliz. 262, 78 Eng. Rep. 518.

37. There were three ways of charging someone with an ecclesiastical crime: (1) the method mentioned in this case, under which at episcopal visitations, persons—normally the churchwardens—were sworn to name those they believed to be offenders, a procedure analogous to common law presentment juries and courts leet; (2) written complaint by a private accuser, procedurally similar to starting a civil suit; and (3) ex officio, which means that the ecclesiastical

court itself is the complainant, proceeding by citation. It is not always possible to tell, but most cases involving self-incrimination, especially those in the High Commission, were ex officio cases. These distinctions are not belabored in the Popham-Coke opinion, but there is a hint in the language that the intent was to cover only ex officio prosecutions; rules 1 and 3 are in any event only relevant for ex officio cases.

38. Anon. (C.P. 1589), Lansd. MS 1,073, fol. 108; Add. MS 25,194, fol. 6v; Add. MS 25,196, fol. 199v; Moore 906.

39. This case was also complicated by other issues, over all of which the Court of Common Pleas was deeply divided.

40. Spendlow v. Sir William Smith (K.B. temp. Jac. I), Hob. 84, 80 Eng. Rep. 234.

41. Gammon's Case (C.P. 1627), Harl. MS 5,148, fol. 142; Het. 18, 124 Eng. Rep. 306. For extension to the High Commission see Birry's Case, supra note 26; Huntley v. Clifford (C.P. 1611), Harg. MS 15, fol. 239, 2 Brownl. and Golds 14, 123 Eng. Rep. 787, sub nom. Huntley v. Cage; Bradshawe's Case (K.B. 1614), Add. MS 25,213, fol. 163, and 2 Bulst. 300, 80 Eng. Rep. 1138, sub nom. Bradstone v. High Commission Court.

42. Bullocke v. Hall (C.P. temp. Jac. I), Harl. MS 1,631, fol. 365.

43. Quaere with what criminal consequences, but at any rate he would have done something shameful.

44. Parson Wransfield's Case, supra note 26; Darrington's Case, supra note 30—MS report only for this point; Huntley v. Clifford, supra note 41.

45. The document is Stowe MS 424, fols. 158–64v. It is given weight in Levy, Origins 245, but seriously misunderstood. For detailed analysis of the document, see 2 Gray, Writ of Prohibition 377–99.

46. Although it was unusual, nothing prevented use of both writs in the same case, provided a party was imprisoned at some point in his dealings with the High Commission.

47. (K.B. 1607), reported in Add MS 25,206, fols. 55 and 59v; Harl. MS 1,631, fols. 353v and 358v. The printed version of Fuller's argument (see text infra) is The Argument of Master Nicholas Fuller in the Case of Thomas Lad, and Richard Maunsell, his Clients, Wherein it is plainly proved, that the Ecclesiastical Commissioners have no power, by Vertue of their Commission, to Imprison, to put to the oath Ex Officio, or fine any of his Maiesties Subjects (1607).

48. The reports show no lawyers arguing against the prisoners' release and in favor of the High Commission, only a dialogue between the prisoners' counsel and the court. This was the usual pattern in habeas corpus cases.

49. The other notable instance is Darcy v. Allen, or "The Case of Monopolies" (best known from 11 Co. Rep. 84v, 77 Eng. Rep. 1360 (1601–3)). Fuller's argument against the legality of the monopoly in question in that case was after

the fact adopted by Coke (who in the actual case argued on the other side) and represented as the opinion of the court. A complete MS report (Add. MS 25,203, fols. 543v, 558, 570, and 678v) shows that the court, while giving judgment Fuller's way, deliberately avoided arguing the case openly on the Bench, thus leaving it ambiguous whether the decision rested on Fuller's grounds or on others (principally the point that infringing a monopoly, even one conferred by an intrinsically lawful royal patent, was not a common law tort, whatever protection the monopolist might be entitled to outside the common law system, as in the Star Chamber). Aside from Coke's misleading report, the only printed evidence of Darcy v. Allen consists in Fuller's argument (reproduced as such in Moore). In Darcy v. Allen as in Maunsell & Ladd, Fuller was principled, thorough, and radical; his success in the long run of history has in both instances been greater than that he enjoyed in the case at hand.

50. Apart from the manuscript reports, Fuller's published argument is the only direct source for Maunsell & Ladd.

51. See, e.g., the discussion in Norman Doe, Fundamental Authority in Late Medieval English Law 30–31 (1990).

52. It was chapter 29 in the reissued version found in the statute books. See Faith Thompson, The First Century of Magna Carta 10 (1925); J. C. Holt, Magna Carta 460 (2d ed. 1992).

53. Needless to say, I speak of what can be made of Magna Carta as understood in the seventeenth century (and abiding historical mythology), not the actual thirteenth-century document, which antedates common law criminal procedure as it came to be and therefore cannot be said to guarantee it in any nonmythic sense.

54. That is, as opposed, say, to having an evidentiary formalism that would have been functionless under a radically different system of fact ascertainment.

55. There might of course have been *some* purpose: an additional court with only ordinary powers might be vigorous in ex officio prosecution of crimes that the diocesan courts were reluctant to prosecute and might construe the ecclesiastical law more correctly by the supreme governor's lights.

56. At least this held true for the powers of imprisoning and fining.

57. 2 Hen. 4 c. 15 (1401).

58. Burrowes, Cox, and Dyton v. The High Commission Court (K.B. 1616), 3 Bulst. 49, 81 Eng. Rep. 42; 1 Rolle 220, 337, 410, 81 Eng. Rep. 445, 527, 572 (sub nom. Roy v. Dighton, Dighton and Holte, and Holt and Dighton's Case); Harg. MS 47, fols. 66 and 114; Moore 840 (Deyton's Case); Harl. MS 4,561, fol. 251v.

59. Finch originally objected that in addition to language sufficient to show jurisdiction the return contained an open-ended phrase—the words "and other matters," suggesting that the charges went beyond the *infra vires* offenses but not giving any indication of what they were. But an affidavit was also put in,

affirming that at least some of the parties were not informed of the articles of inquiry.

60. This case has a sequel. At least some of the parties were imprisoned again, this time for not, in the High Commission's view, making the "submission" on which their bail was conditioned. They brought another habeas corpus before Coke's King's Bench. High Commission methods were in question in the second case, but not self-incrimination properly speaking, since the prisoners were not asked to take an oath. Rather, on reporting to the commission, as they were required to do, they were asked without oath, by way of testing their submissiveness, whether they were willing to conform to the church and receive communion kneeling. They were jailed for refusing to answer. Their counsel (now Serjeant Harvey) contended that it was unlawful to put them in the position of having either to lie or to commit schism by the very act of saying no, where there was no prior charge of schism. Harvey got nowhere with this claim; the prisoners were remanded. The judges gave very little sign of disapproving of the commission's tactics, but even if they did they saw no legal basis for interference. Although the disposal does not in strictness speak to self-incrimination, it is not easy to believe that a court so unready to do anything about such a form of "making criminals" would have forced a general exemption from compulsory examination for lay defendants on the High Commission.

FOUR

I wish to express my gratitude for the advice of Christopher Allen, Albert Alschuler, Akhil Amar, David Brown, Richard Friedman, Paul Gewirtz, Abraham Goldstein, Thomas Green, Richard Helmholz, Richard Lempert, Michael Macnair, and William Twining. When drawing on English and antiquarian sources, I have modernized and Americanized the spelling, except in the titles of books and pamphlets.

1. In "the reign of Queen Mary . . . the earliest trials of which we have detailed accounts took place . . . ." 1 Stephen, History 319.

2. See infra text accompanying note 93.

3. "How say you, Throckmorton, did not you send Winter to Wyat into Kent, and did devise that the Tower of London should be taken . . . ?" 1 State Trials 869, 872 (1554). "But how say you to this, that Wyat and you had conference together sundry times at Warner's house, and in other places?" Id. at 874.

4. Thomas Smith, De Republica Anglorum, bk. 2, ch. 23, at 114 (Mary Dewar ed., 1982) (1st ed. 1583, written c. 1565).

5. Id.

6. The prohibition on defense counsel was a rule applied to cases of treason and felony. The rule did not extend to misdemeanor. The main rationale for exempting misdemeanor from the prohibition was that some of what was prosecuted as misdemeanor was regarded as essentially civil in character, for example, the question of whether a property owner was responsible for maintaining particular roadside ditches. See Michael Dalton, The Countrey Justice 51–55 (London 1619); see also Beattie, Crime and the Courts 339 and n. 62.

In the reform movement that ultimately led to the use of defense counsel in cases of serious crime, critics of the prohibition contrasted the liberty of defense that was allowed in civil litigation and in misdemeanor. "[W]hat Rule of Justice is there to warrant [the] Denial [of counsel], when in a Civil Case of a Halfpenny Value the Party may plead either by himself or Advocate[?]" Sir Bartholomew Shower, Reasons for a New Bill of Rights 6 (London 1692). Blackstone wrote: "For upon what face of reason can that assistance [of counsel] be denied to save the life of a man, which yet is allowed him in prosecutions for every petty trespass?" 4 Blackstone, Commentaries 355.

7. Some of the discussion that follows is outlined in Langbein, Criminal Trial 307–11.

8. "[T]he Court ought to be . . . of counsel for the prisoner, to see that nothing be urged against him contrary to law and right . . . ." Edward Coke, The Third Part of the Institutes of the Laws of England: Concerning High Treason, and Other Pleas of the Crown, and Criminal Causes 29 (1644) (posthumous publication, written 1620s–1630s).

9. Nicholas Throckmorton, 1 State Trials 877. The same report discloses that "[t]hen the Chief Justice Bromley remembered particularly all the Depositions and Evidences given against the prisoner, and either for want of good memory, or good will, the prisoner's Answers were in part not recited: whereupon the prisoner craved indifferency, and did help the Judge's old memory with his own recital." Id. at 897.

10. John Lilburne, 4 State Trials 1269, 1382 (1649). Lilburne's defense did not change Keble's mind. After hearing Lilburne, Keble told the jury, "[Y]ou will clearly find that never was the like treason hatched in England." Id. at 1402. The jury disagreed. See infra note 123 for further discussion of Lilburne's 1649 trial.

11. Act of Settlement, 12 & 13 Will. 3 c. 2, §3 (1701). For background on the act, see Barbara A. Black, Massachusetts and the Judges: Judicial Independence in Perspective, 3 Law & History Review 101, 103–12 (1985).

12. John Hawles, Remarks Upon the Tryals of Edward Fitzharris, Stephen Colledge, Count Coningsmark, the Lord Russel, Collonel Sidney, Henry Cornish and Charles Bateman 22 (London 1689).

13. On the provenance and contents of the State Trials, see Langbein, Criminal Trial 264–67.

14. The Old Bailey Sessions Papers are discussed id. at 267–72; see also Langbein, Ryder Sources 3–18. Regarding an equivalent series of pamphlet assize reports for the county of Surrey, see Beattie, Crime and the Courts 23–25, 649–51; see also id. at 99–106 (discussing murder trials reported there). The pamphlet reports originated as popular literature to entertain nonlawyers, and the accounts of the trials omit much of the detail that historians wish to know.

15. "[T]he common practice clearly was for the judge to take [the victim and any accusing witnesses] through their testimony line by line, acting as both examiner and cross-examiner, until he was satisfied that the fullest possible case had been presented." Beattie, Crime and the Courts 342; see id. at 345 (commenting on "the judge's immense influence on the way the jury received the evidence and the impression it made on them," including his exercise of the power "to comment on the testimony as it was being given").

16. John Twyn, 6 State Trials 513, 516 (1663). Jermin, J., put the matter quite differently, telling Lilburne from the bench that "the court are of your counsel so far as to fact" but that if a matter of law arises, "you may, and ought to have other counsel assigned." John Lilburne, 4 State Trials 1297–98.

17. John M. Beattie, Scales of Justice: Defense Counsel and the English Criminal Trial in the Eighteenth and Nineteenth Centuries, 9 Law & History Review 221, 223 (1991).

18. Id. (emphasis added).

19. Id.

20. Id. at 233. As late as 1827, a prominent judge—Baron William Garrow, who had come to renown as an Old Bailey defense counsel in the 1780s and 1790s (see id. at 236–47)—explained to a grand jury that, although the judges were counsel for the defendants, " 'they could not suggest the course of defence [that] prisoners ought to pursue.' " Id. at 254 (quoting Garrow).

21. For discussion of criminal caseloads and caseload pressures on the bench, see Beattie, Crime and the Courts 376–78; Langbein, Criminal Trial 274–78; Langbein, Ryder Sources 115–23.

22. Sir Edward Coke tossed off a different rationale, a one-liner about the standard of proof, that did not resonate in later discussions about denying defense counsel. He thought that "the testimonies and the proofs of the offense ought to be so clear and manifest, as there can be no defense of it." Coke, supra note 8, at 29. (I owe this reference to Michael Macnair.) The notorious Chief Justice Scroggs resurrected this idea in one of the Popish Plot cases, explaining that the accused was not entitled to counsel because "the proof belongs to [the Crown] to make out these intrigues of yours; therefore you need not have counsel, because the proof must be plain upon you, and then it will be in vain to deny the conclusion." Edward Coleman, 7 State Trials 1, 14 (1678), cited in 1 Stephen, History 382. The idea that affirmative "full proof" precludes

defensive disproof has a long history in Continental procedure. See, e.g., A. Esmein, Histoire de la procédure criminelle en France 146–47 (1882).

23. Volume 1 of this manual had appeared in 1716. The book underwent seven editions through 1795 and an eighth in 1824. See 2 Sweet and Maxwell's Complete Law Book Catalogue 116 (1931).

24. 2 Hawkins, Pleas of the Crown, ch. 39, §2.

25. Id.

26. Beattie, Crime and the Courts 350–51 (footnote omitted).

27. Langbein, Ryder Sources 124.

28. See supra text accompanying note 24.

29. By *testimonial,* I mean that defendants spoke to the merits, even though, until 1898, they were forbidden from speaking on oath. Regarding the background of the English legislation of 1898 and corresponding American enactments, see Graham Parker, The Prisoner in the Box—The Making of the Criminal Evidence Act, 1898, in Law and Social Change in British History: Papers Presented to the Bristol Legal History Conference 156 (J. A. Guy and H. G. Beale eds., 1984); Joel N. Bodansky, The Abolition of the Party-Witness Disqualification: An Historical Survey, 70 Kentucky Law Journal 91, 105–29 (1981–82); see also Zelman Cowen and P. B. Carter, Unsworn Statements by Accused Persons, in Essays on the Law of Evidence 205–18 (1956).

30. See infra text accompanying notes 82–86.

31. 6 & 7 Will. 4 c. 114 (1836) ("An Act for enabling Persons indicted of Felony to make their Defense by Counsel or Attorney").

32. Russen, OBSP (Oct. 1777), at 374, cited in Stephan Landsman, The Rise of the Contentious Spirit: Adversary Procedure in Eighteenth Century England, 75 Cornell Law Review 497, 534 n. 183 (1990).

33. Murdock, OBSP (Oct. 1755, no. 377), at 333, 335, extracted in Langbein, Ryder Sources 130. For another example, see id. at 130 n. 516. Beattie reports an instance from Surrey assizes in 1752 in which the accused tries to leave his defense to his counsel, who declines it. The judge then explains: "Your counsel knows his duty very well, they may indeed speak for you in any matter of law that may arise on your trial, but cannot as to matter of fact, for you must manage your defense in the best manner you can yourself." Beattie, Crime and the Courts 360, citing the case of Derby, Surrey Assize Proceedings (Lent 1752), at 2–11.

34. Woodcock, OBSP (Jan. 1789, no. 98), at 95, 107.

35. See, e.g., Mirjan R. Damaska, The Faces of Justice and State Authority: A Comparative Approach to the Legal Process 128 (1986); Mirjan R. Damaska, Evidentiary Barriers to Conviction and Two Models of Criminal Procedure: A Comparative Study, 121 University of Pennsylvania Law Review 506, 526–30 (1973).

36. Nicholas Throckmorton, 1 State Trials 884–85; John Udall, 1 State Tri-

als 1271, 1281, 1304 (1590). These cases are discussed in Peter Westen, The Compulsory Process Clause, 73 Michigan Law Review 71, 83 n. 40 (1974); James B. Thayer, A Preliminary Treatise on Evidence at the Common Law 158–59 (1898).

37. Criminal Evidence Act, 61 & 62 Vict. c. 36 (1898). Sir Edward Coke, writing in the 1620s or 1630s, criticized the rule forbidding defense witnesses to be sworn: "And to say the truth, we never read in any Act of Parliament, ancient Author, Book case, or Record, that in Criminal cases the party accused should not have witnesses sworn for him; and therefore there is not so much as *scintilla juris* against it. . . . And when the fault is denied, truth cannot appear without witnesses."Coke, supra note 8, at 79. He pointed with approval to the act that provided for the trial in England of felonies committed across the Scottish border and allowed defense witnesses to be examined on oath "for the better information of the consciences of the Jury and Justice." 4 Jac. 1 c. 1, §6 (1606). The act is discussed in Michael R. T. Macnair, The Law of Proof in Early Modern England 238–40 (1991) (unpublished Ph.D. dissertation, Oxford University), drawing on The Parliamentary Diary of Robert Bowyer: 1606–07, at 300–63 (David H. Wilson ed., 1931).

38. Throckmorton, who was acquitted, seems, if the report can be credited, to have been trying to call the jury's attention to the unfairness of the court's excluding his witness. When the court refuses the witness, John Fitzwilliams ("Go you [*sic*] ways, Fitzwilliams, the court hath nothing to do with you; peradventure you would not be so ready in a good cause," Nicholas Throckmorton, 1 State Trials 885), Throckmorton turns to the jury and says, "Since this gentleman's Declaration may not be admitted, I trust you of the Jury can perceive, it was not for any thing he had to say against me; but contrarywise, that it was feared he would speak for me." Id. On the defects of the State Trials as historical sources and the particular shortcomings of the Throckmorton report, see G. Kitson Clark, The Critical Historian 92–114 (1967).

39. John Lilburne, 4 State Trials 1312.

40. Treason Act of 1696, 7 Will. 3 c. 3, §§1, 7, discussed infra text accompanying notes 81–89.

41. 1 Anne st. 2, c. 9, §3 (1702) (part of an omnibus criminal law revision act).

42. See the authorities collected in Westen, supra note 36, at 90 n. 73.

43. See Charles T. McCormick, Handbook of the Law of Evidence §321, at 681–82 and n. 3 (1st ed. 1954). The beyond-reasonable-doubt formula appears to have been employed in Massachusetts in the 1770s. See Anthony A. Morano, A Reexamination of the Development of the Reasonable Doubt Rule, 55 Boston University Law Review 507, 516–19 (1975). I have noticed a tendency to instruct Old Bailey juries in the 1780s that they must acquit if they "have any doubt," Bowman, OBSP (Dec. 1783), at 2, 5; "any reasonable

doubt," Higginson, OBSP (Apr. 1783), at 481, 499; "a reasonable doubt," Corbett, OBSP (Jul. 1784), at 879, 895.

44. Barbara J. Shapiro, "Beyond Reasonable Doubt" and "Probable Cause": Historical Perspectives on the Anglo-American Law of Evidence 1–41 (1991).

45. Beattie, Crime and the Courts 341, 349 (footnote omitted). Trial judges conveyed to defendants their expectation that they should speak for decades after Beattie's example. In 1784 Heath, J., sitting at the Old Bailey, advised a defendant: "Can you give any account how you came by this money that was found in your possession, that will be very material for you. " Ash, OBSP (Jan. 1784), at 227, 232.

Notice as well that Parliament enacted measures in the eighteenth century enhancing the summary jurisdiction of the justices of the peace for lesser thefts that placed on the defendant the burden to provide a "satisfactory account" of how he came to possess goods that might be stolen. 15 Geo. 2 c. 27 (1742) (theft of woolen goods); 29 Geo. 2 c. 30 (1756) (theft and receiving of lead and other metals). (Bruce Smith brought these statutes to my attention.)

46. On the wretched jail conditions in the eighteenth century, see Beattie, Crime and the Courts 288–309. "Gaols in the sixteenth and seventeenth centuries were notoriously decrepit—unfit to 'keep the prisoners free from wind and weather,' as an Essex grand jury put it—and almost always overcrowded and insanitary." James S. Cockburn, A History of English Assizes: 1558–1714, at 107 (1972) (footnote omitted). For data on "prison mortality" in the suburban London jails, see James S. Cockburn, introduction, Calendar of Assize Records: Home Circuit Indictments Elizabeth I and James I, at 36–39 (1985) (noting 1,291 deaths in the Home Circuit jails between 1559 and 1625).

47. Speaking of the great state trials of the century before the Interregnum, Stephen wrote:

> The part of the early criminal procedure which seems to me to have borne most hardly on the accused was the secrecy of the preliminary investigation, and the fact that practically the accused person was prevented from preparing for his defense and from calling witnesses. . . . The one great essential condition of a fair trial is that the accused person should know what is alleged against him, and have a full opportunity of answering either by his own explanations or by calling witnesses, and for this it is necessary that he should have a proper time between the trial and the preparation of the evidence for the prosecution.

1 Stephen, History 356–57.

48. 7 & 8 Will. 3 c. 3, §§1, 9. The ostensible ground for this astonishing rule was to prevent the defendant from making assignments of error based on faulty Latin or comparable technicalities. When the Treason Act of 1696 abrogated the rule against granting the accused a copy of the indictment (for treason

only), it imposed a quid pro quo: it precluded the defense from making assignments of error based on indictment drafting defects unless the defense moved to quash the indictment in the trial court before the taking of any evidence.

49. See, e.g., 2 Hawkins, Pleas of the Crown 402. For discussion of the practice from 1664 into the early nineteenth century, see Douglas Hay, Prosecution and Power: Malicious Prosecution in the English Courts 1750–1850, in Policing and Prosecution in Britain 1750–1850, at 343, 352 (Douglas Hay and Francis Snyder eds., 1989).

50. Another practice that the Treason Act of 1696 eliminated, but only for the case of treason, was nondisclosure of the venire, that is, of the list of prospective jurors. 7 & 8 Will. 3 c. 3, §7. This step was meant to facilitate the exercise of the defendant's challenge rights. In cases of ordinary felony challenge rights were virtually never exercised. See Langbein, Criminal Trial 275–76; see also Beattie, Crime and the Courts 340. Without counsel and without opportunity for defensive preparation, such as investigating potential jurors, it is not surprising that challenge rights were of little use. I suspect that the exercise of challenge rights by the ordinary felony defendant was regarded as an affront to the challenged jurors, who were commonly the social superiors of the accused, and that the defendant understood that he ought not to risk offending the remaining jurors by striking some of their peers.

51. See generally Albert W. Alschuler, Plea Bargaining and Its History, 79 Columbia Law Review 1 (1979).

52. Levy, Origins 325.

53. 2 & 3 Phil. & M. c. 10, §2 (1555).

54. John H. Langbein, Prosecuting Crime in the Renaissance: England, Germany, France 5–125 (1974).

55. Langbein, Ryder Sources 56–57. See generally John P. Dawson, A History of Lay Judges 136–45 (1960); Sidney Webb and Beatrice Webb, English Local Government: The Parish and the County 294–304, 319–446 (1906).

56. 2 & 3 Phil. & M. c. 10, §2 (1555).

57. Sir Thomas Smith describes the Marian pretrial system of around 1565, indicating that the JP's written summary of the pretrial examination was routinely read in court at the criminal trial. Smith, supra note 4, at 109, 113. A generally reliable manual of assize procedure dating from the Restoration says that the JPs routinely surrendered their pretrial examination documents to the clerk of assizes, who studied each, "and if it be Evidence for the King, [the clerk] readeth it to the Jury." T.W., The Clerk of Assize 14 (London 1660), quoted in Langbein, Ryder Sources 82, 315. For discussion of this and other editions of the manual, see Langbein, supra note 54, at 28 n. 15.

By the mid-eighteenth century, the pretrial examinations were not being read at trial routinely, partly as a consequence of a "best evidence" notion that preferred the oral evidence of the victim and the other accusing witnesses, whom the Marian statute required the JP to bind over to testify at trial. The pretrial examinations continued to be consulted at trial for impeachment and for exceptional circumstances, such as the death of the victim or of a witness. In the early nineteenth century, MacNally was still emphasizing that "[t]he confession of the defendant himself, taken upon an examination, in writing, before justices of the peace, in pursuance of the statutes of Philip and Mary . . . is legal evidence against the party confessing." 1 Leonard MacNally, The Rules of Evidence on Pleas of the Crown *37 (Philadelphia 1811) (1st ed. 1802). Regarding the strictures against allowing the accused's pretrial statement to be taken on oath, see infra note 134.

58. 2 & 3 Phil. & M. c. 10, §2 (1555).

59. Barlow's JP manual patiently explains that, while the examining JP ought not to suppress evidence favorable to the accused when such evidence is part of the statement of a prosecution witness, the JP ought not to "examine Witnesses that expressly come to prove the Offender's Innocence." Theodore Barlow, The Justice of Peace: A Treatise Containing the Power and Duty of That Magistrate 190 (London, Lintot 1745).

60. Pretrial depositions were used extensively at the subsequent trials—for example, the notorious early case of Nicholas Throckmorton, 1 State Trials 869.

61. Edmund M. Morgan, The Privilege against Self-Incrimination, 34 Minnesota Law Review 1, 14 and n. 57 (1949), citing state trials occurring in 1664 and 1682.

62. 11 & 12 Vict. c. 42. See generally David Freestone and J. C. Richardson, The Making of English Criminal Law: Sir John Jervis and His Acts, 1980 Criminal Law Review 5.

63. See Morgan, supra note 61, at 14. MacNally reports Irish authority from as late as 1799 that there was no duty to warn. Chamberlain, J., an Irish King's Bench judge sitting on assize, "admitted in evidence, on an indictment for felony, the confession of the prisoner, taken by a justice of the peace, in an examination in writing, though it appeared, on the justice's admission, that he had not warned the prisoner of the legal consequences of his making such confession." MacNally, supra note 57, at *38.

64. Morgan, supra note 61, at 18.

65. Levy, Origins 325.

66. Id. (footnote omitted).

67. Precursors of this jury-operated system of mitigation can be traced back to the medieval common law. Thomas A. Green, Verdict According to Conscience 97–102 (1985).

68. This is a major theme of Beattie, Crime and the Courts; see especially 450–519.

69. Langbein, Ryder Sources 52. Another common exercise of jury sentenc-

ing power concerned the charge of grand larceny—that is, the theft of goods valued at a shilling or more but not alleged to be one of the aggravated forms of theft such as burglary or stealing from specially protected premises. In the eighteenth century, transportation was the prescribed penalty for grand larceny, whereas for petty larceny (theft of goods worth less than a shilling) mere whipping was the usual sanction. Here, too, if the jury wished to impose the lesser sanction, it framed the verdict to downvalue the goods. Id. at 52–53.

70. 4 Blackstone, Commentaries 239.

71. See Beattie, Crime and the Courts 419–30; see also 1 Leon Radzinowicz, A History of English Criminal Law and Its Administration from 1750, at 83–106, 138–64 (1948).

72. See Langbein, Ryder Sources 52. From a much larger sample of Surrey cases, including lesser crime as well as felony, Beattie found comparable partial verdict rates (24.9 percent) in the period 1700–39, then a decline to 12.7 percent for the period 1740–79 and 7.5 percent for the years 1780–1802. Beattie, Crime and the Courts 419 n. 32.

73. See Langbein, Ryder Sources 53.

74. Id.

75. Id. at 41.

76. For discussion of the judicially dominated pardon process as a routine aspect of criminal procedure in the eighteenth century, see Beattie, Crime and the Courts 430–49; Radzinowicz, supra note 71, at 107–37; Langbein, Ryder Sources 19–21; John H. Langbein, Albion's Fatal Flaws, 98 Past & Present 96, 109–14 (1983).

77. This issue is discussed with examples in Langbein, Criminal Trial 278–79. See also Beattie, Crime and the Courts 336–37 and n. 52, concluding: "Virtually every prisoner [in Beattie's Surrey sample for the years 1663–1802] charged with a felony insisted on taking his trial, with the obvious support and encouragement of the court. There was no plea bargaining in felony cases in the eighteenth century."

The tradition of discouraging guilty pleas was already ripe for mention in Sir Matthew Hale's (d. 1676) History of the Pleas of the Crown. Hale says that "it is usual for the court . . . to advise the party to plead and put himself upon his trial, and not presently to record his confession . . . ." 2 Matthew Hale, The History of the Pleas of the Crown 225 (1st ed., S. Emlyn ed., London 1736) (posthumous publication). Cockburn has documented an outbreak of plea bargaining on the Home Circuit for a period of three decades beginning in 1587, Cockburn, Calendar, supra note 46, at 65–70, 105, but the practice appears not to have endured into the age of Hale and Hawkins. See also Neil H. Cogan, Entering Judgment on a Plea of Nolo Contendere, 17 Arizona Law Review 992, 999–1016 (1975) (tracing some use of nolo-type pleas in early modern practice).

So long as trial procedure remained informal and lawyer-free, an assize court or its London equivalent, the Old Bailey, conducted trials extremely rapidly, at the rate of a dozen or more felony jury trials per day. Sources treating criminal caseloads and the caseload pressures on the bench are cited supra note 21. I report that "an average of twelve to twenty [felony] cases per sessions day went to jury trial" at the Old Bailey after 1678. Langbein, Criminal Trial 277; see also id. at 274–78. Beattie reckons jury trial caseloads of about fifteen felony cases per day at Surrey assizes in the second half of the eighteenth century, for an average trial time of about half an hour per case. Beattie, Crime and the Courts 378. Hence, caseload pressures were not yet causing the courts to want to elicit guilty pleas. Rather, the courts repeatedly urged criminal defendants not to plead guilty.

78. Quoted in John M. Beattie, Crime and the Courts in Surrey: 1736–1753, in Crime in England 155, 173 (J. S. Cockburn ed., 1977). See generally Beattie, supra note 17, at 232 (discussing "the importance of having the accused speak for themselves" and noting that "[i]t is this need for a trial—and a trial of a certain kind—that explains the extraordinary fact that judges did everything in their power in the eighteenth century to prevent the accused, especially those on capital charges, from pleading guilty"). What Beattie calls "a trial of a certain kind" is, I think, what I have been calling in this chapter the "accused speaks" trial.

The movement toward encouraging guilty pleas that is so familiar to us today in both English and American practice was, in my view, primarily a response to the complexity and time demands of full-dress adversary jury trial. Little is known about the timing of this event. The ordinarily astute French observer, Cottu, who studied English practice in the post-Napoleonic period, says that it "often happens" that "the prisoner pleads guilty" because he is certain that the death penalty will be commuted, but that, even then, "the judge cautions him that the crime alleged is capital, and that it is his interest to defend himself; the clerk, the gaoler, almost all the counsel, even the prosecutor's persuade him to take the chance of an acquittal. . . ." C. Cottu, On the Administration of Criminal Justice in England 73 (anon. trans., London 1822) (translating De l'administration de la justice criminelle en Angleterre (Paris 1820)).

79. Langbein, Criminal Trial 283. But see the discussion in infra note 134 regarding sensitivity in the contemporary sources about not conducting pretrial examinations on oath.

80. Beattie, Crime and the Courts 348–49.

81. 7 & 8 Will. 3 c. 3, §1 (1696).

82. See generally Alexander H. Shapiro, Political Theory and the Growth of Defensive Safeguards in Criminal Procedure: The Origins of the Treason Trials Act of 1696, 11 Law & History Review 215 (1993); see also James R. Phifer, Law, Politics, and Violence: The Treason Trials Act of 1696, 12 Albion

235 (1980); Samuel Rezneck, The Statute of 1696: A Pioneer Measure in the Reform of Judicial Procedure in England, 2 Journal of Modern History 5 (1930).

83. 7 & 8 Will. 3 c. 3, §1.

84. Id.

85. This step, allowing counsel to address the jury, was not taken for ordinary felonies until the legislation of 1836. See supra text accompanying note 30.

86. 7 & 8 Will. 3 c. 3, §1 ("to make any proof . . . by lawful witness or witnesses, who shall then be upon oath").

87. Id. §7 ("to compel their witnesses to appear for them at any such trial or trials, as is usually granted to compel witnesses to appear against them").

88. See Langbein, Criminal Trial 309–10 (discussing the reasons for restricting defense counsel to treason cases).

89. Serjeant Hawkins, defending the rule forbidding defense counsel to persons accused of routine felony, explained to his readers in 1721 that the Treason Act of 1696 allowed defense counsel in treason cases because "[e]xperience [had revealed] that Prisoners have been often under great Disadvantages from the Want of Counsel, in Prosecutions of High Treason against the King's Person, which are generally managed for the Crown with greater Skill and Zeal than ordinary Prosecutions." Hawkins, Pleas of the Crown 402.

90. Langbein, Criminal Trial 311–13.

91. Suggested on thin evidence, id. at 311–12; substantially amplified in Beattie, Crime and the Courts 352–56.

92. Langbein, Criminal Trial 313; see also Beattie, Crime and the Courts 359.

93. The sources are not good enough to allow us to measure with precision how frequently defense counsel appeared in the eighteenth century. Beattie's cautious account points to the 1780s. See Beattie, supra note 17, at 226–30. His calculations reckon percentages of defense counsel at the Old Bailey as low as 2.1 percent in the 1770s, increasing to 20.2 percent in 1786 and to a high of 36.6 percent in 1795. Id. at 227 (table 1); see also Landsman, supra note 32, at 607.

94. Cottu, supra note 78, at 105.

95. See Langbein, Ryder Sources 84–114.

96. See Beattie, Crime and the Courts 361–62, 374–75; Beattie, supra note 17, at 233–35, 244.

97. Beattie, Crime and the Courts 375. Beattie has drawn attention to the daunting reputation of William Garrow as an Old Bailey defense counsel in the 1780s and 1790s. "[T]he greater participation of lawyers in criminal trials in the 1780s led not merely to more defendants being represented by counsel, but to a more committed advocacy of their cases in the courtroom and a new emphasis on their rights." Beattie, supra note 17, at 238.

98. Noticed obliquely in Cottu, supra note 78, at 98–99.

99. See supra text accompanying note 43.

100. Beattie, supra note 17, at 235.

101. See William Twining, The Rationalist Tradition of Evidence Scholarship, in Rethinking Evidence 32 (1990) (discussing the development of treatise writing on evidence law); John H. Wigmore, A General Survey of the History of the Rules of Evidence, in 2 Select Essays in Anglo-American Legal History 691, at 695–97 (Association of American Law Schools) (1908) (emphasizing the role of *nisi prius* reporting).

102. See David Philips, Good Men to Associate and Bad Men to Conspire: Associations for the Prosecution of Felons in England, 1760–1860, in Hay, supra note 49, at 113–70.

103. John H. Langbein, Book Review, 9 Law & History Review 398, 402 (1991) (discussing Philips, supra note 102).

104. See Langbein, Ryder Sources 128–29.

105. Cottu, supra note 78, at 88. Another scrap of evidence for the possibility that the levels of representation by counsel were higher at provincial assizes than in the Old Bailey appears in Lord Mansfield's papers. He wrote to Justice Wilmot from the Lancaster summer assizes in 1758 that he "had an enormous" criminal calendar and that "I think I had not a single Trial without counsel on both Sides." 1 James Oldham, The Mansfield Manuscripts and the Growth of English Law in the Eighteenth Century 137 (1992). I wonder whether the circuit bar that traveled with the assize judge was more willing to represent indigent defendants (and indigent prosecutors).

106. Cottu, supra note 78, at 88.

107. Id. at 88, 90.

108. 32 Geo. 3 c. 60 (1792). The act completed the immunization of jurors who determined to return verdicts of acquittal in defiance of the applicable law. Such verdicts occurred infrequently, mostly in political cases.

109. On the older patterns of jury control, see Langbein, Criminal Trial 284–300.

110. Bentham's critique is notable for linking the privilege against self-incrimination to the interests of counsel. "In plain English," says Bentham, "the maxim [*Nemo tenetur*] is neither more nor less than so much nonsense." 5 Bentham, Rationale 208. Canvassing with scorn what he treats as the current justifications for the privilege, Bentham disparages the "old woman's reason," that it is "hard" to oblige a man to incriminate himself, id. at 230, and the "fox-hunter's reason," the sportsman's idea of fairness, id. at 238. As fox-hunters need to preserve some foxes to keep hunting, lawyers need to release some criminals. The "persons whose interest is served by the exclusion" of self-incriminating evidence are "evil-doers of all sorts, and . . . lawyers of all sorts . . . ." Id. at 248–49.

Bentham also notices the tension between the Marian pretrial procedure, which provided for systematic examination of the accused, and the privilege against self-incrimination. Id. at 255. He points approvingly to the practice of the long-defunct Star Chamber, "not to speak of the nursery-chamber, and every other room in which common sense was listened to . . . ." Id. at 256. The Marian procedure is "a sprig of common sense, imported from the continent of Europe, and planted in a bed of nonsense and hypocrisy, by which it has been nearly choked . . . ." Id. at 289. (For an account of why it is mistaken to treat the Marian statutes as entailing a reception of Continental procedure, see Langbein, supra note 54, at 21–34.)

Bentham takes up the privilege against self-incrimination as part of his broader critique of exclusionary rules of evidence. 5 Bentham, Rationale 207. For discussion of Bentham's hostility to rules of exclusion, see Twining, supra note 101, at 39–40. Bentham emphasizes the modern safeguard of cross-examination as the superior safeguard. "Against erroneous or mendacious testimony, the grand security is cross-examination. . . ." 5 Bentham, Rationale 212.

Even if Bentham was right to regard cross-examination as superior to exclusion for the purpose of safeguarding against suspect evidence when the concern is to promote accuracy in adjudication, that campaign hardly bears on a rule of supervening policy such as the privilege against self-incrimination, which is meant to subordinate truth-seeking to other values.

As usual, Bentham does not describe the practice of the courts nor the case law of the time, and accordingly, it would be hazardous to draw any conclusions from Bentham's critique about how entrenched or systematically applied the privilege was in Bentham's day.

On Bentham and the privilege see A. D. E. Lewis, Bentham's View of the Right to Silence, 43 Current Legal Problems 135, 138 (1990); see also A. D. E. Lewis, The Background to Bentham on Evidence, 2 Utilitas 195, 203–16 (1990).

111. See supra note 92.

112. Michael R. T. Macnair, The Early Development of the Privilege against Self-Incrimination, 10 Oxford Journal of Legal Studies 66 (1990), confirms in important respects this finding, which Helmholz developed critically in R. H. Helmholz, Origins of the Privilege against Self-Incrimination: The Role of the European *Ius Commune,* 65 New York University Law Review 962 (1990).

113. See generally Mary H. Maguire, Attack of the Common Lawyers on the Oath Ex Officio as Administered in the Ecclesiastical Courts in England, in Essays in History and Political Theory in Honor of Charles Howard McIlwain 199 (Carl Wittke ed., 1936).

114. 16 Car. 1 c. 11 (1640), revised at the Restoration as 13 Car. 2 c. 12 (1661).

115. See Henry J. Friendly, The Fifth Amendment Tomorrow: The Case for Constitutional Change, 37 University of Cincinnati Law Review 671, 696–98 (1968).

116. Id.

117. 8 Wigmore, Evidence §2250, at 267. Wigmore's volume 8, the so-called McNaughton revision, is the currently available edition. As McNaughton explains, Wigmore's account of the history of the privilege against self-incrimination originated in two articles, John H. Wigmore, Nemo Tenetur Seipsum Prodere, 5 Harvard Law Review 71 (1891), and John H. Wigmore, The Privilege against Self-Crimination: Its History, 15 Harvard Law Review 610 (1902); it was then revised across the editions of the treatise. See 8 Wigmore, Evidence §2250, at 267 n. 1.

Wigmore worked before the vast outpouring of research on the history of criminal law and procedure that has occurred since World War II. The later scholarship has materially altered and enriched our view of many of the subjects that Wigmore confronted unaided. Wigmore worked almost entirely from the State Trials and the nominate law reports. He did not, for example, know the Old Bailey Sessions Papers, the extensive series of pamphlet trial "reports" (on which see supra note 14 and sources cited therein). In the paragraphs that follow, I undertake to correct Wigmore, but I do not mean to fault him. I revere Wigmore. At the time it was written, Wigmore's historical account constituted a remarkable advance in knowledge. All who take an interest in these issues stand on his shoulders.

We can now see, as a general matter, that Wigmore tended to project the origins of the rules of evidence further back than the historical record reasonably supports. The modern law of evidence is largely a product of the period from the mid-eighteenth to the mid-nineteenth century. Hazard has shown that the attorney-client privilege, which Wigmore dated to Elizabethan sources, 8 Wigmore, Evidence §2290, at 542–43, is effectively a product of the late eighteenth century. Geoffrey C. Hazard, Jr., An Historical Perspective on the Attorney-Client Privilege, 66 California Law Review 1061, 1080 (1978). Wigmore places the modern hearsay rule in the late seventeenth century. See generally John H. Wigmore, The History of the Hearsay Rule, 17 Harvard Law Review 437 (1904), which is substantially reproduced in 5 Wigmore, Evidence §1364, at 12–28 (James H. Chadbourn rev. ed. 1974), based extensively on the State Trials. For indications that this supposed hearsay rule was ignored well into the eighteenth century, see Langbein, Criminal Trial 301–2; James Oldham, Truth-Telling in the Eighteenth-Century English Courtroom, 12 Law & History Review 95, 103–4 and n. 46, 113–16 (1994). See also Beattie, supra note 17, at 232. I treat this topic extensively in John H. Langbein, Historical Foundations of the Law of Evidence: A View from the Ryder Sources, 96 Columbia Law Review 1168 (1996).

118. 8 Wigmore, Evidence §2250, at 289.

119. Id.

120. Id.

121. I am not alone in remarking on Wigmore's emphasis on serendipity in the common law's absorption of the privilege against self-incrimination. Macnair describes "Wigmore's classic account" as one that "saw the privilege as creeping in 'by indirection' into the common law in the mid-seventeenth century in the wake of the fall of Star Chamber and High Commission, [i.e.,] almost by accident." Macnair, supra note 112, at 66 (quoting 8 Wigmore, Evidence §2250, at 292).

122. 8 Wigmore, Evidence §2250, at 289–90. In the concluding footnote to this passage, Wigmore cites the seventeen cases that I discuss infra in the text accompanying notes 127–39.

123. Levy, Origins 325. Levy tells what is, for practical purposes, a version of Wigmore's story. Levy singles out John Lilburne for adulation: "[M]ore than any other individual [Lilburne] was responsible for the acceptance of the principle that no person should be compelled to be a witness against himself in criminal cases." Id. at 313.

In truth, Lilburne was an insignificant figure in the development of the privilege. Lilburne was prosecuted criminally on several occasions from the first proceedings against him in Star Chamber under Charles I, 3 State Trials 1315 (1637), to his last common law trial in the Commonwealth period, 5 State Trials 407 (1653). Lilburne's reputation derives mainly from his spirited defense to treason charges brought against him during the Commonwealth period at a common law trial convened in 1649; the trial is extensively reported in 4 State Trials, at 1269 (1649). Lilburne raised two important themes in his defense— the need for defense counsel and the jury's power to engage in law nullifying— themes that would have a robust future. Lilburne complained incessantly about being denied the opportunity to consult counsel, id. at 1293–1318, 1329–30, 1373–79, 1394–95, 1404, and he asserted the claim that juries are judges of law and fact. See, e.g., id. at 1379–81. The latter aspect of Lilburne's defense in the 1649 trial has been meticulously studied and related to the surrounding tract literature in Green, supra note 67, at 153–99.

Compared to these insistent themes of the trial, Lilburne's mention of the maxim about not having to be a witness against oneself was quite peripheral. According to the verbatim report of the State Trials, Lilburne adverts to the idea twice. First, at the arraignment, not the trial, hence in a setting not strictly relevant to trial procedure, Lilburne announces that "by the Laws of England, I am not to answer to questions against or concerning myself." 4 State Trials 1292. Keble, J., presiding, plays along, telling him, "You shall not be compelled." Id. at 1293.

Second, during the course of the trial, Keble has a handwritten document exhibited to Lilburne and asks him to acknowledge the handwriting. Lilburne refuses, saying he will not look at prosecution papers, "neither shall I answer to any questions that concern myself." Id. at 1340. A witness thereupon testifies to Lilburne's authorship, which makes it inconsequential that Lilburne had declined to stipulate to the point. Lilburne, however, links up his refusal to answer the question with his larger strategy, which was to put the prosecution to its proofs. "I have said, Sir, prove it." Id. The exchange with Lilburne continues in this vein, the attorney general chiding him for not acknowledging his hand, Lilburne saying, "Sir, I deny nothing . . . but prove it first." Id. at 1341. Again: "I shall deny nothing I do. And yet I have read the Petition of Right, Sir, that teaches me to answer to no questions against or concerning myself, and I have read of the same to be practiced by Christ and his Apostles." Id. Lilburne was drawing not so much on the notion of a privilege against self-incrimination as upon the nascent concept of the prosecutor's burden of proof.

In this respect, Lilburne's claim was truly precocious, and it shows how the newer theory of the trial always lay close to the surface in the old. The old "accused speaks" trial could easily be converted to the "testing the prosecution" trial if the defendant was willing to risk it. If Lilburne had been on trial for a homicide or a theft, he would have hanged himself with these tactics. Lilburne's ploy was designed to put the prosecution on trial. Without counsel that risk could be taken only in a political case in which the defendant had reason to suspect that he could evoke the sympathy of the jury.

Apart from these two asides, Lilburne responds at his trial to prosecution evidence and prosecution questioning as did other defendants of the age. For example, "I shall proceed on to answer your Proof to the Indictment. . . ." Id. at 1382. "In answer to whose testimony I return this. . . ." Id. at 1382. "[A]nd therefore I can answer to that nothing more than what I have said already." Id. at 1388. About certain books, he notes, "I do not own [i.e., admit] a jot, a line, a word, a syllable of any one of them." Id. at 1389. "I hope I have so clearly and fully answered all and every of your proofs, that not any one thing sticks." Id.

This behavior is quite difficult to reconcile with Levy's claim that Lilburne was insisting on a privilege against self-incrimination. In truth, like every other defendant of the age before defense counsel, Lilburne was obliged to defend himself in ways quite inconsistent with a privilege to remain silent.

124. See, for example, the compacted version of Wigmore's account in the leading textbook, Charles T. McCormick, McCormick on Evidence §114, at 424 (John W. Strong ed., 4th ed. 1992).

125. 8 Wigmore, Evidence §2250, at 290.

126. Id. at 290 n. 105.

127. African Co. v. Parish, 2 Vern. 244, 23 Eng. Rep. 758 (Ch. 1691); Bird v. Hardwicke, 1 Vern. 109, 23 Eng. Rep. 349 (Ch. 1682); Anonymous, 1 Vern.

60, 23 Eng. Rep. 310 (Ch. 1682); Penrice v. Parker, Rep. Temp. Finch 75, 23 Eng. Rep. 40 (Ch. 1673). For the flavor of these cases, consider the first, African Co. v. Parish. The dispute concerned a charter party (for the hire of a ship) that contained a noncompetition clause obliging the defendant to pay certain sums to the plaintiff "if the defendant traded in the goods the [plaintiff] company dealt in." 2 Vern. at 244, 23 Eng. Rep. at 758. The company sought discovery of the defendant to determine if he had traded in any such goods. "The defendant pleads the charter-party, by which it appears that the sums therein mentioned, were of double the value of the goods themselves, and so was in the nature of a penalty, and that he ought not to be compelled to make a discovery by answer touching the same, so as to subject himself to such penalties." Id. The court rejected the defense and ordered discovery. The cursory report explains: "The defendant must be bound by his own agreement, having agreed it shall be deducted out of the freight, he ought to discover . . . ." Id.

Macnair has now linked such chancery sources to a larger set of equity cases, extending well back into Elizabethan times, that draw on canonist sources. Macnair, supra note 37, at 38–56; see also Macnair, supra note 112.

128. Firebrass's Case, 2 Salk. 550, 91 Eng. Rep. 465 (K.B. 1700) (granting prohibition against a bill of discovery in a duchy court touching the quantities of deer and timber that the chief ranger of a forest had taken).

129. Francis Jenkes, 6 State Trials 1189 (1676). The report concerns an investigation conducted by the king and his advisors at the council board into remarks that Jenkes uttered during an election campaign speech on the hustings. Wigmore includes the case in his list of supposed instances of the privilege against self-incrimination because Jenkes said at one point that he wished "to be excused all farther answer to such questions; since the law doth provide, that no man be put to answer to his own prejudice." Id. at 1194.

In truth, there was no recognition of the privilege against self-incrimination in the pretrial process until the nineteenth century. Levy acknowledges this point. See supra text accompanying note 66.

130. See Titus Oates, 10 State Trials 1079, 1099, 1123 (1685); Thomas Rosewell, 10 State Trials 147, 169 (1684); Earl of Castlemaine, 7 State Trials 1067, 1096 (1680); Richard Langhorn, 7 State Trials 417, 435 (1679); Nathanael Reading, 7 State Trials 259, 296 (1679). A student's seminar paper alerted me to the point developed above in text. See Mary D. Scott, The Dubious Existence of the Privilege against Self-Incrimination in the Seventeenth Century (1978) (unpublished seminar paper, University of Chicago Law School).

131. Nathanael Reading, 7 State Trials 259, 296.

132. Wigmore mistakenly says that Reading was trying to cross-examine Titus Oates. The actual witness was Oates's co-conspirator, Bedloe. These revolting characters are the subject of a masterful book, John Kenyon, The Popish Plot (1972).

133. Nathanael Reading, 7 State Trials 296.

134. Recall that prosecution witnesses testified under oath, whereas defense witnesses were forbidden to do so and thus spoke unsworn until the legislation of 1702, discussed in supra text accompanying note 41. The defendant spoke unsworn until 1898. See supra note 37. North's reference to the oath of the prosecution witness may have been intended to invoke the distinction between sworn and unsworn witnesses. Under this interpretation, the defendant should not derive advantage from a witness testifying under oath, even when the testimony favorable to the defendant is elicited under cross-examination rather than under direct examination.

In separate correspondence, three scholars who read a prepublication draft of this chapter (Christopher Allen, David Brown, and Michael Macnair) cautioned that concern with oath taking in the pretrial process played a larger role in the development of the privilege against self-incrimination than our trial-centered literature has thus far recognized. Brown and Macnair each point to the murder trial of Sarah Malcolm, OBSP (Feb. 1733), at 90–91, extracted in Langbein, Criminal Trial 283 n. 58, in which the court refused to allow the prosecution to use the JP's pretrial examination of the defendant because the document had been taken on oath. The judge said: "If [the examination] is upon Oath it cannot be read [at trial], for Persons are not to swear against themselves; all Examinations ought to be taken freely and voluntarily, and not upon Oath, and then we can read [th]em." OBSP (Feb. 1733), at 90–91. Beattie reports a comparable case from Surrey assizes in 1743 in which, according to the pamphlet report, the defendant's pretrial confession was offered: "[T]he confession was produced; but it being taken on oath, it could not be read. If it had been taken voluntarily it would have been admitted as good evidence; but the law supposes that an oath is a compulsion; and consequently that no man is obliged to swear against himself in cases where it affects his life." Beattie, Crime and the Courts 365–66 n. 129 (extracting pamphlet report of 1743). Macnair directs attention to Dalton's 1619 JP manual (see Dalton, supra note 6, at 273), in which Dalton explains that "the accused was to be examined without oath, citing *nemo tenetur* for this, and this statement was repeated by most subsequent authors; but the accused continued to be required to answer incriminating questions by the justices, though not on oath, until the nineteenth century." Macnair, supra note 112, at 79 n. 99; see also Barlow, supra note 59, quoted in infra note 149.

135. William, Viscount Stafford, 7 State Trials 1293, 1314 (1680).

136. Id. 1293; Earl of Castlemaine, 7 State Trials at 1067; Richard Langhorn, 7 State Trials at 417; Thomas Whitebread, 7 State Trials at 311; Nathanael Reading, 7 State Trials at 259.

On the Popish Plot, see generally Kenyon, supra note 132. For a succinct account, see 1 Stephen, History 383–92, concluding that "in two years, and in connection with one transaction, six memorable failures of justice, involving the sacrifice of no less than fourteen innocent lives, occurred in trials held before the highest courts of judicature under a form of procedure closely resembling that which is still in force amongst us."

137. Thomas Whitebread, 7 State Trials at 311 (Scroggs, Lord Chief Justice [hereinafter LCJ]); Titus Oates, 10 State Trials at 1079 (Jeffreys, LCJ); Thomas Rosewell, 10 State Trials at 147 (Jeffreys, LCJ); Earl of Castlemaine, 7 State Trials at 1067 (Scroggs, LCJ); Richard Langhorn, 7 State Trials at 417 (Scroggs, LCJ). Regarding Scroggs and Jeffreys, see infra note 142.

138. Dr. Oliver Plunket, 8 State Trials 447, 480–81 (1681).

139. Thomas Whitebread, 7 State Trials at 311, 361; Penn & Mead, 6 State Trials 951, 957 (1670); John Crook, 6 State Trials 201, 205 (1662); Adrian Scroop, 5 State Trials 1034, 1039 (1660).

140. For example, "[a]lthough the legal profession customarily refers to the right against self-incrimination as a 'privilege,' I call it a 'right' because it is one." Levy, Origins xv.

141. 8 Wigmore, Evidence §2250, at 290.

142. On Scroggs and Jeffreys, see Biographical Dictionary of the Common Law 274–77, 466–67 (A. W. B. Simpson ed., 1984); 6 William Holdsworth, A History of English Law 504–8, 527–30 (2d ed. 1937); compare the adulatory G. W. Keeton, Lord Chancellor Jeffreys and the Stuart Cause 24–25 (1965). On the judicial politics of the era, see Alfred F. Havighurst, James II and the Twelve Men in Scarlet, 69 Law Quarterly Review 522 (1953); Alfred F. Havighurst, The Judiciary and Politics in the Reign of Charles II, 66 Law Quarterly Review 62, 229 (1950).

143. Levy, Origins 318. Levy seems to think that the privilege was part of a broader movement of safeguard in the seventeenth century. He admits that the "adversary system in criminal proceedings had always been a one-sided affair, with the crown enjoying advantages denied to the accused. Procedural reforms of the very late seventeenth century redressed the imbalance, giving to the accused a greater measure of parity." Id. at 320–21. He mentions compulsory process in 1696 and 1701 and copy of the indictment and right to counsel in 1696 and thereafter. Id. at 321–23. "Accordingly, by the early eighteenth century both judicial and statutory alterations in procedure made it possible for a defendant to present his defense through witnesses and by counsel. As a result . . . he was no longer obliged to speak out personally in order to get his story before the jury . . . ." Id. at 323. Thus, claims Levy, "[b]y the early eighteenth century, the [privilege against self-incrimination] prevailed supreme in all [trial] proceedings . . . ." Id. at 325.

Levy is correct to notice that the Treason Act of 1696 entailed a fundamental movement toward more balanced criminal procedure. What he overlooks is the highly exceptional character of the act. The reforms applied to a minuscule subset of cases, prosecutions for treason. The object of the 1696 legislation was to do criminal procedural business as usual except for treason. See supra text accompanying notes 39, 47–48, 82–87. The momentous change for the history of ordinary criminal procedure was the allowance of defense counsel, which began as a trickle in the 1730s and which does not seem to have unsettled the basic "accused speaks" trial until well into the second half of the eighteenth century. See supra text accompanying notes 89–92.

144. 8 Wigmore, Evidence §2250, at 291.

145. Id. at 292.

146. Id.

147. 7 & 8 Will. 3 c. 3; see also supra text accompanying notes 81–89, discussing the act.

148. 8 Wigmore, Evidence §2251, at 297, 310–18.

149. Barlow's JP manual of 1745 makes the connection between not torturing and the *Nemo tenetur* maxim:

> The Law of England is a Law of Mercy, and does not use the Rack or Torture to compel Criminals to accuse themselves; since these Methods are cruel, and at the same Time uncertain, as being rather Trials of the Strength and Hardiness of the Sufferer, than any Proof of the Truth, by the Confession which is extorted from him, or by his Perseverance in his Denial. I take it to be for the same Reason, that it does not call upon the Criminal to answer upon Oath. For, this might serve instead of the Rack, to the Consciences of some Men, although they have been guilty of Offences. And the Proof could not all be depended on, unless it was a Confession; and it would be hard, and unequal to rack a Man's Conscience with the Religion of an Oath, and make his Discovery tend to his Condemnation, but not allow his Denial on Oath to have any Weight towards his Exculpation or Acquittal. . . . The Law has therefore wisely and mercifully laid down this Maxim, *Nemo tenetur seipsum prodere.*

Barlow, supra note 59, at 189.

Concern that the accused not be pressured to commit perjury as the precondition of mounting a defense was a prominent theme in the nineteenth-century debate about whether to permit the defendant to testify on oath. See Bodansky, supra note 29, at 110–15.

150. The English authorities used torture in eighty-one documented cases between 1540 and 1640. John H. Langbein, Torture and the Law of Proof: Europe and England in the Ancien Regime 81–128 (1977). The practice ceased in the 1640s, with no evident invocation of any privilege against self-incrimination. Id. at 135–36.

151. Griffin v. California, 380 U.S. 609 (1965). It is also controversial; see chapter 1, section I.A.

FIVE

1. See, e.g., 10 American Legal Records, Criminal Proceedings in Colonial Virginia (Peter C. Hoffer and William B. Scott eds., 1984).

2. See, e.g., Douglas Greenberg, Crime and Law Enforcement in the Colony of New York, 1661–1776 (1976); Philip J. Schwarz, Twice Condemned: Slaves and the Criminal Laws of Virginia 1705–1765 (1988); Donna J. Spindel, Crime and Society in North Carolina, 1663–1776 (1989).

3. Julius Goebel and Thomas Naughton, Law Enforcement in Colonial New York: A Study in Criminal Procedure, 1664–1776 (1944). Further context for the qualitative detail Goebel and Naughton provide, along with a reconsideration of some points in light of later scholarship, can be found in Eben Moglen, Settling the Law 170–208 (1993) (unpublished Ph.D. dissertation, Yale University). A less satisfactory reconstruction for colonial Virginia, based almost entirely on statutory materials, can be found in Arthur P. Scott, Criminal Law in Colonial Virginia (1930).

4. On the complex context of processes described as "reception" and "Anglicization" in the early legal development of New York, see Moglen, supra note 3, at 18–63.

5. Massachusetts Charter of 1628, reprinted in 1 Records of the Governor and Company of the Massachusetts Bay in New England 12 (Nathaniel B. Shurtleff ed., 1853).

6. See William Strachey, For the Colony in Virginea Britannia; Lawes Divine, Morall and Martiall, &c. (1612; repr., P. Flaherty ed., 1969).

7. On the commitment to "Englishry" in New York's criminal law, see Moglen, supra note 3, at 170–209. Cf. Edmund S. Morgan, American Slavery, American Freedom: The Ordeal of Colonial Virginia 133–56 (1975), on "settling down" in Virginia, especially the creation of the county courts and related machinery after 1630.

8. The Body of Liberties art. 26 (1641), reprinted in 7 Old South Leaflets 265 (1905).

9. 4 Statutes at Large: Being a Collection of All the Laws of Virginia 404 (William W. Hening ed., 1820); see Scott, supra note 3, at 79.

10. A revealing exception is the extension of the privilege of counsel in treason cases provided by the statute of 7 Will. 3 c. 3 (1696) to the defendants in the famous New York political trial R.v. Bayard (1702), despite the fact that the statute did not apply in the colonies. When the political elite of the colony faced capital charges, employment of counsel was worthwhile. See R. v. Bayard, 14 State Trials 471. It should be noted that counsel was also permitted to Jacob Leisler during the trial that ended with his execution for treason in 1691. See Public Record Office, London, CO 5/1037, fol. 1.

11. See R. v. John Vincent, May 3 1686, MS Mins. N.Y. County Quarter Sessions 1683/84–94, at 112 (N.Y. Hall of Records [hereinafter NYHR]).

12. Goebel and Naughton, supra note 3, at xxv.

13. 2 Records of the Colony of Rhode Island and Providence Plantations in New England 238–39 (John R. Bartlett ed., 1857). Compare Levy, Origins 356–57, where the restriction is ignored, supposedly showing the early establishment of the "right to counsel."

14. See 2 Hawkins, Pleas of the Crown, ch. 46, §29.

15. See 1 Anne st. 2, c. 9 (1702).

16. Thus, defense witnesses testified unsworn in the trial of an indictment for burglary in 1669, according to Goebel and Naughton, supra note 3, at 562. Rough minutes for the August 1685 New York Quarter Sessions show that defense witnesses were sworn in a misdemeanor prosecution, in this case for violation of the Navigation Acts, in conformity with English practice. See Ludgar qui tam v. The Pink Charles (n.p., unclassified papers, NYHR). On such few indications must our conclusions depend, given the scant documentation of trial protocol, in America as in England, during the seventeenth century.

17. See Queen v. Bowen, MS Mins. NY SCJ 1704–5 to 1706, at 165 (NYHR), where defense witnesses were sworn. Subsequent practice is difficult to ascertain, since so few indications exist in the records showing whether witnesses were sworn or not before they testified. It seems that practice was similar in Virginia after 1705. See George Webb, The Office and Authority of a Justice of Peace 135–36 (1736) (repr. ed. 1969).

18. See Goebel and Naughton, supra note 3, at 477–78, where defense and prosecution witnesses are not adequately separated. In New York, through the eighteenth century, prosecution witnesses primarily appeared to testify under recognizances taken at the preliminary examination, providing the Crown with economic leverage to ensure appearance.

19. See Webb, supra note 17, at 112.

20. See, e.g., King v. Lydius (June 23, 1763), and King v. John van Rensselaer (Oct. 26–Nov. 5, 1768), in J. T. Kempe Lawsuits (New-York Historical Society [hereinafter NYHS]).

21. 2 & 3 Phil. & M. c. 10 (1555). On the drafting and implementation of these crucial reforms, see John Langbein, Prosecuting Crime in the Renaissance: England, Germany, France 5–125 (1974).

22. William Smith Jr., who undoubtedly spoke from personal experience, remarked in his history of provincial New York that "there are instances of some [JPs] who can neither write nor read." 1 William Smith Jr., History of the Province of New York 261 (M. Kammen ed., 1972). John Langbein has argued that the quorum clause had ceased to designate legally trained JPs in England by the end of the sixteenth century. Displacement of felony trial, Langbein says, allowed the designation to the quorum to be retained as "a petty embellishment of dignity." See Langbein, supra note 21, at 113–14; see also J. H. Gleason, The Justices of the Peace in England 1558–1640, at 4 (1969).

23. Langbein, supra note 21, at 43.

24. For the history of the editions of Lambarde through 1619, see 1 Sweet and Maxwell's Legal Bibliography of the British Commonwealth of Nations 229 (2d ed. 1955).

25. William B. Nelson, The Office and Authority of a Justice of Peace, etc. (1704); Giles Jacob, The Modern Justice; the business of a Justice of Peace (1716). For the subsequent publication histories of Nelson and Jacob, see 1 Sweet and Maxwell, supra note 24, at 228, 230.

26. Richard Burn, Justice of the Peace and Parish Officer (1755). For subsequent publication history of Burn, see 1 Sweet and Maxwell, supra note 24, at 225–26.

27. Thus the seventeenth edition of Burn's Justice, printed in 1793, provides the text of Dalton's ch. 164: "The examination of the person accused ought not to be upon oath. But if upon his examination he shall confess the matter, it shall not be amiss that he subscribe his name or mark to it." 1 Richard Burn, The Justice of the Peace and Parish Officer 608 (17th ed. 1793).

28. On this source, see chapter 3, note 23.

29. "Inventory of Estate of Gov. John Montgomerie—1740, New York 1732 Acct: Sales of a Collection of Books being the Library and part of the Goods and Chattels of John Montgomerie Esqr. Deceased," John Montgomerie Papers, NYPL, reprinted in Paul M. Hamlin, Legal Education in Colonial New York 193–96 (1939).

30. William Fleetwood, Office of a Justice of Peace, with Instructions how and in What Manner Statutes should be Expounded (1658).

31. The lists of Alexander, Murray, Chambers, and Smith's libraries are also reprinted in Hamlin, supra note 29, at 171.

32. See 23 The Colonial and State Records of North Carolina 346 (W. L. Saunders, S. B. Weeks, and W. Clark eds., 1886–1914). For the scant evidence of the circulation in colonial North Carolina of such materials as George Webb's Office and Authority of a Justice of Peace, see Helen R. Watson, The Books They Left: Some "Liberies" in Edgecombe County, 1733–1783, 48 North Carolina Historical Review 245–57 (1971).

33. See Webb, supra note 17.

34. For the utility of the English manuals in maintaining a sense of uniformity between English and Virginian legal behavior in the earlier period of Virginia's history, see Warren M. Billings, English Legal Literature as a Source of Law and Legal Practice for Seventeenth-Century Virginia, 87 Virginia Magazine of History & Biography 403–16 (1979).

35. For circulation of Webb in North Carolina, see supra note 32.

36. See John Tabor Kempe letter to JPs in R. v. Kelly, dated August 13, 1764, J. T. Kempe Lawsuits, NYHS.

37. Or so Goebel suggests, with slim evidence as to timing. Goebel and Naughton, supra note 3, at 633 and n. 98.

38. The use of confrontation in securing confessions can be seen in full flower in Justice Daniel Horsmanden's account of the investigation of the "Negro Plot" in 1741. See Daniel Horsmanden, New York Conspiracy 7 and passim (T. J. Davis ed., 1971). As the tenor of the description shows, this was plainly established practice, rather than an adaptation to extraordinary circumstances.

39. Levy, Origins 325.

40. See Goebel and Naughton, supra note 3, at 130–33.

41. 2 Statutes at Large, supra note 9, at 422.

42. For example, the freemen's oath, recurrently taken by members of the General Court and others. See 1 Massachusetts Bay Records, supra note 5, at 354.

43. Body of Liberties, supra note 8, art. 3; Lawes and Libertyes 43 (1648), reprinted in 1 The Laws and Liberties of Massachusetts 1641–1691, at 3, 49 (John D. Cushing ed., 1976).

44. See George L. Haskins, Law and Authority in Early Massachusetts 200–1 and 283 n. 59 (1960), drawing the distinction and denying that the modern form of the privilege prevailed in early Massachusetts.

45. See generally Craig W. Horle, The Quakers and the English Legal System 1660–1688 (1988).

46. Haskins, supra note 44, at 201, believes this provision authorized torture only after judicial conviction, to disclose confederates. This seems to be at odds with the implication that under some circumstances a man might be brought to confess "against himselfe." Professor Barbara Black, in private conversation, has urged that the provision should be read so as to deny any power to torture for self-incrimination, and only to incriminate others if, after a guilty verdict, the defendant refused to name accomplices. I believe "conviction" here means certainty of belief, as in the salvational significance of "conviction of sin," rather than judicial determination. Black, whose personal familiarity with the records is authoritative, believes that "conviction" in this sense would never be coupled with "evidence" in the language of a Massachusetts Bay drafter of the period. But compare, in Laws and Liberties, supra note 43, the 1648 Lawes and Libertyes, s.v. Heresie. In the absence of any documented use of judicial torture in Massachusetts Bay, we cannot be sure what was intended by the drafter or understood by the judges; it is with great reluctance that I reach an interpretation contrary to those of Haskins and Black.

47. Levy, Origins 345.

48. John Selden, Table Talk 133 (Frederick Pollock ed., 1927). Selden saw no objection in law to using deceit or other means to force confession in preliminary examination, see id. at §4. For the theory of half proof and full proof, and all other matters connected, see John Langbein, Torture and the Law of Proof: Europe and England in the Ancien Regime (1977).

49. Haskins, supra note 44, at 201, refers to "a wave of vicious criminality."

His dignified reticence about the nature of the offenses does a slight disservice to understanding. The colony's leadership saw that sexual offenses, secretive in their nature, raised the problems of confrontation and evidence-gathering in their most severe form. Where no competent witnesses existed, as in the cases of sexual use of children or animals, confession might well be the only available evidence, and the questions whether confession might be extracted, and might support a conviction without corroboration, became critical.

50. William Bradford, Of Plymouth Plantation 201 (Harvey Wish ed., 1962). Bradford transcribed excerpts from both this response and that of Charles Chauncy into his manuscript. To Bradford and the others involved, the issue was more pressing than academic. In September 1642, Thomas Granger of Duxbury was executed on his own confession to repeated instances of bestiality, made after examination on the basis of suspicion by neighbors. Id. at 202–3.

51. 2 John Winthrop, History of New England 47 (J. Savage ed., 1826).

52. Goebel and Naughton, supra note 3, at 656.

53. See MS Mins. Ulster Co. Sess. 1738–50 Ulster County Clerk's Office.

54. October 9, 1697: "Emot moves in the name of the sheriff that the Judges do move to the city the insufficiency of the City Hall and prison." Mins.SCJ, 1693–1701, at 127, NYHR. For similar complaints in other counties, see Goebel and Naughton, supra note 3, at 337 n. 36.

55. Concerned about a pair of counterfeiters whose arrest in Dutchess County had been reported as imminent, Attorney General John Tabor Kempe wrote to Clear Everitt, the county sheriff, in 1761:

> I know not what Conditions your Gaol is in, but trust that you will keep them secure that they may make not their Escape from Justice. The Reason of my mentioning this to you, is because several Criminals have broke Gaol and made their Escape lately from some of the Counties . . . and I should be very sorry should you be liable to be punished . . . for the Escape of a Felon.

Letter dated May 1, 1761, Kempe Papers, Box BSW 1, NYHS.

56. See Greenberg, supra note 2, at 168 and n. 21.

57. See, e.g., Act of October 17, 1730, 2 Colonial Laws of New York 645 (1894), a bill for public works in the city declaring that "WHEREAS . . . the Common Gaols of the same are now very much out of Repair, and it appearing there is an Absolute Necessity not only to repair but to Enlarge the said Prisons and Gaols," money would be appropriated for new construction; Jail Tax Act of June 24, 1719, 1 id., at 1025 (empowering JPs to impose local assessments for the construction and maintenance of jails).

58. In an apparent attempt to force implementation of the assembly's 1719 statute giving JPs the power to impose taxes for spending on the jails, Attorney General Richard Bradley brought informations against justices in Albany and Queens County in 1723 for failure to levy taxes for the improvement of the jails. See MS Mins. SCJ, March 17, 1723–24, parchment 102 G 8 (NYHR)

(information against Queens JPs). Although the attorney general prudently sought a change of venue to Westchester County and a trial at bar—thus ensuring that the trial would occur in the city, under the watchful eyes of the entire court, but with jurors drawn from Westchester—the defendants in the Queens prosecution were acquitted. See MS Mins. SCJ, October 9, 1723 (NYHR). The case was finally set down for trial on circuit in 1729, after six years' delay; the defendants were acquitted, and the attorney general astonishingly sought and was granted leave to file new informations. See MS Mins. SCJ, December 2, 1729 (NYHR). The case appears again in the minutes, still untried, in August 1734, but no trial appears ever to have taken place. Thus, after at least fifteen years, was ended the quixotic experiment with prosecuting the local judges for failing to raise local taxes to support the jails. The incident not only sheds light on the difficulty provincial managers experienced in securing adequate jails— a difficulty severe enough to goad them to such unlikely measures—it also demonstrates graphically the tension between central authority and the JPs.

59. 2 Colonial Laws of New York 745, 746. One act covered New York City—where summary jurisdiction was vested in the Mayor, Deputy Mayor, Recorder, Aldermen, or any three of them—and the other conveyed the same jurisdiction to the JPs of the countryside and Albany.

60. 2 Colonial Laws of New York 920, 933; 3 id. at 377, 379. The 1736 extension allowed imposition of a fine of up to 40s. as well as corporal punishment; the 1744 act raised the allowable fine to £5 and provided that nonresidents of the colony were to be banished upon conviction.

61. 4 Colonial Laws of New York 669.

62. Minutes of the Meeting of the Mayor, Deputy Mayor and Aldermen of NYC 1733–43, bound with MS Mins. NYCQS 1722–1742/43 (Rough) (NYHR). Representative cases showing the frequency of confession, or what the court called "tacit confession," are summarized in Goebel and Naughton, supra note 3, at 116–17.

63. J. T. Kempe, Letters to Benajah Strong, Selah Strong, and Richard Woodhull, June 9, 1769 (NYHS).

64. Schwarz, supra note 2, at 53–54.

65. Id. at 54.

66. For the treatment of Sarah Hughson, see Horsmanden, supra note 38, at 285; Thomas J. Davis, A Rumor of Revolt: The "Great Negro Plot" in Colonial New York 174 (1985).

67. Goebel and Naughton, supra note 3, at 597. Similar patterns seem to have prevailed in the countryside. Id. at 597 n. 195. For comparison, Goebel and Naughton report that in the same period in the New York Supreme Court, where we are seeing the trials of more serious offenses, the figures are 91 confessions (15 explicitly to secure benefit of clergy), 429 pleas of not guilty, and 54 judgments for want of a plea.

68. Greenberg, supra note 2, at 140.

69. For more extended consideration of the unraveling of the criminal justice system in prerevolutionary New York, see Moglen, supra note 3, at 200–8.

70. 4 Colonial Laws of New York 969.

71. 4 Geo. 3 c. 34.

72. For a review of the effects of imperial trade and taxation policy on one colonial legal system in the 1760s, see Moglen, supra note 3, at 148–69.

73. This discussion is deeply indebted to John Phillip Reid, whose Constitutional History of the American Revolution—especially the first volume, The Authority of Rights—has brilliantly evoked the eighteenth-century legal context in which British and American controversy over rights occurred during the era of the Revolution. See Reid, Constitutional History of the American Revolution (4 vols.) (1986–); John Phillip Reid, The Concept of Liberty in the Age of the American Revolution (1988). Reid's work is by no means unprecedented, but it is invaluable in its sustained attention to the vast literature of constitutional polemic in the fifteen years preceding independence.

74. 1 Reid, Constitutional History of the American Revolution, supra note 73, at 9–16.

75. Id. at 27–46.

76. This complex of ideas, and its role in the literature of the Revolution, has been further explored by Reid in The Concept of Liberty, supra note 73.

77. 1 Reid, Constitutional History of the American Revolution, supra note 73, at 23.

78. Id. at 47.

79. Address to Quebec, October 26, 1774, Journal of the First Congress 121–22 (London, 1775, Cohen Rare Books Collection, NYU Law School).

80. 9 The Political Register, and Impartial Review of New Books 189 (1771), quoted in 1 Reid, Constitutional History of the American Revolution, supra note 73, at 49.

81. Instructions of Boston, September 18, 1765, Boston News-Letter, September 19, 1765, at 2, col. 1.

82. Instructions of May 8, 1769, 6 Boston Town Records [1631]–1822, at 287.

83. Instructions of Providence, August 13, 1765, Boston Evening-Post, August 19 1765, at 2 col. 3.

84. For an extended consideration of the role played by admiralty in the commercial system and the economic health of New York City before 1763, and the alteration of the 1760s, see Moglen, supra note 3, at 127–69.

85. "John English," Boston Evening-Post, January 2, 1769, at 2, col. 1.

86. [William Bollan], The Free Briton's Memorial, to all the Freeholders, Citizens and Burgesses, who Elect the Members of the British Parliament, Presented in Order to the Effectual Defence of their Injured Right of Election 21 (1769). See also Letter from the Continental Congress to the British People, September 5, 1774, 43 London Magazine 630 (1774).

87. 14 Geo. 3 c. 83, §17 (1774).

88. Id. c. 39.

89. Letter, Isaac Watts to James Napier, December 14, 1764, in Letter Book of Isaac Watts, New-York Hist. Soc. Colls. 1928, at 318. For the context of Watts's particular outburst, see Moglen, supra note 3, at 162.

90. Pauline Maier, From Resistance to Revolution: Colonial Radicals and the Development of American Opposition to Britain, 1765–1776, at 175–76 (1974).

91. See 25 Edw. 3 st. 5, c. 2 (1352).

92. 7 Will. 3 c. 3.

93. 7 The Federal and State Constitutions, Colonial Charters, and Other Organic Laws 3813 (Francis N. Thorpe ed., 1909).

94. 5 id. at 3083.

95. Penn, in the Charter of Privileges §5, provided: "That all Criminals shall have the same Privileges of Witnesses and Council as their Prosecutors." 5 id. at 3079. It should be said of William Penn that he and his early brethren in truth gave the "accused speaks" trial a meaning unique in English legal history. See Horle, supra note 45, at 116 and passim.

96. Max Farrand elegantly shows in parallel columns the textual descent of the Delaware bill from the Pennsylvania declaration, and the subsequent modeling of the Maryland document on the Delaware version, in his original publication of the unprinted Delaware bill, 3 American Historical Review 641.

97. Id. at 646.

98. Levy, Origins 409–10.

99. See Proceedings of the Assembly of the Lower Counties of Delaware 1770–1776, of the Constitutional Convention of 1776, and of the House of Assembly of the Delaware State 1776–1781, at 212 (Claudia L. Bushman et al. eds., 1986).

100. 5 Federal and State Constitutions, supra note 93, at 818.

101. 2 id., supra note 93, at 785 (Georgia constitution); 5 id. at 2598 (New Jersey constitution); 5 id. at 2637 (New York constitution); 6 id. at 3264 (South Carolina constitution).

102. Levy, Origins 406–8.

103. It would be particularly interesting, in light of this provision, to have a detailed study of the uses of summary procedure in Maryland before 1776. Levy's suggestion that this exception concerned only cases of pardon or grant of immunity is unsupported by any evidence. Levy, Origins 410. Unfortunately, we have no significant studies of criminal procedure at any level in colonial Maryland.

104. 1 The Debates in the Several State Conventions on the Adoption of the Federal Constitution 328 (2d rev. ed., Jonathan Elliott ed., 1941).

105. See 5 Colonial Laws of New York 10.

106. For the language of section 8, see Federal and State Constitutions, supra

note 93. The crooked and uninformative track of the movement for bills of rights in the state conventions can be followed in 1 Debates in the Several State Conventions, supra note 104. The material relevant to the privilege is accurately summarized in Levy, Origins 416–21.

107. For Holmes, see 2 Debates in the Several State Conventions, supra note 104, at 111; for Tredwell, 3 id. at 447–52.

108. 1 Annals of Congress 434

109. 1 Annals of Congress 753. The Annals do not report a vote on Laurence's motion to amend, but it appears that Madison had no objection to the amendment. Levy, Origins 425–26, speculates that Laurence's comment about conflict between Madison's phrasing and "laws passed" refers to the proposed section 15 of the Judiciary Act of 1789 (then in the process of passage), which provided the federal courts with equity's traditional power to compel production of documents. There is no direct evidence, but this seems a sensible, if somewhat narrow, conjecture.

110. Levy, Origins 409. For the text of section 8, see citations in supra note 93.

111. [James Parker], Conductor Generalis n.p. (Campbell ed., 1792).

112. N.Y. Const. of 1777, art. XXXIV.

113. On the infrequency of criminal business in Hamilton's practice, see 1 Julius Goebel, The Law Practice of Alexander Hamilton 687–88 (1964).

114. Alexander Hamilton, according to his cash books, received fees from defendants in only four criminal cases throughout the entire duration of his practice. Id. at 692. This may well reflect the idiosyncracies of his practice more than the uniformly prevailing approach—the New York bar was highly specialized even before the revolution, and some prewar New York lawyers of eminence, William Smith Jr., for example, eschewed criminal practice in general for the same reason Smith declined the provincial chief justiceship in 1763— it didn't pay well enough. See Moglen, supra note 3, at 229–30.

115. William Waller Hening, The Virginia Justice: Comprising the Office and Authority of a Justice of the Peace 132 (1795).

116. Henry Hitchcock, The Alabama Justice of the Peace, Containing all the Duties, Powers and Authorities of that Office 98 (1822).

117. Anglo-American Law on the Frontier: Thomas Rodney and His Territorial Cases 366 (William B. Hamilton ed., 1953).

118. Augustin S. Clayton, The Office and Duty of a Justice of the Peace 132 (1819).

SIX

1. 1 Den. 236, 169 Eng. Rep. 227 (Cr. Cas. Res. 1847).

2. 11 & 12 Vict. c. 42 (1848).

3. The Marian Committal Statute of 1555 called for the JP to examine prisoners for the purpose of collecting evidence for the prosecution. 2 & 3 Phil. & M. c. 10 (1555).

4. 61 & 62 Vict. c. 36 (1898).

5. In this chapter, the emphasis will be on the privilege in England, with side-glances at American developments during the same period. A full treatment of the development of the privilege in nineteenth-century America would require an examination of immunity statutes. On the importance of nineteenth-century immunity statutes to the history of the privilege, see Akhil Reed Amar and Renée B. Lettow, Fifth Amendment First Principles: The Self-Incrimination Clause, 93 Michigan Law Review 857 (1995).

6. 4 Hawkins, Pleas of the Crown, bk. 2, ch. 46, §37 (7th ed., Leach ed., 1795) ("It also seems clear, that if the confession of a prisoner be taken *upon oath,* it cannot be read in evidence against him," citing Bull. N.P. 242 (emphasis in original)).

7. In 1801 Peake noted that the disqualification had once been even wider but had more recently been limited to apply to those with a direct interest, leaving indirect interest to be treated as a credibility question:

> [T]he rule which has the most extensive operation in the exclusion of witnesses, and which has been found most difficult in its application, is that which prevents persons interested in the event of a suit (unless in a few excepted cases of evident necessity) from being witnesses in it.—What is such an interest, as shall totally exclude testimony, has often been the subject of controversy. The old cases have gone upon very subtle grounds: but, of late years, the Courts have endeavoured, as far as possible, consistent with authorities, to let the objection go to the credit rather than the competency of a witness; and the general rule now established is, that no objection can be made to a witness on this ground, unless he be directly interested, that is, unless he may be immediately benefited or injured by the event of the suit, or unless the verdict to be obtained by his evidence, or given against it, will be evidence for or against him in another action, in which he may afterwards be a party. . . .

Peake, Compendium 93. The 1824 American edition of Peake noted that the earlier rule forbade testimony from one who would be subject to future inconvenience. Thomas Peake, A Compendium of the Law of Evidence 235–36 (Am. ed. from the 5th London ed. 1824). In a footnote, it noted a controversy about whether one can give evidence that would operate against one's interest in another action but asserted that "a witness is not bound to answer any question which would subject him to punishment, or render him infamous or disgraced. . . . Nor where it may involve him in shame or reproach." Id., citing People v. Herrick, 13 Johns. Rep. 82 (N.Y.S. Ct. 1816).

8. 1 S. March Phillips, Treatise on the Law of Evidence 72 (4th Am. ed. from 7th London ed., Cowan and Hills eds., New York 1839).

9. 1 Simon Greenleaf, A Treatise on the Law of Evidence §329 (1842).

10. Id. §330 (justifying use of the maxim by invoking the prevention of perjury rationale and citing R. v. Woburn (K.B. 1808), 10 East 395, 403, 103 Eng. Rep. 825, 828; Worrall v. Jones (C.P. 1831), 7 Bing. 395, 131 Eng. Rep. 153 (Tindal, C.J.); Phillips and Amos on Evidence 157 (8th ed. London 1838); Commonwealth v. Marsh, 27 Mass. (10 Pick.) 57 (1830).

11. 10 East at 403, 103 Eng. Rep. at 828.

12. 7 Bing. 395, 131 Eng. Rep. 153.

13. 103 Eng. Rep. at 828; 131 Eng. Rep. at 154–55. In *Worrall* the court did not need to reach the issue of consent since the testifying party was deemed to have consented to be examined. 131 Eng. Rep. at 155.

14. 7 Mass. (10 Pick.) 57 (1830).

15. Id. at 58.

16. 1 Greenleaf, supra note 9, §225.

17. Id.

18. Indeed Greenleaf's next section is devoted to a lengthy attempt to reconcile these cases of witnesses examined as third parties who find themselves prisoners later, id. §226. See infra section IV.A.

19. See infra section IV.A.

20. See infra section IV.B.3.

21. See infra section II.B.

22. Another example of the use of phrases that sound privilege-like where the privilege against self-incrimination is not involved can be found in the husband-wife privilege. In discussing this privilege, Phillips notes the rule of R. v. Cliviger (K.B. 1788), 2 T.R. 263, 100 Eng. Rep. 143, that "a husband or wife ought not to be permitted to give any evidence that may even *tend to criminate* each other." 1 Phillips, supra note 8, at 78 (emphasis in Phillips); see R. v. Cliviger, 2 T.R. at 268, 100 Eng. Rep. at 146 ("But the ground of her [the wife's] incompetency arises from a principle of public policy, which does not permit husband and wife to give evidence that may even tend to criminate each other"). What the *Cliviger* opinion did was to use a building block of the *Nemo tenetur* maxim to create an addition to the husband-wife incompetency rule. The mere use of the emphasized phrase does not prove that the husband-wife incompetency rule ever was part of or an instance of the privilege against self-incrimination or had the same motivation.

23. Levy, Origins 388 (emphasis in original) (first set of brackets supplied; others are Levy's), citing Report of Committee of Council, Dec. 24, 1760, New York Colonial Manuscripts, LXXXIX, 54 (5), New York State Library; 14 State Trials 503.

24. As we will see in section IV.B, the witness privilege did not carry with it an exclusionary remedy until the mid-nineteenth century.

25. See infra section II.B.2.

26. 1 Leach 263, 168 Eng. Rep. 234 (Cr. Cas. 1783).

27. Id.

28. Id.

29. For a discussion and adoption of the "fruit of the poisonous tree" doctrine in the Fifth Amendment context, see Kastigar v. United States, 406 U.S. 441 (1972).

30. 1 Leach at 263, 168 Eng. Rep. at 234. See also Amar and Lettow, supra note 5, at 895 (noting innocence-reliability rationale in confession rule).

31. 1 Leach at 263–64, 168 Eng. Rep. at 235.

32. Langbein, Ryder Sources 84–105.

33. Id. at 103–5.

34. This rationale was echoed by the treatise writers; see, e.g., 2 Hawkins, Pleas of the Crown, ch. 46, §3 (6th ed., Leach ed., 1788); Peake, Compendium 13.

35. 2 & 3 Phil. & M. c. 10, §2 (1555).

36. 1 Phillips, supra note 8, at 111 (emphasis in original).

37. Id. (emphasis in original).

38. The full passage from Phillips reads as follows:

> Lambard, a writer in the reign of Elizabeth, in noticing the statute of P. & M. writes thus: "There also you may see, if I am not deceived, the time when the examination of the felon himself was first warranted in our law. *For at the common law, his fault was not to be wrung out of himself,* but rather to be proved by others." Eirenarcha, cap. 21, p. 208. See also Dalton Just. chap. 164. p. 544, and Cromp. 193. The passage, above cited from Lambard, shows how the law was then understood, though it also proves that the power, given by the statute, was exercised with great harshness.

Id. (emphasis in original).

39. 1 Mood. 186, 189, 168 Eng. Rep. 1235, 1236 (Cr. Cas. 1828).

40. Id. at 189, 168 Eng. Rep. at 1236.

41. Id. at 204, 168 Eng. Rep. at 1242.

42. 1 Greenleaf, supra note 9, §225, citing Bull. N.P. 242, and 4 Hawkins, Pleas of the Crown, bk. 2, ch. 46, §37 (n.d.).

43. 8 Wigmore, Evidence §2251(11)(c), at 316–17.

44. Prosecution evidence was excluded under the confession rule in R. v. Drew, 8 Car. & P. 140, 173 Eng. Rep. 433 (N.P. 1837), but with the wrinkle that the court had found an undue inducement in the magistrate's clerk's statement to the prisoner " 'not to say anything to prejudice himself, as what he said [the clerk] should take down, and it would be used for him or against him at his trial.' " Id. at 141, 173 Eng. Rep. at 433. Surprisingly, the court could not "conceive a more direct inducement to a man to make a confession, than telling him that what he says may be used in his favour at the trial." Id. The

Drew case was overruled by R. v. Baldry, 2 Den. 430, 169 Eng. Rep. 568 (1852).

45. 1 Greenleaf, supra note 9, §225, citing Bull. N.P. 242 and 4 Hawkins, Pleas of the Crown, bk. 2, ch. 46, §37 (n.d.).

46. 2 Thomas Starkie, Practical Treatise on the Law of Evidence 51–52 (Metcalf ed., Boston 1826).

47. Id. n. (f). (emphasis in original).

48. Langbein, Ryder Sources 103–5.

49. Holt 597, 171 Eng. Rep. 353 (N.P. 1817) (Richards, C.B.).

50. 2 & 3 Phil. & M. c. 10 (1555).

51. 2 Starkie, supra note 46, at 52, citing Carlisle, Sp. Ass. 1824 (Holroyd, J.).

52. Ry. & Mood. 432, 171 Eng. Rep. 1073 (N.P. 1826).

53. Id. at 432, 171 Eng. Rep. at 1074.

54. See section IV.

55. R. v. Slaney, 5 Car. & P. 213, 172 Eng. Rep. 944 (N.P. 1832); see also 1 J. F. Archbold, A Complete Practical Treatise on Criminal Procedure, Pleading and Evidence, in Indictable Cases 545 (8th ed. with Engl. and Am. decisions, Pomeroy ed., New York 1877) (citing R. v. Slaney) and references infra notes 59–61.

56. R. v. Garbett, 1 Den. 236, 169 Eng. Rep. 227 (Cr. Cas. 1847).

57. See infra section IV.B.

58. The witness privilege is exclusionary in the sense that, if the witness successfully claims the privilege, the testimony he or she would have given is excluded from the proceeding at hand. The confession rule, however, was associated with exclusion as a *remedy* for a violation of the rule. If a prisoner was "compelled" to confess, the confession was excluded from a later trial. But the witness privilege seems not to have been exclusionary in this remedial sense until the mid-nineteenth century. See infra section IV.B.

59. Even as late as 1839, the American edition of Phillips's treatise gave four areas the privilege covers: (1) penalties or criminal charges; (2) potential civil suit; (3) forfeiture; and (4) answers that might degrade witnesses' character. It noted that considerable doubts had been entertained on (2) (civil liability as a ground for invoking the privilege). 2 Phillips, supra note 8, at 276–79.

60. Peake, Compendium 132, citing Bain v. Hargrave (K.B. 1795, unreported and summarized by Peake) and Raines v. Towgood, 1 Peake Add. Cas. 105, 170 Eng. Rep. 210 (N.P. 1796), in both of which Lord Kenyon was the judge. These rulings and the correctness of Peake's statement were called into question in the debates over the Witnesses Act of 1806, discussed infra section II.C.2.

61. 1 Archbold, supra note 55, at 545. See also 2 S. March Phillips, Treatise on the Law of Evidence 421–30 (6th Am. ed. from 9th London ed., New York 1849) (discussing split of authority).

62. 2 Hawkins, Pleas of the Crown, bk. 2, ch. 46, §§19–20 (London 1721). The passage stands virtually unchanged in the 1788 edition. 2 Hawkins, Pleas of the Crown, ch. 46, §§19–20 (6th ed., Leach ed., 1788) (emphasis added).

63. 2 Hawkins, Pleas of the Crown, ch. 31, §2 (6th ed., Leach ed., 1788); id. ch. 46, §3.

64. In this respect, both rules are very similar, not to the later privilege against self-incrimination but rather to the contemporary law of libel. An emphasis on the potential for wounded honor to lead to socially undesirable conduct lies at the heart of the extended reaches of the witness privilege and of the law of libel. In the case of libel, it was thought that wounded honor leads to violence. Blackstone takes libels to be "malicious defamations of any person, and especially a magistrate, made public by either printing, writing, signs, or pictures, in order to provoke him to wrath, or expose him to public hatred, contempt, and ridicule." 4 Blackstone, Commentaries 150 (citation omitted). He goes on to explain that the resulting harmful victim response is what is to be deterred: "The direct tendency of these libels is the breach of the public peace, by stirring up the objects of them to revenge, and perhaps to bloodshed." Id. Since the aim was to prevent this, and the truth of the libelous statement did not diminish this tendency, truth was not a defense to libel. Id. ("[Since] it equally tends to a breach of the peace . . . it is immaterial with respect to the essence of libel, whether the matter of it be true or false; since the provocation, and not the falsity, is the thing to be punished criminally"); accord De Libellis Famosis (K.B. 1606), 5 Co. Rep. 125a, 77 Eng. Rep. 250 (holding truth to be no defense to libel indictment); see also Trial of Tutchin, 14 State Trials 1095, 1121, 1128–29 (1704) (defense counsel raising truth as defense and judge giving contrary jury instruction). See generally Philip Hamburger, The Development of the Law of Seditious Libel and the Control of the Press, 37 Stanford Law Review 661, 693–97 (1985) (discussing emergence of distinction between libel and seditious libel); id. at 694 (discussing tendency to provoke a quarrel as element of seventeeth-century libel and the bringing of scandal on the government as additional element in seventeenth-century seditious libel); 5 Holdsworth, History 208–12 (discussing treatment of criminal libel in sixteenth- and seventeenth-century England); 8 Holdsworth, History 336–42 (discussing role of tendency to breach of peace in libel and seditious libel).

65. Peake, Compendium 88–89.

66. See infra notes 74–75 and accompanying text.

67. 46 Geo. 3 c. 37 (1806).

68. 6 Parl. Deb. 166–67 (1806) (statement of Lord Hawkesbury, Feb. 13); id. at 170–71 (statement of Lord Eldon, Feb. 17).

69. Id. at 167 (statement of Lord Hawkesbury, Feb. 13).

70. Id. at 223 (Feb. 27).

71. "[H]e could only say, that he had been 30 years in the profession of the law, as counsel, and in a judicial character, and it [the bill] was the first time

he had heard that there was any doubt upon the subject. . . ." Id. at 170 (statement of Lord Eldon, Feb. 17).

72. Id. at 227 (statement of Lord Eldon, Feb. 27).

73. See, e.g., 6 Parl. Deb. 343 (1806) (statement of Lord Eldon introducing debate on second reading of bill, Feb. 12); id. at 222–27 (answer of judges and debate about state of law, Feb. 27); id. at 244–49 (continuation of same, Mar. 1); id. at 343 (statement of Lord Eldon expressing skepticism that "a bill could be so framed as to provide against the exceptions which necessarily occurred to the general rule," Mar. 4); id. at 361–62 (statement of Lord Eldon noting that even minority (of two out of seven judges) who believed witness privilege to cover liability to civil suits would allow exceptions, Mar. 7); id. at 402 (mention by Lord Stanhope of "the established compellability of pawnbrokers to give evidence" and assertion that "horse-dealers should be considered in the same light," Mar. 11); id. at 774–75 (statement of Mr. Secretary Fox that judges' majority opinion had left the door open to certain unexplained "exceptions," Apr. 17); id. at 899 (statement of solicitor general noting "unsettled state" of law, Apr. 23).

74. 6 Parl. Deb. 248 (1806) (statement of Lord Chancellor Erskine, Mar. 1):

> [Y]et. . . he never knew a single objection to have been taken to an interrogatory proposed, because the reply to it would render the witness responsible in a civil suit. It was true, that in Mr. Peake's book, which had been frequently cited on the present occasion, there was a note by which it should appear that an objection of this kind had been taken by the late chief justice Kenyon; but, notwithstanding his high opinion of the minute accuracy and great learning of that reporter, he thought he had, in this instance, been guilty of a mistake on two grounds: 1st, because he [Lord Chancellor Erskine] himself had been counsel in the cause, and had no recollection of the circumstance; 2dly, because, if that note were correct lord Kenyon must have been guilty of an obvious contradiction of his own principles and sentiments, as they appeared even on the face of the same report.

75. The lord chancellor expressed the opinion that

> if the bill passed as a simple declaratory bill, the law would stand thus; that if a witness objected that answering any question stated would render him liable to a civil action, such a naked and general demurrer would immediately be overruled; but if out of the particular situation of the witness, or the circumstances of the case, there should arise any special ground of objection, it would still be in the power of the judge to decide upon such special objection according to the law as it should appear to him, he not being compelled by this declaratory law to over-rule such objection in the first instance.

6 Parl. Deb. 486 (Mar. 19, 1806); id. at 773 (assertion by solicitor general that after the bill became law "the judges would be as much at liberty to protect a

witness from any disclosure, by omission of the conditions of forfeiture, or any defect of title to estates, as they would be, if there were no such law in existence," Apr. 17); id. at 774–75 (statement of Mr. Secretary Fox that judges had given majority opinion that a witness was compellable in the face of threat of civil liability in general terms but open to certain unexplained "exceptions," Apr. 17).

76. Witnesses Act of 1806, 46 Geo. 3 c. 37 (1806).

77. 6 Parl. Deb. 401 (1806) (statement of the lord chancellor, Mar. 11).

78. Id. at 771–72 (statement of the master of the rolls, Apr. 17).

79. See, e.g., Peake, Compendium 132 (witness privilege); id. at 13 (confession rule); 1 Starkie, supra note 46, §79, at 105 (witness privilege); 2 id. pt. 4, at 47–54 (confession rule).

80. East v. Chapman, 2 Car. & P. 570, 172 Eng. Rep. 259 (N.P. 1827); Dixon v. Vale, 1 Car. & P. 278, 171 Eng. Rep. 1195 (N.P. 1824).

81. 1 Den. 236, 169 Eng. Rep. 227 (Cr. Cas. Res. 1847). Lord Ellenborough summed up his understanding of the law in 1806 during the debates on the witnesses' indemnity bill: "It was true, that where the reply to the question would expose the witness to the consequences of a criminal prosecution, his lordship always felt it his duty to caution him from the bench; but even in that case, partial communications must not be made, the testimony must not be garbled; if a portion were imparted, the whole evidence must be disclosed." 6 Parl. Deb. 249 (1806) (statement of Lord Ellenborough, Mar. 1).

82. Horstman v. Kaufman, 97 Pa. 147 (1881). See infra section IV.B.2. As late as 1877, the American edition of Archbold endorsed the no-testimony-by parts rule: "But if the witness waives his privilege and testifies to part of a transaction in which he was criminally concerned, he is obliged to state the whole." 1 Archbold, supra note 55, at 544–45, citing State v. Foster, 23 N.H. (3 Foster) 348 (1851).

83. 2 Car. & P. at 574, 172 Eng. Rep. at 261.

84. Peake, Compendium 132. The reference is not wholly clear but may be to his discussion of the confession rule. Id. at 13.

85. Peake, Compendium 259 (Am. ed. from 5th London ed. 1824). In a footnote on evidence in libel cases, the edition asserts that "[i]t is the uniform practice of Courts of Justice, to adhere to the maxim, *nemo tenetur seipsum accusare,* both as to witnesses and jurors. Respublica v. Gibbs, 3 Yeates' Rep. 429. S. C. 4 Dall. Rep. 253. S. P. Les. of Galbraith et al. v. Eichelberger, ibid. 545." Id. Peake also notes the earlier broader scope of the witness privilege extending to civil action or debt and notes the history of the impeachment of Lord Melville. Id. at 260.

86. 1 Starkie, supra note 46, §79, at 105 (after the second sentence appears this footnote: "It is partly upon this principle that an examination of a prisoner, taken before a magistrate on oath, cannot be afterwards read against him as a

confession. Another reason is, that the oath is extra-judicial"). Here again Starkie draws out what parallels he can between the witness privilege and the confession rule.

87. 2 id. §4, at 47–54.

88. 2 id. at 50, citing Stockfleth v. Tastet, 4 Camp. 10, 171 Eng. Rep. 4 (N.P. 1814), and R. v. Merceron, 2 Stark. 366, 171 Eng. Rep. 675 (N.P. 1818) (Abbott, J.).

89. See Langbein, Criminal Trial 272–306.

90. On the "accused speaks" trial and how traditional English criminal procedure pressured the accused to speak, see chapter 4 (explaining "accused speaks" mode of trial and citing as an example the Trial of Sir Nicholas Throckmorton (1554), 1 State Trials 869).

91. Zelman Cowan and P. B. Carter, Essays on the Law of Evidence 205, 207 (1956). See also Fifth Report from Her Majesty's Commissioners for Revising and Consolidating the Criminal Law 128, §8, art. 8 (1849): "An accused person cannot claim, as of right, to address a jury by counsel, and also in person," citing as examples R. v. Boucher, 8 Car. & P. 141, 173 Eng. Rep. 433 (N.P. 1837); R. v. Burrows, 2 M. & Rob. 124, 174 Eng. Rep. 236 (N.P. 1838). According to Stephen, lawyers would often make the argument that their clients' mouths were shut, even if this was not strictly true. 1 Stephen, History 440.

92. 11 Parl. Deb. (2d ser.) 180 (1824) (motion to introduce bill by Mr. Lamb, Apr. 6); id. at 220 (failure of motion, Apr. 6).

93. 15 Parl. Deb. (2d ser.) 589 (1826) (motion to introduce bill by Mr. Lamb, Apr. 25); id. at 633 (failure of motion, Apr. 25).

94. 16 Parl. Deb. (3d ser.) 1199 (1833) (motion to introduce bill by Mr. Ewaert, Mar. 28).

95. 6 & 7 Will. 4 c. 114 (1836) ("An Act for enabling Persons indicted of Felony to make their Defence by Counsel or Attorney").

96. In addition to some of the examples to be discussed shortly, one can point to the vague invocation of Magna Carta by the sponsor of the bill, George Lamb:

> In Magna [Carta] itself, it was expressly stated, that no man should be put upon his trial unless "per judicium parium aut legem terrae" a proof, as he [George Lamb] conceived, that from the very foundation of the Common Law, a man was intitled [*sic*] to full use of counsel and advice upon his defence.

15 Parl. Deb. (2d ser.) 590 (1826). The proponents' arguments often focus on truth-seeking, but it might be doubted whether this predominated in their thinking or was done to forestall the objection that their proposal was too lenient on defendants and would allow the guilty to escape. See, e.g., Second Report

from His Majesty's Commissioners on Criminal Law 2, 6, 12, 16 (1836) [herein-after Second Report].

97. Second Report 3. See also Second Report 2, 17, 18; 11 Parl. Deb. (2d ser.) 181 (1824) (statement of Mr. Lamb, Apr. 6); id. at 187; id. at 202 (statement of Sir James Mackintosh on disadvantage to less educated defendants, Apr. 6); id. at 210 (statement of Dr. Lushington: "Not one prisoner in five thousand could be competent to such an undertaking," Apr. 6); id. at 211; id. at 217; 15 Parl. Deb. (2d ser.) 605 (1826) (statement of Mr. Williams, Apr. 25); 28 Parl. Deb. (3d ser.) 632–33 (1835) (statement of Mr. Twiss, June 10); 35 Parl. Deb. (3d ser.) 179 (1836) (statement of Lord Lyndhurst, July 14).

98. 28 Parl. Deb. (3d ser.) 632 (1835) (statement of Mr. Twiss, June 10).

99. 15 Parl. Deb. (2d ser.) 593 (1826) (statement of Mr. Lamb, Apr. 25).

100. See supra note 90.

101. 11 Parl. Deb. (2d ser.) 217 (1824) (statement of Mr. Denman, Apr. 6); 15 Parl. Deb. (2d ser.) 609 (1826) (statement of Mr. Twiss: "Any statement on the merits must be made by the prisoner's own lips. But the prisoner might be disabled by illness, blindness, deafness or some such other such visitation," Apr. 25); id. at 630 (statement of Mr. Denman, Apr. 25); id. at 631 (describing plight of foreigners); 16 Parl. Deb. (3d ser.) 1202 (1833) (statement of solicitor general, Mar. 28); 35 Parl. Deb. (3d ser.) 178 (1836) (statement of Lord Lyndhurst, July 14); id. at 613 (statement of attorney general, July 28).

102. 15 Parl. Deb. (2d ser.) 631 (1826) (statement of Mr. Denman, Apr. 25). See also Second Report at 3, 15.

103. 35 Parl. Deb. (3d ser.) 184 (1836) (statement of the Earl of Devon, July 14).

104. 16 Parl. Deb. (3d ser.) 1200 (1833) (statement of Mr. Poulter, Mar. 28).

105. Id.

106. Mr. Poulter prefaced the remarks quoted in the text with the following: "It was not sufficient that guilt should be probable—and even morally certain—but the evidence was required to be of that overwhelming and decisive character, as to take away almost all possibility of innocence before a conviction could be obtained." Id. at 1199–1200. For more on the hyperbolic invocations of the burden of proof in criminal trials, see infra section III.A.5.

107. Cowan and Carter, supra note 91, at 210. Some authorities did not count unsworn statements by the accused as evidence, and others counted it as evidence of lesser weight. However, regardless of its legal status, so long as the jury might actually use it, the unsworn statement functioned as evidence in a nontechnical sense.

108. Second Report at 3.

109. 28 Parl. Deb. (3d ser.) 632–33 (1835) (statement of Mr. Twiss, June 10). See also 15 Parl. Deb. (2d ser.) 594 (1826) (statement of Mr. Lamb citing

case where "[t]he Judge, upon that, observed, that he considered it a very bad sign when such men as they [defendants] were seen so well versed in the knowledge of the intricate parts of cross-examination [a laugh]," Apr. 25) (bracketed phrase in original).

110. 11 Parl. Deb. (2d ser.) 196 (1824) (statement of Mr. North, Apr. 6). See also the synopsis of the "accused speaks" trial that is presented for subsequent rebuttal in Second Report at 6 (quoting Hawkins's position that "the denial of a full defence by Counsel is an actual advantage to an innocent person. 'This exclusion,' he observes [Hawkins, Pleas of the Crown, bk. 2, ch. 39, §2 (volume number and edition not indicated)], 'many have complained of as very unreasonable, yet if it be considered, that generally every one of common understanding may as properly speak to a matter of fact as if he were the best lawyer, and that it requires no manner of skill to make a plain and honest defence, which in cases of this kind is always the best; the simplicity, the innocence, the artless and the ingenuous behaviour of one whose conscience acquits him, having something in it more moving and convincing than the highest eloquence of persons speaking in a cause not their own. . . . Whereas, on the other side, the very speech, gesture, countenance and manners of defence of those who are guilty, when they speak for themselves, may often help to disclose the truth, which probably would not so well be discovered from the artificial defence of others speaking for them' ").

111. 11 Parl. Deb. (2d ser.) 184–85 (1824) (statement of Mr. Lamb arguing against the wisdom of this "maxim," Apr. 6); 15 Parl. Deb. (2d ser.) 611 (1826) (statement of Mr. Twiss: "The maxim was a fanciful one," Apr. 25).

112. See, e.g., 11 Parl. Deb. (2d ser.) 184–85 (1824) (statement of Mr. Lamb, Apr. 6); id. at 210 (statement of Dr. Lushington, Apr. 6); id. at 216 (statement of Mr. Denman, Apr. 6); id. at 219 (statement of Mr. Martin quoting judge as saying to defendant, "I will give you credit for a good character, and proceed to try you," Apr. 6); 15 Parl. Deb. (2d ser.) 592 (1826) (statement of Mr. Lamb, Apr. 25); id. at 611 (statement of Mr. Twiss, Apr. 25); id. at 616 (statement of Mr. Martin, Apr. 25).

113. Second Report at 4 (noting that judge does not have all the facts); id. at 7; id. at 8 (judge is nonadversary).

114. John M. Beattie, Scales of Justice: Defense Counsel and the English Criminal Trial in the Eighteenth and Nineteenth Centuries, 9 Law and History Review 221, 223 (1991); see also discussion in chapter 4.

115. Second Report at 4; 15 Parl. Deb. (2d ser.) 610 (1826) (statement of Mr. Twiss, noting that judge has prosecution information but not defense information, Apr. 25); 28 Parl. Deb. (3d ser.) 629–30 (1835) (statement of Mr. Twiss, June 10); id. at 866 (statement of Mr. Fergusson, June 17); 29 Parl. Deb. (3d ser.) 358 (1835) (statement of Mr. Lennard, July 9); 35 Parl. Deb. (3d ser.) 186 (1836) (statement of lord chancellor, July 14: "He was glad that in the course

of this debate they had at last got rid of the fiction so contrary to the fact, 'that the judge was counsel for the prisoner'—counsel for the prisoner, without having any communication with his client and without having the slightest previous knowledge of what it was for the interest of his client to prove").

116. Barbara J. Shapiro, "Beyond Reasonable Doubt" and "Probable Cause": Historical Perspectives on the Anglo-American Law of Evidence 1–41 (1991).

117. Proponents were often required to address this argument: Second Report at 11; 11 Parl. Deb. (2d ser.) 183 (1824) (statement of Mr. Lamb, Apr. 6); id. at 195 (statement of Mr. North, Apr. 6); 15 Parl. Deb. (2d ser.) 608 (1826) (statement of Mr. Secretary Peel, Apr. 25); id. at 611 (statement of Mr. Twiss, Apr. 25); 16 Parl. Deb. (3d ser.) 1199–1200 (1833) (statement of Mr. Poulter, Mar. 28); 28 Parl. Deb. (3d ser.) 867 (1835) (statement of Mr. Poulter, June 17).

118. Other maxims, no more relevant to the debate than *Nemo tenetur,* are mentioned as well, but *Nemo tenetur* is not. One proponent of the measure admonished the House of Commons that "[t]hey ought not to lose sight of the old maxim, that it was better to let ten guilty men escape than to make one innocent man suffer." 24 Parl. Deb. (3d ser.) 825 (1834) (statement of Mr. Bernal, June 24). This is called a maxim, just as elsewhere *Nemo tenetur* is known as a maxim. But the ten-guilty-men maxim is hardly a rule of evidence or even a right of the accused. It is at most a general policy. That a maxim can stand for such a general policy rather than a specific right should alone make one wonder what the status of the maxim *Nemo tenetur* was at the time.

119. This "traditonal" indulgence was a historical fiction. See Langbein, Criminal Trial 283.

120. See, e.g., 11 Parl. Deb. (2d ser.) 182 (1824) (statement of Mr. Lamb noting that Blackstone "in commenting upon the rule, that no counsel shall be allowed a prisoner upon his trial upon the general issue in any capital crime, observes 'that it is not at all of a piece with the rest of the humane treatment of prisoners by the English law,' " Apr. 6); id. at 217 (statement of Mr. Denman, Apr. 26); Second Report at 5–6 (contrasting denial of full right of counsel to "the spirit of indulgence which characterizes the law on all criminal charges with the exception of Felony, and in respect of civil proceedings without exception").

121. See, e.g., 11 Parl. Deb. (2d ser.) 189–98 (1824) (statement of Mr. North, Apr. 6); id. at 206 (statement of attorney general, Apr. 6); see also 15 Parl. Deb. (2d ser.) 619–20 (1826) (statement of Mr. Tindal quoting Cottu as observing that in England defendants were not demonized, Apr. 25).

122. 24 Parl. Deb. (3d ser.) 161 (1834) (statement of Mr. Hill, June 4).

123. 15 Parl. Deb. (2d ser.) 621 (1826) (statement of Mr. Tindal, Apr. 25, rebutting argument that defense by counsel was permitted in other countries

by pointing out that "[b]oth in France and in Scotland there were public prose-cutors, whose duty it was to conduct a prosecution, and who, in France, at least . . . first examined a prisoner, and so became acquainted with the means of his defence. Now, he wished to know, whether the supporters of this measure would clog their proposal with the condition of the creation of such an officer, armed with such a power, or whether they would not rather leave the prisoners as they now stood?"); 35 Parl. Deb. (3d ser.) 172 (1836) (statement of Lord Wharncliffe comparing English system to French system of "personal examina-tion" and "endeavors . . . made to extricate from the prisoner a confession of his guilt" and to Scottish system of nonunanimous verdicts, July 14); id. at 232 (statement of Duke of Richmond deploring system of ex parte depositions against defendants, July 15).

124. See 15 Parl. Deb. (2d ser.) 620 (1826) (paraphrase of statement of Mr. Tindal describing Cottu, a French observer of the English criminal justice sys-tem, as "[coming] from a country in which a system, exactly the opposite of our own, was practiced," Apr. 25).

125. 24 Parl. Deb. (3d ser.) 164 (1834) (statement of Mr. O'Connell, June 4).

126. Certainly the party-witness disqualification removed much of the po-tential scope of such a right, but this opponent's point would have been even more forceful if stated in the most sweeping terms that the facts of criminal procedure would have supported.

127. The participants were also aware that the measure was part of the in-creasing lawyerization of the criminal trial, see, e.g., 15 Parl. Deb. (2d ser.) 598–603 (1826) (statement of attorney general noting experience in other courts with lawyers' statements to jury, arguing that trials would become too adversar-ial and asserting that allowing defense counsel to address jury would be irrevers-ible step, Apr. 25).

128. 11 & 12 Vict. c. 42 (1848). For a brief discussion of the history of the act, see David Freestone and J. C. Richardson, The Making of English Criminal Law: Sir John Jervis and His Acts, 1980 Criminal Law Review 5 (1980).

129. See supra notes 2–3 and accompanying text.

130. 1 Stephen, History 440.

131. Id.

132. Id.

133. Id. at 440–41.

134. Id. at 441.

135. Freestone and Richardson, supra note 128, at 5.

136. As chapter 5 demonstrated, a similar state of affairs obtained in the United States through the early nineteenth century; no one saw a contradiction between *Nemo tenetur* and its constitutionalized version in the Bill of Rights on the one hand and Marian-type pretrial and the contemporary "accused speaks" trial on the other.

137. 1 Den. 236, 169 Eng. Rep. 227 (Cr. Cas. Res. 1847).

138. On the other hand, the early-nineteenth-century witness privilege, though weaker in these respects, protected against a wide range of questions; a third-party witness could invoke the privilege not only against questions tending to incriminate but also against those tending to expose the witness to civil liability or damage to his reputation. The 1806 statute narrowed the scope of the dangers protected against, to the possibility of a future criminal prosecution. See supra section II.C.2.

139. 1 Greenleaf, supra note 9, §225; see also supra note 45 and accompanying text.

140. A famous but somewhat unclear example of a witness not being allowed to refuse to testify is presented by R. v. Merceron, 2 Stark. 366, 171 Eng. Rep. 675 (N.P. 1818). In that case, the defendant had given evidence before a committee of the House of Commons. At his trial for official misconduct as a magistrate, the defendant objected that the statements given into evidence had been made under compulsory process and on pain of contempt and were therefore involuntary (under the confession rule). Nonetheless the court accepted the statement into evidence and the defendant was found guilty. Id. at 367, 171 Eng. Rep. at 675. However, this evidence before the committee of the House of Commons may not have been on oath. Lord Tenterden, the judge in R. v. Merceron, expressed doubts in Gilham's Case, 1 Mood. 186, 203, 168 Eng. Rep. 1235, 1241 (Cr. Cas. 1828), about the report in R. v. Merceron and asserted that "the evidence must have been given without oath, and before a committee of enquiry where the witness would not be bound to answer." Id. But even if Lord Tenterden is right, R. v. Merceron still stands as an example of testimony being admitted despite great pressure—if not legal compulsion—having been applied. No explicit warning or waiver seems to have been required.

141. 1 M. & Rob. 297, 174 Eng. Rep. 101 (N.P. 1833).

142. 2 Mood. 45, 169 Eng. Rep. 18 (Cr. Cas. 1838).

143. The defendant had been informed that he need not answer incriminating questions and had made objections to some questions on that ground. Those objections were sustained, but objections that he had made to other questions were disallowed and, the report notes, "he had been compelled to answer. The examination was upon oath." Id. at 46, 169 Eng. Rep. at 19. Note that *compelled* is used here in a sense distinct from that used in the confession rule; the answer was not voluntary in the everyday sense since the witness had expressed a desire not to answer. Rather, voluntariness in the legal sense for purposes of the witness privilege only was satisfied.

144. Id. at 49, 169 Eng. Rep. at 20.

145. Id. at 51, 169 Eng. Rep. at 20.

146. Id. at 51, 169 Eng. Rep. at 21 (Lord Abinger, C.B.). Lord Abinger dissented from the court's decision.

147. 4 Car. & P. 253, 172 Eng. Rep. 693 (N.P 1829).

148. Id. at 256, 172 Eng. Rep. at 694.

149. 5 Car. & P. 530, 172 Eng. Rep. 1084 (N.P 1833).

150. 6 Car. & P. 161, 172 Eng. Rep. 1190 (N.P. 1833).

151. Id. at 162, 172 Eng. Rep. at 1190.

152. Id.

153. 9 Car. & P. 238, 173 Eng. Rep. 818 (N.P. 1839).

154. Id. at 240–41, 240 n. (a)^2, 173 Eng. Rep. at 818–19, 818 n. (a)^2.

155. See infra section IV.B.

156. 1 Den. 236, 169 Eng. Rep. 227 (Cr. Cas. 1847).

157. 169 Eng. Rep. at 227.

158. East v. Chapman, 2 Car. & P. 570, 172 Eng. Rep. 259 (N.P. 1827); Dixon v. Vale, 1 Car. & P. 278, 171 Eng. Rep. 1195 (N.P. 1824). See supra notes 80–83 and accompanying text.

159. 1 Car. & P. 278, 171 Eng. Rep. 1195.

160. 2 Car. & P. 570, 172 Eng. Rep. 259.

161. 1 Den. at 257, 169 Eng. Rep. at 235.

162. Id. at 257–58, 169 Eng. Rep. at 235–36.

163. See infra sections IV.B.2–3.

164. Lawrence Herman, The Unexplored Relationship between the Privilege against Compulsory Self-Incrimination and the Involuntary Confession Rule (pt. 1), 53 Ohio State Law Journal 101 (1992). Herman argues that the privilege should be identified with the confession rule from an early date. He lumps together confession-rule and witness-privilege cases and therefore (not surprisingly) finds an early implied exclusionary remedy for *Nemo tenetur*. Id. at 159–60, nn. 303–4. The fact that *Garbett* was the first case to apply an exclusionary remedy for wrongfully compelled testimony from a witness presents a major problem for his account. The confession rule did not secure a generalized right to silence (see supra section II.B) and was a rule distinct from the witness privilege (see supra section II.C.3). None of Herman's evidence, tempting though it is in phraseology, suggests the contrary. Instead Herman falls into the trap of equating *Nemo tenetur* rhetoric with a meaningful right to silence.

165. 97 Pa. 147 (1881), also cited in James Fitzjames Stephen, A Digest of the Law of Evidence, art. 120 (Chase Am. ed. from 4th Engl. ed., New York 1885). That the witness privilege was exclusionary was at least asserted in dictum in Hendrickson v. People, 10 N.Y. 13, 31 (1854). The court claimed (id. at 31), without citing supporting authority, that

[i]n all cases, as well before coroners' inquests as on the trial of issues in court, when the witness is not under arrest, or is not before the officer on a charge of crime [and so eligible for the greater confession-rule protection], he stands on the same footing as other witnesses. He may refuse to answer, and his answers are to

be deemed voluntary, unless he is compelled to answer after having declined to do so; in the latter case only will they be deemed compulsory, and excluded.

166. 97 Pa. at 147.

167. Id. at 151–52.

168. Id. at 152.

169. Id.

170. James Fitzjames Stephen, A Digest of the Law of Evidence, art. 23 (London 1876) (citing *Garbett*).

171. In 1864, defendants became qualified to testify in Maine. See 2 Wigmore, Evidence §579; Joel N. Bodansky, The Abolition of the Party-Witness Disqualification: An Historical Survey, 70 Kentucky Law Journal 91, 105–6 (1981–82). Other states, with the notable exception of Georgia, soon followed Maine's lead. Bodansky, supra, at 106.

172. Stephen, supra note 165, art. 23 (citations omitted). It is noted that some states follow the old rule for pretrial that the pretrial examination must not be on oath and must be excluded as evidence if it is.

173. Id. Also cited are 1 Greenleaf, supra note 9, §451, and Hendrickson v. People, 10 N.Y. 13, 27, 31 (1854).

174. Stephen, supra note 165, art. 120, also citing Horstman v. Kaufman, 97 Pa. 147 (1881). It also discusses the practice of many states of allowing a party to become a witness but requiring that the witness then be required to undergo full cross-examination. See infra part V.

175. 14 & 15 Vict. c. 99 (1851). Section 2 of that act removed the disqualification for parties in all suits with the exception, spelled out in §3, of criminal proceedings. On the step-by-step removal of the disqualification of parties for interest, see Bodansky, supra note 171, at 70.

176. 1 Stephen, History 440.

177. 1 Phillips, supra note 8, at 72. See also supra section II.A for a discussion of this derivation of noncompellability from incompetence.

178. 1 Phillips, supra note 61, at 59. See also 1 S. March Phillips and Thomas J. Arnold, Treatise on the Law of Evidence 57 (4th Am. ed. from 10th Engl. ed., New York 1859) (same). The passage in the 1849 edition continues: "It may be doubted, whether it is altogether consistent with the general administration of impartial and severe justice." 1 Phillips, supra note 61, at 59. This complaint has a Benthamite sound to it, and it may well be that the editor was straining to find instances of exclusion to criticize in the Benthamite mode. Even so, the passage may furnish weak evidence that there was a privilege to which the author could even attempt to assimilate the party-witness disqualification.

179. 1 S. March Phillips and Thomas J. Arnold, Treatise on the Law of Evidence 30 (5th Am. ed. from 10th Engl. ed., New York 1868).

180. Bodansky, supra note 171, at 91.

181. Id. at 107.

182. Id. at 114 and n. 97, citing William A. Maury, Validity of Statutes Authorizing the Accused to Testify, 14 American Law Review 753, 762–63 (1880).

183. Id. at 107.

184. An Act to Amend the Law of Evidence: Evidence in Criminal Cases Bill, 61 & 62 Vict. c. 36, §1(a) (1898).

SEVEN

I am grateful to the Leonard Sorkin Faculty Fund and the Sonnenschein Fund at the University of Chicago Law School for research support and to Penelope Bryan, George Fisher, Dick Helmholz, Dan Kahan, Nancy King, Dan Klerman, John Langbein, Stephen Schulhofer, and Welsh White for comments on an earlier draft of this chapter.

1. U.S. Const. amend. V.

2. Miranda v. Arizona, 384 U.S. 436, 460 (1966) (quoting Malloy v. Hogan, 378 U.S. 1, 8 (1964)).

3. Garner v. United States, 424 U.S. 648, 657 (1976) (quoting Lisenba v. California, 314 U.S. 219, 241 (1941)).

4. See Joseph D. Grano, Confessions, Truth, and the Law 141–43 (1993).

5. Griffin v. California, 380 U.S. 609 (1965), in which the Supreme Court held that the Fifth Amendment "forbids either comment by the prosecution on the accused's silence or instructions by the court that such silence is evidence of guilt," id. at 615, is the Supreme Court decision most clearly endorsing the "right to silence" interpretation of the Fifth Amendment. The majority opinion in *Griffin* invoked the language of unconstitutional conditions, declaring that comment "is a penalty imposed by courts for exercising a constitutional privilege. It cuts down on the privilege by making its assertion costly." Id. at 614. The dissenters replied that "[c]ompulsion is the focus of the inquiry" and that "the Court in this case stretches the concept of compulsion beyond all reasonable bounds." Id. at 620 (Stewart, J., dissenting).

The decision most clearly endorsing the "improper interrogation methods" interpretation of the amendment is Colorado v. Connelly, 479 U.S. 157, 170 (1986) ("The sole concern of the fifth amendment . . . is governmental coercion").

The majority opinion in Miranda v. Arizona appeared to embrace both views. The first *Miranda* warning—"You have a right to remain silent"— strongly indicated the Court's approval of the "right to silence" interpretation. So did the Court's expansive accusatorial rhetoric and its demand for a knowing and intelligent waiver of the privilege as a prerequisite to the admission of any statement made by a suspect at the stationhouse. The Court, however, did not direct law enforcement officers to provide the *Miranda* warnings whenever they asked a person suspected of crime to incriminate himself. Only suspects in custody were entitled to the warnings, and the Court referred repeatedly to the "inherently compelling nature" of custodial interrogation. This language and other aspects of the *Miranda* opinion (for example, the Court's discussion of the stratagems that interrogation manuals encouraged law enforcement officers to use while questioning suspects) suggested that the Court was still concerned with the quality and extent of the pressure brought to bear on a suspect and that the Fifth Amendment might not prohibit every inducement to speak. At the same time, much of the Court's discussion of stationhouse interrogation indicated that it was compelling only because it undercut the right to remain silent. A reader attempting to infer from *Miranda* whether the Fifth Amendment mandated neutrality toward a suspect's decision to speak or remain silent could have become confused.

Post-*Miranda* decisions have permitted prison officials to treat a suspect's silence as an indication of his guilt in prison disciplinary proceedings, Baxter v. Palmigiano, 425 U.S. 308, 316–20 (1976), and have allowed prosecutors to impeach the testimony of defendants at trial by showing their earlier failures to speak. See Jenkins v. Anderson, 447 U.S. 231 (1980) (pre-arrest silence); Fletcher v. Weir, 455 U.S. 603 (1982) (postarrest silence). But see Doyle v. Ohio, 426 U.S. 610 (1976) (a suspect's silence following *Miranda* warnings may not be used to impeach him because the warnings themselves might have caused him to remain silent). Even after *Griffin* and *Miranda,* the privilege against self-incrimination does not entirely assure suspects that they will suffer no adverse consequences for refusing to speak.

6. R. Kent Greenawalt, Silence as a Moral and Constitutional Right, 23 William & Mary Law Review 15 (1981).

7. A common response to Greenawalt's argument is that private interrogation cannot be analogized to governmental interrogation because interrogation leading to a criminal conviction has substantially more severe consequences than questioning leading to a private sanction. See, for example, Myron Moskovitz, The O. J. Inquisition: A United States Encounter with Continental Criminal Justice, 28 Vanderbilt Journal of Transnational Law 1121, 1140 (1995). Some private sanctions, however (for example, a discharge from employment), are more severe than some criminal sanctions (for example, unsupervised probation). More important, if someone is guilty of a crime, it seems as appropriate for the government to punish her as for her employer to discharge her. Greenawalt's critics have not explained why a difference in the severity of the threatened sanction should cause a turnabout in the principles of justice that he articulated; these critics presumably do not contend that one should be privileged to frustrate deserved governmental punishment but not deserved private punish-

ment. Although the position of these critics reflects the almost intuitive liberal sense that the public and private realms are "just different," the critics' argument seems seriously incomplete.

8. But see California v. Byers, 402 U.S. 424, 427 (1971) (opinion of Burger, C.J., joined by three other justices) (endorsing balancing).

9. For example, the Supreme Court once maintained that the privilege against self-incrimination expresses "our respect for the inviolability of the human personality and . . . the right of each individual 'to a private enclave where he may lead a private life.' " Murphy v. Waterfront Commission, 378 U.S. 52, 55 (1964) (quoting United States v. Grunewald, 233 F.2d 556, 581–82 (2d Cir. 1956)). The Court has since recognized that the privilege protects privacy only haphazardly. See Fisher v. United States, 425 U.S. 391, 400–1 (1976). Even the most expansive view of the privilege would not protect the privacy of an intimate diary that contained no matter tending to incriminate its owner. If, however, the act of producing a grocery list or other impersonal document would tend to incriminate the person ordered to produce it, she need not respond. Moreover, a grant of immunity lifts the protection of the privilege altogether; with it, a person can be forced to tell all. The privilege does not protect this person's privacy; it protects him only from being forced to incriminate himself.

For convincing responses to most of the justifications that the Supreme Court has asserted for the privilege, see Walter V. Schaefer, The Suspect and Society 59–76 (1967); Lewis Mayers, Shall We Amend the Fifth Amendment? (1959); Henry J. Friendly, The Fifth Amendment Tomorrow: The Case for Constitutional Change, 37 University of Cincinnati Law Review 671 (1981); John H. Wigmore, Nemo Tenetur Seipsum Prodere, 5 Harvard Law Review 71 (1891); Charles T. McCormick, Some Problems and Developments in the Admissibility of Confessions, 24 Texas Law Review 239, 277 (1946); Donald A. Dripps, Against Police Interrogation—And the Privilege Against Self-Incrimination, 78 Journal of Criminal Law & Criminology 699 (1988); Donald A. Dripps, Self-Incrimination and Self-Preservation: A Skeptical View, 1991 University of Illinois Law Review 329; Akhil Reed Amar and Renée B. Lettow, Fifth Amendment First Principles: The Self-Incrimination Clause, 93 Michigan Law Review 857, 889–95 (1995).

10. For sophisticated defenses of the privilege, see Robert S. Gerstein, Privacy and Self-Incrimination, 80 Ethics 87 (1970); Robert S. Gerstein, Punishment and Self-Incrimination, 16 American Journal of Jurisprudence 84 (1971); Robert S. Gerstein, The Demise of *Boyd:* Self-Incrimination and Private Papers in the Burger Court, 27 UCLA Law Review 343 (1979); William J. Stuntz, Self-Incrimination and Excuse, 88 Columbia Law Review 1227 (1988). For responses, see David Dolinko, Is There a Rationale for the Privilege against Self-Incrimination?, 33 UCLA Law Review 1063, 1122–37 (1986); Stephen

J. Schulhofer, Some Kind Words for the Privilege against Self-Incrimination, 26 Valparaiso Law Review 311, 320–21, 322–23 (1991).

11. Schulhofer, supra note 10, at 311. For Schulhofer's justification and defense of the privilege (that it protects innocent defendants who might be unconvincing on the witness stand), see id. at 325–33. But see Tehan v. Shott, 382 U.S. 406, 415-16 (1966) (refusing to apply Griffin v. California retroactively because "the basic purposes that lie behind the privilege against self-incrimination do not relate to protecting the innocent from conviction" and because "the Fifth Amendment's privilege against self-incrimination is not an adjunct to the ascertainment of truth").

12. Amar and Lettow, supra note 9, at 895.

13. See 384 U.S. at 460; 382 U.S. at 414; Malloy v. Hogan, 378 U.S. 1, 7 (1964).

14. See, for example, Withrow v. Williams, 507 U.S. 680, 692 (1993); Pennsylvania v. Muniz, 496 U.S. 582, 595 (1990); Couch v. United States, 409 U.S. 322, 328 (1973); 384 U.S. at 460; 378 U.S. at 55 (quoting 8 Wigmore, Evidence §2251, at 317).

15. See, for example, 425 U.S. 391; United States v. Doe, 465 U.S. 605 (1984) (Doe I).

16. Williams v. Florida, 399 U.S. 78 (1970).

17. United States v. Nobles, 422 U.S. 225 (1975).

18. Schmerber v. California, 384 U.S. 757 (1966).

19. United States v. Dionisio, 410 U.S. 1 (1973).

20. Baltimore City Department of Social Services v. Bouknight, 493 U.S. 549 (1990). Although the Court viewed the body of the suspected homicide victim as nontestimonial evidence, it recognized that the act of producing the body might supply testimonial evidence that the Fifth Amendment would permit a suspect to withhold. In *Bouknight* itself, however, the Court declared the privilege unavailable because a court had adjudicated the suspected homicide victim a child in need of assistance. His mother, the woman suspected of killing him, therefore held him only as a representative of the state. More than five years after the Supreme Court decision and more than seven years after Jacqueline Bouknight was imprisoned for failing to produce the body of her son Maurice, she was released from a Baltimore jail. In our accusatorial system, she had served more time for failing to produce evidence of the suspected but unproved killing than she would have served if she had been convicted of manslaughter. See Mother Ends 7-Year Jail Stay, Still Silent about Missing Child, New York Times, Nov. 2, 1995, sec. A, p. 18, col. 1.

21. When one considers the issue as a matter of abstraction, the gain in human dignity afforded by a right to silence may seem to justify the substantial burdens on law enforcement that the right imposes. The balance, however, may appear more problematic when one focuses on a specific case. For example,

shortly before midnight on May 26, 1996, a driver in Will County, Illinois, killed three teenaged pedestrians, then left the scene of the accident. Effective police work located the 1987 Chevy Blazer involved in the accident, but its owner refused to speak to the authorities about whether he or someone else had been driving the vehicle. See Jerry Shnay, More Charges Are Expected in Fatal Hit-and-Run, Chicago Tribune, June 7, 1996, at 1. One could imagine a case in which this refusal would make it impossible to establish beyond a reasonable doubt the owner's guilt of any crime. In this situation, the owner's refusal to answer might seem more a triumph of incivility than a triumph of human dignity. One wonders whether the Constitution truly affords a suspect the right to thumb his nose at an aggrieved community in this fashion and, if it does, how the framers could have viewed the right as noble and inspiring.

Similarly, one wonders whether it would have been cruel or unfair to ask O. J. Simpson to explain the strong proof of guilt that prosecutors presented at his trial—and to draw an inference adverse to Simpson if he declined. Simpson's lawyers evidently concluded that he would increase his chances of acquittal by not discussing before the jury why telephone company records indicated that he was making calls from his Bronco at a time when he claimed to have been at home, why he told the limousine driver who saw him enter his darkened doorway that he had been asleep, whether Nicole Simpson had ever given him a pair of Aris Isotoner gloves, where he had been planning to go at the time of the chase that everyone watched on television, how his blood could have been found on his driveway before any blood sample had been obtained from him, and other troublesome, unresolved questions.

The lawyers' judgment might well have been correct; Simpson probably improved his chances of acquittal by remaining silent. Encouraging jurors to use their common sense rather than the "artificial reason" of the law to assess the sounds of Simpson's silence could conceivably have altered the outcome of the trial.

22. For a description of the intimidating techniques used by police officers to obtain confessions in the post-*Miranda* era, see David Simon, Homicide: A Year on the Killing Streets 199–220 (1991); Richard A. Leo, *Miranda*'s Revenge: Police Interrogation as a Confidence Game, 30 Law and Society Review 259 (1996).

23. Bureau of Justice Statistics, Sourcebook of Criminal Justice Statistics 1994, at 486 Table 5.49 (1995) (NCJ-154591).

24. U.S. Sentencing Commission, Sentencing Guidelines Manual §3.E1.1 (b)(1) (1995 ed.).

25. Schaefer, supra note 9, at 59. See also Charles T. McCormick, Law and the Future: Evidence, 51 Northwestern University Law Review 218, 222 (1956) ("Ordinary morality . . . sees nothing wrong in asking a man, for adequate reason, about particular misdeeds of which he has been suspected and charged. . . . I predict that the weaknesses of the privilege in point of policy and morality will become more widely understood").

26. Champions of the right to remain silent may wonder about it, too.

27. 384 U.S. 436 (1966).

28. See Max Radin, Handbook of Roman Law 468 (1927). Early Jewish law, however, forbade nearly all self-incriminating testimony and excluded nearly all self-incriminating out-of-court statements. See Irene Merker Rosenberg and Yale L. Rosenberg, In the Beginning: The Talmudic Rule against Self-Incrimination, 63 New York University Law Review 955 (1988); Levy, Origins 433–41.

29. See Amar and Lettow, supra note 9, at 896.

30. Earlier, the church may not have recognized any sacrament for the remission of sins other than baptism. See "Penitential Controversy," in 2 Encyclopedic Dictionary of Religion 2721, 2722 (Paul Kevin Meagher, Thomas C. O'Brien, and Consuelo Maria Ahene eds., 1979); "Penance," in Encyclopedia of Early Christianity 708 (Everett Ferguson ed., 1990).

31. Compare "Confession of Sin," in Encyclopedia of Early Christianity, supra note 30, at 223, 224 ("By the fifth century, the practice of public confession had been replaced by private confession . . ."); 1 Henry Charles Lea, A History of Auricular Confession and Indulgences in the Latin Church 217 (1896, repr. 1968) ("[D]uring the early centuries the only confession recognized by the Church was . . . made by the sinner in the congregation of the faithful, unless, indeed, he might be on trial before his bishop and then it was public in the episcopal court . . ."); R. S. T. Haslehurst, Some Account of the Penitential Discipline of the Early Church in the First Four Centuries 100 (1921) (reciting substantial circumstantial evidence that confession in the early church was public); and J. N. D. Kelly, Early Christian Doctrines 216 (5th ed. 1977) (in the third century, penitential discipline "was wholly public, involving confession, a period of penance and exclusion from communion, and formal absolution and restoration") with "Rites and Ceremonies," in 26 The New Encylopedia Britannica 790 (15th ed. 1993) (In the third century, when penitential exercises included fasting, wearing sackcloth, lying in ashes, and other forms of mortification, "details of the sins committed were confessed in secret to a priest, who then pronounced absolution and imposed an appropriate penance"); "Confession, Auricular," in 1 Encyclopedic Dictionary of Religion, supra note 30, at 868 ("More recent historians of penance are in general agreement that public confession was never obligatory in the early Church, although penitents may well have confessed publicly the major sins for which they were doing penance"); John Halliburton, "A Godly Discipline: Penance in the Early Church," in Confession and Absolution 40, 45 (Martin Dudley and Geoffrey Rowell eds., 1990) ("Those who write of 'public confession' in the early Church normally fail to distinguish between the terms 'exhomologesis' and 'confessio' "); Joseph A. Favazza, The Order of Penitents: Historical Roots and Pastoral Future 214–17 (1988) (in the third century, private confession to a priest was followed by public confession that was liturgical rather than informative in nature).

32. See chapter 2, note 50 and accompanying text.

33. Id. Chrysostom also wrote, "[I]f a man hasten to confess his crimes and show the ulcer to a doctor, who will heal and not reproach, and receive the medicines from him, and speak with him alone, no one else knowing of it, and carefully tell him all, he shall easily be quit of his sin." Quoted in Haslehurst, supra note 31, at 101.

34. Quoted in "Confession, Auricular," in 1 Encyclopedic Dictionary of Religion, supra note 30, at 868. Cyril of Jerusalem wrote, "[T]he Master . . . saith, 'I do not compel thee to come into the midst of the theatre, in the presence of many witnesses: tell the sin to Me, alone, and in private, that I may heal the sore.' " Quoted in Haslehurst, supra note 31, at 102 (collecting many similar sources at 100–5).

35. Wigmore wrote, "The whole rule was embodied in the maxim, 'Licet nemo tenetur seipsum prodere, tamen proditus per famam tenentur seipsum prodere, tamen proditus per famam tenetur seipsum ostendere utrum possit suam innocentiam ostendere et seipsum purgare.' " He translated this sentence as, "Though no one is bound to become his own accuser, yet when once a man has been accused (pointed at as guilty) by general report, he is bound to show whether he can prove his innocence and to vindicate himself." Wigmore concluded, "*Prodere* was used in the sense of 'to disclose for the first time,' 'to reveal what was before unknown.' The whole maxim, far from establishing a privilege of refusing to answer, expressly declares that answers must be given under certain conditions. . . ." Wigmore, supra note 9, at 83–84. For two relatively minor corrections of Wigmore's translation, see Helen Silving, The Oath (pt. I), 68 Yale Law Journal 1329, 1367 (1959). See also 8 Wigmore, Evidence §2250, at 267 n. 1, 275–76; Levy, Origins 95–96.

36. As late as 1886 in fact, the Supreme Court wrote:

> [A]ny compulsory discovery by extorting the party's oath . . . to convict him of crime . . . is contrary to the principles of a free government. It is abhorrent to the instincts of an Englishman; it is abhorrent to the instincts of an American. It may suit the purposes of despotic power; but it cannot abide the pure atmosphere of political liberty and personal freedom.

Boyd v. United States, 116 U.S. 616, 631–32 (1886).

37. "Doctrines and Dogmas, Religious," in 17 The New Encyclopedia Britannica 442, supra note 31. Fifteen centuries before Christ, a cuneiform tablet depicted Mithra, the most important god of pre-Zoroastrian Iran, as the god of oaths. "Mithraism," in 8 id. at 197.

38. Exod. 20:7 (AV (KJ)); see also Deut. 5:11; Lev. 19:12–13.

39. In the Sermon on the Mount (Matt. 5:33–37 (New American Bible, rev. ed.)), Christ said:

Again, you have heard that it was said to the people long ago, "Do not break your oath, but keep the oaths you have made to the Lord." But I tell you, Do not swear at all: either by Heaven, for it is God's throne; or by the earth, for it is his footstool; or by Jerusalem, for it is the city of the Great King. And do not swear by your head, for you cannot make even one hair white or black. Simply let your "Yes" be "Yes," and your "No," "No"; anything beyond this comes from the evil one.

40. The quoted phrase, and some of what follows, is taken from R. H. Helmholz, The Spirit of Classical Canon Law 145 (1996), making use of Paolo Prodi, Il sacramento del potere: Il giuramento politico nella storia costituzionale dell'Occidente (1992).

41. Compurgation as a mode of trial in common law criminal cases did not survive the Assize of Clarendon in 1166. See J. H. Baker, An Introduction to English Legal History 578 (3d ed. 1990). It persisted, however, as a mode of trial in some civil cases until 1602. See id. at 389–94.

The coercive power of an oath stemmed partly from its mystic and religious significance, a significance that modern observers may not fully appreciate. Even when judged solely in secular terms, however, oaths undoubtedly seemed coercive to seventeenth- and eighteenth-century lawyers. Once a witness was placed on oath, his refusal to answer constituted contempt, punishable by imprisonment, and his false answers constituted perjury, punishable by imprisonment as well. The witness could avoid prison only by telling the truth, and when the truth was incriminating, he was threatened with imprisonment unless he condemned himself. That the architects of the privilege regarded the threat of imprisonment as compulsion should not be at all surprising.

William J. Stuntz's recent account of the history of the privilege attaches less significance to oaths than this chapter does. Although Stuntz recognizes that "people [in the seventeenth century] took oaths and swearing a good deal more seriously than they might today," he comments, "[I]t is hard to believe that the sustained criticism of the oath ex officio rested primarily on the cruelty of the choice it posed; after all, this was an era when real racks, not metaphorical ones, were employed with some regularity. . . ." William J. Stuntz, The Substantive Origins of Criminal Procedure, 105 Yale Law Journal 393, 412–13 (1995).

Stuntz probably overestimates the brutality of English criminal procedure. In England, the rack was never employed with regularity. On occasion, the English Privy Council ordered torture for reasons of state, but its goal usually was to gain information and intelligence about an ongoing conspiracy rather than to gain a confession for judicial use. Torture, a recognized part of Continental criminal procedure, simply had no place in the English common law. Moreover, the last case of officially sanctioned torture in England occurred in

1640, and the use of torture had been very infrequent in the preceding decades. See John H. Langbein, Torture and the Law of Proof: Europe and England in the Ancien Regime 73–123 (1977).

Stuntz's account of the privilege distinguishes between cases of religious persecution and "ordinary" criminal cases. This distinction is indeed significant, and the reverence accorded the privilege today is undoubtedly attributable in part to the fact that its initial champions were courageous defenders of the right to religious freedom rather than murderers, rapists, and highwaymen. Stuntz's version of the tale, however, seems flawed. As he tells it, the privilege, theoretically available to defendants in both heresy and "ordinary" criminal cases, was meaningless in the ordinary cases. Most of these cases were effectively resolved by pretrial questioning, and "the privilege was a trial right. It did not affect pretrial questioning, which was not conducted under oath." Stuntz, supra, at 416. Stuntz may have been unaware that the questioning of common law defendants at trial also was not under oath; the privilege was as unavailable to defendants at trial as it was during their pretrial interrogation.

Stuntz's account fails to consider the fact that heresy and "ordinary" cases were tried in different courts using different procedures; this fact, more than any other, accounted for their different histories. Contrary to Stuntz's hypothesis, the use of oaths in religious courts initially prompted common law enforcement of the privilege. The concern voiced about the coercive character of these oaths was not merely a cover.

42. See chapter 2, notes 31–35 and accompanying text.

43. Although the defenders of the High Commission argued that the commission's actions were warranted by the *ius commune,* they also maintained that a royal commission, authorized by the Act of Supremacy (1 Eliz. c. 1, §8 (1558)), exempted the High Commission from the requirements that the *ius commune* imposed on other religious courts. See chapter 3, note 10 and accompanying text.

44. Some suspects who submitted to the ex officio oath objected later to answering particular questions. These suspects asserted essentially the same principles as those who challenged the authority of the High Commission to administer the oath initially. See chapter 2, section II.B.2, reporting that suspects were required to answer

> where there was public knowledge that a crime had been committed, where the public had an interest in punishing the crime, and where there were legitimate indicia that the defendant being questioned had committed it. . . . This had become an accepted principle in the criminal law of the church. Following its mandate, under accepted principles of the *ius commune,* defendants had no personal right to refuse to plead or to ignore questions about their manifest crimes.

45. The Supreme Court referred to the "cruel trilemma" as a justification for the privilege in Murphy v. Waterfront Commission, 378 U.S. 52, 55 (1964). As suggested in chapter 2, the phrase antedated this opinion. The word *trilemma*

does not appear in most dictionaries, but the Oxford English Dictionary notes uses of the word in 1672, 1690, 1725, 1860, and 1887.

46. That the common law's testimonial disqualification was a "disqualification" and not a "privilege" might lead a modern observer to conclude that the disqualification was not intended to benefit defendants. Being "disqualified" from doing something that other people do does not sound like a favor. Nevertheless, one should resist this conclusion. The testimonial disqualification of defendants served several purposes, one of which was to safeguard the defendants themselves.

The primary purpose of the disqualification probably was to keep untrustworthy evidence from the trier of fact. See Rules of Evidence, No. III, Incompetency of Witnesses from Interest, 6 American Jurist 18 (1831). In addition, the disqualification saved juries from the disturbing task of resolving swearing contests, contests that would have revealed the imperfection of the oath as a guarantor of truth. Letter from George Fisher to the author, June 6, 1996 (noting that common law procedure used several devices to avoid sworn credibility conflicts and suggesting that "our system only quite recently became comfortable with the idea that a jury could resolve credibility conflicts between sworn witnesses").

Finally, the disqualification protected defendants. Whatever the law on the subject, the exercise of a privilege not to testify is likely to give rise to an unfavorable inference, and the temptation to commit perjury rather than to invoke this privilege is likely to be strong. Only an unyielding disqualification ensures that the government will not lead defendants to swear falsely and, perhaps, to condemn themselves to damnation. See infra text accompanying notes 92–95 (describing nineteenth-century opposition to abolition of the testimonial disqualification on these grounds).

One cannot know whether the goal of safeguarding defendants and, initially, other interested witnesses was among the goals prompting their disqualification or whether this purpose was a rationalization and an afterthought. Common law sources, however, asserted this rationale for refusing to permit defendants to testify at least as early as the late sixteenth century. See infra text accompanying notes 51–60.

47. See An Oath before an Ecclesiastical Judge ex Officio, in 12 Co. Rep. 26, 77 Eng. Rep. 1308 (1606); Edwards' Case, 13 Co. Rep. 9, 10, 77 Eng. Rep. 1421, 1422 (1609); Levy, Origins 245–46 (discussing Edwards' Case, supra, and Jenner's Case, Stowe MS 424, fols. 159v–160r (1611)).

48. See chapter 3, section II.C.2.

49. The Fifth Amendment not only sets forth the privilege against self-incrimination but also provides that no person shall be held to answer for a capital or otherwise infamous crime except on presentment or indictment by a grand jury.

50. In one respect, however, the Fifth Amendment's formulation of the

privilege is narrower than the maxim *Nemo tenetur prodere seipsum*. The amendment speaks only of compulsion to be a witness in a criminal case, but the older maxim could be invoked successfully when there was no risk of criminal punishment but merely a risk of civil liability or of injury to reputation. See, for example, Zephaniah Swift, A Digest of the Law of Evidence in Civil and Criminal Cases 77 (1810) ("It is a rule of evidence in civil cases, that no man is compellable to testify against his interest, or to answer any question that will render him liable to an action, charge him with a debt, or subject him to a penalty or forfeiture"); id. at 79 ("[A] witness is not bound to answer questions, the direct object and immediate tendency of which are to degrade, disgrace, and disparage the witness, and shew his turpitude and infamy"); Respublica v. Gibbs, 3 Yeates 429, 437 (Pa. 1802); Levy, Origins 423–24, 427; Wigmore, supra note 9, at 85; Lawrence Herman, The Unexplored Relationship between the Privilege against Compulsory Self-Incrimination and the Involuntary Confession Rule (pt. I), 53 Ohio State Law Journal 101, 164 n. 336 (1992); Ullman v. United States, 350 U.S. 422, 449–54 (1956) (Douglas, J., dissenting); Brown v. Walker, 161 U.S. 591, 631–35 (1896) (Field, J., dissenting).

51. For what may be the earliest example, see Anthony Fitzherbert and Richard Compton, L'Office et Authoritie de Justice de Peace 152 (1584) (P. R. Glazebrook ed., 1972).

Early champions of the privilege against self-incrimination rarely argued that statements made under oath were less reliable than unsworn statements. Nevertheless, Akhil Amar and Renée Lettow, contending that the historic purpose of the privilege was to protect against the use of unreliable evidence, recently proposed a procedure that they called "a solution remarkably like the early scope of the privilege." Amar and Lettow, supra note 9, at 898. Amar and Lettow would permit prosecutors to take the depositions of criminal suspects under oath. "The penalty for refusing to answer would be contempt, and the penalty for lying would be perjury." Id. at 989–99 (footnote omitted). Although the prosecutors would not be allowed to use the suspects' statements against them at trial, they would be permitted to introduce evidence derived from these statements—both physical evidence and the testimony of witnesses whose existence, location, and identity the suspects had disclosed. This "solution remarkably like the early scope of the privilege" seems more closely to resemble the evil that the privilege was intended to remedy. See Donald Dripps, Akhil Amar on Criminal Procedure and Constitutional Law: "Here I Go Down That Wrong Road Again," 74 North Carolina Law Review 1559, 1565–66, 1623–35 (1996) (offering a powerful rejoinder to Amar and Lettow's historical account, suggesting that Amar and Lettow "have it exactly backwards," and demonstrating the odd incentives that Amar and Lettow's proposal would create for law enforcement officers). For a discussion of how sharply Amar and Lettow's proposal departs from a century of more recent history, see Yale Kamisar, On the "Fruits" of *Miranda* Violations, Coerced Confessions, and Compelled Testimony, 93 Michigan Law Review 929 (1995). See also the rejoinder, Akhil Reed Amar and Renée B. Lettow, Self-Incrimination and the Constitution: A Brief Rejoinder to Professor Kamisar, 97 Michigan Law Review 1011 (1995).

52. Michael Dalton, The Countrey Justice 273 (1619; repr. 1973).

53. Theodore Barlow, The Justice of the Peace: A Treatise Containing the Power and Duty of That Magistrate 189 (1745) (quoted in chapter 4, note 149).

54. Augustin S. Clayton, The Office and Duty of a Justice of the Peace (1819) (quoted in chapter 5, note 118 and accompanying text).

55. Starkie, Practical Treatise 51–52 (Metcalf ed. 1826) (quoted in chapter 6, section II.B.2).

56. Quoted in Levy, Origins 177.

57. William Haller, The Leveller Tracts 1647–1653, at 454 (1944).

58. William Bradford, Of Plymouth Plantation, 1620–1647, at 405 (Samuel E. Morison ed., 1952); id. at 407 (response of Ralph Partrich). The second response condemned the oath ex officio and the infliction of punishment for failure to confess but emphasized that "[a] magistrate cannot without sin neglect diligent inquisition into the cause brought before him." This response added, "[I]f it be manifest that a capital crime is committed, and that common report or probability, suspicion or some complaint (or the like), be of this or that person, a magistrate ought to require, and by all due means to procure from the person . . . a naked confession of the fact." The failure of a magistrate to fulfill this duty would "betray his country and people to the heavy displeasure of God." Id. at 405–6 (response of John Rayner).

The third response condemned "extract[ing] a confession from a delinquent by an oath in matters of life or death." Nevertheless, so long as the "presumptions are strong" and the matters are "of highest consequence, such as do concern the safety or ruin of states or countries, magistrates may proceed so far as to bodily torments, as racks, hot irons, etc. to extract a confession." Id. at 412–13 (response of Charles Chauncy). For Charles Chauncy, later the president of Harvard College (see id. at 314 n. 4), placing a suspect on oath apparently was more offensive than torture. Although torture was to be used only sparingly in capital cases, interrogation under oath was impermissible.

59. 2 John Winthrop, History of New England 47 (J. Savage ed., 1826). In 1637, the General Court of Massachusetts summoned John Wheelwright to account for his unorthodox religious views. The General Court assured him, however, that he would not be examined "by any compulsory means, as by oath, imprisonment, or the like." Levy, Origins 342.

60. 2 Statutes at Large: Being a Collection of All the Laws of Virginia 422 (William W. Hening ed., 1820).

61. Although John Langbein maintains that England's prohibition of torture was "effected before the first traces of the privilege at common law" (chapter 4, section III), Americans of the founding generation unmistakably saw the privilege as a safeguard against torture. See Amar and Lettow, supra note 9, at

865 n. 20 (1995); Levy, Origins 430. In addition to the sources cited by these works, see Leonard MacNally, Evidence 275 (1804) (declaring that one purpose of the privilege is to outlaw torture). English sources similarly described the privilege as forbidding torture. See Sollom Emlyn, preface, iv (Mar. 27, 1730), in 1 State Trials (2d ed. 1730) ("In other Countries, Racks and Instruments of Torture are applied to force from the Prisoner a Confession, sometimes of more than is true; but this is a Practice which Englishmen are happily unacquainted with, enjoying the benefit of that just and reasonable Maxim, Nemo tenetur accusare seipsum . . ."); 1 Stephen, History 440 ("[T]he assertion that the maxim, 'Nemo tenetur accusare seipsum,' was part of the law of God and of nature . . . was all the more popular because it condemned the practice of torture for purposes of evidence, then in full use both on the Continent and in Scotland"). Herman, supra note 50, collects and discusses these sources at 178–79.

62. Under the common law of evidence, such threats and promises rendered out-of-court confessions involuntary. See Albert W. Alschuler, Plea Bargaining and Its History, 79 Columbia Law Review 1, 12 (1979). Wigmore insisted that the law of voluntariness developed independently of the principle *Nemo tenetur seipsum prodere.* 8 Wigmore, Evidence §3366. He assailed the Supreme Court for declaring in Bram v. United States, 168 U.S. 532, 540 (1897), that "[i]n criminal trials, in the courts of the United States, wherever a question arises whether a confession is incompetent because not voluntary, the issue is controlled by that portion of the Fifth Amendment to the Constitution of the United States, commanding that no person 'shall be compelled in any case to be a witness against himself.' " See 3 Wigmore, Evidence §823, n. 5.

Recently, however, Lawrence Herman noted several occasions in the seventeenth, eighteenth, and early nineteenth centuries when treatise writers, courts, counsel, and a member of the House of Lords described the requirement that guilty pleas and other confessions be voluntary as one incident of the *Nemo tenetur* principle. See Herman, supra note 50, at 143–47, 152–53, 168–69. Herman advanced other reasons for doubting Wigmore's claim that the privilege and the requirement of voluntariness were entirely independent of one another, including the fact that both doctrines were described as forbidding torture. See id at 177–80. Charles McCormick once remarked that although the two doctrines had arisen at different times, the kinship between them was "too apparent for denial." Charles McCormick, The Scope of Privilege in the Law of Evidence, 16 Texas Law Review 447, 453 (1938).

Even if, as Wigmore claimed, "the privilege" antedated the requirement of voluntariness by one hundred years, the requirement that confessions be voluntary antedated the Fifth Amendment. See, for example, R. v. Rudd (K. B. 1775), 1 Leach 115, 118, 168 Eng. Rep. 160, 161. The framers of the Fifth Amendment might well have assumed that their prohibition of "compulsion" to incriminate oneself included a requirement that confessions be "uncompelled" or voluntary. There is little reason to suppose that the unqualified language of the Fifth Amendment and of other American formulations of the privilege merely reiterated the traditional English understanding of the *Nemo tenetur* principle (whether the Americans knew that they were innovating or not). Wigmore to the contrary notwithstanding, the reading of the Fifth Amendment offered by Bram v. United States seems at least plausible both textually and historically.

63. In seeking the target of an unqualified privilege against compulsory self-incrimination, moreover, inhuman methods of interrogation may be a more promising candidate than the ability to ask questions and expect answers from people accused of crime. Henry Hart and Albert Sacks once wrote that in seeking the meaning of an ambiguous or unclear legislative enactment, one should "assume, unless the contrary unmistakably appears, that the legislature was made up of reasonable persons pursuing reasonable purposes reasonably." Henry M. Hart Jr. and Albert M. Sacks, The Legal Process: Basic Problems in the Making and Application of Law 1378 (William N. Eskridge Jr. and Phillip P. Frickey eds., 1994).

64. One cannot know much, however, about what common law judges would have done if unsworn defendants had refused to answer, for during the centuries prior to the Bill of Rights, almost none did. One who did (the first, apparently) was John Udall. When Udall was tried for seditious libel in 1590, the court invited the jury to consider his silence as evidence of his guilt. He was convicted and sentenced to death, and he died in prison. See Herman, supra note 50, at 120–21; Levy, Origins 168–70.

The most prominent of the common-law defendants to assert a right to silence was John Lilburne, the most famous of the Levellers. Lilburne earlier had objected to ex officio proceedings in the Court of Star Chamber (although he had declined to answer only questions concerning unspecified charges). During his common law trial for treason in 1649, he claimed many nonexistent rights. When Lilburne refused to say at his trial whether he had written a particular document, the attorney general quarreled with him. Other proof of Lilburne's authorship was at hand, however, and the court imposed no formal sanction for his refusal. Trial of John Lilburne, 4 How. St. Tr. 1269, 1340–41 (1649).

At his arraignment, Lilburne had declared, "[B]y the Laws of England, I am not to answer questions against or concerning myself," and the presiding judge had replied, "You shall not be compelled." Id. at 1292–93. This response should not be read as an expression of the court's approval of Lilburne's claim or as a promise that no inference would be drawn from his failure to respond. The statement might simply have recognized that English law authorized no formal, judicially imposed punishment when a person who had not been summoned or sworn as a witness declined to speak. Lilburne was subject to the same informal pressure to speak as other defendants, and he did not remain at all silent at his trial.

With very few exceptions, only suspects brought before the prerogative courts and other sworn witnesses ever invoked the maxim *Nemo tenetur seipsum prodere*. As Lawrence Herman suggests, a common law defendant who remained silent during a pretrial examination would have been denied bail, and silence before or during trial would have been called to the attention of the trier of fact. Herman, supra note 50, at 124 (citing John H. Langbein, Prosecuting Crime in the Renaissance 11 (1974)).

65. The imposition of formal sanctions for silence might have been regarded as "torture" forbidden by the privilege, but there is a difference between withholding punishment for conduct and approval of that conduct. Although a suspect might have a right not to be imprisoned for refusing to answer, his refusal to answer might nevertheless be considered wrongful.

66. See, for example, Abe Fortas, The Fifth Amendment: Nemo Tenetur Prodere Seipsum, 25 Cleveland Bar Association Journal 91, 100 (1954) ("A man may be punished, even put to death, by the state; but if he is an American or an Englishman or a free man anywhere, he should not be made to prostrate himself before his majesty").

67. Compare Beattie, Crime and the Courts 348–49 ("There was no thought that the prisoner had a right to remain silent on the grounds that he would otherwise be liable to incriminate himself. . . . [T]he assumption was clear that if the case against him was false the prisoner ought to say so and suggest why, and that if he did not speak that could only be because he was unable to deny the truth of the evidence").

68. See chapter 4, section I (citing Thomas Smith, De Republica Anglorum, bk. 2, ch. 23, at 114 (Mary Dewar ed., 1982) (1583)).

69. The defendant's statement often was read by the justice of the peace himself; this judicial officer frequently appeared as a witness against the defendant.

70. Accord Julius Goebel Jr. and T. Raymond Naughton, Law Enforcement in Colonial New York: A Study in Criminal Procedure 652–59 (1970) (demonstrating the use at trial of confessions before magistrates and inferring that defendants in colonial New York were "directly vulnerable to questioning from the bench").

71. See chapter 4, section I.H.1. A statute in 1696 had permitted defense counsel to appear in treason trials.

72. Charles Cottu, On the Administration of Criminal Justice in England 73 (1822) (translation of L'Administration de la justice criminelle en Angleterre (1820)) (quoted in id.).

73. At the conclusion of chapter 4, Langbein acknowledges that in denying the existence of the privilege against self-incrimination until the emergence of the lawyer-dominated trial, he has spoken in "a shorthand of sorts."

74. See John M. Beattie, Scales of Justice: Defense Counsel and the English Criminal Trial in the Eighteenth and Nineteenth Centuries, 9 Law and History Review 221, 227 (table 1) (1991).

75. See, e.g., Goebel and Naughton, supra note 70, at 573 ("counsel was only occasionally employed in criminal cases" in eighteenth century New York); Peter C. Hoffer, Law and People in Colonial America 86 (1992) ("[B]y the 1760s, counsel was *permitted* felony suspects in more than half the colonies" (emphasis added)); John M. Murrin, "The Legal Transformation: The Bench and Bar of Eighteenth-Century Massachusetts," in Colonial America: Essays in Politics and Social Development 540 (Stanley N. Katz and John M. Murrin eds., 1983); supra chapter 5, sections II.A and IV.E; Levy, Origins 369.

76. See chapter 5, section IV.C.

77. Id.

78. Beattie, supra note 74.

79. Levy, Origins 369.

80. Perhaps judges of the early American republic would not have pressed this response too hard. True, the resolution of the Virginia House of Burgesses in 1677 declared that "noe law can compel a man to *swear* against himself in any matter wherein he is liable to corporal punishment." 4 Statutes at Large: Being a Collection of All the Laws of Virginia 422 (1820) (emphasis added). The Virginia Declaration of Rights proclaimed a century later, "[N]or can he be compelled to give *evidence* against himself." 7 The Federal and State Constitutions, Colonial Charters, and Other Organic Laws of the States, Territories, and Colonies 3813 (1977) (emphasis added). And the federal Bill of Rights provided, "No person shall be compelled in any criminal case to be a *witness* against himself." U.S. Const., amend. 5 (emphasis added). One doubts, however, that the authors of these provisions would have limited the privilege to sworn statements if the statements of an unsworn defendant who had been tortured were offered at his trial.

81. See Alschuler, supra note 62, at 7–13. See also Beattie, Crime and the Courts 336–37, 446–47.

82. See 1 Simon Greenleaf, A Treatise on the Law of Evidence §§225, 329–30 (1842) (explaining why a pretrial statement made under oath cannot be considered voluntary and linking the testimonial disqualification of defendants both to the *Nemo tenetur* principle and to the concern that defendants should not be tempted to commit perjury).

83. See, e.g., The Conductor Generalis 157 (1794) (compiled by James Parker). See also chapter 5, section II.B.2; chapter 4, note 142.

84. The trial of Sarah Malcolm, OSBP (Feb. 1733), at 90–91 (described in chapter 4); Beattie, Crime and the Courts 365–66 n. 129 (describing the report of a case at the Surrey assizes in 1743).

85. See 8 Wigmore, Evidence §2250 at 284, 289–90. In the trial of Sir John Freind, 13 State Trials 1, 17 (1696), Lord Chief Justice Treby said of a witness, "[N]o man is bound to answer any questions that will subject him to a penalty, or to infamy."

86. Queen v. Arnold, 8 C. & P. 622, 173 Eng. Rep. 645 (1838) (Lord Denman).

87. 11 & 12 Vict. c. 42 (1848).

88. See Mike McConville and Chester Mirsky, The Rise of Guilty Pleas: New York, 1800–1865, 22 Journal of Law and Society 443, 452 (1995).

89. See Act of March 25, 1864, Maine Acts and Resolves ch. 280, at 214, codified as amended at 15 Maine Revised Statutes Annotated §1315 (1994).

90. The Criminal Evidence Act of 1898, 61 & 62 Vict. c. 36 (1899).

91. See Georgia Code Annotated §§24-9-20, 17-7-28 (1995).

92. See Ferguson v. Georgia, 365 U.S. 570, 578–79 (1961); Joel N. Bodansky, The Abolition of the Party-Witness Disqualification: An Historical Survey, 70 Kentucky Law Journal 91, 115 (1981–82).

93. Perhaps the earliest, and certainly one of the most earnest, proponents of this position was Jeremy Bentham. See 5 Bentham, Rationale 381–90, 393–97.

94. See *Ferguson,* 365 U.S. at 578–80; Bodansky, supra note 92, at 115.

95. See, for example, [Seth Ames], Testimony of Persons Accused of Crime, 1 American Law Review 443, 444 (1867) ("In its actual workings, it will be found that this new statute will inevitably *compel* the defendant to testify, and will have substantially the same effect as if it did not go through the mockery of saying that he might testify if he pleased") (emphasis in original). I am grateful to George Fisher for this reference.

96. James Fitzjames Stephen, A General View of the Criminal Law of England 202 (1863). See Ames, supra note 95, at 448 ("The guilty . . . will add the crime of perjury to the crime set forth in the indictment. Even of the innocent, some, under the influence of terror and anxiety, may mix some falsehood with the truth, and so increase the embarrassment and aggravate the danger of their position").

97. 20 Stat. 30 (1878), 18 U.S.C. §3481 (1994).

98. See *Ferguson,* 365 U.S. at 580; Bodansky, supra note 92, at 126.

99. See Ruloff v. People, 45 N.Y. 213, 222 (1871); Staples v. State, 89 Tenn. 231, 233, 14 S.W. 603 (1890); State v. Taylor, 57 W. Va. 228, 234–35, 50 S.E. 247, 249–50 (1905); Price v. Commonwealth, 77 Va. 393, 395 (1883) (indicating that without the no-comment provision, the competency statute would have been incompatible with the presumption of innocence); Bodansky, supra note 92, at 126. The first competency statute—Maine's—did not include a provision forbidding adverse comment on a defendant's failure to testify. The Maine Supreme Court not only upheld the constitutionality of the statute but also held that the privilege against self-incrimination did not preclude juries from considering a defendant's failure to testify as evidence of his guilt. State v. Bartlett, 55 Me. 200 (1867). The court noted that "[f]rom time immemorial the . . . silence of the accused person, when charged, has been

regarded as legitimate evidence" and that "refusals to account for the possession of stolen property . . . are evidences of guilt admitted. . . ." Id. at 217. Ignoring the important limitation that a treatise writer included in his description of the circumstances in which an inference from silence is appropriate, the court quoted this description in support of its ruling: "Where a man at full liberty to speak *and not in the course of a judicial inquiry* is charged with a crime, and remains silent, that is, makes no denial of the accusation by word or gesture, his silence is a circumstance which may be left to the jury." Id. at 218 (citing Wharton's Criminal Law 320) (emphasis added).

The court did not advert to the distinction between drawing an adverse inference from the silence of an unsworn person, which the privilege against self-incrimination never had precluded, and pressing a person to answer incriminating questions under oath, which it had. See also State v. Cleaves, 59 Me. 298, 301 (Appleton, C.J.) ("Extrajudicial non-responsion, when a charge is made, is always regarded as an article of circumstantial evidence. . . . Is [the defendant's] silence of any the less probative force, when thus in court called upon to contradict or explain . . . ?"). In 1879, the Maine legislature, "looking for a more careful protection" of the privilege against self-incrimination than the state's supreme court had provided, see State v. Banks, 78 Me. 490, 492 (1886), declared that a defendant's failure to testify should not be treated as evidence of his guilt. Me. Stat. 1879, ch. 92, §6. The Maine court later declared, "We think the intent of the statute is that the jury, in determining their verdict, shall entirely exclude from their consideration the fact that the defendant did not elect to testify, substantially as if the law did not allow him to be a witness." 78 Me. at 492. I am grateful to George Fisher for leading me to the Maine sources.

100. Criminal Justice Act, 1982, c. 48, §72.

101. It has been seventy years, however, since the Supreme Judicial Court's last reiteration of the defendant's ability to offer an unsworn statement. Commonwealth v. Stewart, 255 Mass. 9, 151 N.E. 74 (1926).

102. In other jurisdictions, the ability to make an unsworn statement did not survive the enactment of competency statutes. See Bodansky, supra note 92, at 117 n. 113.

103. 380 U.S. 609 (1965).

104. Id. at 615.

105. 384 U.S. 436 (1966).

106. 483 U.S. 44 (1987).

107. Id. at 52. The Court's logic was no stronger than its history. Denying an opportunity to testify ensures that testimony will not be compelled. To say that a person cannot be compelled to do what he is not permitted to do may be odd, but the Fifth Amendment plainly did forbid compelling defendants to be witnesses against themselves at a time when they were not permitted to be

witnesses against themselves. The protections of the Fifth Amendment, how-ever, were not limited to criminal defendants. They extended to witnesses who could offer self-incriminating testimony if they chose. The Court in *Rock* may have overlooked this fact when it made the statement quoted in the text.

108. Compare Paul G. Cassell, *Miranda*'s Social Costs: An Empirical Reas-sessment, 90 Northwestern University Law Review 387 (1996), and Paul G. Cassell and Bret S. Hayman, Police Interrogation in the 1990s: An Empirical Study of the Effects of *Miranda,* 43 UCLA Law Review 839 (1996), with Stephen J. Schulhofer, *Miranda*'s Practical Effect: Substantial Benefits and Van-ishingly Small Costs, 90 Northwestern University Law Review 500 (1996), and George C. Thomas III, Is *Miranda* a Real-World Failure? A Plea for More (and Better) Empirical Evidence, 43 UCLA Law Review 821 (1996), and George C. Thomas III, Plain Talk about the *Miranda* Empirical Debate: A "Steady-State" Theory of Confessions, 43 UCLA Law Review 993 (1996).

109. See United States Dept. of Justice, Office of Legal Policy, Report to the Attorney General on the Law of Pretrial Interrogation (Feb. 12, 1986).

110. See Stephen J. Schulhofer, The Fifth Amendment at Justice: A Reply, 54 University of Chicago Law Review 950 (1987).

111. Criminal Justice and Public Order Act, 1994, §35. The Criminal Pro-cedure Act of Norway provides that a criminal defendant need not respond to the charges against him when the state's attorney reads these charges at the outset of his trial. Nevertheless, "[i]f the person charged refuses to answer, or states that he reserves his answer, the president of the court may inform him that this may be considered to tell against him." The Criminal Procedure Act of Norway, ch. 9, §93 (1991) (unofficial English translation) (quoted in William T. Pizzi, Punishment and Procedure: A Different View of the American Crimi-nal Justice System, 13 Constitutional Commentary 55, 61 (1996)).

112. Id. §§34, 36, 37. See generally Ian Dennis, The Criminal Justice and Public Order Act 1994: The Evidence Provisions, 1995 Criminal Law Review 4; Gregory W. O'Reilly, England Limits the Right to Silence and Moves To-wards an Inquisitorial System of Justice, 85 Journal of Criminal Law & Crimi-nology 402 (1994).

113. See Dennis, supra note 112, at 10.

114. See Funke v. France, 16 European Human Rights Rep. 297 (1993). The 1994 act was modeled in large part on the Criminal Evidence (Northern Ireland) Order 1988, and the European Commission of Human Rights has con-cluded that in many applications the Northern Ireland order violates article 6.1 of the European Convention. See Murray v. United Kingdom, 18 European Human Rights Rep., Comm'n Supp. CD1 (1994).

115. Some scholars call this process "reification."

116. Levy, Origins xvi ("The familiar phrase of contemporary usage seems to be of twentieth-century vintage").

117. Compare Wigmore, supra note 9, at 71 ("If one instance better than another serves to exemplify the manner in which history may cover up the origin of a legal principle, destroy all traces of its real significance, change and recast its purpose and its use, while preserving an identify of [*sic*] form . . . , it is this rule that no man shall be compelled to criminate himself").

118. The historians may have been misled by the assumption that criminal defendants ought to have been the principal beneficiaries of the privilege against self-incrimination. Until the mid-nineteenth century, the principal benefit that defendants derived from the privilege was that they were not expected or permitted to give sworn testimony. Accordingly, they could not be formally punished for false answers or for remaining silent. Modern historians have had difficulty seeing the lack of an oath as a significant benefit.

119. 1 Bruce Ackerman, We the People: Foundations (1991).

120. 384 U.S. 436 (1966).

121. See Vincent Bugliosi, Outrage: The Five Reasons Why O. J. Simpson Got Away with Murder 173 (1996) ("[F]or the hundreds of thousands of defendants convicted every year throughout the land for various crimes, it is almost unheard of for there to follow, after their conviction, a prosecution against them for perjury"). This exemption may stem less from sympathy for the defendant's self-preservation efforts than from the limited practical utility of a perjury prosecution following a criminal trial. When an apparently perjurious defendant has been convicted at trial, the sentence imposed for his offense is likely to make additional punishment seem unnecessary. Indeed, the sentencing judge might have increased the defendant's sentence because he apparently lied on the stand. See United States v. Grayson, 438 U.S. 41 (1978). When a defendant who may have testified falsely is acquitted, moreover, the likelihood of a successful perjury prosecution is ordinarily slim.

122. See Lawrence Lessig, Fidelity in Translation, 71 Texas Law Review 1165 (1993).

123. Virtually all other readings of the amendment could be supported in much the same way.

124. Carol S. Steiker, Second Thoughts about First Principles, 107 Harvard Law Review 820, 830 (1994). See Albert W. Alschuler, Fourth Amendment Remedies: The Current Understanding, in The Bill of Rights: Original Meaning and Current Understanding 197 (Eugene W. Hickock Jr. ed., 1991) ("Among the things that did not exist when the Fourth Amendment became part of the Constitution were cocaine, heroin, helicopters, magnetometers, drug-detecting dogs, professional police forces, and the exclusionary rule").

125. See supra notes 96–100.

126. The quoted phrase comes from Lakeside v. Oregon, 435 U.S. 333, 345 n. 5 (1978), in which Justice Stevens commented in dissent that "the roster of scholars and judges with reservations about expanding the Fifth Amendment

privilege reads like an honor roll of the legal profession." See Wigmore, supra note 9, at 75–88; Roscoe Pound, Legal Interrogation of Persons Accused or Suspected of Crime, 24 Journal of Criminal Law, Criminology and Police Science 1014 (1934); Paul G. Kauper, Judicial Examination of the Accused—A Remedy for the Third Degree, 30 Michigan Law Review 1224 (1932); Henry J. Friendly, The Fifth Amendment Tomorrow: The Case for Constitutional Change, 37 University of Cincinnati Law Review 671 (1967); Schaefer, supra note 9, at 74–81; Marvin E. Frankel, Partisan Justice 98–99 (1980). See also Yale Kamisar, Kauper's "Judicial Examination of the Accused" Forty Years Later—Some Comments on a Remarkable Article, 73 Michigan Law Review 15 (1974); Dripps, Against Police Interrogation, supra note 9.

127. See Criminal Justice (Scotland) Act, 1980, ch. 62, §6(2); Alexander v. H. M. Advocate, 1988 Scottish Criminal Case Reports 542, 1989 Scots Law Times 193; Neil Gow, The Revival of Examinations, 141 New Law Journal 680 (1991).

128. Permitting defendants to testify under oath but exempting them from the penalties for perjury would resemble the practice of the High Commission in the early seventeenth century, but despite the infamy of the High Commission, the compromise might be appropriate. Jeremy Bentham once observed that courts need not avoid sitting in chambers decorated with stars merely because the court of Star Chamber met in such a chamber. 5 Bentham, Rationale 241.

The primary reason for retaining the oath despite the absence of a formal sanction for violating it would be to avoid a sharp, unexplained contrast between the testimony of defendants and the testimony of other witnesses. Perhaps a defendant should be allowed to present his testimony with the same solemn promise of truthfulness as other witnesses even if he is not threatened with punishment for falsehood.

Justice Walter Schaefer once said of a regime in which defendants were questioned at trial but not under oath, "These rules seem to me to follow natural assumptions. The silence of the accused is noted and taken into account because of the strength of the inference of guilt that flows from his failure to respond; the refusal to administer an oath to the accused, or to force him to answer, reflects spiritual and physical aspects of the law of self-preservation invoked by John Lilburn before the Star Chamber." Schaefer, supra note 9, at 71.

English statutes from before 1713 are taken from *The Statutes of the Realm* (Record Commission, London 1810–27). Statutes for the United States and other countries are listed at the end of the table.

ENGLAND

UNITED STATES
Federal

Georgia

Maine

New York